T0379044

OPENING WINDOWS

Society & Natural Resources Book Series

**Jill Belsky, Mallika Bose, Ken Caine, Anna Haines,
Rick Krannich, and Marianne Penker**
SERIES EDITORS

This series examines the complexity of interrelationships among human societies, biophysical and built environments, and natural resources and engages emergent issues and informs transformations between society and natural resources toward greater social and environmental justice, health, and sustainability and resilience.

A Community Guide to Social Impact Assessment: 2015 Fourth Edition, Rabel J. Burdge

The Community in Rural America, 2nd ed., Kenneth P. Wilkinson

The Concepts, Process and Methods of Social Impact Assessment, Rabel J. Burdge and Colleagues

Daydreams and Nightmares: A Sociological Essay on the American Environment, William R. Burch Jr.

Diffusion Research in Rural Sociology: The Record and Prospects for the Future, Frederick C. Fliegel with Peter F. Korsching

Energy Impacts: A Multidisciplinary Exploration of North American Energy Development, Jeffrey B. Jacquet, Julia H. Haggerty, and Gene L. Theodori

Man, Mind and Land: A Theory of Resource Use, Walter Firey

Opening Windows: Embracing New Perspectives and Practices in Natural Resource Social Sciences, Kate Sherren, Gladman Thondhlana, and Douglas Jackson-Smith

Rural Sociology and the Environment, Donald R. Field and William R. Burch Jr.

Social Assessment: Theory, Process and Techniques, 3rd ed., C. Nicholas Taylor, C. Hobson Bryan, and Colin G. Goodrich

Society and Natural Resources: A Summary of Knowledge, Michael J. Manfredo, Jerry J. Vaske, Brett L. Bruyere, Donald R. Field, and Perry J. Brown

Three Iron Mining Towns: A Study in Cultural Change, Paul H. Landis

Opening Windows

Embracing New Perspectives and Practices
in Natural Resource Social Sciences

EDITED BY

Kate Sherren,
Gladman Thondhlana,
and Douglas Jackson-Smith

UTAH STATE UNIVERSITY PRESS
Logan
SOCIETY AND NATURAL RESOURCES PRESS
Logan

© 2024 by University Press of Colorado

Published by Utah State University Press
An imprint of University Press of Colorado
1580 North Logan Street, Suite 660
PMB 39883
Denver, Colorado 80203-1942

 The University Press of Colorado is a proud member of
the Association of University Presses.

The University Press of Colorado is a cooperative publishing enterprise supported, in part, by Adams State University, Colorado State University, Fort Lewis College, Metropolitan State University of Denver, University of Alaska Fairbanks, University of Colorado, University of Denver, University of Northern Colorado, University of Wyoming, Utah State University, and Western Colorado University.

∞ This paper meets the requirements of the ANSI/NISO Z39.48-1992 (Permanence of Paper).

ISBN: 978-1-64642-628-7 (hardcover)
ISBN: 978-1-64642-629-4 (paperback)
ISBN: 978-1-64642-630-0 (ebook)
https://doi.org/10.7330/9781646426300

Library of Congress Cataloging-in-Publication Data can be found online.

This book will be made open access within three years of publication thanks to Path to Open, a program developed in partnership between JSTOR, the American Council of Learned Societies (ACLS), University of Michigan Press, and The University of North Carolina Press to bring about equitable access and impact for the entire scholarly community, including authors, researchers, libraries, and university presses around the world. Learn more at https://about.jstor.org/path-to-open/.

Cover photograph © JulPo/iStockphoto

Contents

Section Two: Governance and Power

Section Three: Engagement and Elicitation

Figures

generated these images in part with OpenAI's DALL-E 2 artificial intelligence image-generation program based on the authors' specific descriptions (OpenAI, 2022). The use of this software is also an exploration of how the authors' description of competing place metaphors would interact with rhizomatic connections by hundreds of millions of images and their associated captions by other people, which is how the DALL-E 2 algorithm works (O'Connor, 2022).   292

Boxed Case Studies

Tables

Foreword

RICHARD KRANNICH, WILLIAM STEWART, AND ANNA HAINES

When the International Association for Society and Natural Resources (IASNR) launched the Society and Natural Resources (SNR) Book Series in 2019, our objective was to foster the publication of contemporary works that explore emergent issues and important transformations to the environment/society interface. We hoped to encourage innovative works that shed new light on the ways in which social structures, environmental governance, and decision-making processes create different constraints and opportunities for social justice and environmental health.

With those goals established, the SNR Book Series editorial board was tasked with identifying and encouraging new book projects that would enable us to promote exceptional scholarly work while also enhancing the visibility and impact of IASNR and the SNR Book Series. Our attention turned in short order to the prospect of publishing a new "state of knowledge" volume that would simultaneously examine the breadth and societal relevance of SNR knowledge, explore emergent issues and new directions in SNR scholarship, and capture the increasing diversity of SNR research with respect to disciplinary as well as transdisciplinary foundations, theoretical and methodological approaches, geography, and the divergent interests and backgrounds of contributing scholars.

https://doi.org/10.7330/9781646426300.c000a

To successfully address all, or even most, of these objectives in a single volume is without question a daunting task! Thankfully our efforts to identify a team of well-qualified scholars willing to lead such a project quickly led us to three long-time IASNR members and contributors—Kate Sherren, Douglas Jackson-Smith, and Gladman Thondhlana. Collectively they represent the growing diversity of natural resource social science with respect to nationality, research interests, global experience, and disciplinary perspective. Their commitment to diversity of representation in terms of topics as well as authorship has produced an outstanding set of chapters that effectively illuminate both current insights and new directions for SNR scholarship.

This state of knowledge volume draws its energy from concerns with inequities in access to natural resources linked to power and privilege. The volume is not meant as an exhaustive treatise on the gamut of issues connected with society and natural resources; and such honesty in the development process is admirable. Rather, the state of knowledge herein broadens the representation of voices that have been marginalized from previous research and policy forums with a thoughtful optimism for research-informed sociopolitical change. Seeking chapters that propose new ways of building inclusivity in natural resources decision-making, this state of knowledge reflects an intention to break down traditional boundaries and foster transitions in governance directed at empowerment, environmental stewardship, and equity. Although one layer of interpretation is a provocative collection of literature reviews with critiques tied to various contexts of race, gender, and other identities, an additional layer of interpretation is the unmistakable spirit of hope with strategies for moving forward that characterize positive roles for research in the progress ahead.

On behalf of IASNR we extend our gratitude to Kate, Doug, and Gladman as well as all the chapter authors for bringing focus to equity, power, and privilege in contemporary natural resource social sciences to this state of knowledge.

Acknowledgments

The editors would like to thank the authors as well as the many scholars globally who agreed to act as reviewers of the chapters in this volume, specifically: Nino Antadze, Jevgeniy Bluwstein, Michele Campagna, Clare E. B. Cannon, Jessica Cockburn, Georgina Cundill Kemp, Weston M. Eaton, Marla Emery, David Flores, Jennifer Givens, Divya Gupta, Caitlin Hafferty, Julia Haggerty, Aby Lat Soukabe Sène-Harper, Richard J. Hewitt, Mike Howlett, Julie Keller, Jude Ndzifon Kimengsi, Lincoln Larson, Andrew Lawson, Joseph Elizeri Mbaiwa, Jay Mistry, Chenai Murata, Vivian Nguyen, Hemant Ojha, Jouni Paavola, Tara Quinn, Claudia Radel, Stacia Ryder, Chelsea Schelly, Jeremy Schmidt, Tania Schusler, Bobby J. Smith II, Marc Stern, Carla Trentelman, Chloe B. Wardropper, Renate Wesselink, Simon West, and Melanie Zurba.

The editors also thank research assistants based at Dalhousie University, Mehrnoosh Mohammadi and Polly Nguyen, as well as editor Elizabeth Craig, indexer Emily LeGrand, and the hardworking staff at University Press of Colorado / Utah State University Press. Individuals in the IASNR executive and SNR Book Series editorial board have also provided substantial support, including Rick Krannich and Marianne Penker, who got the ball rolling two years ago. Thank you for entrusting us with this important job.

OPENING WINDOWS

Why Do We Need to Open the Windows?

KATE SHERREN, DOUGLAS JACKSON-SMITH,
GLADMAN THONDHLANA, AND POLLY NGUYEN

What Is the State of Knowledge on Society and Natural Resources?

Over the last thirty years we have increasingly seen that the fate of the earth depends on understanding humans, their varied circumstances, and their complex striving. Over the same time period, the International Association of Society and Natural Resources (IASNR) has grown to become an important global (though predominantly English-language) interdisciplinary association for social science professionals who explore the relationships between people and working landscapes. While still dominated by North American members, the organization currently has members from more than forty-five nations—and newly created regional hubs for East/Southeast Asia and Europe are helping expand international perspectives. The kinds of questions IASNR members ask and the issues they focus on have also evolved with the times and in step with the organization's increasingly broad and diverse community of scholars, policy makers and practitioners. As IASNR's membership evolves, the organization has made efforts to better embrace cultural differences, power disparities,

https://doi.org/10.7330/9781646426300.c000b

and criticism of its historic North American biases. It has been like a breath of fresh air.

In late 2020, we were asked to lead this third decennial volume to bring together examples of recent work on natural resource social science (NRSS). IASNR has done this twice before, in 2004 and 2014, and each time it has produced a very different volume. What was produced at each moment in time tells an interesting story about our trajectory as an organization and field of study. The first decennial volume was released at the 10th International Symposium for Society and Resource Management (ISSRM, now called the IASNR Conference) in 2004, in the US Rocky Mountains (Manfredo et al. 2004). The editors of that volume titled their introductory chapter "Coming in from the Dark," referencing the emergence of a systematic NRSS community of practice that focused on the central role of people in natural resource and land management. The trajectory they described (and the contributing author list) was anchored in the institutions, issues, and public lands of the United States (US). The thirty-one chapters were comprehensive but also somewhat siloed, a reflection of the disparate work of that era. Diversity was demonstrated by the impressively wide range of sectors and applications that fit into this still-emerging field. The authorship list included many of the best-known and established scholars in NRSS that often get tapped for such synthetic work.

The second decennial volume was released at the 20th ISSRM in 2014 in Hannover, Germany (Manfredo et al. 2014). That volume was inspired by the surge of intellectual energy around integrated social-ecological systems (SES) that had captured the imagination of social and natural sciences over the previous decade. Focused on presenting the state of the art of and potential for new theoretical and methodological approaches—such as interdisciplinarity, systems thinking, ecosystem services, and multi-scalar analysis—the book presented a roadmap to integrate SES approaches from across the social sciences to better represent human dimensions in models of coupled human-natural systems. Their preface was titled "AND not OR," speaking to growing interest in multifunctionality and balance in landscapes and the need to simultaneously use *and* protect natural resources in a crowded world. This eleven-chapter 2014 volume was less retrospective and featured contributions from invited "leading authors," including some non-US scholars. In this volume, diversity was represented through the different disciplinary lenses applied to SES scholarship. The volume sought to draw together the disparate threads of this evolving field while allowing it to be more useful and commensurate with progress in the natural sciences.

In late 2020 when we got started with this volume, we each were grappling with the challenges of the COVID-19 pandemic, deeply affected by the Black Lives Matter and Decolonization movements and concerned about the lessons of this transformative moment in history for scholarship on NRSS. Antiracism and decolonization, as lenses, bring to the fore colonial processes that resulted in the oppression of people's minds, worldviews, and knowledges as much as they disenfranchised them of their land and resources. In using these lenses, we become more conscious of and committed to addressing issues related to: (i) the impacts of colonial history, racism, classism, gender and inequality, and to avoid "othering" in how we think and do research; (ii) biases in thinking and in whose voices dominate and count; (iii) challenging the status quo and hegemonic and unjust discourses; and (iv) recognizing the value of greater inclusivity and cultural, embodied, and spiritual ways of seeing the world. We were thus guided by central questions of equity, power, privilege, social structure, and resilience; for instance, who has power and who doesn't in shaping research and the trajectory of natural resource transitions, and how do these imbalances propagate? Within NRSS scholarship and practice, we were struck by the energy and leadership on these topics from a younger generation of scholars and practitioners, and by the critical importance of perspectives from outside the dominant Western colonial, white, male academic community. The work that has emerged over the last decade marks a shift in the field toward a greater understanding of the diversity of lived experiences in relation to natural resources and increased attention to how to manage them justly.

In response, our call for contributions to this volume deliberately emphasized a desire to open the windows of NRSS to emerging scholars, perspectives, practices, and opportunities. In crafting the field of potential contributions, we solicited submissions from the community at large, rather than reaching out to authors in our own personal and professional networks. We provided a list of themes of particular interest (global voices, power and privilege, and relevance and impact), but adapted the organization of the final volume based on the mix of submissions. Readers looking for chapters on particular topics will find that we didn't seek to generate a comprehensive tour of NRSS research activity. However, we felt that a volume focused on broadening the voices and perspectives on these pressing issues would be of most value at this time. In addition, our ethos has been one of equity of opportunity and diversity of representation, not just in the substance of the collection but in its editors and contributors. The invitation for proposals explicitly called for author teams that represented diversity in geographies, sectors, identities, and career stages. Most chapters are written by multiple authors with complementary perspectives: a solid majority are non-male, over a third are from non-US institutions, a fifth are from non-academic sectors, and many are early career, including more than a quarter who were graduate students at the time of writing. Authors are also of non-dominant genders and sexualities and Indigenous and non-white identities. Chapters also vary in length and purpose. Commentaries are the shortest, grounded in previous work but focused on making a well-framed argument for new directions for research and application in NRSS. Reviews are longer and are designed to synthesize and identify gaps in the current literature and to make a case for a future research agenda and practice. We hope that the final product is provocative and helpful and that it opens the windows even further to new ideas and voices within IASNR.

Opening Windows

Compared to previous volumes, this collection spends less time looking backward (to the "state of the field") and places more of a premium on creating a roadmap for the future. Most authors included a critical review of previous work but were encouraged to focus on the work that remains to be done. The four themes in which the following fifteen chapters are grouped were induced from the submissions themselves but are also conceptually overlapping and illustrative of the "fresh air" invigorating the field. Upon reflection, we recognized that these themes also reflect shifts in language, concepts, and methods we had observed in the scholarship published in our flagship journal *Society and Natural Resources* (*SNR*) over the last decade. Below we reflect on some of these trends, as indicated in the frequency with which different concepts appear in titles, abstracts, and keywords in *SNR*, and highlight their connections to the various contributions in this volume.

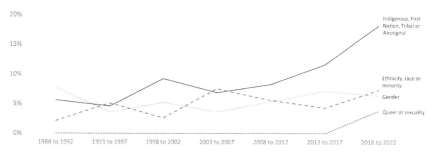

FIGURE 1.1. Selected diversity-related term use in *SNR* papers over time based on the proportion of papers in which the term is present in title, abstracts, and keywords.

Diversity and Justice

In the first decennial volume, the editors included among priorities of the young field, "diverse and local voices in natural resource decision making," described later as moving "past mere public input to active participation" and "communities and collaboration" (Manfredo et al. 2004, 7). Attention to issues of diversity and justice are not new to the social sciences (indeed, they reflect key axes of theoretical reflection in classical sociology), but their application in the natural resource arena as reflected by scholarship in *SNR* has evolved over time (figure 1.1). Gender has been an ongoing interest to *SNR* authors but has yet to climb back up to where it started in *SNR*'s first five years, when it featured in over 8 percent of papers. *Ethnicity* has stayed relatively level as a keyword, but *queer/sexuality* only really received significant attention in the last five-year period, largely thanks to a special issue on sexuality in agriculture. Most dramatic is an increase in the use of terms such as *Indigenous* and *First Nation*, which appeared in almost 20 percent of publications between 2018 and 2020, reflecting a growing appetite for decolonial action within NRSS.

Our first set of chapters reflect the above patterns, both in substance and authorship, and demonstrates the energy and leadership that early career researchers bring to our field. It starts with a commentary by Mejía-Duwan and Hoffelmeyer (chapter 1) advocating for a "queer agroecology" because of the ways that productivist agriculture replicates inequity in access not only to food but to farming, and how embedded ideas of heterosexism also dominate and degrade the ecosystem on which we all depend. Carter and Roesch-McNally (chapter 2) highlight the need for more intersectional analyses of gender and power within agricultural conservation research and programs. Using examples from US-based women in agriculture programs, they show positive outcomes including self-empowerment and conservation decision-making but also highlight the potential of replicating gender inequalities if gender is conceptualized as a simple demographic variable rather than one facet of a more complex system of exclusion. Schelhas et al. (chapter 3) present an overview of the recent empirical and theoretical work on the intersection of racial and ethnic identities and natural resource management that updates an earlier synthesis from twenty years earlier. The chapter points to the similarities *and differences* in how American Indian/ Indigenous, Black, Asian American, and Latinx communities have intersected with natural resource systems and institutions in the United States. Finally, Andrews et al. (chapter 4) provide a perspective on the challenges of and need for building capacity for human dignity to support and empower NRSS researchers during their training and as they seek careers, so they can simultaneously pursue their goals and well-being. Among those challenges are overcoming unreasonably high workloads for emerging faculty (academic staff), limited budgets, unfamiliarity with NRSS, and organizational cultures. They highlight the concept of human dignity as central to meaningfulness, freedom, and health, and as a yardstick for equity and inclusion. They conclude by providing a framework for developing capacity for building human dignity. All four of these chapters not only speak to the importance of opening the windows to new voices and ideas but also provide specific tools and guidance for doing so.

Governance and Power

One of the most dramatic changes in the last decade of NRSS is the growing focus on the concept and approaches to governance. Since 2018 the term *governance* has been present in almost half of *SNR* titles, abstracts, and keywords (47%), up from 19 percent the five years before and almost nonexistent before 2000 (figure 1.2). Over the same period, use of the term *decision-making* has been relatively flat (roughly 10% of papers), while *power* has increased from about 4 percent of *SNR* papers before 2000 to 14 percent. These are

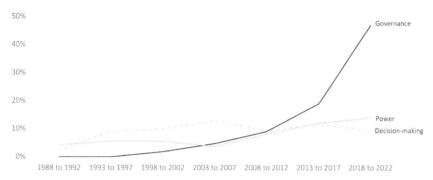

FIGURE 1.2. Selected governance and power term use in *SNR* papers over time based on the proportion of papers in which the term is present in title, abstracts, and keywords.

all indications that our language is shifting toward interrogating the mechanisms of decision-making, rather than taking those mechanisms as given and navigating them.

The chapters in the second section of the book dig deeply into issues of governance, power, and the way that specific policies or models of natural resource management play out for those most affected. Kestikalo (chapter 5) focuses on the role of theory in environmental change studies, particularly the importance of institutionally based perspectives in understanding how responses to emerging environmental issues should consider ways that existing systems already select and bias decision paths. She argues for a broader institutional perspective that views actors as formed, enabled, and constrained by the larger social systems in which they act. Thus, discussions of change must be informed by how institutional systems may be self-reinforcing and costly to change. Consistent with Keskitalo's call, Kiaka et al. (chapter 6) take a critical look at the community-based natural resource management (CBNRM) model that has come to dominate conservation in parts of Africa. Although CBNRM was designed to tackle poverty and marginalization, it has created opportunities for certain actors to benefit over others in the resulting commodification of natural resources. Understanding the mechanisms that keep this model so prominent is important when assessing its value. Finally, Sapkota et al. (chapter 7) use a relational lens to contrast government-community relationships for forest management in Nepal and Australia. They propose a four-part typology of relationships that emphasizes the role of practice, problem framing, and worldview in shaping the ways in which community actors are involved in forest governance across diverse settings. These chapters triangulate upon the importance of examining our institutions as limiting mechanisms for achieving a just future.

Engagement and Elicitation

Keywords in *SNR* publications also reflect some interesting shifts in how we talk about our work with stakeholders and the public. IASNR was born in the US public land management context, where "human dimensions" specialists sought to understand the values, concerns, behaviors, and preferences of land managers, recreationalists, community leaders, and the public, with a significant focus on participatory methods to consult with them in natural resource decision-making. There has been a commensurate shift in terminology from *participation* and *collaboration* toward *engagement,* a trend we believe reflects greater appreciation of multiple knowledge systems including local and Indigenous knowledge and the value of two-way modes of communication (figure 1.3). The approaches used for such engagement have also become more diverse, with increasing attention to visual and digital methods.

The third section of this volume includes chapters that explore some of the emerging theoretical and methodological approaches that reflect our contemporary understanding of engagement and the importance of eliciting local or community knowledge and local control over natural resource management. When institutions fail, or are seen to fail, the public increasingly can turn to resistance rather than engagement in the modes made available by governments. Parkins (chapter 8) explores this by highlighting the diversity of ways that public participation is conceptualized and practiced, mapping out three distinct modes of scholarship on participatory environmental governance: (i) generative and relational pragmatic approaches rooted in trust-building, collaboration, and inclusive decision-making; (ii) critical approaches characterized by confrontation and debate; and (iii) more radical and activist approaches with resistance as a form of governance from the ground up. He stresses that each conceptualization has implications for how governance issues are understood and addressed and how public participation success is measured. Jadallah et al. (chapter 9) describe how early work on public or community engagement failed to appreciate the important power differentials between

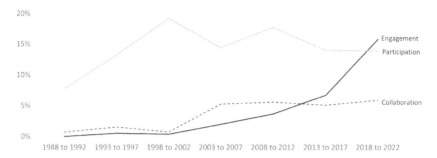

FIGURE 1.3. Selected engagement-related term use in *SNR* papers over time based on the proportion of papers in which the term is present in title, abstracts, and keywords.

decision-makers and the public, and between different groups within society. They challenge scholars working in this area to be more attentive to issues of power and privilege in their work. Whether the engagement techniques used are novel or long-established, Jadallah et al. remind us of the importance of designing participatory approaches that support individual and collective social learning processes, which offer more lasting and greater mutual value than simply social license to make resource-management decisions. Hafferty et al. (chapter 10) and Lamoureux et al. (chapter 11) provide critical reviews and conceptual frameworks that help us better understand how digital, visual, and arts-based methods are (or should be) deployed in NRSS. They point to the significant role of changes in communication technology, including the ubiquity of smartphones (and built-in cameras), artificial intelligence and cloud computing, and online collaborative technologies such as Zoom. Recognizing that a digital divide remains globally, these tools present both challenges and opportunities to shrink distances and empower new voices to improve engagement and elicitation of perspectives for decision-making. These chapters present important systematizations of established and emerging concepts and methods to inform the next decade of NRSS.

Relationships and Place

The way in which human relationships to nature and places have been conceptualized and discussed in NRSS scholarship has also evolved over time,

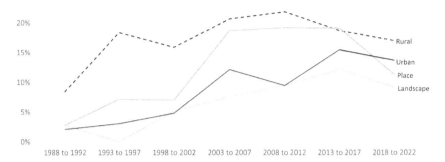

FIGURE 1.4. Selected place-related term use in *SNR* papers over time based on the proportion of papers in which the term is present in title, abstracts, and keywords.

consistent with the above transitions. While attention to the significance of place or local context in shaping human attitudes and behaviors around natural resources peaked a decade ago, attention to landscape-scale work has grown, and our collective scholarship has expanded to encompass more urban settings alongside traditional foci on pristine natural or rural areas (figure 1.4). While not yet captured in our search of *SNR* keywords, the contributions to this volume reflect a growing embrace of the concept of relationality, which often rejects a strict duality of humans and nature and instead focuses attention on the deep material, cultural, and spiritual relationships that link human and nonhuman actors in natural resource landscapes.

The last section of this volume presents work that challenges NRSS scholars to think more systematically and broadly about social science concepts and theories that link biophysical settings to human attitudes and behaviors toward the environment and natural resource management. Initially, Jones and Walton (chapter 12) provide a thorough review of the evolution of theoretical constructs used in the vast pro-environmental behavior literature. They organize this complex body of work into an integrated model aimed at being more adaptable to diverse communities, groups, settings, and contexts. Their work illustrates the culmination of decades of largely Global North scholarship on the individual and collective drivers of environmental concern and a look forward to how this area of research may become more inclusive. The rest of these authors in this section embrace a more relational approach in response to the legacies of colonization, oppression, and exploitation that have defined much of our shared Western natural resource management theories and practices. West et al. (chapter 13) opine about the ways that our practices of theorizing need to change to deal with such responsibilities during the Anthropocene. They describe three ways to decolonize our knowledge practices to avoid strengthening the modernist practices that have fueled our current challenges: situating theory, practicing theory, and theorizing together. Cockburn et al. (chapter 14) problematize the concept of stewardship and highlight the specificity and role of place and culture in unpacking what it means to be a steward of natural resources. Williams and Miller (chapter 15) conclude the section by noting how dominant ideas of place in NRSS have (until recently) explicitly or implicitly privileged notions of stability in which human actors are rooted in familiar social and biophysical landscapes. Recognizing the rapid pace of global migration and change, as well as the arguments for de-centering humans in studies of place, the authors propose the metaphor of rhizomes as a preferred model to capture the nonlinear interconnections between human and nonhuman actors, linkages across both time and space, and the role of resilience and adaptation as a complement to permanence and stability.

Concluding Thoughts

We present with humility what we see as a fresh picture of a field in reflection and transition, that focuses on *how* we do what we do more than *what* we do (figure 1.5). Together, these chapters evidence an increasing willingness to question the foundations of our field to respond to the scale of challenges we collectively face. There are many connections between the sections, and the chapters could have been assembled in different ways. We chose the book sections based on the natural clusters we saw in the submissions—themselves undoubtedly influenced by the approach we took to encourage diversity in authorship—and in our own reflections on trends in our field. As a group, these chapters cross-cut the typical approach in IASNR to focus on different natural resource sectors (e.g., forestry, recreation, agriculture, energy) and instead present a suite of theoretical concepts, methods, and critiques of our shared practices that can be easily applied across multiple domains. Consistent with today's diversity discourse, the chapters also deploy their

FIGURE 1.5. Word cloud visualization of extended chapter abstracts prepared for this volume.

own norms and vocabularies in the naming and capitalizing of various identities being discussed; as editors, we embrace this diversity of usage and look forward to the emergence of new ideas, perspectives, and methods shaped by the fresh winds blowing in our open NRSS windows.

References

Manfredo, M. J., J. J. Vaske, D. R. Field, P. J. Brown, and B. L. Bruyere, eds. 2004. *Society and natural resources: A summary of knowledge.* Jefferson City, MO: Modern Litho.

Manfredo, M. J., J. J. Vaske, A. Rechkemmer, and E. A. Duke, eds. 2014. *Understanding society and natural resources: Forging new strands of integration across the social sciences.* New York: Springer Open.

Section One

Diversity and Justice

1

Queer Agroecology

Exploring Nature, Agriculture, and Sexuality

JAYE MEJÍA-DUWAN AND MICHAELA HOFFELMEYER

The field of queer ecology has broad potential to expand natural resource and agricultural studies through novel conceptualizations of how gender, sexuality, race, and ability collectively mediate human-nature relationships. This chapter highlights an emerging body of scholarship we refer to as queer agroecology, which critiques the cisheteropatriarchy[1] embedded in productivist agri-food systems. This scholarship offers expanded theoretical and practical insight into the relationship between sexuality, gender, nature, and agriculture, and has clear directions for continued development.

Introduction

The International Association for Society and Natural Resources and the bodies of literature produced in this area of focus have, thus far, sparingly engaged with queer theory and queer people. In the field of queer theory,

---

1. Cisheteropatriarchy: Intertwined systems of transphobic, queerphobic, and patriarchal power and oppression.

https://doi.org/10.7330/9781646426300.c001

the term *queer* has been used not only as an adjective to refer to subjects of diverse gender and sexual identities but also as a verb, where "queering" refers to the theoretical and political action of challenging and deconstructing hegemonic norms and assumptions (Gosine 2010). Queer ecology takes up this definition of queerness to investigate the ways in which environmental degradation and the oppression of queer people are intimately linked, both in ideology and in material impacts, especially as mediated across axes of race, class, gender, ability, and species. Through theories and practices that contest these intersecting oppressions, queer agricultural workers[2] and members of eco-queer projects advance movements for queer justice while simultaneously contesting cisheteropatriarchy and other systems of oppression in nature and agriculture. For this reason, we identify queer agroecology as an emerging field that merits increased attention.

Productivist agriculture is defined by intensification, industrialization, and the prioritization of increased yields and profits (Gordon, Davila, and Riedy 2022). In contrast, agroecology promotes lessened environmental degradation through practices such as organic pesticides, cover crops, and agroforestry. Further, agroecology promotes widespread small-scale and peasant production and genetic biodiversity (Perfecto, Vandermeer, and Wright 2019). Agroecology is not *only* an alternative to productivist agricultural production but a divergent ontological approach to farming and the environment. As such, we utilize the terminology of *agroecology* not simply as a categorization of technical practices but as a broader challenge to the productivist paradigm of monocultural agricultural practices.

We thus use the term *queer agroecology* to refer to a loose constellation of research and practice taking shape through a nascent body of literature in the past decade. Scholarly work in this field has covered a broad range of areas, spanning the investigation of queer agricultural workers' identities and experiences (Lizarazo et al. 2017); the implications of cisheteropatriarchy in organizing land, labor, and capital (Leslie 2019); queer environmental and agricultural resistance strategies (Sbicca 2012); and structural interrogations of the roles of gender, sexual, and racial hierarchies in shaping the agri-food

---

2. In this chapter, we use the term *agricultural worker* as a more expansive term than *farmer* in reference to all individuals involved in agricultural production, who may or may not own the land on which they work and who may or may not be engaged in for-profit activities.

system (Leslie, Wypler, and Bell 2019). More work is required, however, especially in relation to the intersectional impacts of racism, colonialism, and sexuality on land and agriculture. We argue that the growing field of queer agroecology has broad implications and applications, as gender and sexuality are intimately woven throughout agriculture and the environment (Leslie, Wypler, and Bell 2019). An engagement with queer agroecology, therefore, presents opportunities for a step-change in natural resource studies. In this chapter, we highlight the strengths of the growing literature, applications to other fields, and directions for future research.

Delineating Queer Agroecology

Increasingly, scholars are engaging with gender and sexuality as central, rather than marginal, to rural and agrarian studies (Keller 2014). Scholars have attended to the generative implications of queer studies for critical food studies, the study of farm policy, and the study of rural communities (Sbicca 2012; Leslie, Wypler, and Bell 2019; Hoffelmeyer 2021). A 2019 special issue in *Society and Natural Resources* foregrounds the influence of queerness on human-nature-agricultural relations. Centrally, Leslie, Wypler, and Bell (2019) argue that queerness and cisheteropatriarchy play key roles in shaping agriculture at both the individual and structural levels; the authors additionally investigate the role of queerness in the transition to just and sustainable agri-food systems. Building from the ideas presented by the authors included in this special issue, we propose queer agroecology as a body of scholarship that explores the alignment of queer theory and politics with agroecological theory and practice.

Several scholars have drawn explicit parallels between queerness and principles of agroecology. For example, Edward (2018) argues that agroecology is deeply linked to queer values of "collective efficacy, the refutation of normativity . . . , alliance with greater social justice movements . . . , balance, the promotion of biodiversity, and enhanced biological intersection." Sbicca (2012) discusses "eco-queer movements," arguing that such movements align ecological, sexual, and anti-capitalist efforts in both rural and urban spaces, illustrating the potential for queer agroecologists to advance revolutionary resistance to foundational values of the current capitalist agricultural system.

Queerness and agriculture are deeply linked in relation to both oppression and resistance. Rosenberg (2016), for instance, points to the 4-H program[3] as a biopolitical tool used by the state to regulate agriculture but also to regulate the family and human sexuality while pathologizing queerness as deviant. Wilms-Crowe (2020) investigates queer agroecological practices in Puerto Rico that "offer a grounded critique of US colonial violence, inherently linked to ecological destruction, cisheteropatriarchy, and disaster capitalism." As a result of these connections to a wide array of systems of oppression and exploitation, queer agroecology provides a compelling organizing principle for broad liberatory coalitions that confront environmental degradation and sociopolitical marginalization.

Drawing on Queer Ecology

While queer ecology has emerged as a key theoretical lens through which queer and feminist scholars explore relationships between humans and the more-than-human world, we argue that the corresponding theoretical insights have thus far been underutilized by scholars of natural resource and agricultural studies. Queer ecological theory directly confronts hegemonic constructions of "human," "nature," and the "natural," and is thus uniquely well-suited for application in natural resource studies (Seymour 2020). We point to several key pieces of literature within the field of queer ecology and highlight their potential contributions to natural resource and agricultural studies, with a particular emphasis on works that intersect with studies of race, colonialism, gender, and ability.

Scholars of queer ecology trouble foundational understandings of humanity, animality, and materiality as well as the ways in which these categories are differentially assigned to humans, more-than-human beings, and other constituent elements of the natural world. In the introduction to a special issue of *GLQ* entitled "Queer Inhumanisms," Luciano and Chen (2015) outline the broad contributions of queer ecological scholarship to studies of the human and the "sub-human, in-human, [and] non-human" as well as the fluid

---

3. 4-H is an international collection of youth organizations based in the United States, where it is overseen by the National Institute of Food and Agriculture and is funded by federal, state, and local governments. Historically centered on rural and agricultural education, the program has since broadened to encompass a wider array of youth development and experiential learning initiatives.

relationships and hierarchies of power that exist between these constructed categories. Analyzing visual and literary artistic production by African diasporic subjects, Jackson (2020) interrogates the centrality of anti-Blackness in Western distinctions of "human identity from that of the animal, the object, and the nonhuman more generally," particularly in tandem with racialized hierarchies of gender and sexuality. Chen (2012) argues that notions of animacy and inanimacy are not innate but rather are "relentlessly produced and policed," whereby systems of power assign life, agency, and humanity to nonhuman subjects in surprising ways while simultaneously refuting the life, agency, and humanity of particular human subjects. Accordingly, anxieties around race, gender, sex, class, nation, and ability impact the biopolitical management of diverse human, animal, and material objects as they are assigned fluctuating inscriptions of purity, toxicity, productivity, and value.

Queer ecological literature additionally emphasizes the important roles of gender, sexuality, race, and ability in shaping environmental violences as well as movements for intersectional environmental justice. Yusoff (2015) recounts narratives of queer ecological resistance to the extractive logics of colonial and capitalist geographies and geologies. In the introduction to a special issue of *Imaginations* entitled "Critical Relationality: Queer, Indigenous, and Multispecies Belonging Beyond Settler Sex & Nature," TallBear and Willey (2019) describe the centrality of sexuality and desire in structuring colonial and capitalist relations between humans and more-than-human beings. In contrast, they advance a variety of Indigenous ontologies and epistemologies of intimacy and relationality between humans, more-than-human kin, land, and the natural world that contest ecological degradation while simultaneously asserting Indigenous sovereignty. Similarly, Gómez-Barris (2017) advances a "decolonial queer femme methodology" to explore Indigenous resistance to destructive capitalist projects of natural resource extraction in South America. Combining trans and Indigenous theories, Wölfle Hazard (2022) explores the possibilities of multispecies solidarity to advance river justice. Lastly, Clare (2017) employs a queer lens to examine the nuanced tensions and coalitional possibilities between movements for environmental and disability justice. These works, among others, advance novel conceptualizations of human-nature relationships and present scholars of natural resource and agricultural studies with alternative frameworks for exploring such relationships in diverse contexts.

Future Growth for Queer Agroecology

The queer agroecological literature thus far offers a basis for examining the following questions, among others: Are queer agricultural workers building coalitions with other marginalized groups? Do queer agricultural workers view the farm as a place of sexual freedom or as a site of cisheteropatri- archal oppression? What are the similarities and differences between queer agricultural workers engaging in agroecological systems and those in pro- ductivist agriculture? Are queer individuals disproportionately exposed to environmental injustices through the agri-food system? Do cisheterosexual agricultural workers bring queer perspectives to their farming practices? A queer agroecological body of knowledge serves as the primer for exploring these and other questions through future research.

However, we caution that queerness should not be romanticized as inher- ently transgressive. Abelson (2016) describes the phenomenon of rural trans men making claims to white working-class masculinity in an effort to rein- force their gender positionality at the expense of BIPOC people. Morgensen (2009) similarly highlights how members of rural queer separatist commu- nities may construct their sexual and gender identities in ways that rein- force nationalist and settler-colonial relationships to occupied Indigenous lands. To date, little work has investigated the impacts of colonialism on queer agriculturalism despite the reality that ongoing colonization founda- tionally defines relationships between settlers, Indigenous peoples, land, and more-than-human beings. Works by Indigenous scholars and by scholars of Indigenous studies are critical to include here; one notable point of depar- ture is TallBear's (2015) application of Indigenous queer theory to studies of nature and sexuality.

Relatedly, the primary foundational weakness of the existing queer agro- ecology literature is the oversampling of white queer agricultural workers and a lack of sufficient attention to race and racism. Race has major impli- cations for the distribution of land, food, labor, and capital, and significantly shapes social and political relationships; for example, Lizarazo et al. (2017) find that queerness and agriculture are collectively mediated through race, ethnicity, and immigration status. As a result, this lack of explicit atten- tion to race and racism prohibits a thorough understanding of sexuality and agriculture. Not only should studies intentionally sample BIPOC agri- cultural workers but scholars should also employ diverse epistemologies and ontologies, such as the "Queer Black South geographies" developed by Eaves (2017).

To date, queer agricultural studies has predominantly focused on North America, overlooking the complex ways in which sexuality interacts with agriculture across the rest of the globe. Also, essential to include in the evolving literature are deeper engagements with the lives and sociopolitical relationships of trans people in agriculture, which may be similar to yet distinct from the experiences of cisgender queer people. Engagements with disability studies provide a further opportunity to interrogate the foundational roles of ability and disability in defining and distributing agricultural land, labor, and capital.

Recent work in the field of queer agroecology has emphasized the connections between queerness, agriculture, and sustainability. In the next decade, we hope to see an expansion into other areas of human-nature relationships that have been emphasized by queer ecological literature, including the impacts of queerness and cisheteropatriarchy on natural resource extraction and climate change.

Finally, future studies must continue to focus not only on queer subjects and communities but also on cisheterosexual subjects and the role of institutional cisheterosexism in shaping political institutions and social worlds.

Conclusion

The endeavor to incorporate queer theory—and people—into theories of nature and agriculture involves more than highlighting the presence of queer people and practices within these fields. Queer agroecological scholarship has the potential to investigate the profound ways in which cisheteropatriarchy and exploitative agricultural systems are co-constructed, generating interrelated mechanisms of oppression as well as corresponding responses that advance socially and ecologically sustainable futures. Queer agroecology, when analyzed with careful attention to race, class, gender, and ability, may offer a beginning body of knowledge to imagine liberatory movements that end the oppression of diverse peoples through a reorientation of human-nature-agricultural relations. This body of queer agroecological scholarship offers profound insights concerning the relationship between agriculture, nature, queerness, and oppression, thereby offering new pathways for examining alternatives to the dominant exploitative agri-food system.

References

Abelson, M. J. 2016. "You aren't from around here": Race, masculinity, and rural transgender men. *Gender, Place & Culture* 23 (11): 1535–46.

Chen, M. Y. 2012. *Animacies: Biopolitics, racial mattering, and queer affect.* Durham, NC: Duke University Press Books.

Clare, E. 2017. *Brilliant imperfection: Grappling with cure.* Durham, NC: Duke University Press Books.

Eaves, L. E. 2017. Black geographic possibilities: On a queer Black south. *Southeastern Geographer* 57 (1): 80–95.

Edward, J. B. 2018. *Uncommon grounds: LGBTIQ farmers, agriculture, and ecologies of social difference.* PhD diss., University of British Columbia.

Gómez-Barris, M. 2017. *The extractive zone: Social ecologies and decolonial perspectives.* Durham, NC: Duke University Press Books.

Gordon, E., F. Davila, and C. Riedy. 2022. Transforming landscapes and mindscapes through regenerative agriculture. *Agriculture and Human Values* 39 (2): 809–26.

Gosine, A. 2010. Non-white reproduction and same-sex eroticism: Queer acts against nature. *Queer Ecologies: Sex, Nature, Politics, Desire* January: 149–72.

Hoffelmeyer, M. 2021. "Out" on the farm: Queer farmers maneuvering heterosexism and visibility. *Rural Sociology* 86 (4): 752–76.

Jackson, Z. I. 2020. *Becoming human: Matter and meaning in an antiblack world.* New York: NYU Press.

Keller, J. C. 2014. Rural queer theory. In *Feminisms and ruralities*, ed. B. Pini, B. Brandth, and J. Little. Lanham, MD: Lexington Books.

Leslie, I. S. 2019. Queer farmland: Land access strategies for small-scale agriculture. *Society & Natural Resources* 32 (8): 928–46.

Leslie, I. S., J. Wypler, and M. M. Bell. 2019. Relational agriculture: Gender, sexuality, and sustainability in U.S. farming. *Society & Natural Resources* 32 (8): 853–74.

Lizarazo, T., E. Oceguera, D. Tenorio, D. P. Pedraza, and R. M. Irwin. 2017. Ethics, collaboration, and knowledge production: Digital storytelling with sexually diverse farmworkers in California. *Lateral* 6 (1).

Luciano, D., and M. Y. Chen. 2015. Introduction: Has the queer ever been human? *GLQ: A Journal of Lesbian and Gay Studies* 21 (2–3): 183–207.

Morgensen, S. L. 2009. Arrival at home: Radical faerie configurations of sexuality and place. *GLQ: A Journal of Lesbian and Gay Studies* 15 (1): 67–96.

Perfecto, I., J. Vandermeer, and A. Wright. 2019. *Nature's matrix: Linking agriculture, biodiversity conservation and food sovereignty.* 2nd ed. London: Routledge.

Rosenberg, G. N. 2016. *The 4-H harvest: Sexuality and the state in rural America.* Philadelphia: University of Pennsylvania Press.

Sbicca, J. 2012. Eco-queer movement(s): Challenging heteronormative space through (re)imagining nature and food. *European Journal of Ecopsychology* 3: 33–52.

Seymour, N. 2020. Queer ecologies and queer environmentalisms. In *The Cambridge Companion to Queer Studies*, ed. S. B. Somerville. 1st ed., 108–22. Cambridge, UK: Cambridge University Press.

TallBear, K. 2015. An Indigenous reflection on working beyond the human/not human. *GLQ: A Journal of Lesbian and Gay Studies* 21 (2–3): 230–35.

TallBear, K., and A. Willey. 2019. Critical relationality: Queer, Indigenous, and multispecies belonging beyond settler sex & nature. *Imaginations: Journal of Cross-Cultural Image Studies* 10 (1): 5–15.

Wilms-Crowe, M. 2020. "Desde abajo, como semilla": Puerto Rican food sovereignty as embodied decolonial resistance. Undergraduate thesis, University of Oregon.

Wölfle Hazard, C. 2022. *Underflows: Queer trans ecologies and river justice*. Seattle: University of Washington Press.

Yusoff, K. 2015. Queer coal: Genealogies in/of the blood. *PhiloSOPHIA: A Journal of Continental Feminism* 5 (2): 203–29.

2

Gender, Land, and Agricultural Sustainability

Working toward Greater Intersectionality for Equity, Inclusion, and Justice

ANGIE CARTER AND GABRIELLE ROESCH-MCNALLY

A more inclusive agricultural system requires researchers, practitioners, and educators to reckon and engage with questions of power in relation to social and ecological diversity. Programs working to address gender equity in agriculture run the risk of replicating existing inequalities if an intersectional approach is not adopted. This chapter identifies how to move beyond focusing on gender alone as a barrier in agricultural conservation and instead work toward more transformative possibilities.

Introduction

Control of agricultural land has been a source of social inequality in the United States since its founding and continues to be a source of gender and racial domination (Dunbar-Ortiz 2014; White 2018; Sachs 1983). Ongoing social and ecological injustices in agriculture continue to exclude people and exploit land, resulting in environmental degradation and contamination including climate change vulnerabilities (Farrell et al. 2021), water pollution

https://doi.org/10.7330/9781646426300.c002

(Helmers et al. 2007), soil loss (Cox, Hug, and Bruzelius 2011), pesticide drift (Harrison 2011), and degraded community health (Wing and Wolf 2020). Mainstream agriculture in the United States today is best characterized as a chemical-intensive, large-scale, industrial monoculture that is highly input dependent and heavily subsidized and vertically integrated (Hendrickson and James 2005). Prioritizing ecological and social diversity in US agriculture is of global consequence as these practices are exported in agricultural aid and policies, destabilizing agricultural systems well beyond US borders, the green revolution and associated technologies being a prime example (e.g., Stone and Glover 2017).

Even as natural resource scientists recognize the importance of both eco-logical and social diversity, too often environmental degradation is studied as separate from rather than coexisting with, and often codependent upon, systems of social exclusion. This chapter identifies how gender inequalities in agriculture help to maintain heteropatriarchal and white control of land (Leslie, Wypler, and Bell 2019; Penniman and Washington 2018) through ongoing violence (Whyte 2018) enabled through institutionalized discrimina-tion[1] (Carpenter 2012). As white, cisgender women conducting agricultural sustainability research in the United States, we call on our colleagues to bet-ter engage questions of power as we work to address agricultural challenges.

Using examples from our own research with women's agricultural pro-grams, we call for shifts in agricultural research and program development from "studying gender" as a variable or "including women" as a demographic category to recognizing how gender, as a system of power, works to exclude some while privileging others. Programs and the creation of alternative spaces for agricultural women may preserve the status quo if we are not also working to create a more relational and equitable agricultural system (Carter, Chennault, and Kruzic 2018; Leslie, Wypler, and Bell 2019) founded in respect for the earth and one another (Whyte 2018). We apply the sociological theory of intersectionality (Collins 2016) to highlight opportunities for agricultural conservation to move beyond treating gender or race as categorical or demo-graphic variables and instead to better implement systemic understandings

---

1. See *Pigford v. Glickman* (class action of African American farmers), *Keepseagle v. Veneman* (class action of Native American farmers), as well as the subsequent USDA 2010 claims process instituted after *Garcia v. Johanns* (Hispanics sought and denied class status) and *Love v. Johanns* (women sought and denied class status) (Carpenter 2012).

of these as systems of oppression limiting conservation research design and outreach implementation and, thus, our progress toward conservation goals. In conclusion, we offer ideas for institutional and programmatic interventions and transformations for more inclusive paths forward.

Why Is an Intersectional Understanding of Power Important to Creating a More Equitable Agricultural System?

In the United States, white male control of land has been legitimized through federal policies, such as the enslavement of African Americans and Indigenous genocide, and legislative actions, such as the 1862 Homestead and Morrill Acts, 1887 Dawes Act, California's 1913 Alien Land Law, and the internment of Japanese Americans in the 1940s. Combined, these policies dispossessed Black,[2] Indigenous, Asian American, and other non-white racial groups of both land and livelihoods while consolidating control of land among whites. For example, Black farmers have lost around 90 percent of their farmland over the past century, and economists estimate that this represents billions of dollars lost in intergenerational wealth (Presser 2019). The United States Department of Agriculture (USDA) has further institutionalized racial and gender-based discrimination in agriculture through discriminatory lending practices, as acknowledged through the largest civil rights settlement in the United States (*Pigford v. Glickman*) and subsequent claims processes for Black, Native, Latinx, and women farmers (Carpenter 2012). Given these historical and ongoing discriminations, it is of little surprise that today women, Black, Native, and other farmers of color[3] are underrepresented in farming and farmland ownership (USDA NASS 2019).

2. We follow the Associated Press's style guide in our capitalization of the word *Black* to describe people rather than color, capitalization of the words *Indigenous* and *Native* to refer to original inhabitants of places, and long-standing custom to capitalize other racial and ethnic groups who share histories in the United States. We also choose to follow the Associated Press's style guide in not capitalizing the word *white* to describe white people in the United States, who do not collectively share a history or culture in the United States, nor a shared history of exclusion. See Daniszewski (2021) for further explanation.

3. In the context of US white supremacy and racial relations, the term *people of color* is used in a contemporary context to describe those who are racialized as non-white but may identify as mixed race, Latinx, Asian American, or other racialized identities other than Black. In the United States, the term *Black* is used to describe those who are of African descent, no matter their country of origin.

Agricultural land control has supported and continues to support cultural, political, and ecological hegemony (Horst and Marion 2019; Leslie 2019; Penniman and Washington 2018; Sachs et al. 2016). Nationally, white land-owners make up 98 percent of total farmland owners (USDA NASS 2019) while, women, in aggregate, own approximately 36 percent of all agricultural land, and most of these women are white (USDA NASS 2019). Still, the USDA considers white women landowners as historically underserved because of their over-representation as operators of beginning and limited resource farms (USDA ERS 2022). Gender continues to be a barrier in agricultural conservation adoption, as patriarchal expectations of land control normalize co-owners', tenants', and conservation advisors' implicit and explicit diminishment of agricultural women's contributions, including questioning their authority, limiting access to conservation networks or information, and even engaging in threats or coercion (see Carter 2019; Eells and Soulis 2013; Petrzelka et al. 2018; Sachs et al. 2016). These means of social control are not specific only to gender but also work to support white supremacy. For example, the 1862 land grant universities continue to profit from land theft that funded their founding (Brayboy and Tachine 2021; Lee and Ahtone 2020) and continue to receive greater federal funding than their 1890 Black land grant institutional counterparts (Thompson 1990). Maintaining racial power among whites and gendered power among men has been and continues to be a fundamental condition of the dominant agricultural system. Given these realities, racial and gender equity must be addressed as fundamental conditions of work toward more diverse and resilient agricultural systems.[4]

The continued maintenance of white supremacy, heterosexism, and patriarchy within the agricultural conservation movement, often by scholars' and practitioners' refusal to acknowledge or engage in analyses of these interlocking systems of power, limits conservation potential and progress. Much of the existing research on gender and sexuality in agriculture focuses disproportionately on white farmers and applies these analyses equally across all races to all farmers (Leslie, Wypler, and Bell 2019). Such research often acknowledges but does not fully reckon with the absence of non-white

---

4. See Farrell et al. (2021) and Whyte (2018) for further discussion of historical and ongoing examples of how land dispossession, through settler colonialism, and its related loss of bio- and social diversity, continues to contribute to ecological and social vulnerabilities, or Carlisle (2022) or Leslie, Wypler, and Bell (2019) for discussion of the importance of ecological and social diversity for more resilient socioecological systems.

farmers in the development of extant theories of social change in agriculture (e.g., see Sachs et al.'s [2016] feminist agrifood theory discussion). Further, research about rural life often treats race as a demographic category rather than a system of power and source of domination (Carillo, King Quisumbing, and Schaft 2021); for example, focusing on the underrepresentation of one racial group without investigating or working to interrupt the means by which white supremacy may exclude farmers of other races. Recognizing the importance of systemic analyses is fundamental to understanding how and why whiteness, as a system of domination, has strategically used gender to uphold white supremacy in control of the land.

Both in practice in the field and in knowledge production across the disciplines of conservation and agriculture, scholars and practitioners have often ignored women (Eells and Soulis 2013; Petrzelka, Sorensen, and Filipiak 2018), rendered them invisible (Sachs 1983), or co-opted their narratives in mainstream agriculture (Sachs 1983; Sachs et al. 2016). When gender is included in agricultural or conservation research, it is, like race, often treated as a reductive binary category rather than a system of power used to uphold white and heteropatriarchal control of land (Leslie, Wypler, and Bell 2019). Women's agricultural organizations, too, have fallen into this trap, upholding racial status quo while protecting heteronormative narratives about agriculture (Carter 2020; Devine 2013; Fink 1986). Even as they have been marginalized, white women have benefitted from their racial privilege as a means of protecting their class privilege as landowners (Devine 2013). It has been the work of Black women, such as Fannie Lou Hamer's Freedom Farm Cooperative (White 2018) and Leah Penniman's Soul Fire Farm (Penniman and Washington 2018), as well as queer farmers, such as Hannah Breckbill's Queer Farm Convergence (Jansen 2020; see also Mejía-Duwan and Hoffelmeyer in chapter 1 of this volume), who offer alternative farming models prioritizing ecological practices as resistance to extractive and exclusive agricultural systems. These ecological practices prioritize diversified crops, livestock integration, and relationality with natural systems. For example, prior to the US government's genocidal policies destroying the buffalo upon which many Indigenous people depended, Indigenous management of the buffalo incorporated management of healthy rangelands. Today, these practices inform new conservation efforts for sustainable grazing in the United States to foster more healthy rangelands providing livestock nutritional needs, as well as healthy and diverse forages and wild-life habitat (see Carlisle 2022).

Further, dominant social norms in mainstream agriculture are such that women, if engaged or visible in agricultural conservation, are expected to cede authority to men, for example, deferring decision-making to male family members, tenants, or advisors (Carter 2019; Sachs 1983; Sachs et al. 2016). Even as new paradigms of agricultural practices emerge, for example, organic or regenerative agriculture, these often lack critical analysis concerning the intersections of race, sexuality, and power and so result in the replication of conditions that contribute to greater inequality (Leslie, Wypler, and Bell 2019; Peter et al. 2000). This has tremendous consequences for conservation implementation and the future of agricultural management. A more diverse agriculture requires that conservation professionals provide better outreach to the white women landowners who own large amounts of farmland, particularly in areas of concern such as the US Corn Belt, while also making sure their outreach inspires critical thinking and fosters greater connections between land justice and conservation goals. The work of Soul Fire Farm in New York, through its partnership with Northeast Farmers of Color Network and the National Black Food and Justice Alliance, provides one example of how farmers of color are creating space for both action and learning on the topic of land justice and conservation. In the Corn Belt, conservation professionals could employ a similar model in coalition with other partners inviting participants to learn more about the history of their land, as well as providing actionable steps for landowners to transform their own relationships to land and support greater equity in agriculture.

How Might Gender-Specific Programs Be an Important Part of Transforming Agriculture?

Creating networks and spaces for those often excluded in agriculture is a first step in creating community and building power among excluded groups. Agricultural women, no matter their race or gender, are already strong partners in conservation despite the extra work they must do to navigate, confront, and upend white supremacy and patriarchy in mainstream agriculture (Carter 2019; Petrzelka, Sorensen, and Filipiak 2018; Petrzelka et al. 2020; Dentzman et al. 2021; Penniman and Washington 2018; White 2018). Women,

particularly Black, Indigenous, and other women of color have been leading the practices of regenerative agriculture (Carlisle 2022). However, merely
extending resources to those excluded in mainstream agriculture is not
enough; there must be interventions in the exclusionary forces if we are to
be successful in increasing agricultural equity (Leslie, Wypler, and Bell 2019).
To support such transformation, institutions and agencies need to extend
institutional resources to support a more socially and functionally diverse
agriculture.

We draw upon our research with the Women, Food and Agriculture
Network's (WFAN) Women Caring for the Land (WCL) and American
Farmland Trust's (AFT) Women for the Land (WFL) programs to analyze
how the creation of gender-based affinity groups and non-hierarchical networks among agricultural women contributes important steps toward meeting ecological and social equity goals in agriculture. WFAN and AFT are
both national nonprofit organizations in the US; while their philosophical
origins differ, both are committed to addressing the gender injustice structurally embedded in the US agricultural system and have specific programs
engaging women landowners and farmers in conservation outreach and
education. WFAN began piloting learning circles and peer-to-peer learning
with agricultural women in Iowa with its WCL program in 2001 (Wells 2004)
and has since expanded it throughout the Midwest, Kentucky, and Maine.
AFT's collaborations with WFAN's WCL program inspired its own national
Women for the Land program in 2019 (although programming in this vein
has been delivered since 2008) and is engaged in nearly twenty states working with women in agriculture. Carter currently serves on the board of direc-
tors of WFAN and has collaborated with WFAN in past research projects,
and Roesch-McNally currently works as the director of AFT's Women for
the Land program.

Agriculture has long been dominated by men and by institutions that support their success. Recent trends suggest that women are taking on more
leadership in agriculture although trends are hard to assess (Pilgeram et al.
2020). While these trends are encouraging, researchers still note that agriculture may be one of the most unequal occupations when it comes to
gender and income (Fremstad and Paul 2020). Given these inequities and
the underrepresentation of women in agriculture, organizations and educational institutions have created programs to connect women more directly

to resources that might support their success. Both WFAN's WCL and AFT's WFL programs (box 2.1) engage peer-to-peer learning circles to foster network connections, dismantle hierarchies, and connect women with technical information on conservation and other relevant topics (Carter et al. 2017; Petrzelka et al. 2020). Research conducted by both WFAN and AFT finds using peer-to-peer learning in agricultural outreach can help women both increase knowledge about conservation practices and develop the relationships needed to support the implementation of these practices (Carter 2017; Eells 2008; Petrzelka et al. 2020).

The learning circles' peer-to-peer learning model addresses practical gender needs (Moser 1993) by bringing women together to gain valuable and needed experience, validation, and information about their land. In doing so, the programs operate from an asset model, rather than remedial model, in their approach to education. Research findings from both organizations identify learning circles, and the connected networks of women in agriculture they foster, as effective tools in building power among agricultural women and in inspiring action to support sustainability on their land (Carter et al. 2017; Carter 2019; Eells and Soulis 2013; Petrzelka et al. 2020; Wells 1998). Learning circle topics have included soil health, climate resilience, and other regenerative agricultural topics that encourage women to adopt practices such as no-till, cover crops and diversified production systems. These networks have the possibility of inspiring women to adopt practices that foster both social and ecological resilience (Gosnell 2021; Roesch-McNally, Arbuckle, and Tyndall 2018).

Why Must Gender-Specific Programming in Agriculture Be Intersectional?

Networks for agricultural women have increased at local, regional, and national scales over the past few decades (Hassanein 1999; Sachs 1983; Sachs et al. 2016), including Pennsylvania's Women and Agriculture Network (PA-WAgN), the Women's Agricultural Network based at the University of Vermont, Extension's Women in Ag state-based programs, Women, Food and Agriculture Network (WFAN), and American Farmland Trust's Women for the Land program (WFL). These networks "provide on-going opportunities to build trust, share information, and build agency" (Trauger et al. 2008, 438). The efforts profiled here from WFAN and AFT reaffirm the benefits of gender-based networks and the engagement of peer-to-peer learning, rather than traditional "expert"-driven model, as a mode of sharing and collective power building (Sachs et al. 2016).

Box 2.1. Case studies: Gender-based conservation education examples.

Women, Food and Agriculture Network developed its Women Caring for the Land[5] (WCL) program to meet the needs of women landowners who are often ignored in mainstream conservation programming. The majority of attendees are commodity agricultural landowners in the US Corn Belt. The program uses a learning circle methodology that applies the unique connections and knowledge women already have about their land to support greater conservation action; for example, talking to a tenant about conservation for the first time, creating a written lease, or enrolling land in a conservation program. WCL opens doors for greater stewardship on women landowners' own terms. For example, WCL Cover Crops Champions recently used their stories to educate others through a peer-to-peer training program about how to better work with tenants and co-owners to protect the health of their land and communities by adopting cover crops as a conservation practice.

American Farmland Trust's Women for the Land[6] program has emphasized the powerful role women landowners and farmers can play in driving conservation decisions on their land and have adapted the learning circle model of peer-to-peer education as a way to create spaces that connect women, help them realize their potential, build personal and collective power, and guide more sustainable land management. One focus of AFT's program has been to push resource professionals in the public sector to see women as a critical audience and partner with whom to engage on topics of conservation and farmland protection. Participants repeatedly emphasize the critical importance of networking as a benefit of the learning circle model as evidenced in this quote from a woman participant, "You're dealing with such a generous community in terms of sharing information. . . . And then women helping women, which is something I love to see."

---

5. For more information: https://wfan.org/women-caring-for-the-land.
6. For more information: www.farmland.org.

Such networks emphasize collective power through knowledge building and connection with others who can support participants' individual and collective success. This work of supporting a network of connections is critically important given the exclusions, some of them violent, that women continue to experience when attempting to create changes on their land or in their work in agriculture more broadly (Carter 2019; Sachs et al. 2016). Studies of landowner-tenant relations in conservation adoption in Iowa, for example, found that women landowners feel alienated when it comes to decision-making about their farms (Carolan et al. 2004) and may even experience trespass, threats, and property damage when they engage in decisions contrary to the status quo (Carter 2017). The length of time these networks stay connected, their geographic or topical scope, and their ability to influence change at the individual and collective level vary (Sachs et al. 2016). AFT's WFL program has emphasized individual or farm-level change by tracking how program engagement supports participants' farm or farmland goals and has focused less on collective change-making or coalition building. Similarly, WFAN's WCL program assesses success by evaluating participants' conservation actions and also offers additional programs to connect new/interested women and nonbinary farmers to women and nonbinary farm mentors, to develop rural women's political leadership and advocacy, and to support antiracism and rural justice.

Participants in these peer-to-peer learning opportunities find clear value in gaining knowledge, sharing resources, and cultivating networks that aid in personal and professional growth and transformation (Carter et al. 2017; Eells 2008; Petrzelka 2020; Wells, 1998). However, much of the scholarship on the practical engagement within these networks has tended to emphasize gender as a locus of engagement rather than approaching this work with an intersectional approach acknowledging how race, gender, sexuality, citizenship or immigration status, and gender identity work together to provide some women access to more resources while excluding other women. To some extent, these networks have functioned best when supporting white women (see Sachs et al.'s [2016] feminist agrifood systems theory discussion). Further, these programs may exclude queer women and gender nonbinary individuals who may find that even these alternative spaces prioritize heteronormativity and cisgender identity (Leslie, Wypler, and Bell 2019; Hoffelmeyer 2021; Mejía-Duwan and Hoffelmeyer, chapter 1). This suggests that while programing for women in agriculture developed in ways to confront gender inequities, these programs may reinforce informational inequality across race, ethnicity, and sexuality lines (Beaman and Dillon 2018). As Pilgeram (2019, 15) argues, "While sustainable farming may have opened up a space for women to farm, it's a space most available for a very particular kind of women: white, well-educated, heterosexual, and married." The same could be said for many women in agricultural networks, including both WCL and WFL.

Focusing singularly on gender in research and programmatic work without inclusion of an intersectional approach—by not being more explicit about who is included and who is, often tacitly, excluded from these spaces—allows for white women to consolidate power at the expense of Indigenous women and women of color. A lack of intersectionality hides the ways that gender, race, class, ethnicity, sexuality, and nationality form mutually constitutive systems of power (Collins 2016) in ways that affect how power is shared, distributed, and contested in agriculture, including sustainable agriculture. This dynamic produces a context in which women's networks may, in some cases, uphold inequality even as they seek to contest it (Ely and Meyerson 2000).

How Can a More Intersectional Approach to Programming for Women in Agriculture Contribute to Increased Sustainability?

Our research and work in programs for agricultural women makes clear that intentionally designed spaces in which women can openly discuss power and exchange experiences and information can lead to transformational changes on the land. In this way, women are taking steps toward greater leadership in conservation decision-making and improving their understanding of the power they have in stewarding their land (Carter et al. 2017). Such networks can help change gendered social relationships, though care must be taken not to silo the conversation about gender away from the mainstream; such "women-centered" spaces may enable male-dominated institutions to do little to create a more inclusive environment for all people in agriculture (Shortall 2001). Just as male spaces in work environments may perpetuate a specific sort of dominant masculinity that excludes other nondominant men and all women (Bird 1996), women-only networks in agriculture may work to concentrate resources and power-building among white women as the dominant group of women in agriculture unless a more intersectional approach is taken to assess, confront, and dismantle inequities in programming and resource allocation.

Boosting women's participation in conservation or agricultural education programs alone will not change the sexism they experience in agriculture, nor will it change the institutionalized gender-based discrimination they face when accessing loans and education programs. We must be careful not to reinforce the status quo by creating the "illusion of inclusion" rather than real change (Gaventa and Cornwall 2001, 75). Programs for agricultural women can provide space in which women can engage in both "critique and an alternative to the conventional and patriarchal agricultural system" (Sachs et al. 2016, 141), rooted in new ways of being in relation to one another and the earth (Carter, Chennault, and Kruzic 2018; Leslie, Wypler, and Bell 2019). The women who created WFAN in the early 1990s did so in response to both exclusions in agriculture and the recognition of the global struggle for agricultural and rural women's autonomy (Wells 1998). WFAN and AFT are both working primarily in the United States where a white majority dominates land ownership and policy. This means both organizations have a responsibility as they work to engage a ready audience of white women in connecting the conservation and business of their farms to larger goals for improving public health, labor conditions, food access, and land justice. Further, this also highlights the opportunity the organizations providing these programs—be they universities, nonprofits, or agencies—have to include justice in outreach, especially to white audiences.

We challenge ourselves and invite our colleagues to better apply intersectionality in our work toward more ecologically and socially sustainable agricultural systems, even—and especially—when the target community is predominantly white and male. Doing so in the practice of social equity and ecological diversity would inspire more emancipatory scholarship that engages social science to improve the quality of life and opportunities for all in a community (Tieken and Wright III 2021). Just as the agricultural women's networks discussed earlier provide space for reflection and possibilities for solidarity-building, we share some critical and reflective questions to guide our collective work toward more ecologically *and* socially diverse agriculture:

First, how is power made visible or invisible by your work?

In what ways might your research, work, organization, and institution avoid, contribute to, benefit from, confront, question, and/or interrupt the status quo of agriculture?

Finally, how are race and gender (especially whiteness and masculinity) treated and understood in your research design, analysis, and programmatic work?

Working toward a more just agricultural system is a process. These questions can be a place from which to begin to think more critically about the research, outreach, and programs often offered with good intention but that may fall short in providing systems change. Increasing intersectionality in agricultural research, outreach, and programs provides opportunities for women and other excluded groups in agriculture to build solidarity and collective agency. This work is an invitation to our fellow researchers and practitioners to courageously ask more questions that purposefully unpack white supremacy and heteropatriarchal systems of power in agricultural systems in the United States with relevance to international systems of agriculture that have adopted similar approaches to their food systems.

References

Beaman, L., and A. Dillon. 2018. Diffusion of agricultural information within social networks: Evidence on gender inequalities from Mali. *Journal of Development Economics* 133: 147–61.

Bird, S. 1996. Welcome to the Men's Club: Homosociality and the maintenance of hegemonic masculinity. *Gender and Society* 10 (2): 120–32.

Brayboy, B. M. J., and A. R. Tachine. 2021. Myths, erasure, and violence: The immoral triad of the Morrill Act. *Native American and Indigenous Studies* 8 (1):139–44.

Carillo, I., K. King Quisumbing, and K. A. Schaft. 2021. Race, ethnicity, and twenty-first century rural sociological imaginings: A special issue introduction. *Rural Sociology* 86 (3): 419–43.

Carlisle, L. 2022. *Healing grounds: Climate, justice, and the deep roots of regenerative farming.* Washington, DC: Island Press.

Carolan, M., D. Mayerfield, M. M. Bell, and R. Exner. 2004. Rented land: Barriers to sustainable agriculture. *Journal of Soil and Water Conservation* 59 (4): 70A–75A.

Carpenter, S. 2012. The USDA discrimination cases: Pigford, in re Black Farmers, Keepseagle, Garcia, and Love. *Drake Journal of Agricultural Law* 17 (1): 1–36.

Carter, A. 2017. Placeholders and changemakers: Women farmland owners navigating gendered expectations. *Rural Sociology* 82 (3): 499–523.

Carter, A. 2019. "We don't equal even just one man": Gender and social control in conservation adoption. *Society & Natural Resources* 32 (8): 893–910. https://doi .org/10.1080/08941920.2019.1584657.

Carter, A. 2020. Women's farm organizations in the United States: Protecting and transforming agricultural power. In *Routledge handbook of gender and agriculture*, ed. C. E. Sachs, L. Jensen, P. Castellanos, and K. Sexsmith, 275–86. New York: Routledge.

Carter, A., C. Chennault, and A. Kruzic. 2018. Public action for public science: Re-imagining the Leopold Center for Sustainable Agriculture. *Capitalism Nature Socialism* 29 (1): 69–88. https://doi.org/10.1080/10455752.2017.1423364.

Carter, A., B. Wells, J. Soulis, and A. Hand. 2017. Building power through community: Women creating and theorizing change. In *Women in agriculture worldwide: Key issues and practical approaches*, ed. A. J. Fletcher and W. Kubic, 225–39. New York: Routledge.

Collins, P. H. 2016. *Intersectionality*. Cambridge, UK: Polity Press.

Cox, C., A. Hug, and N. Bruzelius. 2011. Losing ground. Accessed May 1, 2022. https://www.ewg.org/losingground/.

Daniszewski, J. 2021. AP Stylebook updates race-related terms. Accessed May 1, 2022. https://aceseditors.org/news/2021/ap-stylebook-updates-race-related -terms.

Dentzman, K., R. Pilgeram, P. Lewin, and K. Conley. 2021. Queer farmers in the 2017 US census of agriculture. *Society & Natural Resources* 34 (2), 227–47.

Devine, J. 2013. *On behalf of the family farm: Iowa women's activism since 1945*. Iowa City: University of Iowa Press.

Dunbar-Ortiz, R. 2014. *An Indigenous peoples' history of the United States*. New York: Penguin Random House.

Eells, J. 2008. *The land, it's everything: Women landowners and the institution of agricultural conservation in the U.S. Midwest*. PhD diss., Iowa State University. https://lib .dr.iastate.edu/rtd/15704.

Eells, J. C., and J. Soulis. 2013. Do women farmland owners count in agricultural conservation? A review of research on women farmland owners in the United States. *Journal of Soil and Water Conservation* 68 (5): 121A–23A. https://doi.org/10 .2489/jswc.68.5.121A.

Ely, R., and D. Meyerson. 2000. Theories of gender in organizations: A new approach to organizational analysis and change. *Research in Organizational Behavior* 22: 103–51.

Farrell, J., B. B. Burrow, K. McConnell, J. Bayham, K. Whyte, and G. Koss. 2021. Effects of land dispossession and forced migration on Indigenous peoples in North America. *Science* 374 (6567), eabe4943. https://doi.org/10.1126/science .abe4943.

Fink, Deborah. 1986. *Open country, Iowa: Rural women, tradition and change*. Albany: State University of New York Press.

Fremstad, A., and M. Paul. 2020. Opening the farm gate to women? The gender gap in US agriculture. *Journal of Economic Issues* 54 (1) 124–41.

Gaventa, J., and A. Cornwall. 2001. Power and knowledge. In *Handbook of action research: Participative inquiry and practice*, ed. P. Reason and H. Bradbury, 70–80. London: Sage.

Gosnell, H. 2021. Regenerating soil, regenerating soul: An integral approach to understanding agricultural transformation. *Sustainability Science*, 1–18. https://doi.org/o.1007/s11625-021-00993-0.

Harrison, J. L. 2011. *Pesticide drift and the pursuit of environmental justice*. Cambridge, MA: MIT Press.

Hassanein, N. 1999. *Changing the way America farms: Knowledge and community in the sustainable agriculture movement*. Lincoln: University of Nebraska Press.

Helmers, M. J., T. M. Isenhart, C. J. Kling, and W. W. Simpkins. 2007. Theme overview: Agriculture and water quality in the Cornbelt: Overview of issues and approaches. *Choices* 22 (2): 79–86.

Hendrickson, M. K., and H. S. James. 2005. The ethics of constrained choice: How the industrialization of agriculture impacts farming and farmer behavior. *Journal of Agricultural and Environmental Ethics* 18 (3): 269–91.

Hoffelmeyer, M. 2021. "Out" on the farm: Queer farmers maneuvering heterosexism & visibility. *Rural Sociology* 86 (4): 752–76. https://doi.org/10.1111/ruso.12378.

Horst, M., and A. Marion. 2019. Racial, ethnic and gender inequities in farmland ownership and farming in the U.S. *Agriculture and Human Values* 36: 1–16.

Jansen, J. 2020. LGBTQ+ farmers work to build queer-inclusive rural communities. Accessed May 1, 2022. https://nfu.org/2020/06/24/lgbtq-farmers-work-to-build-queer-inclusive-rural-communities/.

Lee, R., and T. Ahtone. 2020. Land-grab universities: Expropriated Indigenous land is the foundation of the land-grant university system. Accessed May 1, 2022. https://www.hcn.org/issues/52.4/indigenous-affairs-education-land-grab-universities.

Leslie, I. 2019. Queer farmland: Land access strategies for small-scale agriculture. *Society & Natural Resources* 32 (8): 928–46. https://doi.org/10.1080/08941920.2018.1561964.

Leslie, I., J. Wypler, and M. Bell. 2019. Relational agriculture: Gender, sexuality, and sustainability in US farming. *Society & Natural Resources* 32 (8): 853–74. https://doi.org/10.1080/08941920.2019.1610626.

Moser, C. 1993. *Gender planning and development*. London: Routledge.

Penniman, L., and K. Washington. 2018. *Farming while Black: Soul Fire Farm's practical guide to liberation on the land*. New York: Chelsea Green.

Peter, G., M. Bell, S. Jarnagin, and D. Bauer. 2000. Coming back across the fence: Masculinity and the transition to sustainable agriculture. *Rural Sociology* 65: 215–33.

Petrzelka, P., M. Briggs Ott, E. Fairchild, and J. Filipiak. 2020. "From a circle of introductions": Adult learning and empowerment of women agricultural land-owners. *Environmental Education Research* 26 (2): 206–18.

Petrzelka, P., A. Sorensen, and J. Filipiak. 2018. Women agricultural landowners—past time to put them "on the radar." *Society & Natural Resources* 853–64. doi:10.1080/08941920.2017.1423435.

Pilgeram, R. 2019. "How much does property cost up there?": Exploring the relationship between women, sustainable farming, and rural gentrification in the US. *Society & Natural Resources* 32 (8): 911–27.

Pilgeram, R., K. Dentzman, P. Lewin, and K. Conley. 2020. How the USDA changed the way women farmers are counted in the census of agriculture. *Choices* 35 (1): 1–10.

Presser, L. 2019. Their family bought land one generation after slavery: The Reels brothers spent eight years in jail for refusing to leave it. Accessed May 1, 2022. https://features.propublica.org/black-land-loss/heirs-property-rights-why-black-families-lose-land-south/.

Roesch-McNally, G., J. G. Arbuckle, and J. C. Tyndall. 2018. Soil as social-ecological feedback: Examining the "ethic" of soil stewardship among Corn Belt farmers. *Rural Sociology* 83 (1): 145–73.

Sachs, C. 1983. *The invisible farmers: Women in agricultural production.* Totowa, NJ: Rowman and Allanheld.

Sachs, C., M. Barbercheck, K. Brasier, N. Kiernan, and A. R. Terman. 2016. *The rise of women farmers and sustainable agriculture.* Iowa City: University of Iowa Press.

Shortall, S. 2001. Women in the field: Women, farming and organizations. *Gender, Work and Organization* 8 (2): 164–81.

Stone, G. D., and D. Glover. 2017. Disembedding grain: Golden rice, the Green Revolution, and heirloom seeds in the Philippines. *Agriculture and Human Values* 34 (1): 87–102.

Thompson, A. 1990. Obstacles and opportunities: Funding research at the 1890 Land Grant institutions. *Journal of Rural Social Sciences* 7 (1): 3.

Tieken, M. C., and E. Wright III. 2021. Wrestling with the past and mapping the future: A call to the field. *Rural Sociology* 86 (3): 635–39. https://doi.org/10.1111/ruso.12409.

Trauger, A., C. Sachs, M. Barbercheck, N. E. Kiernan, K. Brasier, and J. Findeis. 2008. Agricultural education: Gender identity and knowledge exchange. *Journal of Rural Studies* 24 (4): 432–39.

USDA ERS (United States Department of Agriculture Economic Research Service). 2022. Socially disadvantaged, beginning, limited resource, and female farmers and ranchers. Accessed May 1, 2022. https://www.ers.usda.gov/topics/farm

-economy/socially-disadvantaged-beginning-limited-resource-and-female
-farmers-and-ranchers/.

USDA NASS (United States Department of Agriculture National Agricultural
Statistical Service). 2019. *2017 census of agriculture*. Accessed May 1, 2022. https://
www.nass.usda.gov/Publications/ AgCensus/2017/index.php#full_report.

Wells, B. L. 1998. Creating a public space for women in US agriculture: Empowerment, organization and social change. *Sociologia Ruralis* 38 (3): 371–90.

Wells, B. L. 2004. *Results of survey of Cass County women farmland owners*. Ames, IA:
ISU Sociology Extension.

White, M. 2018. *Freedom farmers: Agricultural resistance and the Black freedom movement*. Chapel Hill: University of North Carolina Press.

Whyte, K. 2018. Settler colonialism, ecology, and environmental injustice. *Environment and Society* 9 (1): 125–44.

Wing, S., and S. Wolf. 2000. Intensive livestock operations, health, and quality of
life among eastern North Carolina residents. *Environmental Health Perspectives* 108
(3): 233–38.

3

Recent Advances in Race, Ethnicity, and Natural Resources

Research and Practice in the United States

JOHN SCHELHAS, JASMINE K. BROWN, MICHAEL DOCKRY,
SARAH HITCHNER, SARAH NAIMAN, AND GRACE WANG

Recent research on natural resource knowledge and practice in relation to racial and ethnic minorities highlights the need to reveal past inequities while also initiating a wide range of inclusive processes that increase diversity and equity in natural resource management. This chapter provides an overview of issues of race, ethnicity, and natural resources from a broad environmental justice perspective. We show how present-day relationships are shaped by the specific histories of inequity, values, and natural resource uses that are unique to different racial and ethnic groups and subgroups. These specifics reveal diversity both within and among groups. Acknowledgment of this diversity can shape inclusive and engaged scholarship as well as provide foundations for more just and equitable natural resource management approaches.

Introduction

Issues and experiences of race and ethnicity in the United States, including both racism and the dominance of white-centered views and policies, are

https://doi.org/10.7330/9781646426300.c003

deeply embedded in the country's history (Feagin 2020), and this is equally true of conservation and natural resource management (Schelhas 2002; Taylor 2016). The natural resource fields have only recently begun to reckon with past and ongoing racism and discrimination, as well as the many distinct cultural relationships that diverse racial and ethnic populations have with natural resources including land, forests, wildlife, fish, water, rangelands, and related ecosystems on both public and private lands (Jacoby 2014; Merchant 2007; Nijhuis 2021; Taylor 2016). Two decades ago, Schelhas's review of the literature on race, ethnicity, and natural resources provided a broad assessment of issues and empirical research (Schelhas 2002), and a recent comment on that paper identifies newer developments (Schelhas 2020). This chapter seeks to provide a closer and more systematic look at recent advances in research and practice related to race, ethnicity, and natural resources in the United States.

Race and ethnicity are related but distinct concepts. In the social sciences, it is generally accepted that there is no biological basis for race (although it is most often erroneously based on perceived physical attributes), but the domain rather understands race as an ever-shifting social construction that has significant material and social outcomes (Harrison 1995; Hill Collins and Solomos 2010; Schelhas 2002; Solomos 2023; Winant 2000). Ethnicity generally refers to cultural groups not based on physical characteristics but rather on regional and national origin and the cultural patterns generally characteristic of these groups (Harrison 1995; Hill Collins and Solomos 2010; Schelhas 2002). The overlapping and shifting concepts of race, ethnicity, and culture are further complicated in the United States by the use in the Census of Population of separate questions for race (American Indian or Alaska Native, Asian, Black or African American, Native Hawaiian or Other Pacific Islander, and White) and ethnicity (Hispanic or Latino, or not). Nevertheless, race and ethnicity are often studied together in the social sciences, and here we focus on four broad racial and ethnic groups: American Indian or Native American, Black or African American, Asian, and Latine[1] or Hispanic.[2]

Social science approaches to race and ethnicity are grounded in several

---

1. The gendered terms Latino/a are increasingly replaced with Latinx, but some see that as originating outside the ethnic group and that the alternative term Latine fits more readily into Spanish language.

2. We recognize that many nationalities and ethnicities are reflected in the cultural patterns within each of these groups, as well as the ways they intersect to form complex identities.

theoretical approaches, including: (1) social relationships, such as the social construction of racial and ethnic categories, racism, discrimination, and inequality; (2) issues of identity, such as narratives imposed by broader society and outside groups, counternarratives originating within racial and ethnic groups, and the resulting detrimental impacts and affordances; and, more recently, (3) critical race theory, which considers race and racism to be structured into all aspects of society and to intersect with other social issues related to class, gender, sexual orientation, and power (Carbado and Roithmayr 2014; Solomos 2023). These theoretical approaches have informed important advances in the ways that natural resource researchers, policy-makers, and practitioners understand discrimination and cultural differences in how various subgroups in the United States conceive of and use natural resources.

Theoretical approaches have been most often applied in the literature regarding outdoor recreation, one branch of natural resource management. For example, under-participation by minorities in recreation has been theorized as based on ethnicity, marginalization, and/or avoidance of negative social encounters (Floyd and Stodalska 2014), reflecting social relations theory. Early studies took white recreation patterns as the norm and assumed that other groups would choose to recreate in the same ways (Schelhas 2002), while later work grounded in identity theory has examined recreation from non-white perspectives (Flores and Kuhn 2018; Izenstark, Crossman, and Middaugh 2022; Johnson and Bowker 2004). Research often uses qualitative and ethnographic research grounded in critical race theory to understand recreation patterns of individuals, breaking away from essentialized race categories (Arai and Kivel 2009; Kivel, Johnson, and Scraton 2009). Furthermore, recreation researchers have sought to broaden the concept of recreation beyond leisure to include a wider range of ways that people engage with natural areas (Blahna et al. 2020) and to broaden the language used in recreation to be more inclusive (Armstrong and Derrien 2020).

What emerges from these findings, and what will guide the most consequential research in the future, is the acknowledgment that empirical research, especially when planned and conducted by scholars with a diversity of backgrounds, experiences, and worldviews, is a necessary precursor to theorizing the roles that race and ethnicity play in natural resource access and utilization. Vera and Feagin (2007) suggest that abstract theorizing closes off many analytical pathways and that most of our conceptual advances (e.g., systematic racism) have come out of empirical studies rather than prees-tablished theorizing (for a contrary view, see West et al., chapter 13). Other scholars similarly caution against overtheorizing in race and ethnicity schol-arship and suggest paying careful attention to empirical research and political engagement by focusing on both the material substance of racial inequalities (Knowles 2010) and decentering white points of view—including the subtle remnants that may remain even after earlier efforts to do so (Feagin 2020).

Our approach here is rooted in the realization that Western scholars have long used dominant white framings that have placed other racial and ethnic groups in inferior positions and have fostered exploitive relationships (Feagin and O'Brien 2010). While there are important advances to be made by add-ing race and ethnicity considerations to a broad range of natural resource research topics, research on race and ethnicity must always grapple with and account for history by rearranging concepts and conducting research *with* diverse groups, not *on* them. Issues of race, ethnicity, and natural resources can be seen as an extension of environmental justice from its more common focus on exposure of minority racial and ethnic communities to environmen-tal hazards to include broader inequities related to natural resources owner-ship, use, management, and conservation (Mutz, Bryner, and Kenney 2002; Sze 2004). The three main tenets of environmental justice—distributive jus-tice, procedural justice, and justice of recognition—point at critical underly-ing questions related to acknowledgment of the diversity of natural resource users, their access to natural resources for a wide range of uses ranging from economic to spiritual, their inclusion in decision-making processes regarding natural resources, and the distribution of costs and benefits from natural resource management decisions (Malin, Ryder, and Lyra 2019; Taylor 2020; Dobbin and Lubell 2021). Implicit in this view is the need for a close exam-ination of the configurations of power that currently exist and attention to the ways that less powerful groups have historically challenged the system or found alternate ways to achieve their goals within it.

Recent research and activism, discussed below, provide a critical lens to look at natural resource challenges in ways that do not normalize historic majority patterns of natural resource use but rather empower communities of color. Importantly, increasing numbers of researchers from diverse racial and ethnic groups (including co-authors of this chapter) are reconfiguring the ways that we think about race, ethnicity, and natural resources from their own perspectives. Our author perspectives are influenced by both our professional expertise and lived experiences, as is evident in our biographies. Our diversity in age, gender/sex, career stage, geographical location, and ethnic and racial background positions us to speak to issues that have not been adequately summarized in the literature. In addition, our collaboration has led to intersectional thinking, creating fertile ground for cross-pollination of ideas through the open sharing of cultures and subcultures of which we are not a part. We would, however, like to explicitly make the point that no one speaks for any racial or ethnic group as a whole. We recognize and celebrate the heterogeneity of perspectives and experiences within population groups, even as we as authors briefly summarize each group's historical and present engagements with nature and natural resources.

American Indian

American Indian populations are often misunderstood by the majority of American citizens, natural resource institutions, and state and municipal governments. One common misconception is that American Indian is a racial category; it is not.[3] American Indian is a political category comprised of sovereign nations and individual tribal citizens. American Indian tribes, as sovereigns, are able to determine citizenship (sometimes called membership, among other terms) just like countries determine citizenship. The reason for this is that American Indian tribes were sovereign entities before the United States was a country. The United States does not grant sovereignty to American Indian tribes, but it has recognized tribes as sovereign from the country's founding. This is the basis for the many treaty agreements made between the United States and American Indian tribes; treaties are binding agreements between sovereign governments. In addition to treaties, the United States recognizes the sovereign nature of American Indian tribes though the US Constitution, Supreme Court decisions, case law, executive orders, and executive branch policies (see, for example, Wilkins and Lomawaima 2001; Wilkinson 2004). At the time of this writing there are 574 tribes recognized by the US government (Bureau of Indian Affairs 2021). Each

---

3. "American Indian or Alaskan Native" is a racial category in the US Census, but we take a different perspective here.

one of these tribes has a unique history, culture, and understanding of the world. They are also diverse internally, as is the case for any sovereign nation.

Despite the foundational principles of tribal sovereignty, American Indian tribes and individual tribal members have faced discrimination in many aspects of natural resource management. The creation of the United States and the federal protected areas (e.g., national parks and forests) was often carried out through genocide and forced removal of American Indian tribes and peoples from their lands (Catton 2016; Keller and Turek 1998; Spence 2000; Waziyatawin 2008). While treaties were used during this initial process, they were often signed through coercion, violence, and corruption (Case 2018). In the wake of American Indian land cessions came massive land loss, forest clearing, fires, and community transformations. This is an ongoing process called settler colonialism, which is defined by the erasure and replacement of Indigenous presence on the land (Whyte 2018; Wolfe 2006). More recently, many states have tried to prevent American Indian people from exercising the treaty rights that were reserved in the original land cessions (e.g., Brown 1994; Nesper 2002; Wilkinson 2005). Today, this dispossession and these ecological transformations contribute to be daily reminders of the discrimination and injustices perpetuated against Indigenous peoples, their cultures, and their ecologies (Dockry and Whyte 2021). All land in the United States today was Indigenous land, and there is a need—morally, legally, and ethically—to confront the ongoing dispossession within society as a whole and within natural resources.

American Indian and Indigenous people have maintained strong relationships to the land and waters of the United States, yet there is a striking dearth of American Indian people, values, and knowledges within natural resource management agencies, education institutions, and research literature. American Indian and Alaskan Native people comprise 1.3 percent of the US population, yet they, like other minoritized groups, are underrepresented in natural resource agencies (Mejicano, Dockry, and Kilgore 2022) and higher education (Sharik et al. 2015). Understanding American Indian recreation patterns is more difficult to tease out from the non-Indigenous society perspective. This is partly because American Indians have different values related to natural resources (Bengston 2004) and outdoor recreation, where often American Indians view things like hunting, fishing, and gathering as cultural responsibilities and not "recreation" (Kimmerer 2013; Reo and Whyte 2012).

Time spent on public lands can also be seen by American Indians as fulfill-ing treaty and spiritual obligations, not as recreational pursuits. One study from California shows American Indian people visit public lands at similar frequencies as white people (Winter et al. 2020), while a study looking at national forest visitation shows that American Indians visit over forty-five times less than white people (Flores et al. 2018). American Indians do not fall easily into "recreation" categories that are developed (and monitored) by public land management agencies, leading to a lack of understanding of the importance of American Indian use. Compounded with the historical legacy of dispossession of land and resources from American Indians, which contin-ues today, the lack of their "participation" in natural resource-based activities as monitored by non-Native institutions is not surprising.

Despite this, American Indian communities have been at the forefront of innovations with regards to natural resource management and responses to our myriad environmental, social, and economic challenges (Dockry and Hoagland 2017). For example, American Indian tribes have built upon gen-erations of knowledge to develop novel strategies to support forest and ecosystem resilience to wildfire (Lake et al. 2017). Tribal natural resource management has proven so effective and innovative that there are some who call for public land management to revert to tribal control (Sessions et al. 2017; Treuer 2021). American Indian innovation has also extended to novel partnerships for natural resource management (Dockry, Gutterman, and Davenport 2018; Donoghue, Thompson, and Bliss 2010), governance (Baumflek et al. 2021), forest inventory (Emery et al. 2014), research (Drawson, Toombs, and Mushquash 2017; Johnson and Larsen 2013; McGregor, Restoule, and Johnston 2018), and education (Gervais et al. 2017; Hoagland et al. 2017). American Indian and Indigenous people are leading the way in biodiversity conservation (Schuster et al. 2019) and climate change adaptation (Townsend, Moola, and Craig 2020; Whyte 2014). Tribal forest management provides numerous examples of balancing complex, multiple objectives in an era of shrinking budgets, novel ecological interactions, and increasing human demands on our natural resources.

None of these innovations happen by chance. American Indian and Indigenous people are poised to usher in a new era for natural resource man-agement and society. With the rise of Indigenous empowerment, natural resource managers and society have a choice in moving forward together:

respect tribal values, sovereignty, and innovations or face the real possibilities of catastrophic ecosystem decline, increased division and litigation, and possibly violence (Dockry 2020). Robin Kimmerer, a Potawatomi scholar, reminds us that we all have a choice in how our world develops and that the integration of broader Indigenous values, like love, respect, and responsibility, is the way forward. She challenges us, "Knowing that you love the earth changes you, activates you to defend and protect and celebrate. But when you feel that the earth loves you in return, that feeling transforms the relationship from a one-way street into a sacred bond" (Kimmerer 2013, 124).

Black American

According to the 2020 US Census Bureau, Black Americans comprise around 12 percent of the US population and are the third largest of the racial and ethnic groups in the United States after whites (58%) and Latines (19%); they are projected to comprise 15–18 percent by 2060 (Jones et al. 2021; Tamir 2021). A shared history of racial violence, dispossession, and disparities directly affects Black American valuations of land, development policies, food justice, and environmental issues such as pollution and climate change. However, as with other racial and ethnic groups, Black Americans are diverse culturally, socially, politically, and economically; attention to nuance is required to avoid the "Black monolith myth" (Ray 2020), especially with regards to natural resource management.

People of African descent have been managing natural resources in what is now the US since they began to arrive as enslaved persons in the late 1500s. While many were forced to labor on white-owned land (following dispossession of Native Americans), some farmed and used natural resources in independent maroon colonies or as freedmen in or near slave territories (Diouf 2016). After Emancipation, some white families deeded land to formerly enslaved persons, some Black families were able to purchase land, and others were granted land through General Sherman's Special Field Order No. 15 in 1865 or through the Southern Homesteading Act of 1866, which allocated land for Black settlers. However, Black Americans have struggled, and are still struggling, to maintain land and fully utilize natural resources (Gordon, Barton, and Adams 2013). Systemic practices such as sharecropping, which restricts ownership of land and was a new form of exploitation following the outlawing of slavery (Schelhas 2002), and historical events such as the Great Migration have had a significant impact on rights, access, and intergenerational connections to land (Reynolds 2002). Black families have also faced obstacles such as land theft, insecure land tenure (primarily in the form of heirs' property, or land held communally by multiple family members in the name of a deceased ancestor), limited access to government programs, and active racial discrimination by lenders and government agencies (Gaither et al. 2019; Gilbert, Sharp, and Felin 2002; Schelhas and Hitchner 2020). Although the commonly used term *land loss* implies the passive disappearance of land-ownership, the dispossession of 98 percent of Black agricultural and forest landowners (Newkirk 2019) can and should be understood as an active, ongoing, and systemic process (Hitchner, Schelhas, and Dwivedi 2021).

The connections between Black Americans, nature, and natural resources are shaped by what Dr. Dorceta E. Taylor calls "eternal stereotypes" (Saha 2018), especially the misconception that Black Americans today are disconnected from nature or exhibit low levels of environmental concern (Mohai 1990, 2003). A growing body of literature (Mohai and Bryant 1998; Parker and McDonough 1999; Jones and Rainey 2006; Jones 2002) describes this characterization as inaccurate (Taylor 2018, 2019), biased, limited in scope (Newell and Green 1997), and overlooking the complexities between Black Americans and nature (Sheppard 2010). Prominent Black American leaders of the environmental justice movement have made direct connections between racism, environmental toxins, and pollution; Black-led activism about these issues further exposes the deeply flawed notion that Black communities lack environmental concern (Bullard 2005; for an international perspective, see Cockburn et al., chapter 14).

One of the reasons that these misconceptions persist is the way that the history of natural resource management in the United States is told. The figures portrayed most prominently in the environmental and conservation movements are white; these include people such as Aldo Leopold, John Muir, Henry David Thoreau, Rachel Carson, and Gifford Pinchot. While they have of course been instrumental in shaping natural resource management, future efforts to present a more inclusive environmental history must consider the efforts of Black American leaders such as Harriet Tubman (naturalist), Paul Logan (first Black forester hired by the USDA Forest Service), and George Washington Carver (naturalist and agricultural scientist) (Alexander

2019; Hersey 2011; Lewis 2005). The environmental histories we share should be reflective of contributions from a diversity of people.

Another reason for the persistence of the myth that Black Americans are disconnected from nature relates to the current disparities in their representation among natural resource management professionals, especially in positions of power to make decisions about resource laws and policies (Brown and Rempel 2020). The historical roots of this inequity can be tied to unequal and limited access to education. The first professional forestry schools (i.e., Yale School of Forestry, Biltmore School of Forestry) were founded in the early 1900s, which predates the Civil Rights Movement and the legally forced integration of educational institutions. Although the first class of Pennsylvania State University's State Forest Academy in 1906 included Ralph E. Brock, the first Black American forester (Manno, Steiner, and Day 2002), Black Americans were excluded from most mainstream forestry academic programs until the 1960s (Bragg 2017). In 1971, Payne and Theoe declared the unequal representation of Black foresters "a professional concern" that could be attributed to barriers such as institutional racism, lack of Black role models, and segregated educational institutions; other barriers include limited awareness of the profession (Wellman 1987; Leatherberry and Wellman 1988), cultural dissonance (Balcarczyk et al. 2015), and discrimination (Schelhas 2002). As reported by Sharik et al. (2015), in 2012 Black Americans represented 3.2 percent of all undergraduate enrollees for forestry, and 2.7 percent for all natural resource fields. However, the demographic statistics do not overshadow the few yet powerful personal experiences of Black natural resources professionals that can be found within literature (for examples, see Richmond, Page, and Blount 1996 and Mobley 1996, 2020).

Research on Black Americans and outdoor recreation has been developing since the 1990s. Early research focusing on underrepresentation, theoretically based in marginality, ethnicity, and social relations / hostility have been reviewed elsewhere (Floyd and Mowatt 2014; Schelhas 2002). New research takes several promising directions. Martin (2004) analyzes images of recreationists across magazines and advertisement to show that recreation is depicted as a white domain. Erickson, Johnson and Kivel (2009) use in-depth qualitative interviews to understand the historical and cultural experiences of Black Americans in relation to Rocky Mountain National Park. Several authors draw on history and personal experience to promote a reimagining of what are often thought of as white outdoor spaces to include Black people (Finney 2014; Johnson n.d.; Lanham 2016; Mills 2014). The approach of increasing representation and awareness of Black outdoor recreationists dovetails with agency efforts to engage these communities (Johnson Gaither, Roberts, and Hanula 2015).

There are currently numerous efforts underway to enhance the engagement of Black Americans with natural resource management. For example, the Uniform Partition of Heirs Property Act (UPHPA) aims to help Black families retain land, while maintaining the rights of individuals to sell their shares (Mitchell 2014). The Justice for Black Farmers Act of 2021 has informed relief efforts for Black farmers in the American Rescue Plan. The Sustainable Forestry and African American Land Retention Network (SFLR), initiated by the US Endowment for Forestry and Communities in 2012, provides access for Black forest landowners to government funding and professional support for forest management in the southeastern United States (Schelhas, Hitchner, and McGregor 2019). One example of telling more inclusive environmental histories is the Maxville Heritage Interpretive Center in Oregon, which tells the stories of multicultural logging towns across the Pacific Northwest, focusing on the contributions of Black loggers to the US timber industry. Organizations seeking to increase the representation of Black Americans in natural resource professions include the Greening Youth Foundation, the Society of American Foresters Diversity Scholars Program, and MANRRS (Minorities in Agriculture, Natural Resources and Related Sciences). The Black outdoors movement is also growing in popularity, led by organizations such as Outdoor Afro, Melanin Basecamp, Joy Trip Project, Get Black Outside, and Taking Nature Black Conference. Together, these policies and initiatives showcase the role of Black Americans in natural resource management history, seek to rectify past discrimination and exclusion, and provide concrete assistance for Black landowners and natural resource managers to more fully engage with both natural resources themselves and the systems of power that have historically restricted their access to them.

Asian American

The term *Asian American* emerged in the 1960s concurrently with the broader Civil Rights Movement (NPS 2005). The Asian American population in the

United States is heterogenous, comprised of individuals of diverse ethnicities, nationalities, histories, and socioeconomic statuses (NPS 2005; Sze 2004; Winter, Jeong, and Godbey 2004). Chinese, Japanese, Filipinos, Koreans, and Asian Indians were among the earliest to settle in the United States and constitute the largest proportion of Asian Americans, while Vietnamese, Cambodians, Laotians, Thais, and Indonesians arrived in significant numbers beginning in the mid-twentieth century (NPS 2005). Asian Americans currently constitute 7 percent of the US population, though their numbers are projected to quadruple by 2060 (Budiman and Ruiz 2021).

Asian Americans, like many immigrant groups, often first found employment in the United States as laborers (NPS 2005). In spite of their important role in western US history, their presence and contributions have often been ignored. For example, at the completion of the transcontinental railroad in 1869, Leland Stanford drove a ceremonial gold spike uniting the Central Pacific and Union Pacific Railroads in Promontory Point, Utah. From historical accounts, the ceremony was festive, but missing were the thousands of Chinese workers, estimated to be up to 90 percent of the workforce, who had built the railroad through the harsh conditions of the High Sierras (Chang 2019). Contemporaneously, Chinese workers mined for gold in California. Yet discriminatory laws, policies, taxes, wage rates, and mob violence aimed to prevent them from mining or allowed them to work only claims yielding low returns (Chung 2011; NPS 2005). Chinese immigrants were familiar with logging, as "cutting timber for fuel and construction was a common occupation in every South China village" (Chung 2015, 3), and many found labor opportunities in migrant farm labor, lumber mills, and logging camps (NPS 2005). Chinese laborers experienced intense discrimination despite their indispensable contribution to the building of modern America (Chang 2019; Graybill 2019). Mob violence forced many Chinese Americans from their lands and communities and further contributed to their erasure from the written history of natural resources in the United States (Pfaelzer 2007). Japanese immigrants also played important roles in agriculture and horticulture on the West Coast; however, their enterprises were interrupted during World War II by Executive Order 9066 that led to their forced removal to internment camps in inland parts of the country (NPS 2005). Koreans found work in agriculture, canneries, and lumberyards, and Vietnamese came to play an important role in the Gulf Coast shrimp fishery (NPS 2005; Schewe et al. 2020).

Asian immigration continued apace following these workers. First coined by sociologist William Peterson in 1966, the "model minority" myth continues to homogenize and stereotype Asians and their "success" in the United States. It is a problematic theory that Asian Americans have overcome barriers of racial discrimination better than other racial groups. Wide disparities in educational attainment have led to deep economic polarization among Asian Americans, more than any other racial or ethnic group; a 2018 Pew Research Center study found that those in the top tenth of the income distribution made 10.7 times more than those in the bottom tenth (Kochhar and Killuffo 2018). The stereotype about Asian success also fails to reflect Asian underrepresentation in all aspects of contemporary society. Asian Americans are significantly underrepresented in senior positions in companies, politics, and media (holding about 3 percent of these positions while comprising 7 percent of the US population; Lu, Nisbett, and Morris 2020). Asian Americans also have the lowest degree of representation in political office compared with any other racial or ethnic group.

Another stereotype that Asian Americans (as with other racial and ethnic groups) have often faced is being erroneously depicted as disinterested in environmental issues (Taylor 2014). Research shows that Asian Americans are strongly pro-environment, with 70 percent considering themselves environmentalists (Ong, Le, and Daniels 2013; Ramakrishnan and Lee 2012). The majority (77%) of Asian Americans support stronger federal policies to combat climate change, and 86 percent agree that acting now on climate change would provide a better life for future generations (Kou-Giesbrecht 2020). Speiser and Krygsman (2014, 24) find that "even though the Asian American population is small in absolute numbers, their growing size and influence on American culture and consumption can help to introduce, steer, and expand climate solutions."

While mainstream environmental narratives have tended to erase or elide the contributions of Asian Americans (Choi 2021), recent work has sought to rectify these omissions and raise important new questions. The important role of Asian Americans in environmental activism and grassroots environmental leadership has been documented (Kim and Matsuoka 2013; Sze 2004). Literature in the last ten years has included further inquiry into and appreciation of Asian labor history in the American West, leading to exploration of how the prejudices faced by their ancestors and historical Asian American engagements with the natural landscape influence their current relationships with natural resources and attitudes toward nature and resources. How do modern Asian Americans process this history as we move forward in making the outdoors more inclusive and representative? In trying to answer this question, we must bear in mind the fact that Asian American conceptions of environmentalism and natural resources are as broad as the ethnicity itself, with each of these distinct groups possessing different attitudes and relationships to natural resources (Ong, Le and Daniels 2013; Winter, Jeong and Godbey 2004).

Diverse Asian American subcultures also have different patterns of outdoor recreation, including both consumptive and non-consumptive uses (Winter, Jeong, and Godbey 2004). Yet mainstream notions of outdoor recreation ignore the divide between recreation as leisure and human connections to nature that include subsistence, cultural connections, spiritual value, and affirming sense of place (Blahna et al. 2020). Outdoor recreational experiences such as hiking, fishing, and camping are the primary ways that people enjoy public lands in the United States (Blahna et al. 2020); however, these mainstream activities omit other types of resource-based enjoyment or use of natural resources, such as the collecting and harvesting of non-timber forest products (NTFPs), particularly on public lands. Chamberlain, Emery, and Patel-Weynand (2018) highlight that harvesters of Asian descent often utilize national forests to gather NTFPs such as mushrooms and ginseng. In addition to providing important cultural and economic benefits, gathering as an activity could contribute significantly to ecological stewardship, as more experienced harvesters tend to have greater depth and breadth of ecological knowledge and use what they perceive to be more sustainable harvesting practices (Ballard and Huntsinger 2006; Richards and Creasy 1996).

Other conservation efforts have drawn on the ecological knowledge of Asian Americans. For example, one contemporary effort to bridge research and practice has used participatory research to engage Vietnamese shrimpers in collaborative natural resource management (Schewe et al. 2020). However, further recognition of the long history of Asian American engagement with natural resources and more representation in positions of decision-making power are necessary elements of a more inclusive future trajectory for Asian Americans.

Latine

Latines/Hispanics are the second largest racial/ethnic group in the United States (after non-Hispanic whites) and are expected to grow from 18 to 28 percent of the population between 2020 and 2060 (Colby and Ortman 2015). In comparison to other racial and ethnic groups, Latines report the highest levels of concern for environmental issues such as climate change, pollution, drought, and so on (Burger et al. 2004; Jones, Cox, and Navarro-Rivera 2014; Pearson et al. 2018; Whittaker, Segura, and Bowler 2005; Williams and Florez 2002). Despite the high levels of environmental concern and their growing power to influence social and environmental change in the United States, they have often been overlooked within environmental scholarship.

Historically, individuals in power have discredited and rejected the concerns of Latines in the United States (Anguiano et al. 2012). As a result, Latines have been subjected to various environmental injustices with regards to land use and ownership (Schelhas 2002), utilization of Latines for low-wage labor (Taylor 2016), exposure to environmental hazards (Crowder and Downey 2010; Hernandez, Collins, and Grineski 2015), access to environmental goods (Flores et al. 2018), discrimination and tokenization in environmental organizations (Naiman, Schusler, and Schuldt 2018; Taylor 2014), and limited participation in environmental decision-making practices (Naiman forthcoming).

Exposure to these various injustices has impacted the ways in which Latines and non-white groups in the United States conceptualize environmental problems. According to Song et al. (2020), non-white individuals in the United States were more likely to report environmental problems as closely tied to human-centered social problems than whites. Latines report a more expansive definition not only of environmental problems but also of what is considered "nature" and "the environment" to extend beyond pristine natural areas and include the built environment where they live or work (Gibson-Wood and Wakefield 2013; Naiman, Schusler, and Schuldt 2018). This appreciation for the connection between environmental and social problems are linked to "environmental justice attitudes," which play a significant role in predicting pro-environmental behavioral intention for both Latines and non-Latines within the United States (Naiman, Stedman, and Schuldt 2023; Song et al. 2020).

Scholars have traditionally treated Latines as a homogenous group despite their diversity in immigration experiences, language, and culture. Research examining these differences has often focused on differences in acculturation (i.e., foreign-born vs. native-born Latines; Macias 2016a, 2016b) or on Mexican Americans as they reflect the largest ethnic group within the United States (Pew Research Center 2021). Historically, scholarship around Mexican Americans in the western United States has highlighted various environmental injustices such as farmworkers' exposure to pesticides (Peña 2005), the use of undocumented labor for forest management (Wilmsen, Bush, and Barton-Antonio 2015), limited access to clean water (Williams and Florez 2002), and historic battles around land use and land rights (Schelhas 2002). Since Hurricane Maria there has been increased attention on Puerto Rico and the historic economic and environmental injustices its citizens continue to face as a consequence of US colonization and capitalism (García 1970; Rodríguez 2004; Rodríguez-Díaz 2018; Schmelzkopf 2008; Willison et al. 2019). As a result, scholars have pointed to the need for and pathways toward achieving energy justice, food sovereignty, decolonization, and resiliency on the island (De Onís, 2018; Garriga-López et al. 2019; Smith-Nonini and Nonini 2019; Wilms-Crowe 2020).

More recently, we have seen increased interest in understanding not only Latine environmental perceptions, concerns, and activism, but also how cultural factors contribute to Latine environmentalism within the United States (Ballew et al. 2019; Macias 2016a, 2016b; Naiman, Stedman, and Schuldt 2023; Pearson et al. 2021). Scholars have found that collectivistic values, social norms, ethnic identity exploration, and Latine social networks—particularly the family—may play a significant role in the ways in which Latines relate to natural spaces, engage in outdoor activities, act on their concern for environmental problems, and express willingness to engage in pro-environmental behaviors (Ballew et al. 2019; Naiman, Stedman, and Schuldt 2023; Naiman forthcoming; Pearson et al. 2021).

These findings build upon previous work demonstrating that Latines enjoyed outdoor recreation activities more when they were able to share them with friends and family and utilize them for heritage practices (Chavez and Olson 2009; Cuevas et al. 2016; Stodolska, Shinew, and Li 2010). Thus, the social aspect of Latine environmentalism is critical to our understanding of Latine interactions with the environment. Similar to other racial and ethnic groups, Latines have had difficulties accessing forests and national parks. Flores et al. (2018) found that forests that were located in highly populated minority areas had some of the greatest inequities in terms of visitorship. To address this large gap, scholars have called for developing meaningful long-term relationships with local communities, actively hiring and retaining diverse staff, creating more tailored programming that centers Latine cultures and identities, and initiating storytelling to promote positive Latine outdoor experiences (Flores et al. 2018; Flores and Sánchez 2020; Flores and Kuhn 2018). Outside of academia, nonprofits such as Latino Outdoors, GreenLatinos, Brooklyn's Latino organization UPROSE, Little Village Environmental Justice Organization, and La Madre Tierra have emerged in the last two decades to promote Latine cultural experiences within nature and to build power to advocate for Latine interests in local and national environmental policy.

Conclusion

This chapter has provided an overview of issues of race, ethnicity, and natural resources from a broad environmental justice perspective, with an emphasis on four broad groups in the United States: American Indian, Black American, Asian American, and Latine. While generalization is important to scholarship, our review generally points in the opposite direction. The lessons and directions for future research and natural resource management often lie in the particulars, which include examining how present-day relationships are shaped by the specific histories of inequity, values, and natural resource uses that are unique to different racial and ethnic groups and subgroups and reflect the landscapes and resource characteristics of specific places. It is incumbent on researchers and managers to be attuned to history and unique socioecological contexts in particular places rather than to rely on generalized and scientific management approaches that have developed without accounting for this diversity. That said, natural resource scholarship also builds on key social science theoretical insights on race and ethnicity more broadly, including social relations, identity, and critical race theory. Further theoretical work that is attuned to the rapidly accruing and changing perspectives from empirical research, activism, and politics can make an important scholarly contribution to the field and enhance practice.

As we have shown with all four racial and ethnic groups discussed, minorities in the United States have been subject to systematic exclusion across a wide range of natural resource contexts. Histories of genocide, land loss, and discrimination have deeply affected members of each of these groups. The results range from preventing people from accumulating wealth to disrupting the ways people have lived or are living their lives within culturally complex socioecological relationships. A wider perspective is important to ensure equity and justice but also to conceptualize and implement more robust policies and management for human livelihoods and ways of living that are connected to forests, wildlife, landscapes, and places. Natural resource management and policy are poorer for having excluded traditional and local knowledge that can enhance sustainability and adaptation to changing environments. Research on different environmentalisms and the varying meaning of natural resources and experiences to people from various groups is critical to provide new foundations for more inclusive approaches to natural resource management and policy.

Conservationists and natural resource managers, even those attuned to complex racial and ethnic dynamics, have many times fallen into various traps that have impeded both sustainable natural resource management and more inclusive resource policies. First, there is often an over-emphasis on the homogenizing effects of mainstream culture (in this case, white-dominated ideals of nature and resource use) that fails to account for innovation and hybridity that comes with intercultural interactions. Brosius and Hitchner (2010, 145) state that policymakers often overlook the fact that "culture is dynamic, that humans exercise agency, and that it is at borders, margins and through zones and processes of hybridity that processes of cultural production are manifested . . . culture is not a timeless entity, but something that is actively produced through processes of articulation." Further, cultural perspectives are not always shared by members of the same racial or ethnic group (or, in the case of a country, a set of ethnic groups), but rather are highly "contextual, polyphonic, disjunctive, negotiated and contested in ways that acknowledge human agency." With this in mind, we have highlighted throughout this chapter the diversity that exists within each broad racial and ethnic group and shown various ways that members of each group are actively engaging with natural resources themselves as well as seeking to influence policies aimed at managing them. Explicit recognition of these displays of agency and intracultural diversity avoids treating subgroups as monolithic and as subjects upon which cultural assimilation is a presumed outcome.

A second main trap involves overtheorizing race when incorporating environmental justice perspectives into resource management (Knowles 2010). While theories of the origins and consequences of race and race relations are important, here we aim to show the benefit of focusing instead on how the main tenets of environmental justice can open new opportunities for the exchange of ideas and a more equitable distribution of the power to make decisions about access to and diverse management of the country's natural resources. As noted by Martin et al. (2020, 20), it is essential to "underline the importance of placing justice at the heart of transformative change," which requires "giving special attention to the treatment of those most vulnerable to the impacts of the climate and ecological crises and to those who are vulnerable to the actions to address these crises." They note the moral impetus of this emphasis on justice: to disrupt the cycle of the "disproportionate burdens to continue to fall on already marginalized groups (current or future), or to suppress their voices and values." They also note the practical benefits, as sustainability goals will only be widely embraced by diverse actors if they are accepted as both legitimate and fair.

Recognition of these traps—and ways out of them—is part of a larger cultural shift in the United States to recognize the ubiquity of white racial frames, lessen their effects, and recognize and elevate the many other racial and ethnic framings in all aspects of society, including natural resource use and management. Governmental agencies, NGOs, and community leaders and organizations are increasingly incorporating deeper understandings of the ways that various groups use and engage with natural resources; these include branching out from traditional views of outdoor recreation as leisure activities to include gathering materials for traditional crafts or medicine, engaging with specific places or species that embody spiritual values or cultural identities, and creating initiatives aimed at encouraging minority youths to participate in outdoor pursuits and natural resource professions. Efforts to build collaborations and support community-based approaches that enable diverse institutions and communities to interact have proven fruitful, and cross-pollination of ideas continues to lead to significant new opportunities for understanding and respecting the many kinds of human connection with nature.

References

Alexander, A. L. 2019: What a strange thing is "race," and family, stranger still. In *Princess of the Hither Isles: A Black suffragist's story from the Jim Crow south*, ed. A. L. Alexander, 306–23. New Haven, CT: Yale University Press.

Anguiano, C., T. Milstein, I. de Larkin, Y. W. Chen, and J. Sandoval. 2012. Connecting community voices: Using a Latino/a critical race theory lens on environmental justice advocacy. *Journal of International and Intercultural Communication* 5 (2): 124–43.

Arai, S., and D. Kivel. 2009. Critical race theory and social justice perspectives on whiteness, difference(s) and (anti)racism. *Journal of Leisure Research* 41 (4): 459–72.

Armstrong, A., and M. M. Derrien. 2020. Language in the recreation world. In *Igniting research for outdoor recreation: Linking science, policy, and action*, ed. S. Selin, L. K. Cerveny, D. Blahna, and A. B. Miller, 51–61. Portland, OR: US Department of Agriculture, Forest Service, Pacific Northwest Research Station.

Balcarczyk, K. L., D. Smaldone, S. W. Selin, C. D. Pierskalla, and K. Maumbe. 2015. Barriers and supports to entering a natural resource career: Perspectives of culturally diverse recent hires. *Journal of Forestry* 113 (2): 231–39.

Ballard, H. L., and L. Huntsinger. 2006. Salal harvester local ecological knowledge, harvest practices and understory management on the Olympic Peninsula, Washington. *Human Ecology* 34 (4): 529–47.

Ballew, M. T., M. H. Goldberg, S. A. Rosenthal, M. J. Cutler, and A. Leiserowitz. 2019. Climate change activism among Latino and white Americans. *Frontiers in Communication* 3: 58.

Baumflek, M., T. Cabe, J. Schelhas, and M. Dunlavey. 2021. Managing forests for culturally important plants in traditional Cherokee homelands: Emerging platforms. *International Forestry Review* 24: 298–314.

Bengston, D. N. 2004. Listening to neglected voices: American Indian perspectives on natural resource management. *Journal of Forestry* 102 (1): 48–52.

Blahna, D. J., L. K. Cerveny, D. R. Williams, J. D. Kline, M. Helmer, S. F. McCool, and F. Valenzuela. 2020. Rethinking "outdoor recreation" to account for the diversity of human experiences and connections to public lands. In *Igniting research for outdoor recreation: Linking science, policy, and action*, ed. S. Selin, L. K. Cerveny, D. Blahna, and A. B. Miller, 65–132. Portland, OR: US Department of Agriculture, Forest Service, Pacific Northwest Research Station.

Bragg, D. C. 2017. Hank Chamberlin and the Arkansas A&M Forestry Program, 1946–1957. *Drew County Historical Journal* 32: 11–38. https://www.srs.fs.usda.gov/pubs/ja/2017/ja_2017_bragg_003.pdf.

Brosius, J. P., and S. L. Hitchner. 2010. Cultural diversity and conservation. *International Social Science Journal* 61 (199): 141–68.

Brown, J. J. 1994. Treaty rights: Twenty years after the Boldt decision. *Wicazo Sa Review* 10: 1–16.

Brown, J. K., and H. G. Rempel. 2020. The discourse of demographic diversity in U.S. natural resources scholarly literature: A multi-methods qualitative study. Master's thesis, Oregon State University.

Budiman, A., and N. Ruiz. 2021. *Key facts about Asian Americans, a diverse and growing population*. Accessed September 25, 2022. https://policycommons.net/artifacts/1526590/key-facts-about-asian-americans-a-diverse-and-growing-population/2214830/.

Bullard, R. D., ed. 2005. *The quest for environmental justice: Human rights and the politics of pollution*. Vol. 19, 32–33. San Francisco, CA: Sierra Club Books.

Bureau of Indian Affairs. 2021. Indian entities recognized by and eligible to receive services from the United States Bureau of Indian Affairs. Accessed November 4, 2022. https://www.federalregister.gov/documents/2021/01/29/2021-01606/indian-entities-recognized-by-and-eligible-to-receive-services-from-the-united-states-bureau-of.

Burger, J., O. Myers, C. S. Boring, C. Dixon, C. Lord, R. Ramos, S. Shukla, and M. Gochfeld. 2004. Perceptions of general environmental problems, willingness to expend federal funds on these problems, and concerns regarding the Los Alamos national laboratory: Hispanics are more concerned than whites. *Environmental Research* 95 (2): 174–83.

Carbado, D. W., and D. Roithmayr. 2014. Critical race theory meets social science. *Annual Review of Law and Social Science* 10: 149–67.

Case, M. 2018. *Relentless business of treaties: How Indigenous land became U.S. property*. Saint Paul: Minnesota Historical Society Press.

Catton, T. 2016. *American Indians and national forests*. Tucson: University of Arizona Press.

Chamberlain, J. L., M. R. Emery, and T. Patel-Weynand, eds. 2018. *Assessment of nontimber forest products in the United States under changing conditions*. Asheville, NC: US Department of Agriculture, Forest Service, Southern Research Station.

Chang, G. H. 2019. *Ghosts of gold mountain: The epic story of the Chinese who built the Transcontinental Railroad*. Boston, MA: Houghton Mifflin Harcourt.

Chavez, D. J., and D. D. Olson. 2009. Opinions of Latino outdoor recreation visitors at four urban national forests. *Environmental Practice* 11 (4): 263–69.

Choi, C. 2021. Why the environmental movement should stop ignoring Asian Americans. Accessed January 7, 2022. https://www.nrdc.org/stories/why-environmental-movement-should-stop-ignoring-asian-americans.

Chung, S. F. 2011. *In pursuit of gold: Chinese miners and merchants in the American West*. Urbana: University of Illinois Press.

Chung, S. F. 2015. *Chinese in the woods: Logging and lumbering in the American West*. Urbana: University of Illinois Press.

Colby, S. L., and J. M. Ortman. 2015. *Projections of the size and composition of the U.S. population: 2014 to 2060*. Current Population Report No. P25–1143, US Census Bureau, Washington, DC.

Crowder, K., and L. Downey. 2010. Interneighborhood migration, race, and environmental hazards: Modeling microlevel processes of environmental inequality. *American Journal of Sociology* 115 (4): 1110–49.

Cuevas, I. L., J. Wingard, M. Purse, and L. Watt. 2016. Heritage in the outdoors-creating a cultural bridge between the Latino community and parks: A case study in Sonoma County. Master's thesis, Sonoma State University.

De Onís, C. M. 2018. Energy colonialism powers the ongoing unnatural disaster in Puerto Rico. *Frontiers in Communication* 3: 2.

Diouf, S. 2016. *Slavery's exiles: The story of American maroons.* New York: NYU Press.

Dobbin, K. B., and M. Lubell. 2021. Collaborative governance and environmental justice: Disadvantaged community representation in California sustainable groundwater management. *Policy Studies Journal* 49 (2): 562–90.

Dockry, M. J. 2020. Indigenous rights and empowerment in natural resource management and decision making as a driver of change in U.S. forestry. In *Drivers of change in U.S. forests and forestry over the next 20 years*, ed. M. J. Dockry, D. N. Bengston, and L. M. Westphal, 76–83. Madison, WI: US Department of Agriculture, Forest Service, Northern Research Station.

Dockry, M. J., S. A. Gutterman, and M. A. Davenport. 2018. Building bridges: Perspectives on partnership and collaboration from the US Forest Service Tribal Relations Program. *Journal of Forestry* 116 (2): 123–32.

Dockry, M. J., and S. J. Hoagland, eds. 2017. A special issue of the *Journal of Forestry*—tribal forest management: Innovations for sustainable forest management. *Journal of Forestry* 15 (5): 339–40.

Dockry, M., and K. Whyte. 2021. Improving on nature: The Legend Lake Development, Menominee resistance, and the ecological dynamics of settler colonialism. *The American Indian Quarterly* 45 (2): 95–120.

Donoghue, E. M., S. A. Thompson, and J. C. Bliss. 2010. Tribal-federal collaboration in resource management. *Journal of Ecological Anthropology* 14 (1): 22–38.

Drawson, A. S., E. Toombs, and C. J. Mushquash. 2017. Indigenous research methods: A systematic review. *International Indigenous Policy Journal* 8 (2).

Emery, M. R., A. Wrobel, M. H. Hansen, M. Dockry, W. Moser, K. J. Stark, and J. H. Gilbert. 2014. Using traditional ecological knowledge as a basis for targeted forest inventories: Paper birch (*Betula papyrifera*) in the US Great Lakes Region. *Journal of Forestry* 112 (2): 207–14.

Erickson, B., C. W. Johnson, and B. D. Kivel. 2009. Rocky Mountain National Park: History and culture as factors in African-American park visitation. *Journal of Leisure Research* 41 (4): 529–45.

Feagin, J. R. 2020. *The white racial frame: Centuries of racial framing and counter-framing.* 3rd ed. New York: Routledge.

Feagin, J. R., and E. O'Brien. 2010. Studying "race" and ethnicity: Dominant and marginalized discourses in the critical North American case. In *The SAGE hand-*

book of race and ethnic studies, ed. P. Hill Collins and J. Solomos, 43–66. London: SAGE.

Finney, C. 2014. *Black faces, white spaces: Reimagining the relationship of African Americans to the great outdoors*. Chapel Hill: University of North Carolina Press.

Flores, D., G. Falco, N. S. Roberts, and F. P. Valenzuela III. 2018. Recreation equity: Is the Forest Service serving its diverse publics? *Journal of Forestry* 116 (3): 266–72.

Flores, D., and K. Kuhn. 2018. Latino Outdoors: Using storytelling and social media to increase diversity on public lands. *Journal of Park and Recreation Administration* 36 (3): 47–62.

Flores, D., and J. J. Sánchez. 2020. The changing dynamic of Latinx outdoor recreation on national and state public lands. *Journal of Park and Recreation Administration* 38 (4): 8–74.

Floyd, M., and R. A. Mowatt. 2014. Leisure among African Americans. In *Race, ethnicity, and leisure: Perspectives on research theory, and practice*, ed. M. Stodolska, K. J. Shinew, M. F. Floyd, and G. J. Walker, 53–74. Champaign, IL: Human Kinetics.

Floyd, M. F., and M. Stodolska. 2014. Theoretical frameworks in leisure research on race and ethnicity. In *Race, ethnicity, and leisure: Perspectives on research theory, and practice*, ed. M. Stodolska, K. J. Shinew, M. F. Floyd, and G. J. Walker, 9–19. Champaign, IL: Human Kinetics.

Gaither, C. J., A. Carpenter, T. L. McCurty, and S. Toering. 2019. *Heirs' property and land fractionation: Fostering stable ownership to prevent land loss and abandonment*, 1–105. Asheville, NC: US Department of Agriculture Forest Service, Southern Research Station.

García, G. 1970. Apuntes sobre una interpretación de la realidad Puertorriqueña. *Revista de Ciencias Sociales* 4 (1): 565–75.

Garriga-López, A., O. Webber, F. Tormos-Apont, and G. Cruz-Mart Ínez. 2019. Puerto Rico: The future in question. *Shima Journal* 13 (2): 174–92.

Gervais, B. K., C. R. Voirin, C. Beatty, G. Bulltail, S. Cowherd, S. Defrance, B. Dorame, R. Gutteriez, J. Lackey, and C. Lupe. 2017. Native American student perspectives of challenges in natural resource higher education. *Journal of Forestry* 115 (5): 491–97.

Gibson-Wood, H., and S. Wakefield. 2013. "Participation," white privilege and environmental justice: Understanding environmentalism among Hispanics in Toronto. *Antipode* 45 (3): 641–62.

Gilbert, J., G. Sharp, and S. M. Felin. 2002. The loss and persistence of Black-owned farms and farmland: A review of the research literature and its implications. *Southern Rural Sociology* 18 (2): 1–30.

Gordon, J. S., A. Barton, and K. Adams. 2013. An exploration of African American forest landowners in Mississippi. *Rural Sociology* 78 (4): 473–97.

Graybill, A. 2019. The forgotten history of the Chinese who helped build America's railroads. *New York Times*, May 10.

Harrison, F. V. 1995. The persistent power of "race" in the cultural and political economy of racism. *Annual Review of Anthropology* 24: 47–74.

Hernandez, M., T. W. Collins, and S. E. Grineski. 2015. Immigration, mobility, and environmental injustice: A comparative study of Hispanic people's residential decision-making and exposure to hazardous air pollutants in Greater Houston, Texas. *Geoforum* 60: 83–94.

Hersey, M. D. 2011. *My work is that of conservation: An environmental biography of George Washington Carver.* Athens: University of Georgia Press.

Hill Collins, P., and J. Solomos. 2010. Situating race and ethnic studies. In *The SAGE handbook of race and ethnic studies*, ed. P. Hill Collins and J. Solomos, 1–16. London: SAGE.

Hitchner S., J. Schelhas, and P. Dwivedi. 2021. Safe havens: The intersection of family, religion, and community in Black cultural landscapes of the southeastern United States. *Landscape and Urban Planning* 214: 104136.

Hoagland, S. J., R. Miller, K. M. Waring, and O. Carroll. 2017. Tribal lands provide forest management laboratory for mainstream university students. *Journal of Forestry* 115 (5): 484–90.

Izenstark, D., K. A. Crossman, and E. Middaugh. 2022. Examining family-based nature activities among Latinx students: Contexts for reinforcing family relationships and cultural heritage. *Annals of Leisure Research* 25 (4): 451–71.

Jacoby, K. 2014. *Crimes against nature: Squatters, poachers, thieves, and the hidden history of American conservation.* Berkeley: University of California Press.

Johnson, C. Y., and J. M. Bowker. 2004. African-American wildland memories. *Environmental Ethics* 26 (1): 57–75.

Johnson Gaither, C., N. S. Roberts, and K. L. Hanula. 2015. *Visitor diversity through the recreation manager lens: Comparing Forest Service Regions 8 (U.S. South) and 5 (California).* Asheville, NC: US Department of Agriculture Forest Service, Southern Research Station.

Johnson, J. T., and S. C. Larsen. 2013. *A deeper sense of place: Stories and journeys of collaboration in Indigenous research.* Corvallis: Oregon State University Press.

Johnson, S. n.d. *Invisible men: Buffalo soldiers of the Sierra Nevada.* Accessed March 14, 2020. http://npshistory.com/publications/seki/invisiblemen.pdf.

Jones, N., R. Marks, R. Ramirez, and M. Ríos-Vargas. 2021. Improved race and ethnicity measures reveal U.S. population is much more multiracial. Accessed March 14, 2022. https://www.census.gov/library/stories/2021/08/improved-race-ethnicity-measures-reveal-united-states-population-much-more-multiracial.html.

Jones, R. E. 2002. Blacks just don't care: Unmasking popular stereotypes about concern for the environment among African-Americans. *International Journal of Public Administration* 25 (2–3): 221–51.

Jones, R. E., and S. A. Rainey. 2006. Examining linkages between race, environmental concern, health and justice in a highly polluted community of color. *Journal of Black Studies* 36 (4): 473–96.

Jones, R. P., D. Cox, and J. Navarro-Rivera. 2014. Believers, sympathizers, & skeptics: Why Americans are conflicted about climate change, environmental policy, and science. Accessed March 14, 2022. https://www.prri.org/research/believers -sympathizers-skeptics-americans-conflicted-climate-change-environmental -policy-science/.

Keller, R. H., and M. F. Turek. 1998. *American Indians & national parks.* Tucson: University of Arizona Press.

Kim, R., and M. Matsuoka. 2013. Building a twenty-first century environmental movement that wins: Twenty years of environmental justice by the Asian Pacific Environmental Network. *AAPI Nexus* 11 (1 & 2): 139–58.

Kimmerer, R. 2013. *Braiding sweetgrass: Indigenous wisdom, scientific knowledge and the teachings of plants.* Minneapolis, MN: Milkweed Editions.

Kivel, D., C. W. Johnson, and S. Scraton. 2009. (Re)theorizing leisure, experience and race. *Journal of Leisure Research* 41 (4): 473–93.

Knowles, C. 2010. Theorizing race and ethnicity: Contemporary paradigms and perspectives. In *The SAGE handbook of race and ethnic studies*, ed. P. Hill Collins and J. Solomos, 23–42. London: Sage.

Kochhar, R., and A. Killuffo. 2018. Income inequality in the U.S. is rising most rapidly among Asians. Accessed March 17, 2022. https://www.pewresearch.org /social-trends/2018/07/12/income-inequality-in-the-u-s-is-rising-most-rapidly -among-asians/.

Kou-Giesbrecht, S. 2020. Asian Americans: The forgotten minority in ecology. *The Bulletin of the Ecological Society of America* 101 (3): e01696.

Lake, F. K., V. Wright, P. Morgan, M. McFadzen, D. McWethy, and C. Stevens-Rumann. 2017. Returning fire to the land: Celebrating traditional knowledge and fire. *Journal of Forestry* 115 (5): 343–53.

Lanham, D. 2016. *The home place: Memoirs of a colored man's love affair with nature.* Minneapolis, MN: Milkweed Editions.

Leatherberry, E. C., and J. D. Wellman. 1988. Black high school students' images of forestry as a profession. *The Journal of Negro Education* 57 (2): 208–19.

Lewis, J. G. 2005. *The Forest Service and the greatest good: A centennial history.* Durham, NC: Forest History Society.

Lu, J. G., R. E. Nisbett, and M. W. Morris. 2020. Why East Asians but not South Asians are underrepresented in leadership positions in the United States. *PNAS* 117 (9): 4590–4600.

Macias, T. 2016a. Ecological assimilation: Race, ethnicity, and the inverted gap of environmental concern. *Society and Natural Resources* 29 (1): 3–19.

Macias, T. 2016b. Environmental risk perception among race and ethnic groups in the United States. *Ethnicities* 16 (1): 111–29.

Malin, S. A., S. Ryder, and M. G. Lyra. 2019. Environmental justice and natural resource extraction: Intersections of power, equity and access. *Environmental Sociology* 5 (2): 109–16.

Manno, E. A., K. C. Steiner, and A. Day. 2002. Ralph E. Brock and the State Forest Academy at Mont Alto, Pennsylvania. *Forest History Today* Fall: 12–19.

Martin, A., T. Armijos, B. Coolsaet, N. Dawson, G. A. S. Edwards, R. Few, N. Gross-Camp, I. Rodriguez, H. Schroeder, M. G. L. Tebboth, et al. 2020. Environmental justice and transformations to sustainability. *Environment: Science and Policy for Sustainable Development* 62 (6): 19–30.

Martin, D. C. 2004. Apartheid in the great outdoors: American advertising and the reproduction of a racialized outdoor leisure identity. *Journal of Leisure Research* 36 (4): 513–35.

McGregor, D., J.-P. Restoule, and R. Johnston. 2018. *Indigenous research: Theories, practices, and relationships*. Toronto: Canadian Scholars' Press.

Mejicano, E., M. J. Dockry, and M. A. Kilgore. 2022. Workforce diversity in federal natural resource organizations. UMN Department of Forest Resources Staff Paper Series. #265. Saint Paul: University of Minnesota. https://hdl.handle.net/11299/226476.

Merchant, C. 2007. *American environmental history: An introduction*. New York: Columbia University Press.

Mills, J. 2014. *The adventure gap: Changing the face of the outdoors*. Seattle: Mountaineers Books.

Mitchell, T. W. 2014. Reforming property law to address devastating land loss. *Alabama Law Review* 66 (1): 1–61.

Mobley, M. S. 1996. Barriers to my participation in SAF. *Journal of Forestry* 94 (11): 16.

Mobley, M. S. 2020. A Black woman who tried to survive in the dark, white forest. *Mountain Journal*, June 18. Accessed March 14, 2022. https://mountainjournal.org/a-woman-recalls-her-nightmare-with-the-united-states-forests-service.

Mohai, P. 1990. Black environmentalism. *Social Science Quarterly* 71 (4): 744–65.

Mohai, P. 2003. Dispelling old myths: African American concern for the environment. *Environment* 45 (5): 10–26.

Mohai, P., and B. Bryant. 1998. Is there a "race" effect on concern for environmental quality? *The Public Opinion Quarterly* 62 (4): 475–505.

Mutz, K. M., G. C. Bryner, and D. S. Kenney. 2002. *Justice and natural resources: Concepts, strategies, and applications*. Washington, DC: Island Press.

Naiman, S. M., Schusler, T. M., and J. P. Schuldt. 2018. Environmental engagement among Latinos: An exploratory study of environmentalists in the greater Chicago area. *Journal of Environmental Studies and Sciences* 9 (1): 109–21.

Naiman, S. M., Stedman, R. C., and J. P. Schuldt. 2023. Latine culture and the environment: How familism and collectivism predict environmental attitudes and behavioral intentions among U.S. Latines. *Journal of Environmental Psychology* 85: 101902.

Naiman, S. M. Forthcoming. U.S. Latines and the environment: Perspectives from Miami, New York City, and San Antonio. *Environmental Communication*.

Nesper, L. 2002. *The walleye war: The struggle for Ojibwe spearfishing and treaty rights*. Lincoln: University of Nebraska Press.

Newell, S. J., and C. L. Green. 1997. Racial differences in consumer environmental concern. *The Journal of Consumer Affairs* 31 (1): 53–69.

Newkirk, V. R. II. 2019. The great land robbery. *The Atlantic*, September 29. Accessed March 14, 2022. https://www.theatlantic.com/magazine/archive/2019/09/this-land-was-our-land/594742/.

Nijhuis, M. 2021. *Beloved beasts: Fighting for life in an age of extinction*. New York: W. W. Norton.

NPS (National Park Service). 2005. *Asian reflections on the American landscape: Identifying and interpreting Asian heritage*. Washington, DC: National Park Service.

Ong, P. M., L. Le, and P. Daniels. 2013. Ethnic variation in environmental attitudes and opinion among Asian American voters. *AAPI Nexus* 11 (1&2): 91–109.

Parker, J. D., and M. H. McDonough. 1999. Environmentalism of African Americans: An analysis of the subculture and barriers theories. *Environment and Behavior* 31 (2): 155–77.

Payne, B. R., and D. R. Theoe. 1971. Black foresters needed: A professional concern. *Journal of Forestry* 69 (5): 295–98.

Pearson, A. R., G. A. Bacio, S. M. Naiman, R. Romero-Canyas, and J. P. Schuldt. 2021. Cultural determinants of climate change amongst Latinos. *Climatic Change* 167 (11). https://doi.org/10.1007/s10584-021-03165-2.

Pearson, A. R., J. P. Schuldt, R. Romero-Canyas, M. T. Ballew, and D. Larson-Konar. 2018. Diverse segments of the U.S. public underestimate the environmental concerns of minority and low-income Americans. *Proceedings of the National Academy of Sciences of the United States of America* 115 (49): 12429–34.

Peña, D. G. 2005. *Mexican Americans and the environment: Tierra y vida*. Tucson: University of Arizona Press.

Pew Research Center. 2021. Hispanic origin groups in the U.S., 2019. Accessed November 4, 2021. https://www.pewresearch.org/fact-tank/2021/09/09/key-facts-about-u-s-latinos-for-national-hispanic-heritage-month/ft_21-09-01_keyfactslatinos_origin_table_final1/.

Pfaelzer, J. 2007. *Driven out: The forgotten war against Chinese Americans*. New York: Random House.

Ramakrishnan, K., and T. Lee. 2012. The policy priorities and issue preferences of Asian Americans and Pacific Islanders. Accessed March 18, 2022. http://naasurvey.com/wp-content/uploads/2015/10/NAAS12-sep25-issues.pdf.

Ray, R. 2020. Black Americans are not a monolithic group so stop treating us like one. *The Guardian* February 14. Accessed March 14, 2022. https://www.theguardian.com/commentisfree/2020/feb/14/black-americans-are-not-a-monolithic-group-so-stop-treating-us-like-one.

Reo, N. J., and K. P. Whyte. 2012. Hunting and morality as elements of traditional ecological knowledge. *Human Ecology* 40 (1): 15–27.

Reynolds, B. J. 2002. Black farmers in America, 1865–2000: The pursuit of independent farming and the role of cooperatives. Report No. 194, Rural Business-Cooperative Service RBS. United States Department of Agriculture.

Richards, R. T., and M. Creasy. 1996. Ethnic diversity, resource values, and ecosystem management: Matsutake mushroom harvesting in the Klamath bioregion. *Society & Natural Resources* 9 (4): 359–74.

Richmond, J. A., M. Page, and L. V. Blount. 1996. Perspective: African Americans in the frame of forestry. *Journal of Forestry* 94 (11): 60.

Rodríguez, H. 2004. A "Long walk to freedom" and democracy: Human rights, globalization, and social injustice. *Social Forces* 83 (1): 391–412.

Rodríguez-Díaz, C. E. 2018. Maria in Puerto Rico: Natural disaster in a colonial archipelago. *American Journal of Public Health* 108 (1): 30–31.

Saha, P. 2018. Do communities of color really feel disconnected from nature? *Audubon News.* May 17. Accessed March 14, 2022. https://www.audubon.org/news/do-communities-color-really-feel-disconnected-nature.

Schelhas, J. 2002. Race, ethnicity, and natural resources in the United States: A review. *Natural Resources Journal* 42 (4): 723–63.

Schelhas, J. 2020. Comment on: Race, ethnicity, and natural resources in the United States: A review—with reprinted article. *Rocky Mountain Mineral Law Foundation Journal* 57 (2): 267–311.

Schelhas, J., and S. L. Hitchner 2020. Integrating research and outreach for environmental justice: African American land ownership and forestry. *Annals of Anthropological Practice* 44 (1): 47–64.

Schelhas, J., S. Hitchner, and A. McGregor 2019. The Sustainable Forestry and African American Land Retention Program. In *Heirs' property and land fractionation: Fostering stable ownership to prevent land loss and abandonment,* ed. C. J. Gaither, A. Carpenter, T. Lloyd McCurty, and S. Toering. Asheville, NC: US Department of Agriculture Forest Service, Southern Research Station.

Schewe, R. L., D. Hoffman, J. Witt, B. Shoup, and M. Freeman. 2020. Citizen-science and participatory research as a means to improve stakeholder engagement in resource management: A case study of Vietnamese American fishers on the U.S. Gulf Coast. *Environmental Management* 65: 74–87.

Schmelzkopf, K. 2008. Scale and narrative in the struggle for environment and livelihood in Vieques, Puerto Rico. In *Contentious geographies: Environmental knowledge, meaning, and scale,* ed. M. K. Goodman, M. Boykoff, and K. Evered, 311–27. Burlington, VT: Ashgate.

Schuster, R., R. R. Germain, J. R. Bennett, N. J. Reo, and P. Arcese. 2019. Vertebrate biodiversity on Indigenous-managed lands in Australia, Brazil, and Canada equals that in protected areas. *Environmental Science & Policy* 101: 1–6.

Sessions, J., J. Gordon, P. Rigdon, D. Motanic, and V. Corrao. 2017. Indian forests and forestry: Can they play a larger role in sustainable forest management? *Journal of Forestry* 115 (5): 364–65.

Sharik, T. L., R. J. Lilieholm, W. Lindquist, and W. W. Richardson. 2015. Undergraduate enrollment in natural resource programs in the United States: Trends, drivers, and implications for the future of natural resource professions. *Journal of Forestry* 113 (6): 538–51.

Sheppard, J. A. C. 2010. The Black-White environmental concern gap: An examination of environmental paradigms. *The Journal of Environmental Education* 26 (2): 24–35.

Smith-Nonini, S., and R. Nonini. 2019. Dis.em.powered: Puerto Rico's perfect storm. Accessed December 4, 2023. https://www.youtube.com/watch?v=7CY9g9H4kT0.

Solomos, J. 2023. *Race, ethnicity, and social theory*. London: Routledge.

Song, H., N. A. Lewis, M. T. Ballew, M. Bravo, J. Davydova, H. O. Gao, R. J. Garcia, S. Hiltner, S. M. Naiman, A. R. Pearson, R. Romero-Canyas, and J. P. Schuldt. 2020. What counts as an "environmental" issue? Differences in issue conceptualization by race, ethnicity, and socioeconomic status. *Journal of Environmental Psychology* 68: 101404.

Speiser, M., and Krygsman, K. 2014. *American climate values 2014: Insights by racial and ethnic groups*. Washington, DC: Strategic Business Insights and ecoAmerica.

Spence, M. D. 2000. *Dispossessing the wilderness: Indian removal and the making of the national parks*. New York: Oxford University Press.

Stodolska, M., K. J. Shinew, and M. Z. Li. 2010. Recreation participation patterns and physical activity among Latino visitors to three urban outdoor recreation environments. *Journal of Park and Recreation Administration* 28 (2): 36–56.

Sze, J. 2004. Asian American activism for environmental justice. *Peace Review* 16 (2): 149–56.

Tamir, C. 2021. Key findings about Black America. Accessed March 14, 2022. https://www.pewresearch.org/fact-tank/2021/03/25/key-findings-about-black-america/.

Taylor, D. E. 2014. The state of diversity in environmental organizations: Mainstream NGOs, foundations and government agencies. Technical report, July 28–31. https://doi.org/10.13140/RG.2.2.34512.40962.

Taylor, D. 2016. *The rise of the American conservation movement: Power, privilege, and environmental protection*. Durham, NC: Duke University Press.

Taylor, D. E. 2018. Racial and ethnic differences in connectedness to nature and landscape preferences among college students. *Environmental Justice* 11 (3): 118–36.

Taylor, D. E. 2019. College students and nature: Differing thoughts of fear, danger, disconnection, and loathing. *Environmental Management* 64: 79–96.

Taylor, D. E. 2020. Mobilizing for environmental justice in communities of color: An emerging profile of people of color environmental groups. In *Ecosystem management: Adaptive strategies for natural resources organizations in the twenty-first century*, 33–67. Boca Raton, FL: CRC Press.

Townsend, J., F. Moola, and M. K. Craig. 2020. Indigenous peoples are critical to the success of nature-based solutions to climate change. *Facets* 5 (1): 551–56.

Treuer, D. 2021. Return the national parks to the tribes. *The Atlantic*, April 12. Accessed January 4, 2022. https://www.theatlantic.com/magazine/archive/2021/05/return-the-national-parks-to-the-tribes/618395/.

Vera, H., and J. R. Feagin. 2007. Epilogue: The future of race and ethnic relations. In *Handbook of the sociology of racial and ethnic relations*, ed. H. Vera and J. R. Feagin, 467–70. New York: Springer.

Waziyatawin. 2008. *What does justice look like?: The struggle for liberation in Dakota Homeland*. Saint Paul, MN: Living Justice.

Wellman, J. D. 1987. Images of a profession. *Journal of Forestry* 85 (3): 18–19.

Whittaker, M., G. M. Segura, and S. Bowler. 2005. Racial/ethnic group attitudes toward environmental protection in California: Is "environmentalism" still a white phenomenon? *Political Research Quarterly* 58 (3): 435–47.

Whyte, K. 2018. Settler colonialism, ecology, and environmental injustice. *Environment and Society* 9 (1): 125–44.

Whyte, K. P. 2014. Justice forward: Tribes, climate adaptation and responsibility. *Climatic Change* 120 (3): 518–30.

Wilkins, D. E., and K. T. Lomawaima. 2001. *Uneven ground: American Indian sovereignty and federal law*. Norman: University of Oklahoma Press.

Wilkinson, C. F. 2004. *Indian Tribes as sovereign governments*. 2nd ed. Oakland, CA: American Indian Resources Institute.

Wilkinson, C. F. 2005. *Blood struggle: The rise of modern Indian nations*. New York: Norton.

Williams, B. L., and Y. Florez. 2002. Do Mexican Americans perceive environmental issues differently than Caucasians: A study of cross-ethnic variation in perceptions related to water in Tucson. *Environmental Health Perspectives* 110 (Suppl. 2): 303–10.

Willison, C. E., P. M. Singer, M. S. Creary, and S. L. Greer. 2019. Quantifying inequities in US federal response to hurricane disaster in Texas and Florida compared with Puerto Rico. *BMJ Global Health* 4 (1): e001191.

Wilms-Crowe, M. 2020. "Desde abajo, como semilla": Puerto Rican food sovereignty as embodied decolonial resistance. Master's thesis, University of Oregon, Eugene. https://scholarsbank.uoregon.edu/xmlui/handle/1794/25828.

Wilmsen, C., D. Bush, and D. Barton-Antonio. 2015. Working in the shadows: Safety and health in forestry services in southern Oregon. *Journal of Forestry* 113 (3): 315–24.

Winant, W. 2000. Race and race theory. *Annual Review of Sociology* 26: 169–85.

Winter, P. L., W. D. Crano, T. Basáñez, and C. S. Lamb. 2020. Equity in access to outdoor recreation—informing a sustainable future. *Sustainability* 12 (1): 124.

Winter, P. L., W. C. Jeong, and G. C. Godbey. 2004. Outdoor recreation among Asian Americans: A case study of San Francisco Bay Area residents. *Journal of Park and Recreation Administration* 22 (3): 114–36.

Wolfe, P. 2006. Settler colonialism and the elimination of the native. *Journal of Genocide Research* 8 (4): 387–409.

4

Human Dignity in Natural Resource
Social Sciences Career Pathways

EVAN J. ANDREWS, CHRISTINE KNOTT, SOLANGE NADEAU, COURTENAY PARLEE,
ARCHI RASTOGI, RACHEL KELLY, MARÍA ANDRÉE LÓPEZ GÓMEZ,
MADU GALAPPATHTHI, AND ANA CAROLINA ESTEVES DIAS

When natural resource social sciences (NRSS) researchers experience human indignity, their ability to contribute and lead NRSS for sustainability outcomes becomes hampered. Therefore, the success of global sustainability agendas requires attention to building capacity for human dignity in NRSS career pathways. This chapter documents experiences and opportunities, including a framework for human dignity.

The Goal: Building Capacity for Human Dignity in NRSS Career Pathways

This commentary explores opportunities to build capacity for human dignity in natural resource social sciences (NRSS) career pathways. Human dignity reflects the ability for individuals to pursue multiple goals and meaning in life, where that pursuit frames their experience and manifests in their behavior (McDougal, Lasswell, and Chen 1980).[1] Human dignity is an overriding

---

1. Human dignity is a contested and complex concept, despite its ubiquity in international and domestic law and discourse (Nagan 2013). According to Malpas and Lickiss (2007),

https://doi.org/10.7330/9781646426300.c004

principle. It is fostered through interpersonal relationships and societal institutions, and as such, reflects both an individual and collective principle (Mattson and Clark 2011). In the context of NRSS career pathways, human dignity refers to autonomy to seek meaningfulness in career experiences, the ability to contribute to sustainability outcomes in ways that reflect researcher goals and skills, and the capacity to experience health, well-being, and intellectual growth, among other values, in the interpersonal relationships and institutions that exist in career pathways (Clark and Wallace 2018). Human dignity for NRSS researchers is about raising the meaningfulness, freedom, and health and well-being for all. It is an important yardstick for goals such as equity (i.e., fairness) and inclusion by understanding and addressing differences in barriers to dignity that arise out of diverse lived experiences (see Byrd and Mason 2021).

In this commentary, we argue that building capacity for human dignity is a neglected yet fundamental part of NRSS career pathways. Attention to NRSS researchers' dignity is important to ensure that they can provide critical research guidance and leadership for sustainability outcomes. Whether they are working in academic, public, nonprofit, and private sectors, NRSS researchers need to be energetic, creative, innovative, emotionally intelligent, and reflective as they conduct high-quality, collaborative, and action-oriented NRSS (Kelly et al. 2019; Kremers, Liepins, and York 2019). We share examples below that show that it is challenging for NRSS researchers to

_____

autonomy and equity are at the core of human dignity. The authors argue, "Human dignity is respected and upheld only when the autonomy of human decision making is itself respected and upheld, and when human beings are treated in ways that are non-hierarchical and non-discriminatory" (2007, 3). The policy sciences literature also argues that human dignity is an overriding principle for all humans. According to this perspective, human dignity is the ability to choose among a range of human values or goals for a meaningful life, such as well-being, wealth, power, and so on. Important to this perspective is that human dignity is expressed in specific institutional settings, such as a university or government (Mattson and Clark 2011). Accordingly, the autonomy to pursue one's values (i.e., human dignity) is mediated by the institution in which values are pursued by individuals or groups (Nagan 2013). In this chapter, we consider human dignity as the autonomy to choose (see Malpas and Lickiss 2007) among multiple human values (Mattson and Clark 2011), in a given institutional setting (Nagan 2013). To understand and foster human dignity, then, we argue that it is important to understand the values being pursued, and the extent to which the opportunities to choose are autonomous and equitable in a given institutional setting (see Nagan 2013; Mattson and Clark 2011).

make these contributions when experiencing indignity and offer a framework to build capacity for human dignity for NRSS researchers. This chapter therefore contributes to an understanding of what human dignity can mean in a dynamic NRSS career pathway, given multiple institutional settings over time, as well as how human dignity can be advanced.

The Problem: Understanding Indignity in NRSS Career Pathways

To build capacity for human dignity in NRSS career pathways, we need to first understand it. However, this is a complicated area for reflection, largely due to five factors. First, NRSS researchers' career pathways are dynamic and may follow less-than-straightforward routes to hiring and job security in academic, public, nonprofit, or private sectors, or even across multiple sectors. Second, the composition of NRSS is diverse, evolving in relation to calls for knowledge integration with and for different knowledge users outside of academia (Buizer et al. 2015). NRSS researchers play different roles including generating science, knowledge brokering, resource mobilization, and policy development. While doing so, they draw on different theories, evidence, and methods from and across alike academic disciplines such as sociology, social anthropology, social psychology, human geography, and feminist approaches. Third, NRSS researchers are increasingly recognizing the need for inter- and transdisciplinary approaches to better understand and respond to complex natural resource challenges (Buizer et al. 2015). Here, interdisciplinarity refers to the means of knowledge production that combines theory, evidence, and methods from multiple disciplines, whereas transdisciplinarity involves and integrates perspectives and knowledge from rightsholders and stakeholders in different phases of interdisciplinary research (see Steelman et al. 2021). In these settings and with different research designs, researchers seek and perform multiple roles (Holden et al. 2019), based on different principles to knowledge co-production, integration, and collaboration (e.g., humility, trust, open-mindedness, creativity, reflexivity; see Renn 2021). Fourth, there is tension between excellence in these inter- and transdisciplinary roles and the standards and metrics for those who are admitted/hired, rewarded, and promoted in different sectors to work on sustainability problems (see Singh 2022). Fifth, human indignity may be embedded in interpersonal and institutional inequities specific to NRSS fields (Burmann et al. 2022). It may also reflect symptoms of broader institutional indignity in certain sectors or in broader society (Clark and Wallace 2018). These trends work together to complicate our understanding, and proposal, of strategies to support human dignity in NRSS career pathways. Yet, as explained below, it is still crucial that we identify entry points if we are to build capacity for human dignity to support NRSS researchers' contributions to critical sustainability outcomes, even if problems of human indignity are more broadly experienced.

The Approach: Combining Experiences and Literature

We explore opportunities to build capacity for human dignity by identifying and combining perspectives from the authorship team and guidance from literature on academic career paths, NRSS researchers training and careers, and transdisciplinarity.[2] The authorship team is a group of NRSS researchers working in academic, public, and private sectors at early and mid-career stages. Through a series of discussions, including at the 2021 International Association of Society and Natural Resources Virtual Conference, we identified and explored our own experiences in seeking to implement our commitments to sustainability outcomes in different sectors, as well as the ideological, interpersonal, and institutional factors that shaped these experiences. We first discuss these experiences and factors in the context of seeking jobs in academia. Then, we move to factors in public and private sectors. We show how these represent a problem of human dignity (see Clark and Wallace 2015). Finally, using these experiences and the literature, we posit a framework to guide capacity building for human dignity in academia.

Experiences in Seeking Academic Employment

Employment in academia is changing worldwide. The ability to land a tenure-track position is increasingly difficult, leading to experiences of indignity. Who succeeds is shaped by who has access to funding (Tricco et al. 2017) and teaching opportunities (Kim 2019). For example, training in higher ranked programs is preferred, where inequities in admissions, support, and advancement are significant (Warner and Clauset 2015). These career challenges are

2. Though we share our experiences, identifying context has been added with care to support privacy. Some of us are working in settings in which we, or our collaborations, are vulnerable.

exacerbated in the context of interdisciplinary and transdisciplinary natural resource research, where research involves time and resources to collaborate across disciplines and outside of academia, collaborative outputs are slower to materialize, and hiring and funding prioritizes disciplinary training and research programs (Karcher et al. 2022; Lyall 2019). During academic training, access to social networks of support varies, including opportunities to engage with effective supervisors and mentors in inter- and transdisciplinary training environments (Andrews and Harper et al. 2020). Interpersonal factors are also critical for a caring and respectful training context (Care et al. 2021). These factors can shape indignities and alienation during training, while NRSS researchers are learning to develop quality and impactful NRSS research and can shape employment outcomes later in academic career paths. For example, variation in supervision, mentorship, and training can result in different levels of experience and preparedness in applying for jobs, conducting interviews, reference letters, and networking, which can be further exacerbated by larger institutionalized societal inequities including race, gender, disability, and class. Thus, attention to institutional change is needed to address structural problems that anchor inequities in academia (Wolbring and Lillywhite 2021). One co-author, a woman of color, a mother, and a PhD candidate reflects:

> Guided by my lived experiences, I strongly believe that a key element of NRSS research lies within our ability to build respectful and reciprocal relationships with the communities we work with. To me, this requires NRSS graduate training that encourages critical reflection on positionalities and power, and provides the ability to question research methodologies and challenge status-quos. This way, our research outputs would be more relevant, context-appropriate, and respectful of local perspectives. I am fortunate to be in a flexible program with a supportive supervisor. Others are not so lucky. How can we support broad structural change?

One ramification of the low availability of inter- and transdisciplinary academic positions relevant for NRSS is the increased prevalence of post-doctoral positions. Postdoctoral fellowships provide opportunities to deepen and broaden training, build leadership capacities, and foster quality research. These positions are often underpaid, may have unrealistic workloads, and yet are focused on increasing NRSS productivity. One co-author reflects on the uncertainty in competing in academia:

During my postdoctoral research position, my expectation was that I was going to end up working as a university professor in an area of my country, near my family. I applied for approximately 25 different teaching positions at various universities, and was not successful in attaining an interview or a position. In speaking to mentors about why I was not being hired, I was told the major reason is that I did not have experience in teaching. It was also explained to me that contract-based courses generally go for first right of refusal to those that have taught the course in the past. So, experience begets experience. I felt totally frustrated and defeated.

Difficulties in hiring are not a new problem, particularly for women and other marginalized groups, but one that comes with precarities associated with postdoctoral positions. Workload expectations are placed on postdoctoral researchers through interpersonal discourse and institutional hiring and reward mechanisms, exacerbating indignities for all, and inequities for those who face additional struggles or responsibilities, such as family obligations (Andrews et al. 2020). This forces a dilemma with implications to research dignity: Compete through uncertainty or languish in precarity.

Opportunities and Challenges in the Public and Private Sectors

Globally, natural resource public and private sectors are slowly changing to foster more opportunities for NRSS researchers. In the public sector, for example, NRSS is needed to advance diverse regulatory obligations in natural resource contexts and foster an integrative science approach (Marshall et al. 2017). For one researcher co-author, the need for more integrative frameworks in the natural resource sector has shaped employment opportunities to contribute impactful NRSS:

In the aftermath of the Brundtland report, my federal government released a comprehensive sector-specific sustainability plan. In my natural resources sector, this led to a shift of framing from sustainable yields to sustainable development. This reframing was supported by various initiatives that opened the path for the hiring of social scientists and nurtured NRSS capacity in a new management network in the 1990s. At the time, it seemed like a whole approach was starting to spread its wings, but progress stalled as government priorities shifted and funding for structural initiatives ended. In the last few years, though, signs show that NRSS might be taking roots in our institutional culture.

Yet, there are barriers in public and private sector institutions that can shape the production and influence of NRSS pathways (Marshall et al. 2017). From our experience, limited budgets, unfamiliarity with NRSS, and organizational cultures can discount qualitative and community-based NRSS researchers and their prospects. As well, researchers' immigration status and local employment experience can block career advancement, even though universities welcome (and profit from) nonresident enrollment:

> I am from Latin America. I completed all my training abroad. I pursued NRSS training related to public health. Ten years after I completed my Master's degree, I am still working in academia, and now as a postdoctoral fellow. This trajectory was partly shaped by my immigration status. Often holding a temporary resident permit, I was not able to switch to the public or private sector. When I was granted a US permanent residency permit after a long eight-year wait, I moved back to the US, but could not secure an interview outside postdoctoral work in academia.

Early career academics, supervisors, and administrators are often not able to understand and foresee job markets outside of academia (McAlpine and Emmioğlu 2015). Academic programs are thus typically not designed to meet needs external to academia (Singh 2022). The skills developed in NRSS programs cannot be assumed to be desired by applied sectors (Hancock 2021). Quality academic training, by academic standards, and internally scoped program designs, then, may not be sufficient to provide students with the range of skills and experiences to find and retain opportunities (McAlpine and Emmioğlu 2015). In the experience of the co-authors, academic training is often insufficient to advance highly structured and applied objectives, to develop the ability to make solution-oriented decisions based on limited information, and to fully understand the need for negotiation, diplomacy, and tact.

There is no doubt that current graduate training provides essential skills, such as analytical skills, systematic thinking, methodological rigor, and communication. However, often it is left to the early career academic to bridge these skills with the needs of an applied career. For instance, it may be expected but not guaranteed that NRSS graduates have the skills required to network, identify the transferability of their skills, and write for a variety of communication outlets. Using experiences from the private sector, one NRSS researcher co-author reflects:

> There is a need to better understand the private sector. In the private sector, hiring schedules are determined by annual work plans, which in turn tend to be heavily scrutinized by governing bodies. There is a general tendency among governing bodies to hesitate [to make] extensive staff increases. The nature of new positions is determined by the short- and medium-term vision of skills and experiences required. Virtually every position requires a combination of skills beyond academic specialization. While NRSS researchers may have expert-level specialization in one subject area, the position may require additional functions. In other words, there needs to be a balance between specialization and generalization, which may not be fostered in academic training.

While NRSS researchers play and even create new roles with diverse skills in the context of inter- and transdisciplinarity (see Holden et al. 2019), training still may not prepare them well for mobility in different career paths. This can lead to human indignity coupled with a sense of vulnerability (Andrews et al. 2020).

Building Capacity for Human Dignity in NRSS Career Pathways

If academic institutions, governments, and private companies want to develop NRSS to guide sustainability outcomes, then academia needs to nurture the broadest distribution of integrated problem-solving NRSS skills and shape NRSS researchers capable of contributing and leading inter- and transdisciplinarity in academic, public, and private sectors. Above, the perspectives and literature reveal complexities and heterogeneities across the NRSS career pathways but point to opportunities and possibilities in academia to advance human dignity for NRSS researchers in a transdisciplinary setting. Drawing on the experiences above, and offering more in the next paragraphs, we imagine a framework that focuses on support during training that can help supply quality, critical, and impactful NRSS research from healthy and well researchers based on the core goal of human dignity (figure 4.1).

The perspectives in this chapter reveal that NRSS career pathways include push factors in academic training and pull factors in public and private sectors, characterized in figure 4.1. For the push factors, training NRSS to embody

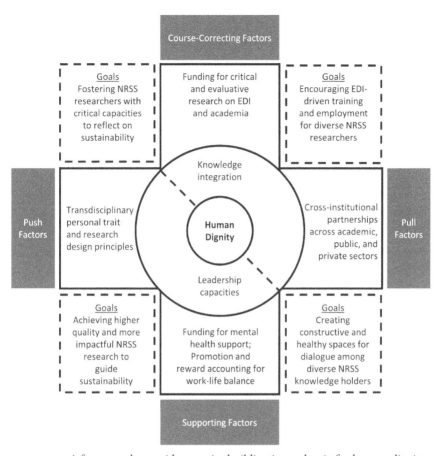

FIGURE 4.1. A framework to guide capacity-building in academia for human dignity.

personal and research principles related to human dignity in transdisciplinary research contexts is a key strategy to reimagine what is important for understanding NRSS contributions to sustainability (Clark and Wallace 2015). This strategy reimagines both ideological and institutional values associated with quality cross-disciplinary work, rather than numbers and metrics associated with research excellence that currently dominate academic training, hiring, and rewarding. One NRSS researcher co-author working in academia makes this connection in the context of interdisciplinarity:

> Engaging in interdisciplinary research has hugely shaped my career—especially in terms of collaboration and the opportunities. I've had to connect with

diverse groups of researchers and marine stakeholders locally and internationally. My experience so far has been very positive. In my experience, interdisciplinary work demands that you become humbler and more open-minded to different knowledge types and perspectives.

The creation of human dignity–informed NRSS training can be shaped by social networks as well as institutional changes that function as pull factors. Transdisciplinary skills, cross-institutional partnerships, and knowledge-transfer lessons are needed to prepare for impactful work in public and private sectors. For instance, training on process facilitation, conflict mediation, effective communication, and cross-cultural communication are relevant in this domain (Holden et al. 2019; Rosenberg, Lotz-Sisitka, and Ramsarup 2018). In addition, metrics for knowledge generation and dissemination beyond scientific publications are indispensable in the context of social and transdisciplinary research. Related research-evaluation strategies can combine questions about credibility, legitimacy, and salience of research with those related to human dignity, such as assessment of ethical research conduct, including involvement of diverse authors, the roles for key rightsholders and stakeholders, and appropriateness of communication strategies (e.g., Mårtensson et al. 2016). Senior and established researchers and supervisors can "champion" these inter- and transdisciplinary skills, principles, and research characteristics (Kelly et al. 2019). One co-author shared the following institutional initiative (Blythe and Cvitanovic 2020), which is centered on the unique needs and challenges of an NRSS career pathway:

> The Centre for Marine Socioecology (CMS) at the University of Tasmania is an institutional alternative that brings together emerging and established NRSS researchers to collaborate, network, train, and innovate for contemporary and future ocean challenges. A unique feature of CMS is its strong female leadership, which has supported the centre's ability to nurture and support emerging NRSS researchers as they enter an NRSS career pathway. The strong female leadership in CMS is demonstrated to have (i) encouraged innovation, (ii) cultivated a more inclusive research and working environment, and (iii) removed hierarchical power imbalances which have the potential to derail inter/transdisciplinary research collaborations.

The research community can benefit from critical reflection about EDI programs and academic norms, as well as assessments of opportunities to help foster stronger relationships through cross-institutional partnerships (Buizer et al. 2015). Constructive, kind, respectful, and ethical interactions among NRSS leaders and diverse knowledge holders are needed to help integrate knowledge and action and facilitate co-learning (Black and Dwyer 2021; Care et al. 2021). Furthermore, leveraging diverse experience in academia and connecting it to the public sector can be tricky but not impossible (Marshall et al. 2017). The goals are to not only address effective career pathways among academic and other sectors but also create equitable and inclusive spaces for underrepresented scholars including female researchers (Shellock et al. 2022). One co-author describes a program alternative:

> The Federal Student Work Experience Program in Canada, by design, is inclusive of both youth, and adults, in an effort to diversify the workforce in public service. The program also provides the option to self-declare identity markers (e.g., gender, Indigenous status, visible minority status, and disability status) with hiring practices that reserve selected employment opportunities to persons belonging to these marginalized groups.

Institutions, metrics, and requirements of research positions and collaborative networks need to evolve accordingly if they are to inform and contribute to sustainability outcomes. Human dignity can be a guiding principle for fostering change in NRSS career pathways, including to ensure the wellbeing of NRSS researchers during their training and as they pursue careers. Such approaches can provide them the much-needed space for critical and quality research development, including supporting visioning, implementing, and evaluating sustainability initiatives. To this end, we contribute a framework that places human dignity at the heart of NRSS training, with an aim to help foster effective, equitable, and inclusive NRSS career pathways.

References

Andrews, E. J., S. Harper, T. Cashion, J. Palacios-Abrantes, J. Blythe, J. Daly, S. Eger, C. Hoover, N. Talloni-Alvarez, L. Teh, et al. 2020. Supporting early career researchers: Insights from interdisciplinary marine scientists. *ICES Journal of Marine Science* 77 (2): 476–85. https://doi.org/10.1093/ICESJMS/FSZ247.

Black, A. L., and R. Dwyer, eds. 2021. *Reimagining the academy: Shifting towards kindness, connection, and an ethics of care.* Cham, Switzerland: Palgrave Macmillan.

Blythe, J., and C. Cvitanovic. 2020. Five organizational features that enable success-ful interdisciplinary marine research. *Frontiers in Marine Science* 7: 981. https://doi.org/10.3389/FMARS.2020.539111/BIBTEX.

Buizer, M., K. Ruthrof, S. A. Moore, E. J. Veneklaas, G. Hardy, and C. Baudains. 2015. A critical evaluation of interventions to transdisciplinary research. *Society & Natural Resources* 28 (6): 670–81. https://doi.org/10.1080/08941920.2014.945058.

Burmann, L. L., M. C. Kelly, C. Schelly, and T. L. Bai. 2022. Formative interests and pathways to natural resources careers among historically underrepresented peo-ple. *Society & Natural Resources* 35 (3): 260–80: https://doi.org/10.1080/08941920.2022.2028046.

Byrd, C. D., and R. S. Mason. 2021. *Academic pipeline programs: Diversifying pathways from the bachelor's to the professoriate.* Amherst, MA: Lever Press. https://doi.org/10.3998/MPUB.12216775.

Care, O., M. J. Bernstein, M. Chapman, I. Diaz Reviriego, G. Dressler, M. R. Felipe-Lucia, C. Friis, S. Graham, H. Hänke, L. J. Haider, et al. 2021. Creating leadership collectives for sustainability transformations. *Sustainability Science* 16 (2): 703–08. https://doi.org/10.1007/S11625-021-00909-y.

Clark, S. G., and R. L. Wallace. 2015. Integration and interdisciplinarity: Concepts, frameworks, and education. *Policy Sciences* 48: 233–55. https://doi.org/10.1007/S11077-015-9210-4.

Clark, S. G., and R. L. Wallace. 2018. The integrity problem in higher education: description, consequences, and recommendations. *Higher Education Review* 50 (2): 127–51.

Hancock, S. 2021. What is known about doctoral employment? Reflections from a UK study and directions for future research. *Journal of Higher Education Policy and Management* 43 (5): 520–36. https://doi.org/10.1080/1360080X.2020.1870027.

Holden, P., J. Cockburn, S. Shackleton, and E. Rosenberg. 2019. Supporting and developing competencies for transdisciplinary postgraduate research: a PhD scholar perspective. In *Developing Change Agents*, ed. K. L. Kremers, A. S. Liepins, and A. M. York. Minneapolis: University of Minnesota Libraries Publishing.

Karcher, D. B., C. Cvitanovic, R. Shellock, A. J. Hobday, R. L. Stephenson, M. Dickey-Collas, and I. E. van Putten. 2022. More than money—the costs of knowledge exchange at the interface of science and policy. *Ocean & Coastal Man-agement* 225: 106194. https://doi.org/10.1016/j.ocecoaman.2022.106194.

Kelly, R., M. Mackay, K. L. Nash, C. Cvitanovic, E. H. Allison, D. Armitage, A. Bonn, S. J. Cooke, S. Frusher, E. A. Fulton, et al. 2019. Ten tips for developing interdisciplinary socio-ecological researchers. *Socio-Ecological Practice Research* 1 (2): 149–61. https://doi.org/10.1007/s42532-019-00018-2.

Kim, K. 2019. *Gender bias in teaching evaluations.* PhD diss., Purdue University.

Kremers, K. L., A. S. Liepins, and A. M. York. 2019. *Developing change agents.* Minne-apolis: University of Minnesota Libraries Publishing.

Lyall, C. 2019. *Being an interdisciplinary academic: How institutions shape university careers.* Cham, Switzerland: Palgrave MacMillan. https://doi.org/10.1007/978-3-030-18659-3.

Malpas, J., and N. Lickiss, eds. 2007. *Perspectives on human dignity: A conversation.* Dordrecht, Netherlands: Springer.

Marshall, N., N. Adger, S. Attwood, K. Brown, C. Crissman, C. Cvitanovic, C. De Young, M. Gooch, C. James, S. Jessen, et al. 2017. Empirically derived guidance for social scientists to influence environmental policy. *PLoS ONE* 12 (3): 1–9. https://doi.org/10.1371/journal.pone.0171950.

Mårtensson, P., U. Fors, S. Wallin, and U. Zander. 2016. Evaluating research: A multidisciplinary approach to research practice and quality. *Research Policy* 45: 593–603. https://doi.org/10.1016/j.respol.2015.11.009.

Mattson, D. J., and S. G. Clark. 2011. Human dignity in concept and practice. *Policy Sciences* 44, 303–20. https://doi.org/10.1007/s11077-010-9124-0.

McAlpine, L., and E. Emmioğlu. 2015. Navigating careers: Perceptions of sciences doctoral students, post-phd researchers and pre-tenure academics. *Studies in Higher Education* 40 (10):1770–85. https://doi.org/10.1080/03075079.2014.914908.

McDougal, M. S., H. D. Lasswell, and L. Chen. 1980. *Human rights and world public order: Basic policies of an international law of human dignity.* New Haven, CT: Yale University Press.

Nagan, W. 2013. *Contextual-configurative jurisprudence: The law, science and policies of human dignity.* Lake Mary, FL: Vandeplas.

Renn, O. 2021. Transdisciplinarity: Synthesis towards a modular approach. *Futures* 130: 102744. https://doi.org/10.1016/j.futures.2021.102744.

Rosenberg, E., H. B. Lotz-Sisitka and P. Ramsarup. 2018. The green economy learning assessment South Africa: Lessons for higher education, skills and work-based learning. *Higher Education, Skills and Work-Based Learning* 8 (3): 243–58. https://doi.org/10.1108/HESWBL-03-2018-0041.

Shellock, R. J., C. Cvitanovic, M. Mackay, M. C. McKinnon, J. Blythe, R. Kelly, I. E. van Putten, P. Tuohy, M. Bailey, A. Begossi, et al. 2022. Breaking down barriers: The identification of actions to promote gender equality interdisciplinary marine research institutions. *One Earth* 5 (6): 687–708. https://doi.org/10.1016/j.oneear.2022.05.006.

Singh, G. G. 2022. We have sent ourselves to Iceland (with apologies to Iceland): Changing the academy from internally-drive to externally partnered. *Frontiers in Sustainable Cities* 4. https://doi.org/10.3389/frsc.2022.832506.

Steelman, T., A. Bogdan, C. Mantyka-Pringle, L. Bradford, M. G. Reed, S. Baines, J. Fresque-Baxter, T. Jardine, S. Shantz, R. Abu, et al. 2021. Evaluating transdisciplinary research: Insights from social network analysis. *Sustainability Science* 16: 631–45. https://doi.org/10.1007/s11625-020-00901-y.

Tricco, A. C., S. M. Thomas, J. Antony, P. Rios, R. Robson, R. Pattani, M. Ghassemi, S. Sullivan, I. Selvaratnam, C. Tannenbaum, et al. 2017. Strategies to prevent or reduce gender bias in peer review of research grants: A rapid scoping review. *PLoS ONE* 12 (1): e0169718. https://doi.org/10.1371/JOURNAL.PONE.0169718.

Warner, J., and A. Clauset. 2015. The academy's dirty secret: An astonishingly small number of elite universities produce an overwhelming number of America's professors. *Slate*, February 23.

Wolbring, G., and A. Lillywhite. 2021. Equity/equality, diversity, and inclusion (EDI) in universities: The case of disabled people. *Societies* 11 (2): 49. https://doi.org/10.3390/SOC11020049.

Section Two

Governance & Power

5

Understanding Institutions

*The Role of Broadly Institutional Perspectives for Understanding
Environmental Change and Natural Resource Use*

E. CARINA H. KESKITALO

Institutionally based perspectives may help us understand how responses to climate change, or any other emerging issues, need to include the ways the existing system already selects and biases particular decision paths. The chapter highlights the potential understandings of multilevel governance and embedded and persistent social logics that are possible through institutionally oriented perspectives.

Introduction

It is almost a given to say that the field of environmental change studies grew out of environmental studies in the natural sciences. But in this also lies what is today one of the major problems in environmental change studies—that the social understanding in natural resource studies is not always based in the social sciences.

Framings, as understandings of what is even relevant to understand, are often persistent over a long time, and can be hard to change (e.g., Weaver

https://doi.org/10.7330/9781646426300.c005

2007). One assumption in the framing of environmental change has long been that better *scientific knowledge about the environment will lead to action*. This assumption has even been seen as just "the way science is practiced" and has even been given its own label: *the linear model of scientific knowledge or expertise*. The assumption here, as Böcher and Krott summarise, is that "if scientific facts are available, then this availability automatically leads to the use of science in practice. In linear models, political actors demand scientific knowledge, and it is supplied by the science community: this knowledge flows directly from science into practice, in which it is utilised by political decision makers and stakeholders with the aim of producing 'rational' solutions. Decisions are then based on scientific information without being altered by the policy process or practical considerations" (Böcher and Krott 2014, 3643).

The crucial issue with gaining social change is, thus, obscured by the model. Social science studies of how to achieve change are not needed in this model, as change is not only automatic but assumed to be requested by policy makers in relation to the best available knowledge in science. The model has been disproven, and Intergovernmental Panel of Climate Change (IPCC) assessment reports now acknowledge that "simply producing more and better knowledge is not sufficient" (Mimura et al. 2014, 887). However, authors have noted that its continued practice (an "undead" model; Durant 2015, 17) continues to obscure the enormous research field, where not only stakeholder interaction is needed to achieve change, but where a social analysis of possibilities and incentives for change is needed.

The Role of Theory

As a framing of what knowledge is needed and what problem understanding is promoted, the linear model of scientific knowledge or expertise is for all intents and purposes working as a theory, with the problem that it is both disproven and not always explicitly recognised (Grundmann 2009; Briggle 2008; Pielke 2007). What may be needed, then, is to both recognise what this type of assumption excludes and try to find ways of including a fuller description and analysis of reality.

In social science studies, of course, theories are explicitly formed and used to understand selected parts of the social world (see, for instance, Jones and

Walton in chapter 12 of this volume). They are often both derived from multiple cases—often while recognising the variety among cases—and broadly applicable. This means several things. It means that understanding the role of theory is crucial, as the social world can never be grasped all at once. But it also means that, in best practice, cases are never only single cases. They can say something about what theory is applicable and where, as results from a case can, for instance, be generalised to theory (e.g., Flyvbjerg 2006).

What much of environmental change study—built on natural science—has done, however, is fail to consider this role of both theory and social study in specific cases. The focus has instead, given the background related to assumptions in the linear model, been placed on direct interaction to promote knowledge, and thereby on lower and sometimes individual-level interaction such as learning among stakeholders or in local communities, or on more composite concepts such as capacity (e.g., Wellstead, Rayner, and Howlett 2014).

This has often resulted in an omission of the more structural or higher-level social context, as well as the role of power in real-life situations. Power, although it has a crucial impact on social and not least political and decision-making situations, is not acknowledged in the linear model of scientific knowledge or expertise, as science is simply to be transmitted to assumedly interested decision-makers (Keskitalo and Preston 2019). The political role of knowledge, and the system or structural conditions, are thus less often placed in focus.

For these types of reasons, it is crucial to also understand the structural or higher level contexts of decision-making, in which the real-life role of power is included—and which encompass and influence lower-level and individual action as well. Taking a broad institutional perspective can be one way to do this. Highlighting the features of the systems in which change is to be implemented does not assume change but rather asks how change can be developed.

A Broad Institutional Perspective

The focus on institutions here is not taken only to refer to specific theories but rather as a focus on institutional logics. This is the broad notion that the social world is institutionalised in a way that it cannot be assumed to change with, for example, improved knowledge only (Thornton, Ocasio, and Lounsbury 2012). Rather, actors or stakeholders are seen as formed, constrained, and enabled in what options they can choose depending on the larger social systems in which they act. In regular application, decision-making is thus often assumed to operate not necessarily through making conscious, assessed choices based on information only, but based on assumption and perhaps "muddling through" in relation to organisationally available information and practice (March and Olsen 1996, Lafferty and Cohen 2001). This means that systems may be self-reinforcing and also that there may be large system costs of change (e.g., Pierson 2000). Some changes may also not work, given the incentive structures or motivations in different systems.

Systems—for instance, levels or sectors—are thereby typically both historically developed and nested, which means that the local level, for example, is typically influenced by decisions at a regional, national, or even international level, and that different sectors are connected to each other. Different systems may also be part of other systems and require these to also change in order to enable change (e.g., Liebowitz and Margolis 1995). All of this means that different levels, sectors, and organisations may be internally dependent on each other, creating "lock-in" effects that may make change to established routines or practices difficult. Incremental, smaller changes may thus not only simply be what is possible in some cases, but can also even be more effective, given that sequences of incremental changes may be more acceptable to actors than transformational change (Greener 2005; Olsen 2009).

This historically developed, interest- and position-based, partially integrated nature of institutions can be seen as a foundational part of understanding what change may be possible even at more local or individual levels. Thus, rather than being able to look past or avoid interest, it is crucial to conceive of interests, values, and motivations to understand the potentials and possible means for change. Logics and interests that are embedded into institutions over time can thereby largely determine the responses to change, including environmental change.

This has significance in multiple areas. Multilevel governance has often been defined as the participation of not only the state but also different levels from subnational to supranational, as well as private and citizen interests, in decision-making (Marks and Hooghe 2004). While governance has often been seen as a more open model, potentially integrating different interests, a broad understanding of institutional workings can support a problematisation of governance as well. From a more institutional perspective, actors that have come into existence because of specific institutional conditions can typically be seen as having been naturalised into sustaining these conditions (North 1996). Consequently, the current distribution of power as well as the different instruments, sectoral traditions, and practices that exist in an area will influence what role new measures take on even within systems that include additional actors (e.g., Skelcher 2005).

Understanding governance through an eye of being implemented in and through existing institutions thus means that one must problematise the ways in which steering can be made to work. Several studies illustrate the implications of such a perspective. Among other things, it has been shown that the use of new environmental policy instruments (Jordan, Wurzel, and Zito 2013) such as more soft or private governance measures will be delimited through incentivisation and what is possible and workable in different institutional contexts (Keskitalo and Pettersson 2012). Private, voluntary arrangements can thus not be assumed to work in the absence of a context where they are strongly incentivised (Lenschow 2014; Marsden et al. 2014; Jordan, Wurzel, and Zito 2013). This also implies that the study of governance must also include social analysis of both the specific institutional context as well as theories that allow for broad understandings of the multiple influences on decision-making on multiple levels and beyond what any individual stakeholder may be able to directly express (Keskitalo and Preston 2019).

Conclusion

To avoid treating the social system like a blank page or "black box" (Wellstead, Howlett, and Rayner 2013; Wellstead, Rayner, and Howlett 2014) into which the climate change or environmental change issue is inserted, a broad, institutionally based understanding may help us understand how responses to climate change or any other new emerging issues need to include the ways the existing system already selects and biases particular decision and non-decision paths, through an integrated social analysis (e.g., Sovacool et al. 2015). This would mean, for instance, that adaptation paths can be chosen that resonate with different decision-makers and within different sectors, even without explicitly making the environment or climate the focus of study.

Taken together, these types of perspectives illustrate significant difficulties with much business-as-usual environmental change research. For instance, communication and learning need to be seen as socially and structurally embedded. Change is delimited by stakeholders' assumptions and socially constructed needs as well as broader decision-making systems rather than being related to an assumption of knowledge as directly leading to change. A focus also needs to be placed on power and institutions as a given in interest structures and thereby as something that needs to be understood and studied rather than avoided.

Acknowledgment

This article summarises some of the arguments in Keskitalo's (2022) *The Social Aspects of Environmental and Climate Change.*

References

Böcher, M., and M. Krott. 2014. The RIU model as an analytical framework for scientific knowledge transfer: The case of the "decision support system forest and climate change." *Biodiversity and Conservation* 23 (14): 3641–56.

Briggle, A. 2008. Questioning expertise. *Social Studies of Science* 38 (3): 461–70.

Durant, D. 2015. The undead linear model of expertise. In *Policy legitimacy, science and political authority: Knowledge and action in liberal democracies*, ed. M. Heazle and J. Kane, 17–38. London: Routledge.

Flyvbjerg, B. 2006. Five misunderstandings about case-study research. *Qualitative Inquiry* 12 (2): 219–45.

Greener, I. 2005. The potential of path dependence in political studies. *Politics* 25 (1): 62–67.

Grundmann, R. 2009. The role of expertise in governance processes. *Forest policy and economics* 11 (5–6): 398–403.

Jordan, A. R. K., W. Wurzel, and A. R. Zito. 2013. Still the century of "new" environmental policy instruments? Exploring patterns of innovation and continuity. *Environmental Politics* 22 (1): 155–73.

Keskitalo, E. C. H., and M. Pettersson 2012. Implementing multi-level governance? The legal basis and implementation of the EU water framework directive for forestry in Sweden. *Environmental Policy and Governance* 22 (2): 90–103.

Keskitalo, E. C. H., and B. L. Preston. 2019. Climate change adaptation policy research and its role in understanding climate change. In *Research handbook on climate change adaptation policy*, ed. E. C. H. Keskitalo and B. L. Preston. 475–91. Cheltenham, UK: Edward Elgar.

Lafferty, W. M., and F. Cohen. 2001. Conclusions and perspectives. In *Sustainable communities in Europe*, ed. W. M. Lafferty. London: Earthscan.

Lenschow, A. 2014. Innovations through sector integration and new instruments. In *The problem-solving capacity of the modern state: Governance challenges and administrative capacities*, ed. M. Lodge and K. Wegrich, 144–62. Oxford, UK: Oxford University Press.

Liebowitz, S. J., and S. E. Margolis. 1995. Path dependence, lock-in, and history. *Journal of Law, Economics, & Organization* 11 (1): 205–26.

March, J. G., and J. P. Olsen. 1996. Institutional perspectives on political institutions. *Governance* 9 (3): 247–64.

Marks, G., and L. Hooghe. 2004. Contrasting visions of multi-level governance. In *Multi-level governance*, ed. I. Bache and M. Flinders, 15–30. Oxford, UK: Oxford University Press.

Marsden, G., A. Ferreira, I. Bache, M. Flinders, and I. Bartle. 2014. Muddling through with climate change targets: A multi-level governance perspective on the transport sector. *Climate Policy* 14 (5): 617–36.

Mimura, N., R. S. Pulwarty, D. M. Duc, I. Elshinnawy, M. H. Redsteer, H. Q. Huang, J. N. Nkem, and R. A. Sanchez Rodriguez. 2014. Adaptation planning and implementation. In *Climate change 2014: Impacts, adaptation, and vulnerability. Part A: Global and sectoral aspects*, ed. C. B. Field, V. R. Barros, D. J. Dokken, K. J. Mach, M. D. Mastrandrea, T. E. Bilir, M. Chatterjee, K. L. Ebi, Y. O. Estrada, R. C. Genova, et al., 869–98. Cambridge, UK: Cambridge University Press.

North, D. C. 1996. Institutional change: A framework of analysis. In *Social rules*, ed. D. Braybrooke, 189–201. Boulder, CO: Routledge.

Olsen, J. P. 2009. Change and continuity: An institutional approach to institutions of democratic government. *European Political Science Review: EPSR* 1 (1): 3–32.

Pielke, R. A. 2007. *The honest broker: Making sense of science in policy and politics.* New York: Cambridge University Press.

Pierson, P. 2000. Increasing returns, path dependence, and the study of politics. *American Political Science Review* 94 (2): 251–67.

Skelcher, C. 2005. Jurisdictional integrity, polycentrism, and the design of democratic governance. *Governance* 18 (1): 89–110.

Sovacool, B. K., S. E. Ryan, P. C. Stern, K. Janda, G. Rochlin, D. Spreng, M. J. Pasqualetti, H. Wilhite, and L. Lutzenhiser. 2015. Integrating social science in energy research. *Energy Research & Social Science* 6: 95–99.

Thornton, P. H., W. Ocasio, and M. Lounsbury. 2012. *The institutional logics perspective: A new approach to culture, structure and process.* Oxford, UK: Oxford University Press.

Weaver, D. H. 2007. Thoughts on agenda setting, framing, and priming. *Journal of Communication* 57 (1): 142–47.

Wellstead, A. M., M. Howlett, and J. Rayner. 2013. The neglect of governance in forest sector vulnerability assessments: Structural-functionalism and "black box" problems in climate change adaptation planning. *Ecology and Society* 18 (3): 23.

Wellstead, A. M., J. Rayner, and M. Howlett. 2014. Beyond the black box: Forest sector vulnerability assessments and adaptation to climate change in North America. *Environmental Science & Policy* 35: 109–16.

6

The *CBNRM-isation* of East and Southern Africa

A Critical Review of the Community Conservancy Model

RICHARD DIMBA KIAKA, PAUL HEBINCK, AND RODGERS LUBILO

Community-based natural resource management (CBNRM) in East and Southern Africa has had mixed evaluations. On the one hand, CBNRM is said to have achieved some ecological success by expanding landscapes for conservation and advancing the recovery of wildlife populations. On the other hand, CBNRM is argued to have largely failed in its economic empowerment objective—the incentive that should drive communities to participate in conservation. Whereas the critique anticipates the end of CBNRM in the region, the conservation model continues to spread and draws support from global conservation NGOs and donors. Taking the example of community conservancies, this chapter argues that the continuous flux of CBNRM institutions in east and southern Africa is underpinned by new meanings and purposes that various actors ascribe to them.

Introduction

Since the mid-1980s, community-based natural resource management (CBNRM) has been undertaken in East and Southern Africa and beyond to

https://doi.org/10.7330/9781646426300.c006

curtail the alarming losses in biodiversity and address the enduring poverty of many rural people who reside in areas bordering protected and conservation areas (IUCN, UNEP, and WWF 1980; Silva and Mosimane 2013; Western, Waithaka, and Kamanga 2015). Intellectually aligned with sustainable development policies that emerged from the international Earth Summit in 1992 (Agrawal 2001), CBNRM demanded a new paradigmatic orientation to provide local people access to the benefits of nature. New policies and actions taken at the local level turned CBNRM into a promising "triple-win" option, for and by the people, to sustainably use natural resources, restore biodiversity, and reduce poverty (Noss 1997; Western, Wright, and Strum 1994). With substantial support from a coalition of conservation NGOs, donors, domestic elites, local community leaders, group ranch leaders,[1] and national and regional policymakers, CBNRM trickled down to the local level (Roe, Nelson, and Sandbrook 2009). We refer to the process by which CBNRM has been introduced and spread in east and southern Africa as the *CBNRM-isation* of conservation. *CBNRM-isation* is being perpetuated to address the historical inequalities and injustices and the imperfections of state-mandated fortress-style conservation to adequately protect biodiversity (Nelson 2010; Schreckenberg et al. 2016; Brockington 2002). Fortress conservation refers to a protectionist conservation model that creates protected areas where wildlife is conserved in isolation of human disturbance (Brockington 2002). *CBNRM-isation* is not a linear process but rather one that entails negotiations and struggles, and one whose outcome may mean the practices deviate from the original intentions.

We focus here on communal conservancies, a form of CBNRM for managing wildlife and other natural resources, which are praised for their contribution to empowerment and democratisation and for providing alternative livelihood opportunities. Roe, Nelson, and Sandbrook (2009) document ecological, economic, and institutional achievements of CBNRM. In Namibian communal conservancies, wildlife has increased in both numbers and diversity, implying conservancies are an essential tool for wildlife conservation and ecological success (Bollig 2020; Naidoo et al. 2016). Critics argue that

1. In East Africa, especially Kenya, group ranches are collectively owned lands with defined membership; that is, portions of communal land are jointly owned and managed by a group of pastoralists, usually organised according to large extended families (Galaty 1992).

ascribing this success entirely to communal conservancies is inaccurate, as many factors have contributed to it, including the temporarily favourable climatic conditions and reduced conflicts in some pastoral areas, as well as increased security surveillance by governments (Sullivan 2012; Bersaglio and Cleaver 2018). The many critical appraisals of CBNRM in Namibia provide evidence that *CBNRM-isation* has occurred in contested spaces. Rather, community-based conservation projects emerged as sites of competition, manipulation, and inequality between conservancy actors operating at different scales (Hebinck, Kiaka, and Lubilo 2020). The actors in these projects have not been as homogenous a group as the CBNRM discourse assumes. Rather, actors have been differentiated by their ability to exert power and authority and to flout the rules. The global appeal, reach, and influence of actors have also varied in class, race, and gender.

The claimed socioecological successes of CBNRM are often overshadowed by negative outcomes. There have been accusations of financial mismanagement, elite capture,[2] and corruption in the allocation of salaried positions in conservancies (Lubilo 2018; Muyengwa, Child, and Lubilo 2014; Roe, Nelson, and Sandbrook 2009). Additionally, withdrawal and resistance by some community members within conservancies can arise from undemocratic decision-making, such as patriarchal politics and the role of community leaders (Alexander and McGregor 2000; Sullivan 2003; Lubilo and Hebinck 2019; Rabe and Saunders 2013). In some cases, the contractual relationship between private investors and communities has also been found to be unfair and not transparent (Cavanagh, Weldmichel, and Benjaminsen 2020; Mittal and Moloo 2021). The political economy of tourism and trophy hunting also severely constrains local communities, who may wish to set up their own businesses to capture the revenue from tourism and hunting (Nelson 2012). Poaching and "illegal" hunting continue (Lubilo and Hebinck 2019), and the lack of compensation for loss of rights evoke different forms of resistance to the *CBNRM-isation* of conservation (Gargallo 2021). CBNRM also facilitated the creation of "new symbolic and material spaces" for foreign investors and consumers (Corson 2010).

---

2. Elite capture refers to the process through which social, economic, and politic elites capture resource distribution, project implementation and decision-making to their advantage. In community-development discourse, it is usually seen as a form of corruption (Musgrave and Wong 2016).

Trophy hunting is a good example of how such spaces generate controversies (Novelli and Humavindu 2005; Lindsey et al. 2007; Batavia et al. 2018; Dickman et al. 2019). Global campaigns against trophy hunting and economic instabilities caused by the COVID-19 pandemic threaten to redirect the flow of conservation funding (Lindsey et al. 2020). The distribution of trophy hunting revenue has generated thorny debates about the inadequate economic returns for local communities (Humavindu and Stage 2015; Homewood, Nielsen, and Keane 2022; Sullivan 2006; Silva and Mosimane 2014). As communities foster and protect wildlife and bear the costs of human-wildlife conflicts, the lion's share of the revenues accrues to the private sector (Schnegg and Kiaka 2018; Drake et al. 2020). Kalvelage, Diez, and Bollig (2020) show that most of the value addition for Namibia's CBNRM is realised outside the region. These critiques, we argue, are the outcome of interconnected processes, which are systemic for CBNRM, including its design and mode of implementation. Indeed, as Ribot (2004) argued, efforts to truly devolve the rights over natural resources to the local level have been superficial and frustrated by a variety of actors. Many of the required institutional reforms to enable CBNRM to live up to its promises have been counterproductive.

The intention of this chapter is not to summarise the details of the criticisms. Rather, we focus on coming to grips with the fact that, despite the critiques and general perception that CBNRM has failed to deliver on most of its promises—especially in providing sufficient and equitable economic incentives for local communities (Hutton, Adams, and Murombedzi 2005; Blaikie 2006)—the conservation model still enjoys the support of many actors, especially the international conservation and donor communities. Conservancies (or their equivalents) in East and Southern Africa continue to be defended and operated in their present forms through international funding. If the continuity of the conservancy model were based only on community economic outcomes, CBNRM would no longer be used as a model for conservation in the region. Considering these dynamics, how can we explain the continuity of CBNRM-isation in the region? We postulate here that conservancies provide room for certain key social actors to manoeuvre, allowing them to either meet their existing sociopolitical, cultural, and economic interests or identify and defend newly emerging opportunities that conservancies (re)present. These actors deploy their agential capacities to repurpose conservancies and take advantage of opportunities that did not exist before CBNRM.

We continue by first elaborating on conservancy enactment as our analytical entry point. Next, we briefly depict the development of communal conservancies in East and Southern Africa. We then explore four areas that together contribute to an explanation of why conservancies are still favoured. We end with some concluding remarks about how conservancy enactment enhances *CBNRM-isation* and argue for their place in literature.

The Role of Conservancy Enactment and Repurposing

CBNRM-isation includes establishing a market-driven type of conservation—one that is neoliberal in orientation and organisation and that deepens the commodification of nature (Igoe and Brockington 2007). In this way, CBNRM-*isation* emerges through the processes of neoliberal *environmentality*, where conservationists endeavour to incentivise local people to behave in conservation-friendly ways (Fletcher 2010). Across East and Southern Africa, achieving economic growth is foremost in CBNRM policies (Cavanagh, Weldemichel, and Benjaminsen 2020; Schnegg and Kiaka 2018). Mechanisms of redistribution and co-management are designed to empower local people to reap the benefits of living and working with nature. All this is financed by revenues from ecotourism, trophy hunting, and the marketing of other natural resources; the private sector; and philanthropists channelled through international civil society organisations and NGOs (Roe, Nelson, and Sandbrook 2009). The state's role is to create an enabling environment through policy and legislative reforms that secure ownership rights of land and the products of nature (Roe, Nelson, and Sandbrook 2009). Democratic decision-making and collaboration with experts are the new norm (Fabricius et al. 2004; Nelson 2010). Local, indigenous, or "traditional" people thus become conservation partners and enrolled as parabiologists to assist in the struggle for conserving biodiversity (Sheil and Lawrence 2004; de Cunha and de Almeida 2000).

Community-based or communal conservancies are the institutional embodiment of the *CBNRM-isation* of the management of wildlife and other natural resources in the communal lands in East and Southern Africa, notably in Kenya, Zambia, Botswana, Zimbabwe, and Namibia (Roe, Nelson, and Sandbrook 2009). In Kenya, a community conservancy is described as land protected by a community for wildlife protection and other sustainable land uses that can lead to improved livelihoods (Reid et al. 2016). In Zimbabwe, where the Communal Areas Management Program for Indigenous Resources (CAMPFIRE) pioneered the application of CBNRM in wildlife management, communal conservancies can be defined as communal lands that are set aside for collective management of wildlife to achieve both improved livelihoods of communities and ecological sustainability (Muzvidziwa 2013). In Namibia, a communal conservancy is a legally registered and self-governed community-based institution that has obtained conditional rights to use the wildlife occurring within a self-defined area, as set out in Nature Conservation Amendment Act of 1996 (Republic of Namibia 1996).

While the enactment of community conservancies varies, the overall meaning and objectives are similar. Community conservancies are fixed portions of communal land where conservation of wildlife is promoted as a land use alongside other livelihood practices. Organisations enact institutions, constitutions, or articles of associations that govern these spaces to facilitate wildlife conservation as a land use (Campbell and Shackleton 2001). In Namibia, these organisations are also referred to as conservancies (Schnegg and Kiaka 2018; Hebinck, Kiaka, and Lubilo 2020). Conservancies are legally fashioned and bestowed with rules, procedures, and obligations to manage the resources and secure the sharing of benefits. These rules enact redistribution of conservation benefits and codify the roles of managers and elected committees in the day-to-day management (de Vette, Kashululu, and Hebinck 2012; Neumann 2001).

The crafting of institutions, as the CBNRM experiences underscore, is a complex and conflictive process. Conservancy enactment entails considering how social actors perform and (re)shape institutions and compete for authority through a process of bricolage (Lund 2006; Cleaver 2012). The enactment process is fluid and continuously in the making rather than something introduced through legislation or by applying design principles (Ostrom 1990). Conservancies unfold as arenas (Long 2001) where struggles and negotiations take place and political power and authority are played out. An arena is intrinsically sociomaterial and historical and structured by what Latour (2005) conceptualises as "micro-politics." This does not simply mean an exclusive focus on the "micro" level of the conservancy *per se*. Conservancies involve the strategic financial, technical, and discursive support of a wide array of NGOs and international organisations and collaboration with private sector partners in the conservation sector (Kiaka 2018; Schnegg and Kiaka 2018; Hebinck, Kiaka, and Lubilo 2020). Conservancies evolve as sites where different (e.g., local and global) discourses of conservation and development are produced, debated, and contested, and where a variety of discursive means are employed by the actors involved, forging different kinds of alliances (Arce and Long 2000).

Repurposing or reworking conservancies is one of the discursive means by which actors influence or manipulate conservancy enactment. Reworking conservancies may be analysed as a form of resistance by actors contesting and resisting reforms such as the forming of conservancies and their inherent disciplining mechanisms. Van der Ploeg (2010) refers to this form of resistance as "resistance of the third kind." Such resistance does not follow a blueprint. It also involves actively constructed and local(ised) responses to confront or challenge the current ordering of society (e.g., how benefits are distributed, how rights are defended) or the reforms that are initiated to transform decision-making and (re)distribution. Resisters of the third kind use a repertoire of political and culturally embedded strategies that are shaped by history. They do not distance themselves from the conservation project, but by collaborating and participating in it they aim to alter the *modus operandi* of the conservancy. Arce and Long (2000) coined the term *counterwork* to express that (reform) policies are neither fixed nor static; they evolve and shift and, above all, are negotiated and reworked by (some of the) beneficiaries (Long 2001, 2008; Scott 2009).

Well-situated beneficiaries (i.e., elites) navigate the conservancies and "capture" the conservancy by creating opportunities to influence conservancy politics and the distribution of revenue (Hebinck, Kiaka, and Lubilo 2020). These elites include representatives of conservancy governance structures, local entrepreneurs, and traditional authorities and leaders, as well as individual bureaucrats, NGOs, and international organisations. Such repurposing is usually debated under the heading of "elite capture," which concerns the harnessing of collective resources and manipulation of the decision-making processes by elites (Platteau 2004). We argue that elites' resistance, repurposing, or counterwork manifests in diverse ways, ranging from corruption and land grabbing to defending the commons from being pillaged by outsiders. Repurposing also includes practices of commoners or ordinary members of conservancies, whose everyday forms of resistance as Scott (1985) labelled them, cannot be ignored (Kiaka 2018).

Repurposing is also the embodiment of a process that Lund (2016) refers to as "authority in the making." This is the process by which the different normative orders of property and rights (e.g., customary and state laws, mechanisms of [re]distribution) that underlie the performance of CBNRM institutions are aligned with the new norms initiated by legislative reforms. This is essentially a process of political negotiations and a display of power. Ostrom's design principles (Ostrom 1990) only guide the settling of authority, as there is no predefined authority. In situations where different governing institutions are involved, there will be competition over authority. This is particularly relevant when competition over land and resources intersects with relations of authority and opportunity in contemporary Africa (Berry 2017; Hammar 2007; Herbst 2014). *CBNRM-isation*, we argue, fosters such situations. The question of who the legitimate authority is becomes contested and (re)negotiated in the conservancies—and often also in court (van der Wulp and Hebinck 2021).

Development of Community-Based Conservation and Conservancies in Africa

CBNRM-isation finds its roots in addressing situations like those prevalent in East and Southern Africa, where rights and responsibilities over wildlife outside protected areas were severely restricted during colonial administrations. In colonial Kenya and Namibia, for example, laws and policies that restricted the direct benefit of wildlife by governing hunting largely favoured a minority of white settlers and foreign hunters, whose interests were protected by the colonial government (Steinhart 1989; Botha 2005). White settlers had exclusive access to and use of wildlife on their private farms (Jones and Weaver 2008). Local communities, who had a long history of sharing habitats, whether in pastoral lands or in areas of hunting and gathering, were considered by the state to be decimators of the very wildlife that they had protected for centuries (Nelson 2003; Neumann 1996). In the 1970s and 1980s, politically moderate conservationists like Garth Owen-Smith (Owen-Smith 2010) in Namibia, Graham Child (Child 2008) and Marshall Murphree (Murphree 2009) in Zimbabwe, and Michael Wright and David Western (Western, Wright, and Strum 1994) in Kenya began to argue that wildlife and its habitats would be decimated if local communities residing on communal lands were excluded from the rights to use and access them. The wildlife conservation discourse in colonial and post-colonial Africa included many critiques of the system's racial inequality, furthering the call for the lifting of these restrictions (Adams and Mulligan 2003). This paved the way for community conservancies to manage wildlife outside parks and on private land. CAMPFIRE in Zimbabwe pioneered the establishment of communal conservancies in Southern Africa (Child 1996). Through legislation, the newly independent Zimbabwe granted rights over natural resources to the Rural District Councils to manage and devolve resource utilisation rights to the local communities (Child 1996; Dzingirai 1994; Murphree 2009). These district councils directly distributed income from safari accommodation and trophy hunting to households in participating villages.

The early success attributed to CAMPFIRE inspired many conservationists across East and Southern Africa. In Namibia, efforts to devolve restricted usufruct rights over wildlife to communities increased in the early 1990s after several pilot projects. In 1996, the Nature Conservation Amendment Act was introduced to repeal discriminative sections of the Nature Conservation Ordinance of 1975. The amendment saw a subsequent increase in the establishment of conservancies on communal land (Nuulimba and Taylor 2015). Over the past twenty-five to thirty years, communal conservancies mushroomed in the country to a current total of eighty-six, covering more than 20 percent of the country. Similar developments are documented for Zambia, where *CBNRM-isation* began in the mid-1980s as a possible panacea for bushmeat hunting and poaching that was believed to be motivated by local poverty and exclusion. A national programme, Administrative Management Design for Game Management Areas (ADMADE), was initiated to pioneer the development of CBNRM in game management areas in Zambia (Lubilo and Child 2012). The Luangwa Integrated Resources Development Project (LIRDP) was established to protect wildlife resources in South Luangwa National Park and to support the sustainable-use approach in the local communities residing in the Lupande Game Management Areas (Child and Dalal-Clayton 2004). Through these programmes, a portion of revenues generated from hunting and tourism operations were allocated to local chiefs of the areas where the wildlife conservation areas were located. Concerns were raised that these initiatives were still not addressing the urgent issue of improving rural livelihoods and changing attitudes toward conservation.

This paved the way for the current CBNRM programme to ensure a devolution and retention of 100 percent of the revenues for the local communities (Lubilo and Child 2012).

In East Africa in the 1980s, particularly in Kenya, *CBNRM-isation* coincided with demands for political and land tenure reforms (Cockerill and Hagerman 2020). Like elsewhere, the push in Kenya for CBNRM was fuelled by pressure from the international conservation community to address the historical misalignment of social development and wildlife preservation. Substantial bilateral donor funding and the authority of NGOs laid the foundations for CBNRM in the country (Cockerill and Hagerman 2020; Western, Waithaka, and Kamanga 2015). The state agency created to oversee wildlife conservation in the country, Kenya Wildlife Service (KWS), initiated "Parks beyond Parks" and "Parks for Kenyans" campaigns for sharing revenues with local communities affected by wildlife conservation (Western, Waithaka, and Kamanga 2015). These programs, coupled with growing support for land tenure reform to establish group ranches and investment opportunities for ecotourism enterprises, encouraged the growth of community organisations and their participation in conservation (Baskin 1994). With political goodwill and support from KWS, *CBNRM-isation* began to take shape in the mid-1990s. The drive was also fuelled by communities demanding more benefit-sharing from conservation and ecotourism. Legislative amendments in 2013 to enact CBNRM made donors decide to increase their funding. Since then, community conservation has expanded to account for at least 60 percent of all land under conservation in Kenya (Cockerill and Hagerman 2020).

Why Do Conservancies Continue to Exist?

The continuity of *CBNRM-isation* in East and Southern Africa, we posit, cannot be fully explained by economic successes. *CBNRM-isation* occurs because key actors manage to repurpose the meanings of and motivations for conservancies. We discuss four ways that CBNRM projects have been repurposed and given new meanings: (1) elite capture; (2) protecting land rights; (3) legitimising local authority; and (4) NGO career-building. These motivations underscore how repurposing can overtly and sometimes covertly epitomise the struggles and contestations that occur in conservancies. Sometimes this repurposing involves redirecting the flow of benefits to elites or making use of a conservancy as a vehicle to demonstrate and exercise authority. In other cases, it involves capturing and defending career opportunity and space.

Elite Capture

Most pioneer community conservation initiatives like the CAMPFIRE programme performed well in the early stages of their implementation (Roe, Nelson, and Sandbrook 2009). Elites, however, began to position themselves strategically in the flow of money from conservancy management boards and committees and managed to capture most of the benefits (Balint and Mashinya 2006). Many cases of elite capture of community conservation illustrate the gradual shift from relative success to a crisis and, in some cases, collapse, which casts doubt on the merit of devolving management rights of natural resources (Dzingirai 2003; Dzingirai, Manhamo, and Mangwanya 2019). Accumulated evidence suggests that benefits from conservancies rarely reach community members equitably. Schnegg and Kiaka (2018); Dressler and Büscher (2008); and Cavanagh, Weldemichel, and Benjaminsen (2020) show that conservancies benefit the private sector more than they do rural populations. Igoe and Croucher (2007) note that benefits rarely flow to community members and, if they do, these benefits only reach a few well-placed community members. Silva and Mosimane (2014) and Lubilo (2018) both find that Namibian conservancies do provide economic benefits to some members but fail to deliver community-wide improvements (e.g., improved infrastructure and services), and thus improve the livelihoods of a relatively small proportion of members. The type of benefits (i.e., monetary or non-monetary) and how they are distributed are important because these factors influence the perception of whether benefits are meaningful, appropriate, sufficient, and equitable (Silva and Mosimane 2013; Scanlon and Kull 2009).

Elite capture in conservancies in Kenya partly has its roots in the institutional transformation of post-colonial pastoral land tenure. Between 1960 and 1980, donors funded the registration of group ranches as a way to commercialise pastoralism in areas dominated by Maasai pastoralists (Galaty 1992). Crafted as market-oriented institutions to govern pastoral land, group ranches lasted only two decades before they started dissolving into private tenure (Wairimu and Hebinck 2017). Several group ranches dissolved on grounds of financial corruption and mismanagement from committee officials. Disgruntled individuals embraced the subdivision of group ranches into individualised private tenure (Mwangi 2007). Parallel to the collapse of group ranches, conservancies were created. The conservancies' promises of economic benefits attracted former group ranch officials, who had become local economic elites (Thompson and Homewood 2002). Their desire to bring in ongoing donor funding and rent payments from investors, as well as enhance their reputations, necessitated that they support and push for the development of conservancies in pastoral lands.

Protecting Land Rights

Colonialism in East and Southern Africa left behind land injustices that independent governments have not successfully addressed. Chunks of pastoral lands were converted to government land as national parks and game reserves (Nelson 2003). Pastoral communities on whose land most of the conservancies are located have precarious land tenure in the face of the transformation to individual tenure (Mwangi 2007; Galaty 2012). Land grabbing, for example, has characterised most of the pastoral land tenure transformation in Kenya since independence (Galaty 2012). Allocation of land for mining concessions in communal areas in Namibia also makes communities unsure about the security of their communal land (Odendaal and Hebinck 2020). In southern Kenya and northern Tanzania, in the steppes of Kilimanjaro for example, there is infiltration of well-connected networks of local and international investors to convert Maasai pastoral land into crop production, especially for the export market (Okello et al. 2011). All these developments are justified by viewing pastoral land as underutilised, but they are also made possible through opportunities for selling land that subdivision and individualised titling have necessitated (Nkedianye 2020). Some local Maasai communities see increased opportunities to sell land as carrying the threats of future landlessness and decline of pastoralism (Seno and Shaw 2002). Although the establishment of conservancies around the area leads to lease payments to landowners (Cavanagh, Weldemichel, and Benjaminsen 2020), the Maasai also view the conservancies as a way of protecting their land against loss to *outsiders* through rampant sale after subdivision and individual titling (Galaty 2013, 2016). This scenario is not universal in pastoral communities in northern Kenya but occurs where land is not subdivided into individual titles to contest formation of conservancies (Greiner 2012). In those areas, communities view conservancy establishment as a way of turning grazing land to conservation, for example, as a form of green grabs (Bersaglio and Cleaver 2018) or reintroducing the group ranches model. In these complex and precarious contexts of land tenure, community conservancies offer institutional arrangements for local communities to stop land sales, protect grazing areas, and preserve their pastoral lifestyle (Reid et al. 2016).

In Namibia, where boundaries of community land are contested by communities, smaller conservancies with low tourism potential are often established in order to secure communal land against potential land grabbers, especially for mining concessions granted by the government to private companies (Bollig 2016; Odendaal and Hebinck 2020). The N‡a Jaqna Conservancy Committee in east Namibia employs the conservancy institution as a vehicle to seek protection for its land rights and to fight against the fences built by land grabbers. This fight is being waged in the conservancy as well as in the High Court (van der Wulp and Hebinck 2021).

Legitimising Local Traditional Leadership

In Southern Africa, and especially in Zimbabwe and Namibia, the Traditional Authority (TA) under the leadership of a chief is a significant player in local governance and politics. TAs are reminiscent of administrative practices of the colonial regime of apartheid (Düsing 2002), when Black people were clustered in native or communal land and placed under the second-tier administration governed by a TA (Botha 2005). In post-colonial Namibia, a TA has no legal jurisdiction over land anymore (Kiaka 2018); nevertheless, territorial claims over land remain an important political tool for traditional leaders to establish and/or retain legitimacy and to exercise authority over their subjects (Behr, Haer, and Kromrey 2015).

Since the establishment of conservancies, TAs must compete with the democratically elected Conservancy Committees (Hitchcock, Babchuk, and Frost 2021). Their relationships are complex. Not only do they tap different political repertoires (traditional vs. democratic) but, more importantly, their relations are complicated by the fact that their authority overlaps (van der Wulp and Hebinck 2021). TAs and Conservancy Committees both claim control over land (and people). Establishing a conservancy therefore emerged as an opportunity to effect such a claim (Bollig 2016). This emergence was clearly fed by the belief that the mandate of conservancies was a lot broader than only conservation and included matters of land governance. The state, however, retained control over land matters. Through official recognition of TAs and by paying them monthly emoluments, the state attempts to control traditional leadership.

Conservancy formation gave a strong impetus to traditional leaders by establishing new TAs, even without the formal consent of the central government. Registering a conservancy would mean establishing and proving their authority and control over land and people (Bollig 2016). Their co-existence is, however, not without complications: they compete with one another. In the Nǂa Jaqna conservancy in Namibia, the chief allowed land grabbers from outside the conservancy to illegally fence off land and to graze cattle therein. The fencers paid their customary fees to the chief to register their claim. The Conservancy Committee filed a court case to remove the fences. The High Court ordered the TA and chief to remove them, but these orders are yet to be complied with (van der Wulp and Hebinck 2021).

NGO Career-Building

The role played by NGOs remains essential for the continuity of most community conservancies in both East Africa and Southern Africa. They channel donor funds, which are still an important part of the budgets of most community conservancies. International conservation NGOs continue to justify to the donor community the importance of community participation in ensuring sustainable natural resource management. As markets for conservation and communities became the cornerstones for the success (or failure) of CBNRM, international NGOs also play the role of advising on contracts between conservancies and private tourism investors and trophy hunters (for Southern Africa). In Namibia, for example, WWF advises groups of conservancies through the Namibian Association of CBNRM Support Organisations (NACSO) on development of conservation enterprises and negotiating trophy hunting contracts (Kiaka 2018). In East Africa, particularly in Kenya, international NGOs themselves have become the markets for community conservation. The Big Life Foundation and International Fund for Animal Welfare (IFAW), using funds from donors and philanthropists, have leased land for community conservancies to conserve wildlife (Mugo, Visseren-Hamakers, and van der Duim 2020; Mugo, Visseren-Hamakers, and van der Duim 2021). In addition to paying lease fees to communal land-owners, these NGOs also organise other payments to communities, such as bursaries and compensations for damages accruing from human-wildlife conflicts (Mugo, Visseren-Hamakers, and van der Duim 2021).

By and large, the *CBNRM-isation* of East and Southern Africa has been a venture of conservation NGOs with funding support of donors and philan-thropists (Wondirad, Tolkach, and King 2020). Conservation funding also supports overhead and personnel costs (Brockington and Scholfield 2010). NGOs have created a niche for stable and financially rewarding careers in com-munity conservation. These lucrative jobs may act as motivations for their relentless work with community conservancies, acting as the link between the donor and community conservancy organisations. Local NGOs, which serve as the link between international NGOs and local communities, are just as important (Pellis, Lamers, and van der Duim 2015). These include NACSO in Namibia and, in Kenya, the Kenya Wildlife Conservancies Associations (KWCA) and its regional umbrella bodies, such as the Amboseli Ecosystem Trust (AET) and the Northern Rangelands Trust (NRT). The jobs that these NGOs offer provide significant motivation for their employees to continu-ously present CBNRM as a success story (Koot, Hebinck, and Sullivan 2020); to argue for the support of community conservancies, even when challenges are glaring. We are not arguing that employment and job-seeking in con-servation NGOs are a bad thing, nor do we claim that they are exploitative of communities who have to live with wildlife in conservancies. The point is to demonstrate that, as in many other fields of employment, the idea of participatory conservation has created a livelihood for many proponents of CBNRM in Africa that they would not wish to relinquish. This struggle for career survival pushes proponents of community conservation to justify the continuity of conservancies despite the many critiques and challenges that the conservation model continues to face.

Conclusion

The critical appraisals of CBNRM are not just coincidental outcomes of independent operating processes but are inbuilt and structural. What underlies the systemic nature of the critique on CBNRM is the naivety of the discourse; a belief that institutions can be crafted and designed, and that this crafting is a linear process with a steep but productive learning curve. It has proven to be naive to assume that a globally driven initiative can neutrally land in the local context where authority and institutions are in the (re)making, and where actors flout rules and cause havoc, contestation, and negation. The tensions that arise during *CBNRM-isation* are essentially ontological and political. Tensions arise between actors who see wildlife and other natural resources as common property resources and those who perceive them as commodities for investors, trophy hunters, and philanthropists. Conservancies unfold as opportunities for actors to (attempt to) control land and nature-related resources. Through CBNRM, newly crafted conservancy institutions, in interaction with the neoliberal mode of commoditising nature, blend with "traditional" forms of communal governance of natural resources where tribal leaders performed key roles (e.g., dealing with land issues). This blending generates different types of spaces, where equitable forms of decision-making and benefit distribution are subject to negotiation and reworking. In some of these spaces, actors compete over whose authority counts when it comes to protecting (land) rights and extending favours. In others, new domestic elites, often in an alliance with the old elites, make use of the opportunities to grab resources. While these processes play out at the local community level, at the national and global level CBNRM initiatives become vehicles for actors to achieve their political and economic objectives. These range from generating employment to gaining global public support for *CBNRM-isation* of the conservation project.

The outcome of repurposing or resistance is not always straightforward. The outcomes of a conservation project often deviate from the initial objectives—but this is not always because of powerful, rich, or traditional leaders manipulating the institutional arrangements. Conservancies and commoners also play their parts in the process, meaning that *CBNRM-isation* does not follow a linear and predefined path with the intended and planned outcomes. Below the surface of the CBNRM-*isation* of conservation is a rich experience of practices that deviate from the stated objectives. These practices, however, remain largely out of sight of the many CBNRM evaluators and policymakers and are, as Stuart Marks (2014) argued, not found in textbooks but in everyday practices and arise when least expected. In conclusion, we suggest that a holistic evaluation of the value of CBNRM must consider emerging objectives—protection of land rights, legitimising local leadership, and providing jobs to conservation NGOs—of the conservation initiatives, which transcend economic benefits to local communities (Koot 2019) and ecological outcomes. While these new objectives may not form part of the rationale behind promoting CBNRM, they play a crucial role in its persistence as an alternative paradigm to fortress conservation.

References

Adams, W., and M. Mulligan, eds. 2003. *Decolonizing nature: Strategies for conservation in a post colonial era*. London: Earthscan.

Agrawal, A. 2001. Common property institutions and sustainable governance of resources. *World Development* 29 (10): 1649–72.

Alexander, J., and J. McGregor. 2000. Wildlife and politics: CAMPFIRE in Zimbabwe. *Development and Change* 31 (3): 605–27.

Arce, A., and N. Long. 2000. Reconfiguring modernity and development from an anthropological perspective. In *Anthropology, development and modernities: Exploring discourses, counter-tendencies and violence*, ed. A. Arce and N. Long. London: Routledge.

Balint, P., and J. Mashinya. 2006. The decline of a model community-based conservation project: Governance, capacity, and devolution in Mahenye, Zimbabwe. *Geoforum* 37 (5): 805–15.

Baskin, Y. 1994. There's a new wildlife policy in Kenya: Use it or lose it. *Science* 265 (5173): 733–35.

Batavia, C., M. Nelson, C. Darimont, P. Paquet, W. Ripple, and A. Wallach. 2018. The elephant (head) in the room: A critical look at trophy hunting. *Conservation Letters* e12565.

Behr, D., R. Haer, and D. Kromrey. 2015. What is a chief without land? Impact of land reforms on power structures in Namibia. *Regional & Federal Studies* 25 (5): 455–72.

Berry, S. 2017. Struggles over land and authority in Africa. *Africa Studies Review* 60 (3): 105–25.

Bersaglio, B., and F. Cleaver. 2018. Green grab by bricolage: The institutional workings of community conservancies in Kenya. *Conservation and Society* 16 (4): 467–80.

Blaikie, P. 2006. Is small really beautiful? CBNRM in Malawi and Botswana. *World Development* 34 (11): 1942–57.

Bollig, M. 2016. Towards an arid Eden? Boundary-making, governance and benefit sharing and the political ecology of the new commons of Kunene Region, Northern Namibia. *International Journal of the Commons* 10 (2): 771–99.

Bollig, M. 2020. *Shaping the African savannah: From capitalist frontier to arid Eden in Namibia*. Cambridge, UK: Cambridge University Press.

Botha, C. 2005. People and the environment in colonial Namibia. *South African Historical Journal* 52 (1): 170–90.

Brockington, D. 2002. *Fortress conservation: The preservation of Mkomazi Game reserve, Tanzania*. London: James Currey.

Brockington, D., and K. Scholfield. 2010. The conservationist mode of production and conservation NGOs in sub-Saharan Africa. *Antipode* 42 (3): 551–75.

Campbell, B., and S. Shackleton. 2001. The organizational structures for community-based natural resource management in Southern Africa. *African Studies Quarterly* 5 (3): 87–114.

Cavanagh, C. J., T. Weldemichel, and T. A. Benjaminsen. 2020. Gentrifying the African landscape: The performance and powers of for-profit conservation on southern Kenya's conservancy frontier. *Annals of the American Association of Geographers* 110 (5): 1594–1612.

Child, B. 1996. The practice and principles of community based wildlife management in Zimbabwe: The CAMPFIRE programme. *Biodiversity and Conservation* 5: 369–98.

Child, B., and B. Dalal-Clayton. 2004. Transforming approaches to CBNRM: Learning from the Luangwa experience in Zambia. In *Getting biodiversity projects to work towards more effective conservation and development*, ed. T. McShane and M. Wells. New York: Columbia University Press (Biology and Resource Management Series).

Child, G. 2008. The emergence of modern conservation practice in Zimbabwe. In *Evolution and innovation in wildlife conservation: Parks and game ranches to transfrontier conservation areas*, ed. B. Child, H. Suich, and A. Spenceley. London: Routledge.

Cleaver, F. 2012. *Development through bricolage: Rethinking institutions for natural resource management*. London: Routledge.

Cockerill, K., and S. Hagerman. 2020. Historical insights for understanding the emergence of community-based conservation in Kenya: International agendas, colonial legacies, and contested worldviews. *Ecology and Society* 25 (2).

Corson, C. 2010. Shifting environmental governance in a neoliberal world: US AID for conservation. *Antipode* 42 (3): 576–602.

de Cunha, M. C., and M. W. de Almeida. 2000. Indigenous people, traditional people, and conservation in the Amazon. *Daedalus* 129 (2): 315–38.

de Vette, M., R.-M. P. Kashululu, and P. Hebinck. 2012. Conservancies in Namibia: A discourse in action. In *Forest-people interfaces*, ed. B. Arts, S. van Bommel, M. Ros-Tonen, and G. Verschoor. Wageningen, Netherlands: Wageningen Academic Publishers.

Dickman, A., R. Cooney, P. J. Johnson, M. P. Louis, and D. Roe. 2019. Trophy hunting bans imperil biodiversity. *Science* 365 (6456): 874.

Drake, M. D., J. Salerno, R. E. Langendorf, L. Cassidy, A. E. Gaughan, F. R. Stevens, N. G. Pricope, and J. Hartter. 2020. Costs of elephant crop depredation exceed the benefits of trophy hunting in a community-based conservation area of Namibia. *Conservation Science and Practice* 2 (3): e345.

Dressler, W., and B. Büscher. 2008. Market triumphalism and the CBNRM "crises" at the South African section of the Great Limpopo Transfrontier Park. *Geoforum* 39 (1): 452–65.

Düsing, S. 2002. Traditional leadership and democratisation in Southern Africa: A comparative study of Botswana, Namibia, and Southern Africa. Vol. 6. Münster, Germany: LIT Verlag.

Dzingirai, V. 1994. Politics and ideology in human settlement: Getting settled in the Sikomena area of Chief Dobola. *Zambezia* 21 (2): 167–77.

Dzingirai, V. 2003. The new scramble for the African countryside. *Development and Change* 34 (2): 243–64.

Dzingirai, V., A. Manhamo, and L. Mangwanya. 2019. Continued state monopoly and control of community-based natural resource management in Zimbabwe: The case of Hurungwe's CAMPFIRE programme. In *Nature conservation in Southern Africa: Morality and marginality: Towards sentient conservation?*, ed. J. B. Gewald, M. Spierenburg, and H. Wels. Leiden, Netherlands: Brill Academic Publishers.

Fabricius, C., E. Koch, with H. Magome, and S. Turner. 2004. *Rights, resources & rural development: Community-based natural resource management in Southern Africa.* London: Earthscan.

Fletcher, R., 2010. Neoliberal environmentality: Towards a poststructuralist political ecology of the conservation debate. *Conservation and society* 8 (3): 171–81.

Galaty, J. 1992. The land is yours: Social and economic factors in the privatization, subdivision and sale of Maasai ranches. *Nomadic Peoples* 30 (30): 26–40.

Galaty, J. 2012. Land grabbing in the Eastern African rangelands. In *Pastoralism and development in Africa: Dynamic change at the margins*, ed. C. Andy, Lind Jeremy, and S. Ian. London: Routledge.

Galaty, J. 2013. The collapsing platform for pastoralism: Land sales and land loss in Kajiado County, Kenya. *Nomadic Peoples* 17 (2): 20–39.

Galaty, J. 2016. Reasserting the commons: Pastoral contestations of private and state lands in East Africa. *International Journal of the Commons* 10 (2): 709–27.

Gargallo, E. 2021. Human-wildlife conflict in a "successful" community conservation programme: Economic and territorial impacts on Namibia's conservancies. *Journal of Arid Environments* 193: 104591.

Greiner, C. 2012. Unexpected consequences: wildlife conservation and territorial conflict in northern Kenya. *Human Ecology* 40 (3): 415–25.

Hammar, A. 2007. "The day of burning": Land, authority and belonging in Zimbabwe's agrarian margins in the 1990s. PhD diss., Roskilde University.

Hebinck, P., R. D. Kiaka, and R. Lubilo. 2020. Navigating community conservancies and institutional complexities in Namibia. In *Natural resources, tourism and community livelihoods in Southern Africa: Challenges for sustainable development*, ed. M. T. Stone, M. Lenao, and N. Moswete. London: Routledge.

Herbst, J. 2014. States and power in Africa: Comparative lessons in authority and control. Princeton, NJ: Princeton University Press.

Hitchcock, R. K., W. A. Babchuk, and J. Frost. 2021. San traditional authorities, communal conservancies, conflicts, and leadership in Namibia. In *Challenging authorities*, 267–91. Cham, Switzerland: Palgrave Macmillan.

Homewood, K., M. R. Nielsen, and A. Keane. 2022. Women, wellbeing and wildlife management areas in Tanzania. *Journal of Peasant Studies* 49 (2): 335–62.

Humavindu, M. N., and J. Stage. 2015. Community-based wildlife management failing to link conservation and financial viability. *Animal Conservation* 18 (1): 4–13.

Hutton, J., W. M. Adams, and J. C. Murombedzi. 2005. Back to the barriers? Changing narratives in biodiversity conservation. *Forum for Development Studies* 32 (2): 341–70.

Igoe, J., and D. Brockington. 2007. Neoliberal conservation: A brief introduction. *Conservation and Society* 5 (4): 432–49.

Igoe, J., and B. Croucher. 2007. Conservation, commerce, and communities: The story of community-based wildlife management areas in Tanzania's northern tourist circuit. *Conservation and Society* 5 (4): 534–61.

IUCN, UNEP, and WWF. 1980. *World conservation strategy: Living resource conservation for sustainable development*. Gland, Switzerland: International Union for Conservation of Nature and Natural Resources.

Jones, B., and L. C. Weaver. 2008. CBNRM in Namibia: Growth, trends, lessons and constraints. In *Evolution and innovation in wildlife conservation*, ed. B. Child, H. Suich and A. Spenceley, 241–60. London, UK: Routledge.

Kalvelage, L., J. Revilla Diez, and M. Bollig. 2020. How much remains? Local value capture from tourism in Zambezi, Namibia. *Tourism Geographies* 24 (4–5): 1–22.

Kiaka, R. D. 2018. Environmental (in)justice in Namibia: Costs and benefits of community-based water and wildlife management. PhD diss., Staats-und Universitätsbibliothek Hamburg Carl von Ossietzky.

Koot, S. 2019. The limits of economic benefits: Adding social affordances to the analysis of trophy hunting of the Khwe and Ju/'hoansi in Namibian community-based natural resource management. *Society & Natural Resources* 32 (4): 417–33.

Koot, S., Hebinck, P., and Sullivan, S., 2020. Science for success—a conflict of interest? Researcher position and reflexivity in socio-ecological research for CBNRM in Namibia. *Society & Natural Resources* 36 (5): 1–18.

Latour, B. 2005. Reassembling the social: An introduction to actor-network-theory. Oxford, UK: Oxford University Press.

Lindsey, P., J. Allan, P. Brehony, A. Dickman, A. Robson, C. Begg, H. Bhammar, L. Blanken, T. Breuer, K. Fitzgerald, et al. 2020. Conserving Africa's wildlife and wildlands through the COVID-19 crisis and beyond. *Nature Ecology & Evolution* 4 (10): 1300–10.

Lindsey, P., L. Frank, R. Alexander, A. Mathieson, and S. Romañach. 2007. Trophy hunting and conservation in Africa: Problems and one potential solution. *Conservation Biology* 21 (3): 880–83.

Long, N. 2001. *Development sociology: Actor perspectives*. London: Routledge.

Long, N. 2008. Resistance, agency, and counterwork: A theoretical positioning. In *The fight over food: Producers, consumers, and activists challenge the global food system*, ed. W. Wright and G. Middendorf. University Park, PA: Penn State University Press.

Lubilo, R. 2018. Enactment of "community" in community-based natural resource management in the Zambezi region, Namibia. PhD diss., Wageningen University.

Lubilo, R., and B. Child. 2012. The rise and fall of community-based natural resource management in Zambia's Luangwa Valley: An illustration of micro- and macro-governance. In *Community rights, conservation and contested land: The politics of natural resource governance in Africa*, ed. F. Nelson. London: Routledge.

Lubilo, R., and P. Hebinck. 2019. "Local hunting" and community-based natural resource management: Resistance and livelihoods in Namibia. *Geoforum* 101 (May): 62–75.

Lund, C. 2006. Twilight institutions: Public authority and local politics in Africa. *Development and Change* 37 (4): 685–705.

Lund, C. 2016. Rule and rupture: State formation through the production of property and citizenship. *Development and Change* 43 (6): 1199–1228.

Marks, S. 2014. *Discordant village voices: A Zambian "community-based" wildlife programme*. Braamfontein: University of South Africa Press.

Mittal, A., and Z. Moloo. 2021. Stealth game; Community conservancies devastate land & lives in Northern Kenya. Oakland CA: Oakland Institute.

Mugo, T., I. Visseren-Hamakers, and R. van der Duim. 2020. Landscape governance through partnerships: Lessons from Amboseli, Kenya. *Journal of Sustainable Tourism* 30 (10): 1–19.

Mugo, T., I. Visseren-Hamakers, and R. van der Duim. 2021. Contributions of partnerships to conservation and development: Insights from Amboseli. *Tourism Review International* 25 (2–3): 189–208.

Murphree, M. 2009. The strategic pillars of communal natural resource management: Benefit, empowerment and conservation. *Biodiversity and Conservation* 18 (10): 2551–62.

Musgrave, M. K., and S. Wong. 2016. Towards a more nuanced theory of elite capture in development projects: The importance of context and theories of power. *Journal of Sustainable Development* 9 (3): 87–103.

Muyengwa, S., B. Child, and R. Lubilo. 2014. Elite capture: A comparative case study of meso-level governance in four southern Africa countries. In *Adaptive cross-scalar governance of natural resources*, ed. G. Barnes and B. Child. London: Routledge.

Muzvidziwa, V. N. 2013. Eco-tourism, conservancies and sustainable development: The case of Zimbabwe. *Journal of Human Ecology* 43 (1): 41–50.

Mwangi, E. 2007. Subdividing the commons: Distributional conflict in the transition from collective to individual property rights in Kenya's Maasailand. *World Development* 35 (5): 815–34.

Naidoo, R., C. Weaver, R. Diggle, G. Matongo, G. Stuart-Hill, and C. Thouless. 2016. Complementary benefits of tourism and hunting to communal conservancies in Namibia. *Conservation Biology* 30 (3): 628–38.

Nelson, F., ed. 2010. *Community rights, conservation and contested land: The politics of natural resource governance in Africa*. London: Routledge.

Nelson, F. 2012. Blessing or curse? The political economy of tourism development in Tanzania. *Journal of Sustainable Tourism* 20 (3): 359–75.

Nelson, R. H. 2003. Environmental colonialism: "saving" Africa from Africans. *Independent Review* 8 (1): 65–86.

Neumann, R. P. 1996. Dukes, earls, and ersatz edens: Aristocratic nature preservationists in colonial Africa. *Environment and Planning D: Society and Space* 14 (1): 79–98.

Neumann, R. 2001. Disciplining peasants in Tanzania: From state violence to self-surveillance in wildlife conservation. In *Violent environments*, ed. N. Peluso and M. Watts. Ithaca, NY: Cornell University Press.

Nkedianye, D. K., J. O. Ogutu, M. Y. Said, S. C. Kifugo, J. de Leeuw, P. Van Gardingen, and R. S. Reid. 2020. Comparative social demography, livelihood diversification and land tenure among the Maasai of Kenya and Tanzania. *Pastoralism* 10 (1): 1–25.

Noss, A. J. 1997. Challenges to nature conservation with community development in central African forests. *Oryx* 31 (3): 180–88.

Novelli, M., and M. N. Humavindu. 2005. Wildlife tourism: Wildlife use vs local gain: Trophy hunting in Namibia. In *Niche tourism: Contemporary issues, trends and cases*, ed. M. Novelli. Amsterdam: Elsevier.

Nuulimba, K., and J. Taylor. 2015. 25 years of CBNRM in Namibia: A retrospective on accomplishments, contestation and contemporary challenges. *Journal of Namibian Studies: History Culture Politics* 18 (1): 89–110.

Odendaal, W., and P. Hebinck. 2020. Mining on communal land as a new frontier—a case study of the Kunene Region, Namibia. *Journal of Land Use Science* 15 (2–3): 457–76.

Okello, M. M., E. Buthmann, B. Mapinu, and H. C. Kahi. 2011. Community opinions on wildlife, resource use and livelihood competition in Kimana Group Ranch near Amboseli, Kenya. *Open Conservation Biology Journal* 5 (1).

Ostrom, E. 1990. *Governing the commons: The evolution of institutions for collective action*. Cambridge, UK: Cambridge University Press.

Owen-Smith, G. 2010. *An arid Eden. A personal account of conservation in the Kaokoveld*. Cape Town, South Africa: Jonathan Ball Publishers.

Pellis, A., M. Lamers, and R. van der Duim. 2015. Conservation tourism and landscape governance in Kenya: The interdependency of three conservation NGOs. *Journal of Ecotourism* 14 (2): 130–44.

Platteau, J. P. 2004. Monitoring elite capturing in community-driven development. *Development and Change* 35 (2): 223–46.

Rabe, L., and F. Saunders. 2013. Community-based natural resource management of the Jozani-Pete mangrove forest: Do they have a voice. *Western Indian Ocean Journal of Maritime Science* 12 (2): 133–50.

Reid, R. S., D. Kaelo, K. A. Galvin, and R. Harmon. 2016. Pastoral wildlife conservancies in Kenya: a bottom-up revolution in conservation, balancing livelihoods and conservation? In *Proceedings of the International Rangelands Congress* 18: 22.

Republic of Namibia. 1996. Nature Conservation Amendment Act of 1996.

Ribot, J. 2004. *Waiting for democracy: The politics of choice in natural resource decentralization*. Washington, D. C.: World Resources Institute.

Roe, D., F. Nelson, and C. Sandbrook, eds. 2009. *Community management of natural resources in Africa: Impacts, experiences and future directions*. London: International Institute for Environment and Development.

Scanlon, L. J., and C. A. Kull. 2009. Untangling the links between wildlife benefits and community-based conservation at Torra Conservancy, Namibia. *Development Southern Africa* 26 (1): 75–93.

Schnegg, M., and R. D. Kiaka. 2018. Subsidized elephants: Community-based resource governance and environmental (in)justice in Namibia. *Geoforum* 93: 105–15.

Schreckenberg, K., P. Franks, A. Martin, and B. Lang. 2016. Unpacking equity for protected area conservation. *Parks* (2): 11–26.

Scott, J. 1985. *Weapons of the weak: Everyday forms of peasant resistance*. New Haven, CT: Yale University Press.

Scott, J. 2009. *The art of NOT being governed: An anarchistic history of upland south east Asia*. New Haven, CT: Yale University Press.

Seno, Simon K., and W. W. Shaw. 2002. Land tenure policies, Maasai traditions, and wildlife conservation in Kenya. *Society & Natural Resources* 15 (1): 79–88.

Sheil, D., and A. Lawrence. 2004. Tropical biologists, local people and conservation: New opportunities for collaboration. *Trends in Ecology & Evolution* 19 (12): 634–38.

Silva, J., and A. Mosimane. 2013. Conservation-based rural development in Namibia: A mixed-methods assessment of economic benefits. *Journal of Environment & Development* 22 (1): 25–50.

Silva, J., and A. Mosimane. 2014. "How could I live here and not be a member?": Economic versus social drivers of participation in Namibian conservation programs. *Human Ecology* 42 (2): 183–97.

Steinhart, E. I. 1989. Hunters, poachers and gamekeepers: Towards a social history of hunting in colonial Kenya. *Journal of African History* 30 (2): 247–64.

Sullivan, S. 2003. Protest, conflict and litigation: Dissent or libel in resistance to a conservancy in North West Namibia. In *Ethnographies of conservation: Environmentalism and the distribution of privilege*, ed. E. Berglund and D. Anderson. Oxford, UK: Berghahn Press.

Sullivan, S. 2006. The elephant in the room? Problematising "new" (neoliberal) biodiversity conservation. *Forum for Development Studies* 33 (1): 105–35.

Sullivan, S. 2012. *Financialisation, biodiversity conservation and equity: Some currents and concerns*. Vol. 16 of Environment and Development Series. Penang, Malaysia: Third World Network.

Thompson, M., and K. Homewood. 2002. Entrepreneurs, elites, and exclusion in Maasailand: Trends in wildlife conservation and pastoralist development. *Human Ecology* 30 (1): 107–38.

van der Ploeg, J. D. 2010. The peasantries of the twenty-first century: The commoditisation debate revisited. *Journal of Peasant Studies* 37 (1):1–30.

van der Wulp, C., and P. Hebinck. 2021. Fighting fences and land grabbers in the struggle for the commons in Na Jaqna, Namibia. *African Affairs* 120 (480): 417–43.

Wairimu, W., and P. Hebinck. 2017. Beyond cattle and communal land: How the Maasai accommodate change in land tenure. In *Land law and governance*, ed. H. Mostert, L. Verstappen, and J. Zevenbergen. Cape Town, South Africa: Juta.

Western, D., J. Waithaka, and J. Kamanga. 2015. Finding space for wildlife beyond national parks and reducing conflict through community-based conservation: The Kenya experience. *Parks* 21: 51–62.

Western, D., R. M. Wright, and S. C. Strum, eds. 1994. *Natural connections: Perspectives in community-based conservation*. Washington, D.C.: Island Press.

Wondirad, A., D. Tolkach, and B. King. 2020. NGOs in ecotourism: Patrons of sustainability or neo-colonial agents? Evidence from Africa. *Tourism Recreation Research* 45 (2): 144–60.

7

From Authoritative to Relational

A Typology and Analysis of Government-Community Relationships in Nepalese and Australian Forest Management

PRATIVA SAPKOTA, REBECCA M. FORD, MADDISON MILLER,
ANDREA RAWLUK, AND KATHRYN J. H. WILLIAMS

Uncertainty and injustices are unsettling the authoritative and managerial approaches often seen in forest and fire management. Navigating toward more community-driven approaches requires looking beyond practices like participation to the worldviews and assumptions about power, knowledge, and values that underpin relationships. In this chapter, we present four types of government-community relationships based in those assumptions and clearly distinguish relational thinking from the authoritative and managerial approaches which are common in current policy environments.

Introduction

Relationships between government agencies and local communities in forest and fire management take many forms, commonly characterised with reference to levels of participation that community members are afforded or the degree of centralisation in government decision-making (e.g., Tiwari et al. 2013; Ross, Buchy, and Proctor 2002). They can change over time,

https://doi.org/10.7330/9781646426300.c007

shaped and reshaped by many forces including political discourses, community expectations and conflict within communities, and characteristics of the forested landscape such as climate change (Schultz et al. 2021). While there is much ambition to encourage new forms of government-community relationships—for example, to foster more community-led forest and fire management—realising such change is challenging (Paschen and Beilin 2016). In this context, it is important to understand the diversity of relationships between agencies and communities and ways in which characteristics of relationships might facilitate or resist change.

Several authors have offered what might be considered typologies of government agency-community relationships (e.g., Hill et al. 2012; Leeuwis 2004; Ross, Buchy, and Proctor 2002). Our goal in adding to this literature is twofold. First, others have noted how upheavals and uncertainties associated with climate change and recognition of longstanding social injustices are driving new forms of relationships between agencies and communities (Hill et al. 2012; Schultz et al. 2021). In response, researchers in several fields have sought to expand the ways we envision relationships in environmental management (MacPherson et al. 2021; Beilin and Paschen 2021). *Relationality* has emerged as an important concept that draws attention to (a) ways of being and relating that focus on process, negotiation, and flexibility in the face of change (MacPherson et al. 2021) and (b) holistic attention to assemblages of actors (human and beyond) (West et al. 2020; Tynan 2021). We draw on this recent work to offer an extended typology of government-community relationships. Second, we note that most typologies of government-community relationships are primarily concerned with different types of practice and emphasise observable attributes such as actors, participation, and purpose. Research over the last decade has revealed how practice is shaped and stabilised by deeper problem framings and worldviews (e.g., Paschen and Beilin 2016; Bosomworth, 2015). We seek to enrich understanding of different types of relationship by linking forms of practice with their underpinning perspectives.

In this chapter, we pose the question: How can diverse relationships between government and communities be characterised and differentiated? This question was formed through engagement with forest and fire agency staff in Australia who are seeking new ways of relating to communities and require language and frameworks to inform decisions about how to establish relationships in particular contexts. While we focus on government agencies and their relationships with communities, these cannot be considered in isolation from cross-agency and integrated sector-wide decision-making that underpin environmental governance globally. In this chapter, we first examine how relationships between government and communities have been understood across multiple fields of inquiry, ordering these to distinguish critical aspects of practice, problem framing, and worldview. We then analyse how such relationships are expressed in forest and fire management in Australia and Nepal. These countries provide complementary contexts for exploring the circumstances in which different forms of government-community relationships occur and the forces that both stabilise and shift relationships. Based on our typology and analysis, we discuss opportunities and challenges for moving toward a more relational approach to supporting forest and fire management in the context of uncertainty.

Exploring Government-Community Relationships in Forest and Fire Management

In this section, we propose four types of relationships that we see evident in forest management, and point to differences in practice, problem framing, and worldviews that vary across these categories. The types are authoritative, managerial, interactive, and relational (figure 7.1). Authoritative relationships are typically characterised by government-led, planned decision-making that allows limited roles for community and are grounded in instrumental problem framings and mechanistic worldviews. In managerial relationships, environmental problems are understood to involve contested values and diverse stakeholders, but practices are nevertheless grounded in instrumental and mechanistic worldviews that constrain the degree of community participation. Interactive approaches are associated with increased levels of participation, giving communities a greater role in defining institutions, and they emphasise the use of processes that support negotiation in the context of uncertainty and change. Relational approaches focus on establishing trust as a necessary step toward inclusive and ongoing deliberations among extended communities of actors. They are distinguished from interactive relationships by an extended understanding of community, agency, and knowledge that incorporates the more-than-human world.

		Authoritative	Managerial	Interactive	Relational
Practices	Participation	Low Levels of participation			Community-driven decision making
	Decision Making	Planned, sequential			Focus on process and negotiation
	Institutions	Centralised			Devolved
	Capacity building	Education to support Government action			Building trusting relationships
Problem framing	Recognized actors	*Local communities*	*Stakeholders*	*Networks*	*More than human community*
	Objectives and values	*Uncontested, instrumental*		*Contested, value pluralism*	*Uncontested, relational values*
	Certainty	Predictable consequences			Uncertain consequences
	Power assumptions	Held		Negotiated	*Negotiated among more than human community*
World views	Ontology	More mechanistic			More holistic
	Epistemology	Objective fact		Situated knowledge	*Embodied, extended knowledge*
	Dynamics	Linear change		Complex change	*Constantly unfolding reality*
	Ethics	Utilitarian			Ethics of care ('caring as')

FIGURE 7.1. A typology of government-community relationship types (authoritative, managerial, interactive, and relational) that are expressed through key characteristics (practices, problem framings, and worldviews). Arrows suggest where characteristics can be understood on a continuum, while text in italics suggests where characteristics are qualitatively discontinuous across relationship types.

This typology was developed by the authors in the context of conversations between academics and environmental managers, seeking a shared language for discussing how different ways of relating were and were not "fit for purpose" in the context of rapid social and environmental change. These conversations were driven by agency commitments to build stronger partnerships with Indigenous peoples, and practitioner desires for relationships with communities characterised by deeper understanding and trust. We also reviewed the published literature on community engagement, environmental governance, and human-nature relationships more broadly to identify appropriate concepts that describe variation in government-community relationships. Our proposed conceptualisation builds specifically on two existing typologies: Hill et al.'s (2012) description of four forms of agency-community engagement, and Ross, Buchy, and Proctor's (2002) attention to multiple facets of practice. We extended these frameworks based on contemporary reflections on "relationality" that highlight the problem framings and worldviews that underpin different forms of relationship, and analyses that demonstrate how these often-hidden assumptions serve to stabilise relationships, entrenching power relations (e.g., Paschen and Beilin 2016; McDougall and Ojha 2022).

In the following sections, we identify characteristics of practice, problem framing, and worldviews that can be used to distinguish authoritative, managerial, interactive, and relational approaches to forest and fire management.

Practices of Government-Community Relationships

Analyses of governance and community participation have identified multiple dimensions of variation in the ways that government-community relationships are realised in practice (top third of figure 7.1). The best-known focus is on the degree and nature of *participation*, often characterised as a ladder ranging from information dissemination to full community empowerment (e.g., Arnstein 1969; see also Parkins, chapter 8 of this volume). When participation is narrowly defined, communities are treated as stakeholders permitted to share their views only through formal consultation mechanisms; in more inclusive forms of participation, power relationships are more complex, with the roles of agencies and communities in defining institutional arrangements and decision-making constituted in different ways (Hill et al. 2012).

Leeuwis (2004) distinguishes different forms of *decision-making*. Instrumental approaches (here aligned with authoritative and managerial approaches) use top-down forms of communication as a government moves through a mechanistic process of problem definition, analysis, and option selection. Interactive approaches instead emphasise process, as learning is dynamically negotiated within a network of actors. This distinction is extended by recent reflections on relationality (e.g., West et al. 2020; MacPherson et al. 2021). In relational approaches, negotiation is understood to occur within an extended network of actors, including the more-than-human world (Tynan 2021). The time frames and modes of communication involved are necessarily constituted in ways that diverge radically from mechanistic pathways.

Forms of institutions also vary across the types. Institutions may centralise power and decision-making within a single agency or involve various degrees of decentralisation to include cross-sector institutions, multiple stakeholders, or devolution of authority to local or traditional institutions (Hill et al. 2012; Tiwari et al. 2013). Ceding power to nongovernment actors requires new forms of accountability (Ribot, Agrawal, and Larson 2006), cross-sector engagement (MacPherson et al. 2021), and processes of rules (Hill et al. 2012). Relational approaches in governance place less emphasis on fixed laws or institutions and instead seek to establish "conditions for an open, inclusive, and ongoing dialogue" (MacPherson et al. 2021, 3).

Finally, previous scholarship has identified a range of approaches and purposes associated with *capacity building*. Bosomworth (2015) noted that technocratic approaches to emergency management emphasise community education primarily as a means to secure compliance and support for government action, while sustainability approaches promote building capacity for government and community dialogue about value choices. In the context of government engagement with Indigenous communities, Hill et al. (2012) contrast agency-led collaborations that emphasise community training to ensure their functionality, with Indigenous-led collaborations that emphasise building relationships of trust across groups.

Problem Framings in Government-Community Relationships

Observable practices in government-community relationships are grounded in shared beliefs about the nature of environmental challenges. These problem framings create institutional realities that delimit understanding and stabilise action, even when practice change is directly requested (Bosomworth 2015; Paschen and Beilin 2016).

One must first consider *which actors are recognised* by government and what constitutes "community." Community has often been understood by government actors as a localised or place-based group of people, with community members defined either by personal bonds and shared goals or structures and rules that enable collective action (Ojha et al. 2016). Communities may also be viewed as delocalised, characterised by heterogeneity and connections beyond local areas through stakeholder groups and networks (Ojha et al. 2016). Relational perspectives retain a place-based definition of community but extend membership to the more-than-human world through bonds of kinship and reciprocity (Tynan 2021). Problem framings also define how community is recognised by government, generally through attribution of formal rights and responsibilities (Hill et al. 2012). Agency is most often attributed to human actors, for example, through concepts of self-determination (Muller, Hemming, and Rigney 2019) or shared responsibility (Beilin and Paschen 2020). Alternatively, government can recognise extended forms of community membership; for example, through legal recognition of the personhood of waterways (McPherson et al. 2021).

A second critical aspect of problem framing relates to *objectives and values* (Bosomworth 2015). Hill et al. (2012) noted that government-led collaborations are often organised to achieve a single purpose, for example protecting a certain species. This contrasts with problem framings that consider objectives to be contested, reflecting divergent values among communities and stakeholders (Bosomworth et al. 2017). Where value pluralism is assumed, the goals of environmental management typically include assessing and trading off a range of instrumental and intrinsic values (Ford 2013). In relational approaches, absolute values and goals might be treated as clear and uncontested as the well-being of people and land are considered inseparable rather than tradable (Tynan 2021).

Problem framings also shape how *knowledge* and uncertainty is approached. Bosomworth et al. (2017) observed government decision-making often assumed knowledge is certain and clear, whether the focus is on techno-scientific or multidisciplinary knowledge. They argue this is inadequate for addressing complex problems such as climate adaptation. Scholars addressing complex coupled systems view environmental problems as ones of considerable uncertainty and constant change (e.g., Cook and Wagenaar 2012) while relational approaches may draw on extended forms of knowledge that constitute the wisdom of more-than-human actors (Tynan 2021).

Finally, problem framings incorporate assumptions about *the nature of power*. Power refers to the capacity of actors within a social relationship to determine their circumstances (Boonstra 2016). Environmental planning often assumes power is held by government and deployed in rational ways. Tools such as Arnstein's (1969) ladder of participation imply that government can share its inherent authority, "empowering" communities for specific purposes (Ross, Buchy, and Proctor 2002). Participatory processes often assume participants have equal power, and delegates are able to represent diverse communities (McDougall and Ojha 2022; Renn 2006). Such "power neutral" assumptions jar with evidence that power relations are inevitable, shaped and reshaped through dynamics of structure (institutions, norms, and practices) and the agency of actors (McDougall and Ojha 2022; Caine 2013). Compared to authoritative or managerial relationship types, interactive and relational approaches typically recognise that power is negotiated among actors, often within an extended community involving more-than-human actors (Boonstra 2016; Tynan 2021).

Worldviews in Government-Community Relationships

Divergent problem framings, in turn, are grounded in varying worldviews about the nature of reality (ontology) and approaches to knowledge generation (epistemology). In recent years, there has been helpful reflection on the worldviews that exist within ecosystem management, as part of what has been called a relational turn (West et al. 2020).

West et al. (2020; see also West et al., chapter 13 of this volume) contrast three worldviews in ecosystem management. In modernist approaches, reality is comprised of separate natural and human entities. Relationships between these entities are considered mechanistic, linear, and predictable and can be known through objective scientific methods. Human control over nature motivates change and progress (West et al. 2020). Social-ecological systems (SES) thinking challenges this worldview, viewing change as constant and nonlinear, where relationships between entities are emergent, and knowledge of the system is inherently incomplete and uncertain. While SES thinking is more interactive and integrative, social and ecological entities are generally assumed to be distinct (West et al. 2020). Walsh, Böhme, and Wamsler (2021) have noted that some consider this differentiation essential to analysing social-ecological systems without "dichotomizing or subsuming one into the other" (2021, 76). Finally, West et al. (2020) describe relational approaches in which the focus is on assemblages that are mutually constituted and continually unfolding (Walsh, Böhme, and Wamsler 2021). Knowledge of these relations is not simply subjective and situated but also embedded in place, embodied with an increasing emphasis on emotion, and extended beyond the constraints of human cognition (Walsh, Böhme, and Wamsler 2021).

Environmental management paradigms embedded in government-community relationships also reflect different ethical stances. Mechanistic approaches typically emphasise utilitarian ethics, sometimes in the form of a single goal such as preservationism, and other times in the form of multiple goals that must be balanced or traded (Callicott and Mumford 1997; Perley 2003). Complex systems thinking is less consistently linked to a particular ethical stance. Researchers have variously highlighted principles of justice (Shah et al. 2018), stewardship (West et al. 2020), and the importance of provisional decision-making in the face of uncertainty (Preiser and Cilliers 2010). Relational approaches are more likely to emphasise an ethic of care (West et al. 2020). Suchet-Pearson et al. (2013) outline a more relational conceptualisation of "caring *as* Country" rather than "caring *for* Country." Country is a complex and multidimensional concept that encompasses the land, water, plants, animals, air, humans, and dreaming stories, as well as the interconnected relationships between those elements (Rose 1996).

It is important to note that the typology presented here should not be considered a continuum or spectrum of relationships. First, the typology is multidimensional, and we anticipate that practices, problem framings, and worldviews may be combined or manifest in complex ways. Second, as represented in figure 7.1, while some characteristics may fall on a continuum, others are qualitatively distinct. This is particularly important for representing relational approaches, where worldviews based on extended communities and relationships often breach what for many readers will be a taken-for-granted meaning of government-community relationships.

Contextualising Forest and Fire Management in Nepal and Australia

Nepal and Australia provide complementary contexts in which to explore government-community relationships in forest and fire management. Both countries have large, forested areas and diverse ecosystems, such that forest management is beyond the capacity of governments alone. Community forestry in the middle hills of Nepal evolved as a participatory policy reform responding to the failure of state-centred approaches to forest management to fully protect forests (Gilmour and Fisher 1991) and perceived environmental crises (Blaikie, 1985). Community forestry includes "initiatives, sciences, policies, institutions and processes that are intended to increase the role of local people in governing and managing resources" (RECOFTC 2013, 1), shifting control and authority away from the state to local communities (Agrawal and Ostrom 2008). In Australia, historical conflicts related to colonisation and different values for forests have led to approaches that differ with land tenure and the type of managers (Lane and McDonald 2002; Kanowski 2015). On public land in settled areas, management of forests and fire is highly regulated and professionalised (Kanowski 2015). On private land and in less settled areas, devolution of natural resource management enabled partnerships between government and local groups (Kanowski 2015; Curtis et al. 2014). As part of this shift, Indigenous land management was formalised through Indigenous Protected Areas and other forms of co-management (Hill et al. 2012).

Nepal and Australia have different political histories, which have implications for relationships and power dynamics among people, forests, and governance systems. Nepal has been subject to major changes in political system and the influence of international environmental and economic development institutions (Ojha et al. 2014). The international climate programme, Reducing Emissions from Deforestation and forest Degradation (REDD+) is a recent example. Australia has a recent history of colonisation and the imposition of a British political model, with conflict between Indigenous peoples and British colonisers shaping the context for current forest and fire management relationships (Hill et al. 2012). Negotiations toward treaties between Indigenous peoples and the national and state governments have the potential to change forest management governance in coming years. Australian forest management is also influenced by a context of increasing fire frequency and intensity due to climate change.

FIGURE 7.2. Changing governance of forests during different political systems in Nepal (adapted from Malla [2001] and Ojha [2014]).

Analysing Government-Community Relationships in Forest and Fire Management

In this section, we use our proposed typology framework (figure 7.1) to describe government-community relationships in forest and fire management in Nepal and Australia.

Community Forestry in Nepal

Government-community relationships in Nepal are underpinned by a changing political system and associated shifts in forest governance. We focus our analysis on government-community relationships after the emergence of community forestry in 1978 and its evolution over three distinct political systems (figure 7.2).

Nepal is internationally recognised for its innovations in community forestry, which emerged in the 1970s and the initial efforts were shaped by the legacy of authoritative relationships that created weak local institutions (Malla 2001) affecting the way local communities perceived government's initiative of community forestry. For instance, goals were defined unilaterally by government agencies as ecological restoration of degraded land while also supporting local livelihoods (Blaikie 1985). While legislation formulated during this period (e.g., Panchayat Forest Rules, 1978, Decentralisation Act, 1982) allowed local communities to be involved in forest management and utilisation, government agencies still exerted authoritative control. Reluctance of forestry officials to devolve genuine authority to community members limited opportunities for local people to influence decision-making (Gilmour and Fisher 1991). Such mechanistic and centralised relationships were manifested in practices that were both ecologically and socially problematic; for example, plantation of

pine species in the mid-hill districts without acknowledging ecological variation and differing interests of people in forest products. Subsequent efforts of
community forest user groups (CFUGs) to convert monoculture pine plantation to forests of diverse species underscores communities' dissatisfaction
with this mechanistic arrangement (Sapkota, Keenan, and Ojha 2019).

Over time, government-community relationships in forest management
in Nepal have taken more *interactive* forms. Democratic shifts in the political system that occurred in 1990 helped foster community forestry policy
reforms, creating more space for civic engagement in forest management.
The Federation of Community Forest Users of Nepal (FECOFUN) was
established in 1995 following the idea that all the CFUGs should be connected
to each other. Its formal recognition in establishing legal rights of CFUGs
created space for continued negotiation between government and communities (Ojha et al. 2007). As FECOFUN expanded from its initial registration
with the Kathmandu District Administration Office, government agencies
at both national and district levels started using this network to inform and
communicate with CFUGs. Extensive engagement of FECOFUN and other
national and international agencies was crucial in establishing the formal
rights of CFUGs through advocacy, capacity development, and community
empowerment using radio programmes, providing training courses on policy and legal awareness, forest surveys, record keeping, and facilitation and
leadership skills (Britt 1998; Ojha et al. 2007). These efforts shifted community
forestry from a focus on government-defined conservation and development
goals to a community-led platform of adaptive learning and leadership at the
grassroots level. Increased participation was closely aligned with changes in
problem framings and worldviews, such as the idea that communities are a
part of the system and should be viewed as central to ecosystem management (Ives and Messerli, 1989). Increasingly people's livelihoods and forests
were considered inseparable, reflecting a shift away from mechanistic to
complex systems perspectives and relationships.

CFUGs in Nepal exhibit some characteristics of *relational* types. These
place-based communities have been managing their forests for generations, with intergenerational responsibilities maintained despite sociopolitical disruption and absence of formal institutional recognition. This was
evident during the decade-long civil conflict in Nepal that began in 1996.
Despite wider institutional collapse and obstructed communication with

government-generated challenges for CFUGs (Karna, Shivakoti and Webb, 2010), CFUGs not only sustained but kept evolving during this phase through communities' ability for self-organisation in the face of crisis, a strong characteristic of the relational type. CFUGs have also demonstrated their resilience during the 2015 earthquake, where their self-organising skills supported by a well-established network, trust, and governance mechanism enabled local forest management to continue (Gentle et al. 2020).

While these specific trends reflect examples of shifts in the degree of community participation and control, characteristics of authoritative and managerial approaches have been frequently reasserted in Nepalese community forestry. Attitudes and intentions of forestry bureaucrats have always been crucial in shaping relationships with communities (Gilmour and Fisher 1991; Ojha 2006; Basnyat et al. 2018). The continued reluctance of forestry officials to devolve decision-making power to communities (Agrawal and Ostrom 2008), as evident in multiple attempts to amend forest policies and reinforce national control over forest governance (Paudel and Ojha 2008), have undermined the capacity of communities. Community forestry knowledge systems remain dominated by scientific and professional forestry expertise with little space to integrate local and Indigenous knowledge (Nightingale 2005). In recent years, climate change programmes led from both grassroots and international organisations have often assumed that communities are uninformed, which undermines and devalues the knowledge and ability of local people (Ahlborg and Nightingale 2012). Similarly, increased occurrence of forest fires has provided a basis for forestry officials to reassert mechanistic relationships in CFUGs due to a problematic assumption that people deliberately burn their forests. Such views do not recognise that communities have traditionally used fire as a land-management tool. Most notably, holistic governance of forests is constrained by the socioeconomic inequality in Nepalese society, manifested as unequal distribution of wealth, a discriminatory caste system, and conventional gender roles (Sapkota, Keenan, and Ojha 2018). Addressing those forms of inequalities in community forestry would require ensuring meaningful participation from marginalised groups in society (Sapkota, Keenan, and Ojha 2019).

While international organisations often advocate for stronger community-led approaches, in reality they have a mixed influence in terms of achieving such shifts (box 7.1). They have played a positive role in the development of community forestry at the national and local level in Nepal, but there are cases of unfavourable outcomes in shaping government-community relationships.

Box 7.1. Reducing Emissions from Deforestation and Degradation (REDD+) and an increased threat of recentralisation in forest governance in Nepal.

Implementation of climate policy initiatives such as REDD+ in Nepal may affect community-government relationships through shifts in worldviews, problem framing, and government practices. Shifting worldview is evident in an increased focus of forest management on carbon sequestration, which undermines people's traditional dependence on forests and associated livelihood outcomes. This distinction has also weakened cross-sectoral collaborations between forestry and agriculture, reinforcing historic bureaucratic separation between agencies (Marquardt, Khatri, and Pain 2016) and has been dismissive of local and traditional knowledge while reinforcing scientific forestry narratives (Basnyat et al. 2018).

A shift in problem framing from a local to a global view has resulted in changes in priorities, increasing enthusiasm and involvement in carbon trading through REDD+ but limiting attention to the importance of adaptation in forest-dependent communities, with less priority given to local issues. Moreover, REDD+ has also reduced discussion of the value of forests to a single metric (carbon content), diminishing consideration of a wider range of non-monetary values of forests (Khatri et al. 2018).

Practices associated with REDD+ implementation have narrowed the scope of community participation in forest management. Implementation of REDD+ begins with an awareness campaign on climate change, which implies that community support is ensured through education but also undermines the ability of CFUGs. Domination of REDD+ by technoscientific perspectives has been justified through requirements of meeting international objectives. Moreover, increased alliances of local elites with external actors to ensure accountability for carbon increments has resulted in elite capture of decision-making, increased corruption, and shifted power away from marginalised communities (Bastakoti and Davidsen 2017). Together, these have cumulatively increased the threat of recentralisation in forest governance in Nepal (Bushley 2014), bringing changes in government-community relationship that had previously fostered broader democratic changes and increased people's involvement in forest management.

FIGURE 7.3. Changing governance of forests and natural resource management (NRM) in Australia in response to historical conflicts (adapted from Kanowski [2015]; Pyne [1991]).

Forest and Fire Management in Australia

In Australia, historical conflicts have led to differences in land tenures and management control, which have had implications for government-community relationships. Since colonisation, there have been four distinct phases of forest-related policy (figure 7.3).

Between the 1910s and the 1980s, the forestry profession developed simultaneously with efforts by foresters to understand the unfamiliar (to them) Australian forests and to promote science-based management in contrast to previous ad hoc exploitation. This period was associated with *authoritative* relationships, in which inputs from non-professionals were limited to occasional public inquiries (Kanowski 2015; Pyne 1991). Approaches to silviculture and bushfire planning emerged, including the use of controlled fire. Bushfire suppression methods developed following major bushfires in the 1930s and 1940s, drawing on leftover resources and military experiences after World War II (Pyne 1991). Bosomworth (2015) analysed problem framings associated with bushfire management in Victoria and found *authoritative* relationships still dominant in a "command and control" emergency management framing in which government pursues a primary goal of protecting human life. Relationships with community are focused on education to increase risk awareness and community acceptance of government actions. Multiple authors have demonstrated how these practices are underpinned by mechanistic worldviews, with a focus on technoscientific expertise maintaining centralised power (Neale 2016; Ford, Rawluk, and Williams 2019).

During the 1990s, *managerial* patterns of government-community relationships emerged for forest management on public land. The 1992 National Forest Policy Statement and subsequent development of twenty-year regional forest agreements (RFAs) between commonwealth and state governments recognised multiple goals (Ford 2013; Kanowski 2015). Documentation emphasised participation, but only one state (NSW) enabled high levels of stakeholder participation in preparation of RFAs, with others relying on advisory groups and public consultation. Consideration of multiple values was primarily through technical assessment followed by negotiation among bureaucrats to achieve an acceptable balance. This framing meant production and biodiversity values took prominence, and recreational, cultural, aesthetic, and other experiential values were difficult to incorporate (Ford 2013). A narrow understanding of science also constrained incorporation of other forms of knowledge (local, experiential, and Indigenous) in forest decision-making (Bruekner and Horwitz 2005).

More distinctly *interactive* relationships in natural resource management (NRM) on private lands emerged in the early 1990s. Under the National Landcare Program, voluntary partnerships between local landholder groups and supportive government bodies came to resemble interactive systems in which people with a diversity of roles, interests, and experiences interacted in polycentric networks (Beilin, Reichelt and Sysak, 2013). New elements continue to emerge, most recently regional scale landcare networks. These are a new type of institution. Each network supports several constituent local groups, often deepening relationships between community, governments, and businesses (Curtis et al. 2014). Landcare overall is, however, under constant pressure to shape itself to the ways its government partners operate. A key tension lies between a vision of multiple local actors negotiating their own goals for NRM and neoliberal tendencies to instrumentalise communities as on-ground implementation agents for centralised goals (Kanowski 2015; Curtis et al. 2014; Robins and Kanowski 2011). Despite these recentralising forces, a significant proportion of landowners in Australia engage voluntarily in landcare (Curtis et al. 2014).

In the last two decades, following a series of mega-fires, policy efforts have focused more on achieving integrated bushfire management across public and private land tenures. Bosomworth (2015) noted that the *authoritative* "emergency management" framing discussed above has coexisted with a "sustainability" problem framing, an approach that has some markers of both *managerial* and *interactive* relationships. This latter framing considers multiple values and emphasises living with fire, suggesting a more holistic or systems worldview. In some localities, strong community participation is enabled by community-based bushfire management (CBBM) processes, which bring together different bushfire-management agencies to work with communities under the understanding that local communities can effectively build their own response and resilience to bushfire. CBBM has developed more trusting relationships that appear *interactive* and has built local capacity in bushfire risk planning and management, but examples remain isolated and are typically situated within the dominant disaster-management conceptualisation (Macken 2019). Bushfire planning more typically occurs at a regional scale, with consultation that appears *managerial* (Eckerberg and Buizer 2017; Paschen and Beilin 2016). While public policies require staff of fire-management agencies to manage for multiple values on public land, institutional norms mean that in practice objectives are more narrowly defined (primarily to reduce fire risk to life; Williams, Ford, and Rawluk 2021). Decision-making is thus dominated by scientific-technical modelling practices, which present barriers to other forms of knowledge and consideration of other values of concern to communities (Ford, Rawluk, and Williams 2019; Neale 2016), maintaining power with the agencies.

At the same time, increasing societal and policy attention to reconciliation and self-determination for Indigenous peoples in Australia has led to greater potential for using *relational* approaches for forest and fire management. For Indigenous peoples in Australia, fire is an integral part of culture that plays a vital role in fostering kinship with country. Fire practice and planning is seen as a caring obligation (Fletcher et al. 2021) that is often referred to as "cultural burning" or "cultural fire" in reference to the role that it plays in Indigenous culture and tradition. Indigenous communities share that healthy country does not experience the catastrophic bushfires witnessed in recent years and that by healing country through the reintroduction of cultural burning regimes, the occurrence of catastrophic fire can be reduced.

In response, governments across Australia have been exploring ways to incorporate cultural burning into forest management. Attempts to restore Indigenous-informed and -led approaches take several forms. Superficially, these examples look similar but, in fact, reflect different forms of government-community relationships, and most fall short of enabling relational approaches in line with community aspirations (box 7.2). As Indigenous sovereignty is being understood through contemporary treaty discussions, the relationships between government and Indigenous groups must adapt (First Peoples Assembly of Victoria 2020). Currently, Indigenous-led country management is forced to exist in a regulatory and policy framework that is largely uninformed by Indigenous knowledge systems. A significant shift is required to make space for relational Indigenous management of country.

Box 7.2. Three approaches to cultural fire management in Australia.

We draw on three examples of cultural fire management that illustrate different forms of relationships between the state and Indigenous peoples. First, the New South Wales Cultural Fire Management Strategy (Government of New South Wales 2016) is a government-led document that emphasises the importance of shared knowledge in cultural fire, and positions cultural burning as an activity suited to low-risk conditions. This places cultural fire securely within existing regulatory frameworks, and inhibits Indigenous agency in this space, reflecting a managerial relationship.

Meanwhile, the Victorian Traditional Owner Cultural Fire Strategy (Victorian Federation of Traditional Owners 2019) sets out aspirations for fire as a mechanism to restore the health of country. The strategy calls for an adaptive management framework that accommodates Indigenous knowledge in a regulatory framework. It acknowledges that country is not bound by land tenures, and that these boundaries are a barrier to fire practice. Counter to the New South Wales strategy, the Victorian Traditional Owner Cultural Fire Strategy is published by a Traditional Owners representative body. It shows the characteristics of an interactive system but is aspiring to be relational.

In contrast to these state strategies, the Firesticks Alliance Aboriginal Corporation is an Indigenous-led network of cultural fire practitioners and knowledge holders who advocate for the return of cultural burning on the landscape. Firesticks facilitates the sharing of fire knowledge through grassroots mentoring, networking, and support in navigating regulatory requirements. They recognise that fire occurs across boundaries created by a colonial state. Firesticks is working within a relational type, where power is redistributed, and people and country are irreducible.

Grassroots movements like Firesticks represent the desire of Indigenous communities to reclaim traditional land management and caring practices. The move to Indigenous-led and -informed fire practice requires significant policy shifts to allow for a relational and culturally responsive approach.

Implications and Conclusion

Analysis of forest and fire management in Nepal and Australia demonstrates diverse and changing forms of relationships between government and communities. It is noteworthy that more authoritarian and managerial approaches remain dominant across both contexts, and that the policy often serves to curb the full expression of more interactive relationship forms. In Nepal, community forestry has flourished with a strong network of nongovernment actors (Ojha et al. 2007), but concerns about threat of recentralisation in forest governance abound, particularly with growing attention to carbon sequestration goals (Sunam, Paudel, and Paudel 2013; Basnyat et al. 2018). In Australia, bushfire policy calls for community-centred approaches to balance the technical planning processes of information dissemination (Eckerberg and Buizer 2017; Willams, Ford, and Rawluk 2021; Paschen and Beilin 2016) and there are many programmes to introduce more community-based decision-making. However, these programmes often remain within ontological and epistemological positions defined by the agencies, rather than reflecting the fluid everyday local relationships that occur among individuals, communities, and their landscapes (Reid, Beilin, and McLennan 2020). Observations across both countries illustrate the power of "reactive" imaginaries in which government-community relationships can be planned and ordered in line with established government goals (Beilin and Paschen 2020; McDougall and Ojha 2022).

Each relationship type in our typology has its place and purpose but is aligned with different policy and management paradigms. For example, the authoritative type provides predictive power where both problem diagnosis and knowledge have a high level of certainty and the goal is not contested, such as communication for evacuation in the event of a fire. We note there may be few circumstances in which these conditions apply. While a managerial relationship type enables more opportunities for external input, an interactive type enables negotiation, conversation, and contestation about knowledge and problem diagnosis. We note that discovery of shared goals may be slow, posing challenges where decisions still need to be made in a particular timeframe. The relational type supports government-community relationships as continuous through time, collaborative, and focused on trust-building, yet it requires intensive time commitments from all participants, adequate resources, and a redistribution and reorganisation of power.

The typology developed here clearly distinguishes relational thinking from other approaches to government community relationships. While there is growing appetite for relational approaches, current technocratic policy environments are a barrier to implementation of relational types. Creating change in the relationships between government and communities is not as simple as selecting an ideal type from the typology. Instead, building on McDougall and Ojha (2022), creating meaningful, long-lasting change requires critical consideration of the context and history (such as colonisation and politics) that supports or hinders these relationships. The relational type is thus a radically different alternative to authoritative, managerial, and interactive types, and movement toward relational approaches requires careful attention to knowledge systems, worldviews, and assumptions about power and autonomy. We hope the framework presented in this chapter supports the discovery of practical pathways to expand the use of relational approaches, including clarifying the underpinning worldviews and problem framings that distinguish this approach, and providing insights to what this may look like in practice.

References

Agrawal, A., and E. Ostrom. 2008. Decentralization and community-based forestry: Learning from experience. In *Decentralization, forests rural communities: Policy outcomes in South and Southeast Asia*, ed. E. L. Webb and G. P. Shivakoti, 44–67.

Ahlborg, H., and A. J. Nightingale. 2012. Mismatch between scales of knowledge in Nepalese forestry: Epistemology, power, and policy implications. *Ecology and Society* 17 (4).

Arnstein, S. R. 1969. A ladder of citizen participation. *Journal of the American Institute of Planners* 35 (4): 216–24. https://doi.org/10.1080/01944366908977225.

Basnyat, B., T. Treue, R. K. Pokharel, L. N. Lamsal, and S. Rayamajhi. 2018. Legal-sounding bureaucratic re-centralisation of community forestry in Nepal. *Forest Policy and Economics* 91: 5–18.

Bastakoti, R. R., and C. Davidsen. 2017. Optimism, hopes and fears: Local perceptions of REDD+ in Nepalese community forests. *International Forestry Review* 19 (1): 1.

Beilin, R., and J.-A. Paschen. 2020. Risk, resilience and response-able practice in Australia's changing bushfire landscapes. *Environment and Planning D: Society and Space* 39 (3): 514–33 https://doi.org/10.1177/0263775820976570.

Beilin, R., and J.-A. Paschen. 2021. Risk, resilience and response-able practice in Australia's changing bushfire landscapes. *Environment and Planning D: Society and Space* 39 (3): 514–33.

Beilin, R., N. Reichelt, and T. Sysak. 2013. Resilience in the transition landscapes of the peri-urban: From "where" with "whom" to "what." *Urban Studies* 52 (7): 1304–20.

Blaikie, P. M. 1985. *The political economy of soil erosion in developing countries.* New York, NY: Longman.

Boonstra, W. J. 2016. Conceptualizing power to study social-ecological interactions. *Ecology and Society* 21 (1).

Bosomworth, K. 2015. Climate change adaptation in public policy: Frames, fire management, and frame reflection. *Environment and Planning C: Government and Policy* 33 (6): 1450–66. http://epc.sagepub.com/content/by/year.

Bosomworth, K., P. Leith, A. Harwood, and P. J. Wallis. 2017. What's the problem in adaptation pathways planning? The potential of a diagnostic problem-structuring approach. *Environmental Science & Policy* 76: 23–28.

Britt, C. 1998. Community forestry comes of age: Forest-user networking and federation-building experiences from Nepal. In *Crossing Boundaries: the Seventh Biennial conference of the International Association for the Study of Common Property.* Vancouver, BC: Digital Library of the Commons.

Brueckner, M., and P. Horwitz. 2005. The use of science in environmental policy: A case study of the Regional Forest Agreement process in Western Australia. *Sustainability: Science, Practice, and Policy* 1 (2): 14–24.

Bushley B. R. 2014. REDD+ policy making in Nepal: Toward state-centric, polycentric, or market-oriented governance? *Ecology and Society* 19 (3).

Caine, K. J. 2013. Bourdieu in the north: Practical understanding in natural resource governance. *Canadian Journal of Sociology* 38 (3): 333–58.

Callicott, J. B., and K. Mumford. 1997. Ecological sustainability as a conservation concept. *Conservation Biology* 11 (1): 32–40.

Cook, S. D. N., and H. Wagenaar. 2012. Navigating the eternally unfolding present: Toward an epistemology of practice. *American Review of Public Administration* 42 (1): 3–38.

Curtis, A., H. Ross, G. R. Marshall, C. Baldwin, J. Cavaye, C. Freeman, A. Carr, and G. J. Syme. 2014. The great experiment with devolved NRM governance: Lessons from community engagement in Australia and New Zealand since the 1980s. *Australasian Journal of Environmental Management* 21 (2): 175–99. https://doi.org/10.1080/14486563.2014.935747.

Eckerberg, K., and M. Buizer. 2017. Promises and dilemmas in forest fire management decision-making: Exploring conditions for community engagement in Australia and Sweden. *Forest Policy and Economics* 80: 133–40.

First Peoples Assembly of Victoria. 2020. Discussion paper: Examples of rights available under state-wide and local treaties. Accessed December 15, 2021. https://www.firstpeoplesvic.org/wp-content/uploads/2020/10/Discussion -paper-Examples-of-rights-available-under-statewide-and-local-Treaties-1.pdf.

Fletcher, M., A. Romano, S. Connor, M. Mariani, and S. Y. Maezumi. 2021. Catastrophic bushfires, Indigenous fire knowledge and reframing science in Southeast Australia. *Fire* 4 (3): 61.

Ford, R. M. 2013. Contested social values in decision-making for Australian native forests. *Australian Forestry* 76 (1): 37–49. https://doi.org/10.1080/00049158.2013 .776924.

Ford, R. M., A. Rawluk, and K. J. H. Williams. 2019. Managing values in disaster planning: Current strategies, challenges and opportunities for incorporating values of the public. *Land Use Policy* 81: 131–42. https://doi.org/10.1016/j.landusepol .2018.10.029.

Gentle, P., T. N. Maraseni, D. Paudel, G. R. Dahal, T. Kanel, and B. Pathak. 2020. Effectiveness of community forest user groups (CFUGs) in responding to the 2015 earthquakes and COVID-19 in Nepal. *Research in Globalization* 2: 100025. https://doi.org/10.1016/j.resglo.2020.100025.

Gilmour, D. A., and R. J. Fisher. 1991. *Villagers, forests, and foresters*. Kathmandu, Nepal: Sahayogi Press.

Government of New South Wales. 2016. Cultural fire management policy. Accessed December 15, 2021. https://www.environment.nsw.gov.au/topics/parks-reserves -and-protected-areas/park-policies/cultural-fire-management.

Hill, R., C. Grant, M. George, C. J. Robinson, S. Jackson, and N. Abel. 2012. A typology of Indigenous engagement in Australian environmental management: Implications for knowledge integration and social-ecological system sustainability. *Ecology and Society* 17 (1): 23.

Ives, J. D., and Messerli, B. (1989). *The Himalayan dilemma: Reconciling development and conservation*. London: Routledge.

Kanowski, P. J. 2015. Australia's forests: Contested past, tenure-driven present, uncertain future. *Forest Policy and Economics* 77: 56. https://doi.org/10.1016/j .forpol.2015.06.001.

Karna, B. K., G. P. Shivakoti, and E. L. Webb. 2010. Resilience of community forestry under conditions of armed conflict in Nepal. *Environmental Conservation* 37 (2): 201–09.

Khatri, D. B., K. Marquardt, A. Pain, and H. Ojha. 2018. Shifting regimes of management and uses of forests: What might REDD+ implementation mean for community forestry? Evidence from Nepal. *Forest Policy and Economics* 92: 1–10.

Lane, M. B., and G. McDonald. 2002. Towards a general model of forest management through time: Evidence from Australia, USA, and Canada. *Land Use Policy* 19 (3): 193.

Leeuwis, C. 2004. *Communication for rural innovation: Rethinking agricultural extension*. 3rd ed. Oxford, UK: Blackwell Science.

Macken, F. 2019. Community-based bushfire management in Victoria. *Australian Journal of Emergency Management* 34 (4): 9–10.

Macpherson, E., S. C. Urlich, H. G. Rennie, A. Paul, K. Fisher, L. Braid, J. Banwell, J. T. Ventura, and E. Jorgensen. 2021. "Hooks" and "anchors" for relational ecosystem-based marine management. *Marine Policy* 130. https://doi.org/10 .1016/j.marpol.2021.104561.

Malla, Y. B. 2001. Changing policies and the persistence of patron-client relations in Nepal: Stakeholders' responses to changes in forest policies. *Environmental History* 6 (2): 287–307.

Marquardt, K., D. Khatri, and A. Pain. 2016. REDD+, forest transition, agrarian change and ecosystem services in the hills of Nepal. *Human Ecology* 44 (2): 229–44.

McDougall, C., and H. Ojha. 2022. How does adaptive collaborative management leverage changes in power. In *Adaptive collaborative management in forest landscapes: Villagers, bureaucrats and civil society*, ed. C. J. P. Colfer, R. Prabhu, and A. M. Larson. Abingdon, UK: Routledge.

Muller, S., S. Hemming, and D. Rigney. 2019. Indigenous sovereignties: Relational ontologies and environmental management. *Geographical Research* 57 (4): 399–410.

Neale, T. 2016. Burning anticipation: Wildfire, risk mitigation and simulation modelling in Victoria, Australia. *Environment and Planning A: Economy and Space* 48 (10): 2026–45. https://doi.org/10.1177/0308518X16651446.

Nightingale, A. J. 2005. "The experts taught us all we know": Professionalisation and knowledge in Nepalese community forestry. *Antipode* 37 (3): 581–604.

Ojha, H. R. 2006. Techno-bureaucratic doxa and challenges for deliberative governance: The case of community forestry policy and practice in Nepal. *Policy and Society* 25 (2): 131–75.

Ojha, H. 2014. Beyond the "local community": The evolution of multi-scale politics in Nepal's community forestry regimes. *International Forestry Review* 16 (3): 339–53.

Ojha, H. R., M. R. Banjade, R. K. Sunam, B. Bhattarai, S. Jana, K. R. Goutam, and S. Dhungana. 2014. Can authority change through deliberative politics?: Lessons from the four decades of participatory forest policy reform in Nepal. *Forest Policy and Economics* 46: 1–9.

Ojha, H. R., R. Ford, R. J. Keenan, D. Race, D. C. Vega, H. Baral, and P. Sapkota. 2016. Delocalizing communities: Changing forms of community engagement in natural resources governance. *World Development* 87: 274–90. https://doi.org/10 .1016/j.worlddev.2016.06.017.

Ojha, H. R., D. R. Khanal, N. Sharma, H. Sharma, and B. Pathak. 2007. Federation of community forest user groups in Nepal: An innovation in democratic forest governance. *In Proceedings of an international conference on poverty reduction and forest: Tenure, market and policy reforms*. Bangkok, Thailand: RECOFTC.

Paschen, J.-A., and R. Beilin. 2016. How a risk focus in emergency management can restrict community resilience: A case study from Victoria, Australia. *International Journal of Wildland Fire* 26 (1): 1–9.

Paudel, K., and H. Ojha. 2008. Contested knowledge and reconciliation in Nepal's community forestry: A case of forest inventory policy. In *Knowledge systems and natural resources: Management, policy and institutions in Nepal*, ed. H. Ojha, N. Timsina, R. Chhetri, and K. Paudel, 40–59. New Delhi, India: International Development Research Center.

Perley, C. 2003. Resourcism and preservationism in New Zealand forestry: An end to the dichotomy? *New Zealand Journal of Forestry* 11–17.

Preiser, R., and P. Cilliers. 2010. Unpacking the ethics of complexity: concluding reflections. In *Complexity, difference and identity*, 265–87. Dordrecht, Netherlands: Springer.

Pyne, S. J. 1991. *Burning bush: A fire history of Australia*. New York, NY: Henry Holt.

RECOFTC. 2013. *Community forestry in Asia and the Pacific: pathway to inclusive development*. Bangkok: Center for People and Forests.

Reid, K., R. Beilin, and J. McLennan. 2020. Communities and responsibility: Narratives of place-identity in Australian bushfire landscapes. *Geoforum* 109: 35–43. https://doi.org/10.1016/j.geoforum.2019.12.015.

Renn, O. 2006. Participatory processes for designing environmental policies. *Land Use Policy* 23 (1): 34–43.

Ribot, J. C., A. Agrawal, and A. M. Larson. 2006. Recentralizing while decentralizing: How national governments reappropriate forest resources. *World Development* 34 (11), 1864–86.

Robins, L., and P. Kanowski. 2011. "Crying for our country": Eight ways in which "caring for our country" has undermined Australia's regional model for natural resource management. *Australasian Journal of Environmental Management* 18 (2): 88–108.

Rose, D. B. 1996. *Nourishing terrains: Australian Aboriginal views of landscape and wilderness*. Canberra, Australia: Australian Heritage Commission.

Ross, H., M. Buchy, and W. Proctor. 2002. Laying down the ladder: A typology of public participation in Australian natural resource management. *Australian Journal of Environmental Management* 9 (4): 205–17.

Sapkota, P., R. J. Keenan, and H. R. Ojha. 2018. Community institutions, social marginalization and the adaptive capacity: A case study of a community forestry user group in the Nepal Himalayas. *Forest Policy and Economics* 92: 55–64. https://doi.org/10.1016/j.forpol.2018.04.001.

Sapkota, P., R. J. Keenan, and H. R. Ojha. 2019. Co-evolving dynamics in the social-ecological system of community forestry: Prospects for ecosystem-based adaptation in the Middle Hills of Nepal. *Regional Environmental Change* 19 (1): 179. https://doi.org/10.1007/s10113-018-1392-9.

Schultz, C. A., J. B. Abrams, E. J. Davis, A. S. Cheng, H. R. Huber-Stearns, and C. Moseley. 2021. Disturbance shapes the US forest governance frontier: A review and conceptual framework for understanding governance change. *Ambio* 50: 2168–82. https://doi.org/10.1007/s13280-021-01629-4.

Shah, S. H., L. Rodina, J. M. Burt, E. J. Gregr, M. Chapman, S. Williams, N. J. Wilson, and G. McDowell. 2018. Unpacking social-ecological transformations: Conceptual, ethical and methodological insights. *The Anthropocene Review* 5 (3): 250–65. https://doi.org/10.1177/2053019618817928.

Suchet-Pearson, S., S. Wright, K. Lloyd, and L. Burarrwanga. 2013. Caring as country: Towards an ontology of co-becoming in natural resource management. *Asia Pacific Viewpoint* 54 (2): 185–97. https://doi.org/10.1111/apv.12018.

Sunam, R. K., N. S. Paudel, and G. Paudel. 2013. Community forestry and the threat of recentralization in Nepal: Contesting the bureaucratic hegemony in policy process. *Society and Natural Resources* 26 (12): 1407–21. https://doi.org/10.1080/08941920.2013.799725.

Tiwari, B. K., H. Tynsong, M. M. Lynrah, E. Lapasam, S. Deb, and D. Sharma. 2013. Institutional arrangement and typology of community forests of Meghalaya, Mizoram and Nagaland of North-East India. *Journal of Forestry Research* 24 (1): 179–86.

Tynan, L. 2021. What is relationality? Indigenous knowledges, practices and responsibilities with kin. *Cultural Geographies* 28 (4): 597–610. https://doi.org/10.1177/14744740211029287.

Victorian Federation of Traditional Owners. 2019. The Victorian traditional owner: Cultural fire strategy. Accessed December 15, 2021. https://knowledge.aidr.org.au/media/6817/fireplusstrategyplusfinal.pdf.

Walsh, Z., J. Böhme, and C. Wamsler. 2021. Towards a relational paradigm in sustainability research, practice and education. *Ambio* 50 (1): 74–84. https://doi.org/10.1007/s13280-020-01322-y.

West, S., L. J. Haider, S. Stålhammar, and S. Woroniecki. 2020. A relational turn for sustainability science? Relational thinking, leverage points and transformations. *Ecosystems and People* 16 (1): 304–25. https://doi.org/10.1080/26395916.2020.1814417.

Williams, K. J. H., R. M. Ford, and A. Rawluk. 2021. Changing bushfire management practices to incorporate diverse values of the public. *Environmental Science & Policy* 125: 87–95.

Section Three

Engagement and Elicitation

8

Three Modes of Participatory Environmental Governance Research

JOHN R. PARKINS

In this chapter, I identify three distinct modes of scholarship on participatory environmental governance that coexist, overlap, and experience moments of mutual ascendance and decline over decades of scholarship. Mode one takes inspiration from notions of pragmatism and adult learning. Mode two recognizes the limits of collaborative governance and the retrenchment of power elites. Mode three offers a more radical and activist approach to environmental governance.

Introduction

Governance involves a "set of regulatory processes, mechanisms and organizations through which political actors influence environmental actions and outcomes" (Lemos and Agrawal 2006, 298). A key element of this definition is the idea of influence, and for decades now, researchers have trained their analytical tool kits on defining and understanding the mechanisms and tactics of influence within governance spaces. Although governance is inclusive

https://doi.org/10.7330/9781646426300.c008

of regulatory reforms and law making through electoral politics (what we often call "big-P" politics), this chapter focuses on the everyday "small-p" politics of environmental governance that is commonly reflected in small-group processes, where local residents or stakeholders engage in organized and longer term conversations and debates about how to manage local projects, policies, plans, and associated landscapes (e.g., Sanders, Nielsen, and Abrams 2021; Nenko et al. 2019).

Since the 1990s in particular, research on public participation as an element of environmental governance has taken off within many areas of practice and scholarship, including environmental assessment (O'Faircheallaigh 2010), conservation biology (Day 2017), and disaster management (Hamideh 2020). Yet, in spite of these advances in theory and practice, and an almost complete consensus on the need for public participation, we observe an enduring set of concerns about the overall functioning and effectiveness of participatory processes in achieving fair, equitable, and environmentally friendly outcomes. For decades now, critics (e.g., McCloskey 1996; Ribot et al. 2006) have expressed deep apprehensions about the power imbalances between economic elites and local stakeholders, and these concerns remain a dominant theme in much of the literature on this topic (Miller and Nadeau 2017). While researchers and practitioners continue to seek ways to address these shortcomings and improve participatory processes (Armatas, Borrie, and Watson 2022), others seek to influence change through direct action as a component of the governance process. Research by Gobby and colleagues (2022), for example, reflects a disquieting among citizens who see no value in endless public consultations (e.g., "talk shops") and see direct action as a more effective approach to governance.

Attending to these diverse approaches, the chapter is structured around three modes of scholarship on public participation:

- *Mode one*: Generative and relational—methods and tools for participation
- *Mode two*: Institutional and discursive—critiques and elaborations on theory and practice
- *Mode three*: Resistant and resurgent—from dialogue to direct action

Although I create clear distinctions between these modes and they are also ordered somewhat chronologically, all three of these modes remain active within the published literature and they coexist, sometimes overlapping, and experience moments of popularity and decline over time. This chapter is also more about research than it is about tools and strategies for political action. The chapter offers a reflection on how researchers have approached the subject matter and advanced concepts and empirical methods that contribute to the academic literature.

I approach this review as a long-standing contributor to this literature and one who was schooled in theories of deliberative democracy. But I also come to this review with a lifetime of observing minimal progress on pressing societal and environmental challenges and a growing skepticism of stakeholder engagement as a strategy for change. In this sense, my review is an invitation to reflect on how political actors can influence environmental actions and outcomes, and the potential limits of public participation in advancing many of our most pressing environmental challenges.

In reviewing the corpus of scholarship on public participation, I draw the bulk of materials from the journal, *Society and Natural Resources*. Using the search engine on the publisher's website (*Taylor & Francis*), I found practically no end of material on this topic. Strict search criteria yielded twenty articles published with the phrase "public participation" in the title between 1994 and 2018. Using *Google Scholar*, the same search with this phrase located anywhere in the article yields more than 346 articles from this journal. Similarly, between 2011 and 2021, there were six articles published with the phrase "public engagement," and eighty-one articles with the phrase located anywhere in the article. Other pseudonyms, such as "public consultation," yielded even more material on this topic, not to mention the extensive treatment of this topic in many other journals. For example, in the sections to follow I draw on disciplinary journals (e.g., *Environmental Impact Assessment Review*) and sector-specific journals (e.g., *Canadian Journal of Forest Research*). Specific references to the literature are not intended to be exhaustive but instead illustrative of key points and trends that are observed and highlighted below.

In the sections to follow, I document three modes of public participation as outlined above. In each section, I draw on key articles and examples to illustrate contributions and tensions in the literature—many of which are enduring and highlight the dynamic elements of scholarship in this field.

Mode One: Participation as Generative and Relational

As an entry point to this literature on public participation, one can trace the origins of scholarship to several key historical moments and theoretical traditions. These underpinnings are extensive with complex and contending positions. But broadly speaking, we see the roots of this scholarship in two particular fields of study. First, within the North American tradition of pragmatism, as defined by John Dewey, we take inspiration from a theory of pragmatic politics—one that maligns ideology and dogma in favor of a practical and realist politics of everyday life. This political space is focused on how laypeople and experts are linked within political spaces and how to maintain public engagement and democratization in the face of complexity (Dewey [1927] 2012). Dewey's enduring philosophical tradition gives rise to the urgency of public participation as an essential element of democratic society. It also influences other theoretical work, including theories of adult learning as put forward by Mezirow (2003) and others.

Second, within European scholarship, the work of Jürgen Habermas was influential in defining the historical emergence of a public sphere within seventeenth-century western Europe. The primary text for these ideas is titled *The Structural Transformation of the Public Sphere: An Inquiry into a Category of Bourgeois Society* (Habermas [1962] 1991). Given that the English translation came along decades later, the influence of his work in North America was arguably delayed until the early 1990s. By focusing on the societal conditions that gave rise to the emergence (and decline) of the public sphere, Habermas provided a historically informed understanding of everyday democracy as reflected in the coffee houses and salons of England and France. These so-called penny universities, where common folk mingled with societal elites, offered an alternative mode of public discourse that functioned outside of hegemonic political and economic forces in church and state. Inspired by these historical accounts, Habermas identifies a series of norms, or ideal characteristics, of the public sphere that scholars utilize as the basis of evaluating public participation more generally. Calhoun (1992) clarifies these criteria as (1) the discounting (or bracketing out) of social differences; (2) rational argument as the sole arbiter of public debate, or what Habermas describes as the "unforced force of the better argument"; (3) identifying and debating new areas of public concern; and (4) a commitment to inclusiveness, as reflected in the "penny university" where barriers to entry were low (i.e., mere pennies). Although these possibilities for rational debate and inclusiveness are hotly debated by political theorists (see Fischer, Stenius, and Holmgren 2020 for a critique of Habermas in relation to Swedish discourses on the bioeconomy), arguably, Habermas gives us an enduring sense of optimism, a sense of what is possible and necessary for proper functioning of the public sphere and a basis for evaluating the extent to which contemporary processes of public participation measure up to these ideals. This work by Habermas also informs applications of deliberative democracy that are a fairly common element of the resource management literature (Parkins and Mitchell 2005; Lockie 2007).

From this theoretical tradition, we take some inspiration for a politics of everyday life that must thrive alongside and complement electoral politics as an essential element of democratic societies. At a minimum, these public spheres represent political spaces to test ideas, gain diverse insights, revise personal preferences, and influence decisions on matters of public concern.

In addition to these historical and theoretical starting points, another entry point into the literature on public participation is directly related to the challenges of environmental governance, starting in the post-WWII era. These challenges precipitated regulatory reforms such as the National Environmental Policy Act (NEPA) in the United States and the Federal Environmental Assessment Review Office (FEARO) in Canada during the 1970s. These changes are mirrored in Europe with more recent developments such as the Aarhus Convention that provides a framework for environmental management and public participation. In fact, the first article within the journal *Society & Natural Resources* to use the term *public participation* in the title highlights NEPA as a catalyst for evolving public participation processes in the United States (Gericke and Sullivan 1994).

This 1994 article also notes growing dissatisfaction with land management plans as a motivation for regulation and policy changes. Along these lines, the emergence of regulatory reforms during the 1970s and subsequent decades was largely in response to a series of environmental challenges that scholars and policy makers thought could be addressed by enhancing public participation in the planning and management of natural environments. From the northern spotted owl controversy in the northwest United States (Watson and Muraoka 1992) to the "war in the woods" in British Columbia, Canada (Jackson and Curry 2004), the optimism expressed by theorists noted above was reflected in much of the early thinking on public participation as a catalyst for changing paradigms in environmental management. These changing approaches reflected a growing recognition of the messiness of resource management challenges, the inability of scientists and politicians to find solutions to these challenges, and an enduring set of deep conflicts that are based on competing values systems and oppositional knowledge claims (McCool and Guthrie 2001).

In this regard, a plethora of research is focused on the generative and relational dimensions of public participation. From a generative perspective, participatory processes are intended to offer opportunities for policy and management options to emerge that are in line with the views and experiences of participants. By accessing information, sharing information, participating in the decision-making process, and learning about diverse technical and social dimensions of governance challenges, at a minimum, participatory processes allow participants to understand (if not support) the decisions that are made. Moreover, these same processes can help to generate new ways of thinking about old problems and facilitate new management approaches. Added to the generative dimension is a relational dimension that is focused on trust building between agencies, individuals, and communities, and gaining acceptance of decisions.

Some of my own early influences in this mode of scholarship are reflected in the work of Shindler and Neburka (1997) who offer eight attributes of successful public participation in forest planning. Two of these attributes included (1) the selection of members who have a good understanding of the issues and (2) processes that are structured to promote full group interaction rather than one-way information flows. Other scholars contributed to this body of work, with research on what participants expect of these processes and how to make participation successful within often-messy resource management situations (e.g., Webler 1999; Wondolleck and Yaffee 2000; McCool and Guthrie 2001; Daniels and Walker 2001; Olsen and Shindler 2010). Much of this work formed the body of emerging scholarship during the 1990s and early 2000s—a focus on convivial and pragmatic approaches to public participation that is intended to "turn down the heat" on controversial topics and find solutions that are, if not consensus based, at least understandable to those involved.

Another key component of this first wave of scholarship involved attention to the methods and technique of public participation that are available to practitioners. As an effort to "expand the toolbox" of options, a number of scholars offer ways of doing public participation that extend beyond common (and overused) techniques like town hall meetings and public advisory committees.

In 2000, Rowe and Frewer published an influential paper outlining a suite of public participation methods, including the following: referenda, public hearings/inquiries, public opinion survey, negotiated rule making, consensus conference, citizen jury/panel, citizen/public advisory committee, and focus group. Other researchers developed similar approaches to defining a wide range of public participation methods and ways of evaluating the strengths and weaknesses of these approaches (Lawrence and Deagen 2001; Sinclair and Diduck 2017). For example, Beckley, Parkins, and Sheppard (2006) developed a reference guide for forest mangers on how to assemble a program of public participation methods that are complementary—whereby the representativeness of opinion surveys is matched with focus groups that allow for deliberation and two-way flows of information.

In addition to these review essays and reference guides, scholars are also doing more fine-grained assessments of participatory techniques, such as Carr and Halvorsen (2001), who assess three community-based approaches to citizen participation (surveys, conversations with community groups, and community dinners). As technologies evolve and as social media sources become more ubiquitous, we also observe research that is pushing new ways of integrating public information, such as participatory geographic information systems (Brown, Montag, and Lyon 2012) and the use of websites and social media to assess the inclusiveness of engagement processes by conservation agencies (Fairchild and Petrzelka 2021; see also Hafferty et al. in chapter 10 of this volume).

Mode Two: Participation as Institutional and Discursive

Although *mode one* is decidedly optimistic and pragmatic about the possibilities of participatory environmental governance, there are detractors (e.g., Cupps 1977) and these concerns are more prominent in *mode two*. Another way of understanding the distinction between mode one and mode two is to understand the overarching question that researchers and practitioners are attempting to address. In the generative and relational phase, what is the goal of public participation? What does successful public participation look like? I would argue that the answer to the first question for mode one researchers is to achieve better social and environmental outcomes through engagement. The goal involves getting people to work better together, to reduce conflict by identifying new ideas, new strategies, and engagement techniques to tackle often-intractable challenges. All of this effort is expected to level the playing field. Inserting stakeholders and ideas into the governance process can challenge the status quo and turn policy and management decisions toward more sustainable outcomes. Analogous to positivist traditions in social science, one might argue that mode one reflects a positivist approach to citizen engagement. With thoughtful but straightforward additions of stakeholder and local citizens, governance processes are better for it.

Notwithstanding these claims, however, mode two scholars are more skeptical of participation as is commonly practiced and are more contemplative about the values of participation. Mode two remains committed to the values and benefits of public participation, but with cynicism. What does success look like? Well, it might not be improved environments. Instead, it might be a better understanding about why we disagree, what's at stake, and how hard it will be to affect change.

This shift in focus, away from the outcomes of deliberations to process, is reflected in the words of Dryzek (1990, 22), where the primary emphasis of discursive democracy is "understanding between individuals rather than success in achieving predefined individual goals." With this change of emphasis in mind, this section highlights three particular examples of scholarship along these lines: (1) justice theory, (2) trust theory, and (3) representation and knowledge production.

Justice theory (Taylor 2000) emerged over the last few decades as a key area of focus in the literature on public participation. In its most common formulation, justice theory includes two distinct (but interconnected) domains: procedural justice and distributive justice. Procedural justice involves the fairness of procedures that are used to arrive at final decisions. These procedural elements can include the fairness of representation, consideration of alternative points of view, and the terms and conditions for engagement, including adequate resources and supports for underprivileged and underserved groups. Researchers who study these fairness criteria point to procedural considerations whereby participants are keen to be heard and to know that their ideas are being taken seriously (Smith and McDonough 2001). Although the idea of justice in this context seems more like common sense, the notion of justice does signal a moral imperative that requires more than simply tinkering with procedures.

Distributive justice is about the fairness of outcomes, which is about how costs and benefits are distributed—who wins and who loses. Some authors put more emphasis on the procedural elements because they have such an important impact on distributional justice issues. For example, according to Lauer et al. (2018, 13), "to achieve satisfactory outcomes, stakeholders must have been given an opportunity to participate; however, the opportunity to participate will not affect satisfaction unless stakeholders also see how their participation shaped decisions." Similarly, other researchers confirm that satisfaction with participatory processes are determined by procedural and distributive justice variables (Nenko, Parkins, and Reed 2019). These dimensions of justice are central to recent scholarship within energy social sciences, where scholars point to the centrality of procedural justice in determining support and implementation of renewable energy projects (Simcock 2016; Walker and Baxter 2017).

A second area of scholarship involves trust theory. The literature on this topic is crucially linked to questions of what we are trying to achieve through public participation. For many scholars, particularly within *mode one*, the idea of trust building (as a key input and outcome of public participation) is non-problematic. When local institutions are not trusted, and when people do not trust each other, it's difficult to make progress on difficult issues. In this mode of scholarship, running through almost all of the research on this topic, trust building is deemed to be a key point of focus. Within the journal *Society & Natural Resources*, there are twenty-nine articles with the word *trust* in the title. From the first paper in this series, the authors talk about the role of small-group activities in building mutual trust and education regarding the interests of all participants (Gericke and Sullivan 1994). This message is communicated through many studies, including more recent attention to the dynamic nature of trust as a choice and the implication for cooperative behaviors (Hamm 2017). In differentiating modalities of trust, Hamm also refers to extensive scholarship on the dimensions of trust—the most basic dimensions of which include institutional trust (trust in the process) and individual trust (trust in the people involved). A further delineation of these dimensions is offered by Coleman and Stern (2018) with four types of trust (i.e., dispositional, rational, affinitive, and procedural), each of which is defined and measured uniquely.

Particularly within a world of growing polarization, arguing against the merits of trust building feels like a fool's bargain. Yet, consistent with scholarship on discursive democracy, there is a sense in which trust building can go too far and can have corrosive effects on public engagement. As an entry point into this argument, from a philosophical standpoint, Warren (1999, 310) claims that "distrust is essential not only to democratic progress but also, we might think, to the healthy suspicion of power upon which the vitality of democracy depends." This sentiment emerges from a general concern that democracy suffers in a political milieu of excessive consensus and the associated apathies of busy and distracted citizens (Mouffe 1993). As a counterpoint to distraction, to sharpen the mind, one must feel vulnerable, perhaps threatened, but also have opportunities to engage and effect change.

While these philosophical ideas are as relevant to electoral politics as they are to small group deliberations, the dynamics of trust and distrust can also be examined empirically. Stern and Baird (2015), for example, describe a "complacency threshold" for indicating when too much trust is not beneficial. Within my own work, I draw on concepts from Poortinga and Pidgeon (2003) and the idea of critical trust, "which is the optimal pairing of high general trust in the institutional context of public engagement, plus a high degree of skepticism about the politics of decision making" (Parkins et al. 2017, 938). Our empirical analysis offers evidence that survey respondents who exhibit these characteristics of critical trust are more likely to be engaged; to be more active citizens.

While authors will continue to debate the merits of distrust in participatory processes, my goal in this section is to illustrate the somewhat more complicated approach to research on public participation within mode two. It is not often the case that public participation leads to better environmental outcomes. In fact, scholars are interested in other metrics of success, such as justice or the quality of democratic discourse, as illustrated above. Echoing the words of Dryzek (1990), participation is as much about achieving mutual understanding as it is about achieving specific goals or outcomes.

A final aspect of *mode two* scholarship involves closer attention to issues of public representation, stakeholder analysis, and systems of knowledge production. For example, research by Leach (2002) identifies four categories of stakeholders (i.e., federal and state agencies, local agencies, environmental advocates, and resource users), and then utilizes survey data to understand the partnership's success in achieving goals, trust in other members of the partnership, and other aspects of watershed partnerships in California and Washington.

This approach to stakeholder analysis remains common, but there are other ways of doing stakeholder analysis, including an exploration of "values representation." The work of McFarlane and Boxall (2000) exemplify this approach by analyzing the values and attitudes of stakeholder groups in the Canadian forest sector. Drawing on a typology of forest values put forward by Bengston (1994) and others, their study utilizes survey research to examine the values composition of local stakeholder-based public advisory committees who are sponsored by forest companies. Their analysis shows that although the public advisory committees have diverse memberships (i.e., members of environmental groups, local municipal leaders, labor leaders, etc.), the values of group members are largely in line with the values of registered professional foresters and are not representative of the general public. If these public advisory groups are intended to serve as sounding boards for public interest and concern, results from McFarlane and Boxall (2000) indicate they are not meeting these goals. One can debate the reasons for these outcomes and the extent to which this is a good thing or a bad thing, but the point here is that scholarship on stakeholder analysis can extend beyond interests and constituencies to attitudes and values.

One additional step in this research on stakeholders involves an understanding and appreciation for the contribution of diverse knowledge systems. Knowledge systems are crucial to this discussion, in part because of how knowledge contributes directly to discourses. Within the literature on sociotechnical systems, notions of post-normal science are influential here (Funtowicz and Ravetz 1994). Post normality is defined by situations where decision stakes are high and system uncertainties are high (e.g., forest landscapes in a climate crisis). Under such circumstances, applied scientific methods must give way to post-normal science. Within these post-normal conditions, distinctions between facts and values are blurred and extended peer communities become a crucial component of problem solving. Stated more directly, in complex and uncertain situations where the stakes are high, not only do we need values representation but we also need diverse systems of knowledge production.

Toward this end, there is much to be said here about contributions from the research on citizen science (Fischer 2000) and popular epidemiology (Brown 1997), but we also see growing contributions in the realm of Indigenous knowledge systems. Arguably, some of the most dynamic work in this space is related to fire management in North America and Australia (see, for instance, Sapkota et al. in chapter 7 of this volume). For example, Eriksen and Hankins (2014) illustrate traditional Indigenous fire knowledge and its application to fire management but also highlight the tensions and difficulties in maintaining these knowledge systems in the face of state and federal agency interests. Similarly, Lewis, Christianson, and Spinks (2018) illustrate Indigenous fire use in the Lytton First Nation, a community that experienced devastating fires in June 2021. These insights are foretelling, but they also reflect an urgency for new modes of knowledge production and a need for dramatic shifts in the ways that forest landscapes are managed. Moreover, these knowledge systems are critical to ongoing debates and discursive ways of understanding the value and contribution of public participation in environmental governance.

In summary, I highlight one final and important distinction between *mode one* and *mode two* scholarship. Inasmuch as mode one is about bringing sources of information to the table and utilizing rational thought and the "unforced force of the better argument" to arrive at more sustainable outcomes, mode two scholarship aligns with science and technology studies and the idea that "more environmental science often leads to more controversy," not less (Sarewitz 2004). In this way, new science, traditional knowledge systems, co-design, and co-creation complicate the idea of "evidence-based decision making" by asking hard questions about whose evidence and for what benefit.

Mode Three: Participation as Resistance and Resurgence

A third mode of public participation in environmental governance involves outright resistance and the resurgence of minority communities, as discussed below. If *mode one* and *mode two* reflect variations on how to improve participatory governance, *mode three* represents a wholesale rejection of the talk shops that promise much and deliver little. This approach circles back to *mode one* in the sense that we expect governance processes to lead to improved decision-making—improved social and environmental sustainability. But the tactics around how this gets done are radically altered. *Mode three* speaks truth to power, but it also utilizes power against power. Power is about social mobilization, protest, and resistance, but it is also about emerging economic, political, and cultural resources that are a part of a resurgence in the ways that governance is radically redesigned and reimplemented.

Scholarship on social movements is extensive and is outside the scope of this review chapter, but there is a sense in which political mobilization is a key component of environmental governance. Two papers help to illustrate my point. First, Gobby and colleagues (2022) invert conventional wisdom within the governance literature whereby resistance movements are assumed to eventually evolve into governance processes (i.e., from resistance to governance). In putting forward the argument that resistance is a form of governance, they argue "resistance from communities and social movements in the form of blockades, occupations and other strategies and tactics are powerfully shaping outcomes and processes in Canada . . . these modes of resistance constitute *governance from the ground up*" (Gobby et al. 2022, 2; italics in the original text). Drawing from fifty-seven cases of environmental conflict in Canada, analysis shows the top four most effective forms of resistance are court cases, national and international NGO involvement, shareholder activism and the creation of alternative knowledge. These insights on alternative knowledge systems connect directly to some of the elements of *mode two* governance discussed above, but they are set within a more direct form of resistance rather than cooperative governance arrangements.

In another example, Sovacool and Dunlap (2022, 1) offer an overview of radical approaches to climate protection that include a wide range of tactics. The authors are motivated by the idea that "research needs to examine why and under which conditions transformative change can occur, and which policies, institutional practices, governance structures, and legal regimes can facilitate it." Interestingly, with respect to this paper, in reviewing twenty-six tactics used to protest against large dams (Del Bene, Scheidel, and Temper 2018), including everything from street protests to boycotts, there is nothing in the list of tactics that resembles public participation in environmental governance, as defined in this chapter (mode one or mode two). Instead, the tactics are situated around violent and nonviolent direct action, including strikes and shareholder activism. Similar to Gobby et al. (2022), alternative knowledge creation is an important tactic that includes alternative reports, alternative proposals, and community-based participative research.

While resistance is an important step in transforming longstanding and entrenched economic and environmental governance systems, pathways to something new and more sustainable are not always that clearly articulated. What can a different governance system look like? What should we be trying to achieve through these resistance movements? Some alternative pathways are evident, however, and we can see them in the resurgence movements across North America and within Indigenous communities worldwide. Within Canada, for example, the hashtags #landback and #WetsuwetenStrong represent a movement against fossil fuels and further pipeline infrastructure development on traditional Indigenous territories. They also reflect a broader call for changes in ownership and control of resources and territories. They represent a call for change in how landscapes and resources are governed. In the United States, some authors are calling for national parks to be returned to the tribes, not only in terms of occupation but also in terms of control and management (Treuer 2021; Wolfley 2016). Research is also showing that Indigenous-managed lands in countries such as Brazil, Australia, and Canada have more biodiversity than lands set aside for conservation by state and local governments (Schuster et al. 2019). These studies illustrate a call for change, but also the potential for changes in management and control to translate into more sustainable outcomes.

A final example of resurgence comes from the literature on energy governance. Much like the literature on protected areas management or forest management, there are constant calls for enhanced public participation in the development of new energy systems, including wind and solar. In the case of renewable energy, the concept of community ownership is now a well-established alternative (Brummer 2018). For Indigenous and non-Indigenous communities, the idea of ownership (either through municipally owned corporations or cooperatives or partnerships) is leading to new ways of thinking about participation. Compared to *mode one* and *two*, which are focused on improved dialogue, *mode three* is about a resurgence through equity ownership and community control. We see these developments in the energy sector, but there are also examples in community forestry (Kimengsi and Bhusal

2022). In all cases, notions of environmental governance are expanded well beyond the realm of talk shops and discursive governance to a realm of political action and community mobilization that is quite distinct from other modes of environmental governance.

Inasmuch as these initiatives reflect an important and (sometimes) exciting dimension of public participation, there are real challenges and limits to this emphasis on local ownership and control that are increasingly recognized within the research community. In the forest sector, community forestry is recognized as a key tool for local engagement, yet researchers identify the perpetuation of elite local interests and a lingering lack of devolution from state to community leaders (Ambus and Hoberg 2011). Similarly, within energy social sciences, researchers caution that forms of local ownership, such as co-operatives, may not lead to the kinds of inclusive economic models that one might assume to be the case (MacArthur and Tarhan 2022). These insights reflect a need for caution in terms of how much we can expect to achieve from public participation through these governance modalities.

Conclusion

This chapter reflects on environmental governance through public participation, with attention to three modes of scholarship that continue to be advanced within the published literature. In table 8.1, I summarize these modes with attention to several dimensions of environmental governance that are noted in the sections above. For example, the orientation of *mode two* research is more skeptical and cynical about the value of small-group deliberations, mainly because of the potential for these settings to be manipulated by elite interests. Reflecting on the role of science, *mode one* represents a common view within environmental governance that more scientific information will bring clarity and improve environmental decision-making. This view contrasts sharply with *mode three* understandings of participation where scientific evidence is observed to be secondary (or peripheral) to forms of direct action such as lawsuits or blockades.

In considering all three modes, one can see a continuum of scholarship from *mode one* (where there remains an ongoing focus on tools and methods for improving public deliberations that lead to better outcomes) to mode three (where the focus shifts away from dialogue to direct action). Some

TABLE 8.1. Summary of three modes of research on public participation in environmental governance.

Dimension	Mode one	Mode two	Mode three
Orientation	Optimistic and pragmatic	Skeptical and cynical	Wholesale rejection
Purpose	Improving outcomes	Improving deliberations	Direct action
Relationships	Trusting	Skeptical	Tactical / strategic
Stakeholders	Constituent representation	Values representation	Building a movement
Role of science	Evidence brings solutions	Evidence is contested	Evidence is secondary

readers may quibble with the inclusion of *mode three* as a part of this continuum of public participation because it looks more like social movements than public participation. This is a fair point, but for many community members and stakeholders who are invited to "participate" in environmental governance processes, having a seat at the table is an entirely insufficient basis for influencing environmental outcomes. Influence comes from direct action as well as equity ownership, and in this sense, *mode three* offers a way to influence environmental outcomes through political mobilization, much like the other modes discussed here.

Within each mode of scholarship, there are ongoing challenges and opportunities to advance the field of study, and one key goal of this chapter is to encourage researchers to reflect on the modalities of environmental governance that are central to their research. By doing this, possibilities for advancing theory and methods are enhanced. In *modes one* and *two*, future research can address how to maintain successful participatory processes in the face of increasing political polarization. Research can also explore how to counter the influence of social media, polarization, and disinformation campaigns that threaten to derail constructive dialogue across large differences in knowledge and values. In *mode three*, future research will continue to examine the challenges of transitioning from resistance efforts to post-resistance efforts. At times, these efforts may include new directions, such as community ownership models, but efforts may also include environmental protection or project partnership that reflect deeper connections with local values and priorities. Finally, given the local context and objectives, researchers and practitioners may see examples of *multi-modal approaches* to environment governance, for example where parallel tracks of discursive engagement (*modes one* and *two*) and strategic action (*mode three*) are combined. These areas of research will continue to propel this field of study forward in the decades to come.

References

Ambus, L., and G. Hoberg. 2011. The evolution of devolution: A critical analysis of the community forest agreement in British Columbia. *Society & Natural Resources* 24 (9): 933–50.

Armatas, C. A., W. T. Borrie, and A. E. Watson. 2022. A social science method for public engagement in the context of natural resource planning in the United States. *Society & Natural Resources* 35 (5): 506–26.

Beckley, T. M., J. R. Parkins, and S. R. J. Sheppard. 2006. *Public participation in sustainable forest management: A reference guide*. Edmonton, Alberta: Sustainable Forest Management Network.

Bengston, D. N. 1994. Changing forest values and ecosystem management. *Society & Natural Resources* 7 (6): 515–33.

Brown, G., J. M. Montag, and K. Lyon. 2012. Public participation GIS: A method for identifying ecosystem services. *Society & Natural Resources* 25 (7): 633–51.

Brown, P. 1997. Popular epidemiology revisited. *Current Sociology* 45 (3): 137–56.

Brummer, V. 2018. Community energy–benefits and barriers: A comparative literature review of Community Energy in the UK, Germany and the USA, the benefits it provides for society and the barriers it faces. *Renewable and Sustainable Energy Reviews* 94: 187–96.

Calhoun, C. 1992. Habermas and the public sphere. In *Habermas and the Public Sphere*, ed. C. Calhoun, 1–50. Cambridge, MA: MIT Press.

Carr, D. S., and K. Halvorsen. 2001. An evaluation of three democratic, community-based approaches to citizen participation: Surveys, conversations with community groups, and community dinners. *Society & Natural Resources* 14 (2): 107–26.

Coleman, K., and M. J. Stern. 2018. Exploring the functions of different forms of trust in collaborative natural resource management. *Society & Natural Resources* 31 (1): 21–38.

Cupps, D. S. 1977. Emerging problems of citizen participation. *Public Administration Review* 37 (5): 478–87.

Daniels, S. E., and G. B. Walker. 2001. *Working through environmental policy conflict: The collaborative learning approach*. Westport, CT: Praeger.

Day, J. C. 2017. Effective public participation is fundamental for marine conservation—lessons from a large-scale MPA. *Coastal Management* 45 (6): 470–86.

Del Bene, D., A. Scheidel, and L. Temper. 2018. More dams, more violence? A global analysis on resistances and repression around conflictive dams through co-produced knowledge. *Sustainability Science* 13 (3): 617–33.

Dewey, J. (1927) 2012. *The public and its problems: An essay in political inquiry.* University Park: Pennsylvania State University Press.

Dryzek, J. S. 1990. *Discursive democracy: Politics, policy, and political science.* Cambridge, MA: Cambridge University Press.

Eriksen, C., and D. L. Hankins. 2014. The retention, revival, and subjugation of Indigenous fire knowledge through agency fire fighting in eastern Australia and California. *Society & Natural Resources* 27 (12): 1288–1303.

Fairchild, E., and P. Petrzelka. 2021. The USDA, gender, and race equity: Representation on conservation agency websites and social media. *Society & Natural Resources* 34 (1): 122–32.

Fischer, F. 2000. *Citizens, experts, and the environment: The politics of local knowledge.* Durham, NC: Duke University Press.

Fischer, K., T. Stenius, and S. Holmgren. 2020. Swedish forests in the bioeconomy: Stories from the national forest program. *Society & Natural Resources* 33 (7): 896–913.

Funtowicz, S. O., and J. R. Ravetz. 1994. Uncertainty, complexity and post-normal science. *Environmental Toxicology and Chemistry: An International Journal* 13 (12): 1881–85.

Gericke, K. L., and J. Sullivan. 1994. Public participation and appeals of Forest Service plans—an empirical examination. *Society & Natural Resources* 7 (2): 125–35.

Gobby, J., Temper, L., Burke, M., and N. von Ellenrieder. 2022. Resistance as governance: Transformative strategies forged on the frontlines of extractivism in Canada. *The Extractive Industries and Society* 9: 100919.

Habermas, J. (1962) 1991. *The structural transformation of the public sphere: An inquiry into a category of bourgeois society.* Cambridge, MA: MIT press.

Hamideh, S. 2020. Opportunities and challenges of public participation in post-disaster recovery planning: Lessons from Galveston, TX. *Natural Hazards Review* 21 (4): 05020009.

Hamm, J. A. 2017. Trust, trustworthiness, and motivation in the natural resource management context. *Society & Natural Resources* 30 (8): 919–33.

Jackson, T., and J. Curry. 2004. Peace in the woods: Sustainability and the democratization of land use planning and resource management on crown lands in British Columbia. *International Planning Studies* 9 (1): 27–42.

Kimengsi, J. N., and P. Bhusal. 2022. Community forestry governance: Lessons for Cameroon and Nepal. *Society & Natural Resources* 35 (4): 447–64.

Lauer, F. I., A. L. Metcalf, E. C. Metcalf, and J. J. Mohr. 2018. Public engagement in social-ecological systems management: An application of social justice theory. *Society & Natural Resources* 31 (1): 4–20.

Lawrence, R. L., and D. A. Deagen. 2001. Choosing public participation methods for natural resources: a context-specific guide. *Society & Natural Resources* 14 (10): 857–72.

Leach, W. D. 2002. Surveying diverse stakeholder groups. *Society & Natural Resources* 15 (7): 641–49.

Lemos, M. C., and A. Agrawal. 2006. Environmental governance. *Annual Review of Environment and Resources* 31: 297–325.

Lewis, M., A. Christianson, and M. Spinks. 2018. Return to flame: Reasons for burning in Lytton First Nation, British Columbia. *Journal of Forestry* 116 (2): 143–50.

Lockie, S. 2007. Deliberation and actor-networks: The "practical" implications of social theory for the assessment of large dams and other interventions. *Society and Natural Resources* 20 (9): 785–99.

MacArthur, J. L., and M. D. Tarhan. 2022. Institutionalizing energy democracy: The promises and pitfalls of electricity cooperative development. In *Routledge handbook of energy democracy*, ed. A. M. Feldpausch-Parker, D. Endres, T. R. Peterson, and S. L. Gomez, 172–86. New York: Routledge.

McCloskey, M. 1996. The skeptics: Collaboration has its limits. *High Country News* 28 (9). https://www.hcn.org/issues/59/1839.

McCool, S. F., and K. Guthrie. 2001. Mapping the dimensions of successful public participation in messy natural resources management situations. *Society & Natural Resources* 14 (4): 309–23.

McFarlane, B. L., and P. C. Boxall. 2000. Forest values and attitudes of the public, environmentalists, professional foresters, and members of public advisory groups in Alberta. *Information Report No. NOR-X-374*, Northern Forestry Centre, Edmonton, AB.

Mezirow, J. 2003. Transformative learning as discourse. *Journal of Transformative Education* 1 (1): 58–63.

Miller, L. F., and S. Nadeau. 2017. Participatory processes for public lands: Do provinces practice what they preach? *Ecology and Society* 22 (2).

Mouffe, C. 1993. *The return of the political*. New York: Verso.

Nenko, A., J. R. Parkins, and M. G. Reed. 2019. Indigenous experiences with public advisory committees in Canadian forest management. *Canadian Journal of Forest Research* 49 (4): 331–38.

Nenko, A., J. R. Parkins, M. G. Reed, and A. J. Sinclair. 2019. Rethinking effective public engagement in sustainable forest governance. *Society & Natural Resources* 32 (12): 1383–98.

O'Faircheallaigh, C. 2010. Public participation and environmental impact assessment: Purposes, implications, and lessons for public policy making. *Environmental Impact Assessment Review* 30 (1): 19–27.

Olsen, C. S., and B. A. Shindler. 2010. Trust, acceptance, and citizen–agency interactions after large fires: Influences on planning processes. *International Journal of
Wildland Fire* 19 (1): 137–47.

Parkins, J. R., T. M. Beckley, L. Comeau, R. C. Stedman, C. L. Rollins, and A.
Kessler. 2017. Can distrust enhance public engagement? Insights from a national
survey on energy issues in Canada. *Society & Natural Resources* 30 (8): 934–48.

Parkins, J. R., and R. E. Mitchell. 2005. Public participation as public debate: A
deliberative turn in natural resource management. *Society & Natural Resources* 18
(6): 529–40.

Poortinga, W., and N. F. Pidgeon. 2003. Exploring the dimensionality of trust in risk
regulation. *Risk Analysis* 23 (5): 961–72.

Ribot, J. C., A. Agrawal, and A. M. Larson. 2006. Recentralizing while decentralizing: How national governments reappropriate forest resources. *World Development* 34 (11): 1864–86.

Rowe, G., and L. J. Frewer. 2000. Public participation methods: A framework for
evaluation. *Science, Technology & Human Values* 25 (1): 3–29.

Sanders, A. R., E. A. Nielsen, and J. Abrams. 2021. Does information and deliberation affect ecosystem service judgments? Evidence from tree plantation expansion in Argentina. *Society & Natural Resources* 34 (11): 1433–48.

Sarewitz, D. 2004. How science makes environmental controversies worse. *Environmental Science & Policy* 7 (5): 385–403.

Schuster, R., R. R. Germain, J. R. Bennett, N. J. Reo, and P. Arcese. 2019. Vertebrate
biodiversity on indigenous-managed lands in Australia, Brazil, and Canada
equals that in protected areas. *Environmental Science & Policy* 101: 1–6.

Shindler, B., and J. Neburka. 1997. Public participation in forest planning. *Journal of
Forestry* 95 (1): 17–19.

Simcock, N. 2016. Procedural justice and the implementation of community wind
energy projects: A case study from South Yorkshire, UK. *Land Use Policy* 59:
467–77.

Sinclair, A. J., and A. P. Diduck. 2017. Reconceptualizing public participation in
environmental assessment as EA civics. *Environmental Impact Assessment Review*
62: 174–82.

Smith, P. D., and M. H. McDonough. 2001. Beyond public participation: Fairness in
natural resource decision making. *Society & Natural Resources* 14 (3): 239–49.

Sovacool, B. K., and A. Dunlap. 2022. Anarchy, war, or revolt? Radical perspectives
for climate protection, insurgency and civil disobedience in a low-carbon era.
Energy Research & Social Science 86: 102416.

Stern, M. J., and T. D. Baird. 2015. Trust ecology and the resilience of natural
resource management institutions. *Ecology and Society* 20 (2).

Taylor, D. E. 2000. The rise of the environmental justice paradigm: Injustice framing and the social construction of environmental discourses. *American Behavioral Scientist* 43 (4): 508–80.

Treuer, D. 2021. Return the national parks to the tribes: The jewels of America's landscape should belong to America's original peoples. *The Atlantic*, April 12. Accessed December 4, 2023. https://www.theatlantic.com/magazine/archive/2021/05/return-the-national-parks-to-the-tribes/618395/.

Walker, C., and J. Baxter. 2017. Procedural justice in Canadian wind energy development: A comparison of community-based and technocratic siting processes. *Energy Research & Social Science* 29: 160–69.

Warren, M. E., ed. 1999. *Democracy and trust.* Cambridge, UK: Cambridge University Press.

Watson, R. B., and D. D. Muraoka. 1992. The northern spotted owl controversy. *Society & Natural Resources* 5 (1): 85–90.

Webler, S. T. T. 1999. Voices from the forest: What participants expect of a public participation process. *Society & Natural Resources* 12 (5): 437–53.

Wolfley, J. 2016. Reclaiming a presence in ancestral lands: The return of Native peoples to the national parks. *Natural Resources Journal* 56: 55–80.

Wondolleck, J. M., and S. L. Yaffee, 2000. *Making collaboration work: Lessons from innovation in natural resource management.* Washington, D.C.: Island Press.

9

Social Learning in Participatory Natural Resource Management

Examining the Roles of Power and Positionality

CHRISTOPHER JADALLAH, ELIZA OLDACH,
AND ABRAHAM MILLER-RUSHING

Participatory approaches to natural resource management are pinned on the promise of promoting social learning across diverse actors to improve social-ecological outcomes. However, the role of power and positionality in these social-learning processes is underexplored by managers and researchers, leaving the field largely ignorant of who benefits and who is burdened by decisions made with social learning as their basis. This chapter calls for greater attention to power and positionality in social learning, with implications for how we structure natural resource management processes that support more just and sustainable social-ecological futures.

Introduction

Power dynamics between actors—from scientists to resource managers to community members—play a critical role in shaping nearly all aspects of participatory natural resource management (NRM), an approach to management in which multiple groups participate in collaborative planning and

https://doi.org/10.7330/9781646426300.c009

decision-making processes. Scholars generally agree that participatory NRM can result in greater social and ecological benefits in part because of the underlying process of social learning, whereby diverse actors share ideas and develop new understandings (Fernández-Giménez et al. 2019). But while social learning is increasingly recognized as key to NRM (Gerlak et al. 2018), we see an unmet need to interrogate the roles of power and positionality in this process. Power and positionality—which may be shaped by various factors within diverse social-ecological contexts—influence the trajectory of social-learning processes, and ultimately, who benefits from their outcomes. In this commentary, we urge NRM researchers and practitioners to more explicitly attend to the influence of power and positionality on social learning in participatory NRM.

Power, Positionality, and NRM

Researchers in numerous fields relevant to NRM have grappled with defining and operationalizing power, resulting in distinct yet interrelated definitions of this complex construct (Epstein et al. 2014; Raik, Wilson, and Decker 2008). Some of these researchers, building in particular on studies in the Global South, have pushed for more reflexive and critical analyses of power (Agrawal and Gibson 1999; Kashwan, MacLean, and García-López 2019). Here, we draw from multiple theoretical perspectives in conceptualizing power as the socially structured ability to influence others and institutions. Power-as-influence can be seen in many ways: how individuals are positioned in relation to one another; how statuses are maintained or disrupted; and who has access to particular spaces, actions, and resources—which are themselves imbued with power (Holland and Leander, 2004). Extending beyond an *agent-centered view* that focuses on power solely as individually exercised, we simultaneously take a *structural view* of power that accounts for broader social forces that may shape its emergence (Raik, Wilson, and Decker 2008).

The concept of positionality helps us work from this understanding of power as being rooted in broader social forces. Positionality can be understood as the way that individuals' and groups' standpoints—rooted in their shared histories and social locations—shape their perspectives and influence (Collins 1997; Harding 1992). By recognizing positionality, we see power as partly conferred *structurally* by forces such as authority, resources, and legitimacy (Purdy 2012) that inform individuals' and groups' positionality, while simultaneously being negotiated by *agents* via moment-to-moment interactions between individuals. Ultimately, this brings us to a realist position (Raik, Wilson, and Decker 2008), in which we contend that interactions do not exist in isolation from the ways power has been enacted across time and space (Foucault 1980). In this way, broader systems of privilege and oppression operating along national, racial, gendered, classed, linguistic, and other lines manifest in individuals' positionalities, thus structuring interactions between individuals in participatory NRM and often constraining participation of marginalized groups.

Social Learning and NRM

Social learning can be defined as the process through which diverse individuals develop new understandings and simultaneously co-create shared knowledge through participation in multi-actor initiatives (Reed et al. 2010). Social learning happens at both the individual and group level through interactions between people and their social contexts (Jadallah and Ballard 2021), and in NRM, can help achieve positive social and ecological outcomes as it allows different experiences and knowledges to become the basis for joint decisions (Cundill and Rodela 2012). Individuals can learn regardless of their role—from government official to resource user—and social learning can influence NRM outcomes through many routes, including shaping management decisions, improving trust, opening pathways to previously overlooked evidence and expertise, and changing the behavior of people with the ability to influence resource conditions (Reed et al. 2010). Given that those involved in participatory NRM often come from diverse positionalities, questions remain as to what degree, and in what ways, power mediates their interactions and resultant social learning processes.

Early Evidence of the Importance of Power and Positionality in Social Learning

There is an urgent need for research in which scholars critically interrogate the roles of power and positionality in social learning. In reviewing many studies of social learning, Suškevičs, Hahn, and Rodela (2019) argue that power imbalances hinder learning—though they note that this contextual factor has been under-explored. In examining literature in this field, we find many case studies that point to the importance of power and positionality in social learning and participatory NRM, but few that are designed to investigate these constructs explicitly. Instead, observations around the role of power in learning are mostly indirect. Furthermore, in their meta-analysis on social learning literature, Gerlak et al. (2018) found that clear theories of power were missing. We concur. Though scholars have developed frameworks for exploring power-laden dynamics of NRM (e.g., Purdy 2012) or how learning happens in NRM spaces (e.g., Gerlak and Heikkila 2011), we find no frameworks that clearly link these two concepts.

Nevertheless, these case studies offer implicit insights and drive further questions about power and learning. Some suggest that power imbalances, left unaddressed, negatively influence learning in participatory NRM. Siddiki, Jangmin, and Leach (2017) find that diversity among stakeholders' affiliations hampers social learning, which they attribute in part to "possibly raising the specter of tangible political threats that elicit defensive cognitive and relational postures" (2017, 871). Ballard and Belsky (2010) investigated learning between harvesters of non-timber forest products and land managers in the Pacific Northwest, USA. They find that power imbalances due to "politics and differing socio-economic values and interests . . . may impede efforts at institutional change and reorganization" (2010, 615). Sometimes, rhetoric of social learning may be used to reinforce power imbalances and maintain the status quo, as in cases that reveal the pitfalls of "integrating" Indigenous ways of knowing in Western environmental management (Nadasdy 1999).

Other cases suggest the possibility of designing NRM processes to improve learning even when power imbalances are present. Barnaud and Van Paassen (2013), working in national park management in northern Thailand, critique the idea of a "neutral" facilitator in social learning contexts, instead suggesting that facilitation processes should be reflexive and transparent about assumptions and biases. Turner et al. (2020) similarly describe from their research on collaborative freshwater management in New Zealand how facilitating critical reflection allows participants to identify power imbalances. Identifying these imbalances helped the whole group to prevent powerful subgroups, whose knowledge was initially seen as more credible, from dominating the learning process. Balazs and Lubell

(2014), studying water management in the San Joaquin Valley of California argue that social learning is itself a mechanism for increasing the power of marginalized groups because it can drive broader structural changes to water management.

The Need for Future Research and Application

Examining the links between power and social learning processes can help us attend to critical questions that advance both theory and practice. For instance, how does the distribution of authority, resources, and legitimacy across actors (Purdy 2012) influence who learns, what is learned, and how learning occurs? How do sources of power figure into the collective settings in which learning processes occur, and how does this mediate the outcomes of said learning processes? What methods are effective at disrupting power asymmetries to maximize trust, equitable engagement, and social learning? When is a specter of social learning used to conceal a commitment to maintaining the status quo (Nadasdy 1999)? The answers to these questions are required to improve the processes and outcomes of participatory management, particularly as more institutions adopt participatory NRM approaches (Fernández-Giménez et al. 2019).

In terms of research, fruitful lessons may be found in other fields where the critical study of learning is more fully developed, such as in education (Esmonde and Booker 2017). Educational researchers have turned careful attention to the dynamics of learning given power imbalances, for example, in using micro-ethnographic methods to trace how students gain undue influence in group discussions based on perceived merit, intellectual authority, access to the conversational floor, and spatial privilege (Engle et al. 2014). These approaches may be transferable to research on social learning in NRM; for example, they could clarify why some ideas are taken up and others rejected depending on the social positions of the people who initially raise them during a participatory process.

In terms of practice, lessons can be found in cases of participatory NRM that foreground active reflection and adaptation around power. For example, McGreavy et al. (2021) reflexively examine collaborations between Indigenous and settler groups around the Penobscot River in Maine to offer critical praxis for disrupting uneven power relations associated with colonialism in NRM. Such cases offer practical advice for reshaping power distribution during the collaborative process, for example, by working toward reciprocity and iterative dialogue, recognizing the multiplicity of time, and actively centering Indigenous ways of knowing (McGreavy et al. 2021). Such adjustments could be taken up across various contexts, creating spaces for social learning even against the charged backdrops where participatory NRM takes place.

Integrating the study of power, positionality, and learning in participatory NRM can coalesce currently scattered insights and help inform how we design participatory processes to disrupt power asymmetries and create opportunities for more equitable engagement. Otherwise, even NRM approaches that are participatory in name will continue to experience and reinforce persistent inequities in who is represented, who speaks and who is heard, and what identities, practices, and epistemologies matter. Decisions made in these settings may then result in uneven, inequitable implications as to who benefits and who bears the costs. This portends negative consequences for social and ecological outcomes—and, further, bars us from imagining other possible futures. Even in this commentary, our own academic and government positions limit our imaginations and lead us to call for tweaks to existing research and practice. Radical rethinking of our social, environmental, and learning relationships is needed to address ongoing power imbalances (e.g., in North American settler colonialism; Whyte, 2018). We see attention to power as a starting point for more transformative change. Attending to power in the design, implementation, and evaluation of participatory NRM approaches can ultimately foster social learning that helps cultivate social and ecological flourishing while moving us toward these futures.

Acknowledgments

We would like to thank Hailey Wilmer, as well as two anonymous reviewers, for helpful comments on earlier versions of this manuscript. The findings and conclusions presented in this chapter are those of the authors and do not necessarily reflect those of the US Government or the US Department of the Interior.

References

Agrawal, A., and C. C. Gibson. 1999. Enchantment and disenchantment: The role of community in natural resource conservation. *World Development* 27 (4): 629–49. https://doi.org/10.1016/S0305-750X(98)00161-2.

Balazs, C. L., and M. Lubell. 2014. Social learning in an environmental justice context: A case study of integrated regional water management. *Water Policy* 16 (S2): 97–120. https://doi.org/10.2166/wp.2014.101.

Ballard, H. L., and J. M. Belsky. 2010. Participatory action research and environmental learning: Implications for resilient forests and communities. *Environmental Education Research* 16 (5–6): 611–27. https://doi.org/10.1080/13504622.2010.505440.

Barnaud, C., and A. Van Paassen. 2013. Equity, power games, and legitimacy. *Ecology and Society* 13. http://dx.doi.org/10.5751/ES-05459-180221.

Collins, P. H. 1997. Comment on Hekman's "Truth and method: Feminist standpoint theory tevisited": Where's the power? *Signs* 22 (2): 375–81.

Cundill, G., and R. Rodela. 2012. A review of assertions about the processes and outcomes of social learning in natural resource management. *Journal of Environmental Management* 113: 7–14. https://doi.org/10.1016/j.jenvman.2012.08.021.

Engle, R. A., J. M. Langer-Osuna, and M. McKinney de Royston. 2014. Toward a model of influence in persuasive discussions: Negotiating quality, authority, privilege, and access within a student-led argument. *Journal of the Learning Sciences* 23 (2): 245–68. https://doi.org/10.1080/10508406.2014.883979.

Epstein, G., A. Bennett, R. Gruby, L. Acton, and M. Nenadovic. 2014. Studying power with the social-ecological system framework. In *Understanding society and natural resources*, ed. M. J. Manfredo, J. J. Vaske, A. Rechkemmer, and E. A. Duke. Dordrecht, Netherlands: Springer. https://doi.org/10.1007/978-94-017-8959-2.

Esmonde, I., and A. N. Booker. 2017. Toward critical and sociocultural theories of learning. In *Power and privilege in the learning sciences: Critical and sociocultural theories of learning*, ed. I. Esmonde and A. N. Booker. New York: Routledge.

Fernández-Giménez, M. E., D. J. Augustine, L. M. Porensky, H. Wilmer, J. D. Derner, D. D. Briske, and M. O. Stewart. 2019. Complexity fosters learning in collaborative adaptive management. *Ecology and Society* 24 (2). https://doi.org/10.5751/ES-10963-240229.

Foucault, M. 1980. *Power/knowledge: Selected interviews and other writings, 1972–1977*, ed. C. Gordon, 1st ed. New York: Pantheon Books.

Gerlak, A. K., and T. Heikkila. 2011. Building a theory of learning in collaboratives: Evidence from the Everglades restoration program. *Journal of Public Administration Research and Theory* 21 (4): 619–44. https://doi.org/10.1093/jopart/muq089.

Gerlak, A. K., T. Heikkila, S. L. Smolinski, D. Huitema, and D. Armitage. 2018. Learning our way out of environmental policy problems: A review of the scholarship. *Policy Sciences* 51 (3): 335–71. https://doi.org/10.1007/s11077-017-9278-0.

Harding, S. 1992. Rethinking standpoint epistemology: What is "strong objectivity"? *The Centennial Review* 36 (3): 437–70.

Holland, D., and K. Leander. 2004. Ethnographic studies of positioning and subjectivity: An introduction. *Ethos* 32: 127–39.

Jadallah, C. C., and H. Ballard. 2021. Social learning in conservation and natural resource management: Taking a sociocultural perspective. *Ecology and Society* 24 (4).

Kashwan, P., L. M. MacLean, and G. A. García-López. 2019. Rethinking power and institutions in the shadows of neoliberalism. *World Development* 120 (August): 133–46. https://doi.org/10.1016/j.worlddev.2018.05.026.

McGreavy, B., D. Ranco, J. Daigle, S. Greenlaw, N. Altvater, T. Quiring, N. Michelle, J. Paul, M. Binette, B. Benson et al. 2021. Science in Indigenous homelands: Addressing power and justice in sustainability science from/with/in the Penobscot River. *Sustainability Science* 16 (3): 937–47.

Nadasdy, P. (1999). The politics of TEK: Power and the "integration" of knowledge. *Arctic Anthropology* 36 (1/2): 1–18.

Purdy, J. M. 2012. A framework for assessing power in collaborative governance processes. *Public Administration Review* 72 (3): 409–17. https://doi.org/10.1111/j.1540-6210.2011.02525.x.

Raik, D. B., A. L. Wilson, and D. J. Decker. 2008. Power in natural resources management: An application of theory. *Society and Natural Resources* 21 (8), 729–39.

Reed, M. S., A. C. Evely, G. Cundill, I. Fazey, J. Glass, A. Laing, J. Newig, B. Parrish, C. Prell, C. Raymond et al. 2010. What is social learning? *Ecology and Society* 15 (4): resp 1. https://doi.org/10.5751/ES-03564-1504r01.

Siddiki, S., K. Jangmin, and W. D. Leach. 2017. Diversity, trust, and social learning in collaborative governance. *Public Administration Review* 77 (6): 863–74. https://doi.org/10.1111/puar.12800.

Suškevičs, M., T. Hahn, and R. Rodela. 2019. Process and contextual factors supporting action-oriented learning: A thematic synthesis of empirical literature in natural resource management. *Society & Natural Resources* 32 (7): 731–50. https://doi.org/10.1080/08941920.2019.1569287.

Turner, J. A., W. Allen, C. Fraser, A. Fenemor, A. Horita, T. White, L. Chen, M. Atkinson, and M. Rush. 2020. Navigating institutional challenges: Design to enable community participation in social learning for freshwater planning. *Environmental Management* 65 (3): 288–305. https://doi.org/10.1007/s00267-020-01256-x.

Whyte, K. 2018. Settler colonialism, ecology, and environmental injustice. *Environment and Society* 9 (1): 125–44. https://doi.org/10.3167/ares.2018.090109.

10

Digital Tools for Participatory Environmental Decision-Making

Opportunities, Challenges, and Future Directions

CAITLIN HAFFERTY, IAN BABELON, ROBERT BERRY,
BETH BROCKETT, AND JAMES HOGGETT

Digital technology is continuously transforming participation in research, policy, and practice; however, its effectiveness in delivering meaningful and inclusive outcomes remains uncertain. This chapter examines the use of digital tools for participation in environmental decision-making processes, considering their potentials, challenges, and ethical implications. To promote equitable environmental decision-making in an increasingly digitised world, more informed choices of online, in-person, and hybrid approaches are crucial.

Introduction

Digital technology is continuously transforming participatory approaches in research, policy, and practice. However, there are still many unresolved questions about their effectiveness at addressing the goals of participation. The COVID-19 pandemic has added urgency to the question of whether inclusive, representative, and meaningful participation can be conducted in

https://doi.org/10.7330/9781646426300.c010

online settings. This chapter contributes to debates around the use of digital tools for meeting the principles and criteria of participation in environmental decision-making. We categorise different tools and discuss opportunities for their use in a variety of environmental contexts. Although digital technology can enhance participation, it comes with a particular set of practical and ethical issues, constraints, and barriers. There is no single approach that guarantees successful participation, which is dependent on a variety of contextual factors, design choices, and power relations. We reflect that an informed choice among online, in-person, and hybrid (online and in-person) approaches will help to balance the challenges and opportunities of participatory processes.

Addressing "What Works" in Participation: Rationales, Benefits, and Limitations

Tackling complex environmental issues requires flexible, transparent decision-making processes that incorporate a diversity of knowledges and values. As such, the involvement of public and other stakeholder groups has been increasingly pursued and embedded in research, policy, and practice from local to international scales (Konisky and Bierele 2001; Reed et al. 2018). In this chapter, we define participation after Reed (2008) as a process where groups and individuals can choose to be involved in making decisions that affect them, whether passively (e.g., via information provision) or actively (e.g., via two-way engagement). This terminology is diverse, complex, and fluid throughout the literature, which can be confusing and even contradictory (for example, see Hafferty 2022a, 2022b). We use *participation* as a broad and generic term to increase the accessibility of this chapter for diverse audiences.

A number of rationales and claimed benefits have been identified for participation. Rooted in concepts of deliberative democracy, participatory practices can incorporate diverse knowledge types, lead to better quality decisions, enhance trust and credibility, and help to empower voices that are often marginalised in research and policy decision-making (Dryzek 2002; Fiorino 1989). However, failure to deliver on the benefits of participation continues to create disillusionment amongst practitioners, stakeholders, and members of the public alike (Afzalan and Muller 2018; Cooke and Kothari 2001; Falco and Kleinhans 2018; Reed et al. 2018). This remains a risk for efforts towards participatory environmental decision-making; participation can reinforce unequal power structures, marginalise minority perspectives, increase mistrust, cause delays, amongst other issues and risks (see also Jadallah et al. in chapter 9 of this volume). Central to these debates is the consideration of participant needs and priorities, knowledge prioritisation, fairness and trust, and whose reality "counts" in participatory environmental decision-making processes (e.g., Chambers 2006; Krupa, McCarthy Cunfer, and Clark 2020; Smith and McDonough 2001). The process and outcomes of participation are highly dependent on the context (including societal structures and institutional "fit"), process design, management of power dynamics, and scalar fit (Baker and Chapin 2018; Reed et al. 2018). Drawing from interdisciplinary research from within and beyond academia, this chapter broadly contributes to debates around "what works" by focusing on the effectiveness of digital tools for meeting the goals of participation. First, we provide a synoptic overview of different digital tools and discuss their utility in different environmental decision-making settings. The critical debates around the practical and ethical challenges are then discussed, reflecting on learnings from the COVID-19 pandemic and highlighting considerations for the future.

A Landscape of Digital Tools for Participation

Different types of participation can lead to different outcomes. To help provide clarification and structure for "what works," typologies have been developed to define different levels, what's involved, the role of (public) actors, and the goals or outcomes. Arnstein's classic *ladder of participation* (1969) defines different "rungs" of citizen participation from low to high levels, which has informed frameworks in both research and practice (e.g., IAP2 2018; Pretty 1995). Although it remains central to debates around participation, Arnstein's ladder has been critiqued for its static, linear, and hierarchical structure (Collins and Ison 2009). Participatory processes are dynamic and vary between different contexts, demographics, and purposes. Other approaches have been developed that further incorporate contextual factors in the design, process, and evaluation of participatory processes (e.g., Bell and Reed 2021). This knowledge can help us to understand how different participatory approaches, methods, and tools are "fit for purpose" (Reed et al. 2018), as well as the role of a variety of societal and institutional factors in shaping the process (Baker and Chapin 2018).

Digital tools are used for a wide range of purposes and at different stages in environmental management and decision-making processes, from problem exploration and scoping to feedback on proposals and project evaluation. Møller and Olafsson (2018) provide a synoptic (heuristic, rather than comprehensive) overview of the landscape of digital tools that can be used for participatory environmental decision-making. Importantly, this framework acknowledges a distinction between digital and online/web-based tools. Online means that a technology is used on a computer, tablet or phone that is connected to the internet. Digital can be considered as a format or process, including technology that uses, stores, and processes data or information in the form of digital signals (i.e., digital can be either online or offline). Digital tools for engagement can also be synchronous (taking place in real time) and asynchronous (conducted remotely and at different times). A selection of the tools is displayed in figure 10.1 and discussed in more depth in the following sections. More broadly (but related), there is much we can learn from the array of digital tools that are used for participation in planning and development, healthcare, and technological innovation (e.g., Rawat and Yusuf 2019; Wilson and Tewdwr-Jones 2021). In particular, recent literature highlights the value of "digital ecologies" for participation that consider that the selection and use of tools can be flexibly aligned to the context and purpose, rather than strict prescriptions (Kleinhans, Falco, and Babelon 2021). Additionally, the vast number of typologies of tools and purposes for participatory decision-making suggests that digital tools are versatile and can be classified in many different ways (see, for example, Babelon 2021). The online global network and crowdfunded repository Participedia[1] provides a more comprehensive view of the range of tools available for community engagement and public participation.

To complement figure 10.1, figure 10.2 illustrates one way of categorising digital tools for participatory environmental decision-making along the project lifecycle. There are a variety of different typologies for participation—more than is possible to cover in this review—the stages shown can also vary by discipline, sector, specialism, ambitions, goals, and so forth. Therefore, we use one example of a categorisation inspired by Møller and Olafsson (2018)

1. https://participedia.net/.

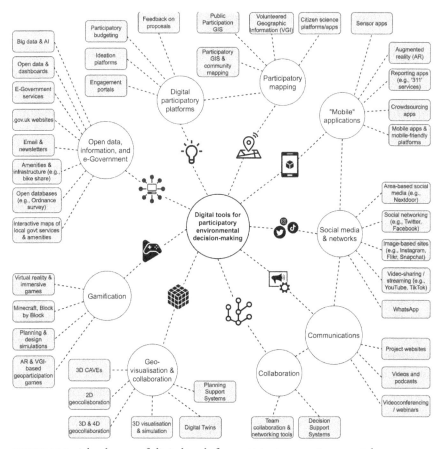

FIGURE 10.1. A landscape of digital tools for participatory environmental decision-making.

(based on Arnstein's ladder, which, despite critiques, remains a widely implemented and recognised typology). Figure 10.2 illustrates how the use of digital tools can be mapped onto different engagement levels or categories, as well as different project stages. Given the breadth of participatory environmental decision-making contexts (e.g., ranging from environmental impact assessment for infrastructure projects to community-led resource management), the suggested project stages are indicative of common stages found in practice and the literature, rather than authoritative (others could include design, implementation, and assessment, and so forth). Additionally, digital

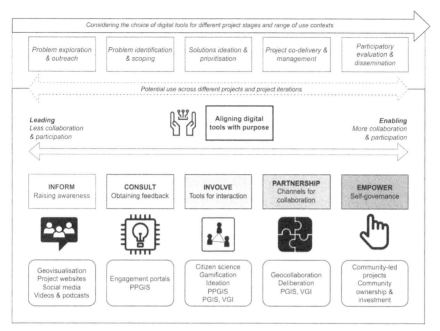

FIGURE 10.2. Aligning the use of digital tools with purpose, including project lifecycle, and intended level of engagement. Inspired by Møller and Olafsson (2018).

tools are becoming increasingly versatile and can therefore be scaled and adapted to many different project stages and use contexts (see for example Babelon 2021).

When referring to figure 10.2, we add an important caveat: the use of different tools should be adapted to the context and purpose in which they are needed. For example, there are many reasons why tools for "partnership and collaboration" might fail to meet desired outcomes, and where tools for information provision and consultation might be more appropriate (e.g., when there is little room for participants to influence a decision). This chapter unpacks some of these complexities.

Communications, Social Media, and Applications

Tools for networking, communications, and collaboration have transformed the way that people communicate with each other, driving new forms of participatory environmental decision-making (Evans-Cowley and Hollander, 2010). Social media, videos, podcasts, and videoconferencing platforms can be useful tools for sharing knowledge, reaching large audiences, and facilitating more transparent and open ways of engaging (e.g., Chivers et al. 2021; Lobe, Morgan, and Hoffman 2020; Sinclair et al. 2017). They have been used by organisations responsible for governance, management, planning, and other environmental decision-making processes to encourage greater levels of public participation. For example, a combination of online tools (including blog posts, Twitter, YouTube, and podcasts) are used by the UK government to communicate information and encourage involvement in farming, agriculture, and conservation issues (DEFRA 2021). Although social media and communications technologies tend to be more suited to one-way sharing of information (see Falco and Kleinhans 2018; Sinclair et al. 2017), they can enable more collaborative and participatory processes. For example, when run by skilled facilitators, videoconferencing platforms (e.g., Zoom and Google Meet) can help meet the goals of participation by promoting more inclusive deliberation, shared learning, and fostering trusting relationships (Marzi 2021; Willis et al. 2023). Reflecting on the effectiveness of online workshops on climate change issues, Willis et al. (2023) conclude that online discussions via Zoom helped create a meaningful and useful process for both researchers and participants by widening opportunities for participation, fostering international collaboration, and reducing travel and carbon emissions. Similarly, Marzi (2021) used remote participatory video techniques with international participants to meaningfully co-produce research during the pandemic.

Many of these tools can be used and integrated with other technologies to enhance participation and collaboration. For example, social media–generated geographic information (SMGI) is used to support different stages of collaborative planning, environmental management, and governance (e.g., Lin 2022). Hybrid approaches, which use a blend of online and in-person techniques, are often advocated (e.g., Chivers et al. 2021). For example, Boone (2015) finds that a combination of videos, media, and arts helped to empower local communities to make decisions for the planning of a park (see also Lamoureux et al. in chapter 11 of this volume). It's important to remember that meaningful participation can be challenging to achieve in virtual environments (Hall, Gaved, and Sargent 2021), particularly when success is dependent on building trust and rapport and nurturing close collaborations over time. We must pay close attention to the opportunity (or its lack) for building and maintaining close social ties, as well as creating spaces for collaboration and reflection.

Digital Participatory Platforms, Participatory Mapping, and Geo-Visualisation

Digital participatory mapping and geographic information systems (GIS) encompasses a wide range of technologies and methodologies. For decades, critical and feminist discourse raised important questions about the value of GIS, including its inadequacy for representing people and places, positivist epistemology, focus on data-driven methods, and its role for top-down power and control (Elwood 2006; Kwan 2002). These critical approaches have become mainstream, with people using mapping and GIS in more diverse and participatory ways than ever before (Pánek 2016; Pavlovskaya 2009).

Enabling different levels of participation, these tools are versatile and can be adapted to a wide range of projects (Billger, Thuvander, and Wästberg 2016; Brown et al. 2017; Møller and Olafsson 2018). The literature differentiates between public participation GIS (PPGIS), participatory GIS (PGIS) and volunteered geographic information (VGI). Different forms of participatory mapping can be effective tools for e-governance (the use of digital devices in the public sector to deliver services, information, and democracy), particularly in environmental policy domains (Rawat and Yusuf, 2019). PPGIS typically consists of map-based surveys; for example, by local authorities to involve residents in decision-making (e.g., Brown, Montag, and Lyon 2012). PGIS, on the other hand, is community-led mapping, which can be supported by researchers (e.g., to provide guidance and technical support). VGI overlaps with PGIS in that it can be led by community members but is typically conducted as a form of "cartographic citizen science" to improve existing spatial data; for example, national geospatial data infrastructure. It is important to note that there is a difference between active and passive VGI; for example, see Haklay (2013). Mapping and GIS tools can also be used to support and enhance comprehensive planning support systems (PSS) for meaningful and effective public participation, promoting transparency and early involvement (Kahila-Tani et al. 2016). Distinguishing participatory mapping as either top-down, bottom-up, and/or scientific in nature is essential in understanding its utility for participatory environmental decision-making in different contexts (Brown, Reed, and Raymond 2020).

Developments in participatory forms of GIS are analogous to the growth of the holistic approach to public participation exemplified by geodesign, which is a process relying on digital geographic methods and tools for integrating analysis, evaluation, design, and public involvement in planning (Haklay, Janowski, and Zwoliński 2018). For example, a number of digital collaborative planning and design technologies are included on the International Geodesign Collaboration website.[2]

Pánek (2016) identifies the origins of community-based mapping in "mental map" sketches and other spatial representations popularised by Kevin Lynch (1960) and successive phases in the democratisation of GIS. These have transformed mapping from an expert-led cartographic practice to one where community participation in land-use planning and management is more possible, with the role of communities changing from being objects of geographical research to decision-makers. Chambers (2006) and others have promoted the involvement of local communities towards more collaborative and co-produced levels of participation. This signifies a shift from maps being traditionally used as tools of power, towards citizen empowerment. Three-dimensional (3D) geocollaboration is a form of geospatial visualisation, map-making and/or modelling that can include a variety of tools such as Google Earth, virtual reality (VR), augmented reality, 3D city models, 4D modelling (i.e., 3D simulation over time), and highly immersive 3D Computational Analytics, Visualisation and Education (CAVE) labs (Billger, Thuvander, and Wästberg 2016; Lovett et al. 2015; Smith, Berry, and Clarke 2019). For example, Smith, Berry, and Clarke (2019) developed and evaluated a 3D "virtual globe" tour (using Google Earth) with local communities for collaborative natural flood management, finding that it was helpful for developing an understanding of the river catchment and issues it faced, as well as demonstrating the potential of different management measures.

Gamification

Gamification is the use of game design elements in a non-game context (i.e., for purposes other than entertainment) such as awarding points, ranks,

2. https://www.igc-geodesign.org/igc-2020-21-projects.

or levels (Galeote et al. 2021). Game-based tools have been used to engage the public and other stakeholders in sustainability education (e.g., climate change), energy reduction, transportation, air quality, waste management, water conservation, placemaking, and sustainable tourism (Galeote et al. 2021). For example, Koroleva and Novak (2020) found that gamification techniques increased the motivation of residents to address complex but otherwise intangible water-related sustainability issues (i.e., issues where effects had not been experienced yet) in their local communities.

Minecraft is one specific game-based tool which has been used to promote engagement in planning, design, and environmental decision-making (e.g., Delaney 2022). It enables players to build creative structures (like buildings, parks, and landscapes) out of coloured blocks and has been employed as an innovative tool for engaging children and young people. For example, de Andrade, Poplin, and de Sena (2020) show how Minecraft can be used to co-create walkable, green, and interactive cities in their study in Tirol Town, Brazil. These approaches have also been applied to more practical settings. For example, as part of UNICEF's national Child Friendly Cities and Communities initiative, Minecraft is being used in Cardiff (Wales, UK) to enable young people to design and share their ideas of how a future city would suit their needs, with a particular focus on preserving and promoting green spaces (Cardiff University 2021).

Practical and Ethical Challenges for Digital Participation

Issues of equity, trust, power, and positionality (amongst others) are inherent to participation, regardless of the (in-person, online, or hybrid) way in which it is conducted. However, the dynamic nature of participatory technologies raises specific questions regarding whether inclusive, equitable, and representative participation can be conducted effectively in online and remote settings. To better understand the practical and ethical issues associated with digital engagement, it is important to develop and apply theoretical frameworks to account for the processes and outcomes involved (Reed et al., 2018). For example, Chewning (2018) identifies the need for new theories of virtual engagement, while Afzalan and Muller (2018) note that theory should aid understanding of what draws participants (and those coordinating engagement) to such tools, what they are used for (and for whose benefit), and how they influence the subsequent knowledge, opinions, and behaviours of participants. Engagement is an inherently social and contextual activity, within which issues of identity, power, legitimacy, social influence, social justice, and social norms play important roles (Fielding et al. 2008; also see Jadallah et al. in chapter 9 of this volume). Theories of virtual engagement must account for such dynamics as well as for those that may be unique to virtual environments, such as online anonymity, online personas, digital accountability and novel issues around data protection, open access, and regulation. Existing theories of engagement should be applied, tested, and developed to further understanding as well as cover the practical and ethical issues discussed in more depth below.

Technical Barriers

There are numerous technical issues that can affect the quality and reliability of digital participatory processes, particularly when those involved are unfamiliar with particular technologies (Hall, Gaved, and Sargent 2021). The risks can include setup and accessibility issues, loss of connection and dropouts, outdated hardware and/or limited functionality, poor video and audio quality, low device battery, background noise, and other disruptions (Afzalan and Muller 2018; Archibald et al. 2019; Hall, Gaved, and Sargent 2021). Although these issues can lead to delays and frustration, they can be overcome by careful planning, including time for participants to familiarise themselves with the technology, and confidence-building through piloting the technology and providing training sessions (Marzi 2021). The shared experience of resolving technical issues may actually help build rapport between participants and facilitators, as well as helping to develop confidence and digital literacy (Archibald et al. 2019).

Equity and Inclusion

Issues relating to inclusivity and equity underpin, and are fundamental to, participation (Reed 2008). On the one hand, the use of digital tools and practices can make participatory processes more inclusive, facilitating engagement across different geographies and organisations (Afzalan and Muller 2018). On the other hand, they can make it more complex and exclusionary as access to and knowledge of technology is not distributed equally across populations (Afzalan and Muller 2018). This can expand the so-called digital divide and (further) marginalise people based on factors such as gender, race, ethnicity, age, disability, education, and income (Panganiban 2019).

Difficulties accessing and utilising the internet can be an exclusionary factor (Hall, Gaved, and Sargent 2021). For example, some communities in remote rural areas experience inconsistent broadband service, which can limit opportunities to engage (Lyon et al. 2020). Digital and spatial literacy can also be a barrier, particularly when tools are unfamiliar and/or require technical knowledge and skills. For example, participatory mapping using GIS can be complex and require high levels of digital, visualisation, and spatial literacy from participants (e.g., Roche 2014). People who are more accustomed to face-to-face engagement may also find it challenging to adapt to a virtual context and learn new skills (Hall, Gaved, and Sargent 2021), which can be improved by online training (Marzi 2021).

Power Relations

Notions of power are inherent to understandings of participation (Reed 2008; Hafferty 2022a). Power relations are complex, fluid, and multi-layered, occurring between different actors and at different stages in participatory processes. Power relations can also play out in different ways in virtual environments compared to face-to-face environments. For example, facilitators may feel a lack of control over online discussions and experience difficulty "reading the room" (e.g., due to reduced visibility of participants, including their body language and facial expressions), which can make it more difficult to ensure everyone has the chance to contribute to discussions, as well as deal with disruptions and technical issues (Hall, Gaved, and Sargent 2021).

Additionally, power differentials can exist between those leading/coordinating the engagement and the participants; for example, children and young people can experience power and environmental change on the ground quite differently from expert researchers (Börner, Kraftl, and Giatti 2021). Digital participation and limits on in-person engagement (particularly during the COVID-19 pandemic) have reinforced the importance of reconsidering roles, expectations, and relationships in participatory research contexts (Börner, Kraftl, and Giatti 2021; Hafferty 2022b; Marzi 2021). This can help challenge power relations (e.g., between those who are more empowered to contribute to the discussion and those who are less so) and help flatten traditional hierarchies between the research team (or other engagement coordinators) and participants.

Trust and Rapport

One key consideration for digital participation processes is the extent to which remote, online environments are effective at creating in-depth dialogue, developing close trusting relationships, and promoting collaboration (Hall, Gaved, and Sargent 2021). Afzalan and Muller (2018) provide empirical evidence that participatory technologies can effectively help build consensus in communities by cultivating trust, fostering social bonds and collective action at the local level in spatial planning. Others have reflected on the challenges of virtual engagement for fostering a sense of trust (Börner, Kraftl, and Giatti 2021); for example, the limited opportunities for spontaneous and informal conversations that are essential for relationship building (Hall, Gaved, and Sargent 2021). However, close bonds can be developed and maintained when engaging online in some situations (e.g., when relationships have already been established); for example, through regular online meetings (Marzi 2021).

The use of open data (data which can be used freely without restrictions) and free and open-source software (accessible online digital platforms or systems) can help build trust with participants by improving the accessibility and reproducibility of decision-making processes. When platforms are made free and accessible online, open data and tools can help promote the transparency and accountability of decisions and the institutions making them (Falco and Kleinhans 2018). Open data can also have important implications for power dynamics regarding who has access and control of the decision-making process and outcomes.

Privacy, Ethics, and Well-Being

Digital forms of participation are also subject to privacy and security issues, which can limit their effectiveness (Lobe, Morgan, and Hoffman 2020). Awareness of these issues has increased in recent years, driven by instances of privacy breaches on private databases and social media platforms, surveillance and tracking, and concerns over the storage and use of data (Le Blanc 2020). Key considerations include ensuring confidentiality and protecting the anonymity of participants (particularly when using community-generated data); bias and inaccurate information (e.g., increased risk of misunderstandings and distortion); data ownership, safe storage, and control over data sharing (e.g., when data are controlled by a third party with different privacy policies; Afzalan and Muller 2018; Hall, Gaved, and Sargent 2021; Lobe, Morgan, and Hoffman 2020). The ethics of digital and data-driven technologies are increasingly pertinent, with key issues for the ethical impact and implications of algorithmic decision-making, artificial intelligence, geospatial tools, and location data (Tsamados et al. 2021).

Digital tools can also blur the lines between public and private spaces, particularly when using videoconferencing and other audio-visual tools to engage with participants in their homes. As Marzi (2021) reflects, special attention needs to be paid to ethical issues that can arise when using digital participatory approaches with women participants, particularly with regards to blurring the lines between public and private spaces. Potential risks include participants disclosing private information (e.g., about themselves or others in their private spaces), excluding people who are unable to participate from home, or even risking their safety (e.g., if particular spaces have the potential to be harmful to participants). Digital well-being and safety is often considered alongside privacy and security risks with the aim of protecting both physical and psychological health (including the risk of digital fatigue and negative impacts on mental health, particularly when in-person interaction is limited), as well as awareness of the environmental impacts of digital technologies and their use (e.g., see Le Blanc 2020). As suggested by Willis et al. (2023), online participation can be beneficial for academics (and practitioners) who aim to reduce the environmental impact of their research.

Institutionalising Digital Participation

The use of digital tools for participatory decision-making by institutions needs to be part of an institutional strategy for undertaking best-practice engagement if such tools are to ultimately help to deliver sustainable decisions (Akhmouch and Clavreul 2016; Baker and Chapin 2018; Hafferty 2022a, 2022b).

For example, institutionalising participatory and deliberative democracy was highlighted as a key goal for the Scottish government in the UK (Scottish Government 2022), with knowledge gaps highlighted regarding the opportunities and constraints for public sector officials working to embed participatory practices (Escobar 2021). Undertaking such an organisational cultural shift is not a simple task (Pallett and Chilvers 2015); any work to initiate and embed such a shift needs to be taken with good understanding of the range of existing reasons for engagement, along with current practices, assumptions, expertise, capacity, capability, and organisational barriers. The temptation to embrace an "all singing and all dancing" digital participation software package as the solution to participation needs without such a strategy runs the risk of unintended negative outcomes, as with any poorly reasoned, designed, and/or delivered engagement process (e.g., see Hafferty 2022b).

Amongst other risks, organisational capacity and capability (both human and digital) need to be explicitly considered. As we have shown in this chapter, digital participatory tools are complex and have multiple, interrelated, and context-dependent challenges and opportunities. Organisations may lack the technical and human capacity to address and manage inherent risks, data analysis requirements, privacy and security issues, and other sociotechnical challenges that underpin the use of digital tools (Afzalan and Muller 2018).

Future Directions and Conclusion

The literature reveals numerous factors that can influence the effectiveness of using digital tools for public and stakeholder participation in research, policy, and practice. Following an overview of digital tools for participation, this chapter explores some of the practical and ethical debates for participatory environmental decision-making scenarios. It is important to understand how the use of digital tools and technologies shape the balance of these challenges and opportunities—identifying and mitigating these can help to ensure that participatory processes will achieve their intended goals. Systematic and comparative evaluations of engagement processes, as well as embedding the resulting learning as part of institutional strategies, are essential parts of this improvement.

This review highlights the importance of understanding the purpose and context within which participatory technology is deployed. While digital participation can be rewarding and meaningful for public participants, researchers, and decision-makers alike, it is clear that there is no one-size-fits-all digital tool or approach that guarantees successful participation in all situations. Those undertaking participatory processes need to carefully consider this complexity and optimise their approach based on participants' needs and priorities (Reed et al. 2018), as well as institutional fit (Baker and Chapin 2018; Hafferty 2022b). By paying attention to this, we can help tackle participation inequalities and work to include the voices of people who hold less power in society, are disproportionately impacted by decisions, and risk being marginalised in environmental decision-making processes.

Looking to the future, we must apply these lessons to make more informed choices of online, in-person, and hybrid approaches within frameworks of evidence-led best practice. This is essential if participation in environmental decision-making is to become more fair, accessible, and inclusive, delivering outcomes that are fit-for-purpose, sustainable, and resilient. Writing this during a global pandemic and following the UN Climate Change Conference in Glasgow (COP26), we reflect that more evidence is needed regarding the effectiveness of participatory technologies for helping us to recover and rebuild in times of simultaneous environmental and societal crisis, disruption, and change.

References

Afzalan, N., and B. Muller. 2018. Online participatory technologies: Opportunities and challenges for enriching participatory planning. *Journal of the American Planning Association* 84 (2): 162–77. https://doi.org/10.1080/01944363.2018.1434010.

Akhmouch, A., and D. Clavreul. 2016. Stakeholder engagement for inclusive water governance: "Practicing what we preach" with the OECD Water Governance Initiative. *Water (Switzerland)* 8 (5): 1–17. https://doi.org/10.3390/w8050204.

Archibald, M. M., R. C. Ambagtsheer, M. G. Casey, and M. Lawless. 2019. Using Zoom videoconferencing for qualitative data collection: Perceptions and experiences of researchers and participants. *International Journal of Qualitative Methods* 18: 1609406919874596.

Arnstein, S. R. 1969. A ladder of citizen participation. *Journal of the American Institute of Planners* 35 (4): 216–24.

Babelon, I., 2021. Digital participatory platforms in urban planning. PhD thesis, University of Northumbria.

Baker, S., and F. S. Chapin. 2018. Going beyond "it depends": the role of context in shaping participation in natural resource management. *Ecology and Society* 23 (1). https://doi.org/10.5751/ES-09868-230120.

Bell, K., and M. Reed. 2021. The tree of participation: A new model for inclusive decision-making. *Community Development Journal*. https://doi.org/10.1093/cdj/bsab018.

Billger, M., L. Thuvander, and B. S. Wästberg. 2016. In search of visualization challenges: The development and implementation of visualization tools for supporting dialogue in urban planning processes. *Environment and Planning B: Urban Analytics and City Science* 44 (6): 1012–35. https://doi.org/10.1177/0265813516657341.

Boone, K. 2015. Disembodied voices, embodied places: Mobile technology, enabling discourse, and interpreting place. *Landscape and Urban Planning* 142: 235–42. https://doi.org/10.1016/j.landurbplan.2015.07.005.

Börner, S., P. Kraftl, and L. L. Giatti. 2021. Blurring the "-ism" in youth climate crisis activism: Everyday agency and practices of marginalized youth in the Brazilian urban periphery. *Children's Geographies* 19 (3): 275–83. https://doi.org/10.1080/14733285.2020.1818057.

Brown, G., K. Kangas, A. Juutinen, and A. Tolvanen. 2017. Identifying environmental and natural resource management conflict potential using participatory mapping. *Society and Natural Resources* 30 (12): 1458–75. https://doi.org/10.1080/08941920.2017.1347977.

Brown, G., J. M. Montag, and K. Lyon. 2012. Public participation GIS: A method for identifying ecosystem services. *Society and Natural Resources* 25 (7): 633–51. https://doi.org/10.1080/08941920.2011.621511.

Brown, G., P. Reed, and C. M. Raymond. 2020. Mapping place values: 10 lessons from two decades of public participation GIS empirical research. *Applied Geography* 116: 102156. https://doi.org/10.1016/j.apgeog.2020.102156.

Cardiff University. 2021. Innovative Minecraft competition for young people to influence Cardiff redesign. *Cardiff University News*, January 21. Accessed May 12, 2023. https://www.cardiff.ac.uk/news/view/2490664-innovative-minecraft-competition-for-young-people-to-influence-cardiff-redesign.

Chambers, R. 2006. Participatory mapping and geographic information systems: Whose map? Who is empowered and who disempowered? Who gains and who loses? *Electronic Journal of Information Systems in Developing Countries* 25 (1): 1–11. https://doi.org/10.1002/j.1681-4835.2006.tb00163.x.

Chewning, L. V. 2018. Virtual engagement a theoretical framework of affordances, networks. In *The handbook of communication engagement*. Wiley-Blackwell.

Chivers, C. A., K. Bliss, A. de Boon, L. Lishman, J. Schillings, R. Smith, and D. C. Rose. 2021. Videos and podcasts for delivering agricultural extension: achieving credibility, relevance, legitimacy and accessibility. *The Journal of Agricultural Education and Extension* 1–25. https://doi.org/10.1080/1389224X.2021.1997771.

Collins, K., and R. Ison. 2009. Jumping off Arnstein's ladder: Social learning as a new policy paradigm for climate change adaptation. *Environmental Policy and Governance* 19 (6): 358–73.

Cooke, B., and U. Kothari, eds. 2001. *Participation: The new tyranny?* London: Zed Books.

de Andrade, B., A. Poplin, and Í. S. de Sena. 2020. Minecraft as a tool for engaging children in urban planning: A case study in Tirol Town, Brazil. *ISPRS International Journal of Geo-Information* 9 (3). https://doi.org/10.3390/ijgi9030170.

DEFRA (Department for Environment, Food and Rural Affairs). 2021. Future farming blog. Accessed March 22, 2022. https://defrafarming.blog.gov.uk/.

Delaney, J. 2022. Minecraft and playful public participation in urban design. *Urban Planning* 7 (2): 330–42. https://doi.org/10.17645/up.v7i2.5229.

Dryzek, J. S. 2002. *Deliberative democracy and beyond: Liberals, critics, contestations.* Oxford, UK: Oxford University Press.

Elwood, S. 2006. Critical issues in participatory GIS: Deconstructions, reconstructions, and new research directions. *Transactions in GIS* 10 (5): 693–708.

Escobar, O. 2021. Between radical aspirations and pragmatic challenges: Institutionalizing participatory governance in Scotland. *Critical Policy Studies* 1–16. https://doi.org/10.1080/19460171.2021.1993290.

Evans-Cowley, J., and J. Hollander. 2010. The new generation of public participation: Internet-based participation tools. *Planning Practice and Research* 25 (3): 397–408. https://doi.org/10.1080/02697459.2010.503432.

Falco, E., and R. Kleinhans. 2018. Beyond technology: Identifying local government challenges for using digital platforms for citizen engagement. *International Journal of Information Management* 40: 17–20. https://doi.org/10.1016/j.ijinfomgt.2018.01.007.

Fielding, K. S., D. J. Terry, B. M. Masser, and M. A. Hogg. 2008. Integrating social identity theory and the theory of planned behaviour to explain decisions to engage in sustainable agricultural practices. *British Journal of Social Psychology* 47 (1): 23–48. https://doi.org/10.1348/014466607X206792.

Fiorino, D. 1989. Environmental risk and democratic process: A critical review. *Columbia Journal of Environmental Law* 14 (2): 501–47. https://doi.org/10.7916/cjel.v14i2.5781.

Galeote, D. F., M. Rajanen, D. Rajanen, N.-Z. Legaki, and J. Hamari. 2021. Gamification for climate change engagement: Review of corpus and future agenda. *Environmental Research Letters* 16 (6). https://doi.org/10.1088/1748-9326/abec05.

Hafferty, C. 2022a. Embedding an evidence-led, best-practice culture of engagement: Learning from the evidence. Natural England Research Report NEER021.

Hafferty, C. 2022b. Engagement in the digital age: Practitioners' perspectives on the challenges and opportunities for planning and environmental decision-making. PhD thesis, University of Gloucestershire. doi:10.46289/MM76Y4T8.

Haklay, M. 2013. Citizen science and volunteered geographic information: Overview and typology of participation. In *Crowdsourcing geographic knowledge*, ed. D. Sui, S. Elwood, and M. Goodchild, 105–22. Dordrecht, Netherlands: Springer.

Haklay, M., P. Jankowski, and Z. Zwoliński. 2018. Selected modern methods and tools for public participation in urban planning: A review. *Quaestiones Geographicae* 37 (3): 127–49. https://doi.org/10.2478/quageo-2018-0030.

Hall, J., M. Gaved, and J. Sargent. 2021. Participatory research approaches in times of Covid-19: A narrative literature review. *International Journal of Qualitative Methods* 20: 1–15. https://doi.org/10.1177/16094069211010087.

IAP2 (International Association for Public Participation). 2018. Spectrum of public participation. Accessed February 2, 2022. https://cdn.ymaws.com/www.iap2 .org/resource/resmgr/pillars/Spectrum_8.5x11_Print.pdf.

Kahila-Tani, M., A. Broberg, M. Kyttä, and T. Tyger. 2016. Let the citizens map: Public participation GIS as a planning support system in the Helsinki master plan process. *Planning Practice and Research* 31 (2): 195–214. https://doi.org/10 .1080/02697459.2015.1104203.

Kleinhans, R., E. Falco, and I. Babelon. 2021. Conditions for networked co-production through digital participatory platforms in urban planning. *European Planning Studies* 1–20. https://doi.org/10.1080/09654313.2021.1998387.

Konisky, D. M., and T. C. Beierle. 2001. Innovations in public participation and environmental decision making: Examples from the Great Lakes regions. *Society and Natural Resources* 14 (9): 815–26. https://doi.org/10.1080/089419201753210620.

Koroleva, K., and J. Novak. 2020. How to engage with sustainability issues we rarely experience? A gamification model for collective awareness platforms in water-related sustainability. *Sustainability (Switzerland)* 12 (2). https://doi.org/10 .3390/su12020712.

Krupa, M. B., M. McCarthy Cunfer, and S. J. Clark. 2020. Who's winning the public process? How to use public documents to assess the equity, efficiency, and effectiveness of stakeholder engagement. *Society and Natural Resources* 33 (5): 612–33. https://doi.org/10.1080/08941920.2019.1665763.

Kwan, M. P. 2002. Feminist visualization: Re-envisioning GIS as a method in feminist geographic research. *Annals of the American Association of Geographers* 92 (4): 645–61. https://doi.org/10.1111/1467-8306.00309.

Le Blanc, D. 2020. E-participation: A quick overview of recent qualitative trends. *DESA Working Paper*, (163), United Nations: Department of Economic and Social Affairs. Accessed March 22, 2022. https://www.un.org/development/desa/ CONTENTS.

Lin, Y. 2022. Social media for collaborative planning: A typology of support functions and challenges. *Cities* 125: 103641.

Lobe, B., D. Morgan, and K. A. Hoffman. 2020. Qualitative data collection in an era of social distancing. *International Journal of Qualitative Methods* 19: 1–8. https://doi.org/10.1177/1609406920937875.

Lovett, A., K. Appleton, B. Warren-Kretzschmar, and C. Von Haaren. 2015. Using 3D visualization methods in landscape planning: An evaluation of options and practical issues. *Landscape and Urban Planning* 142: 85–94. https://doi.org/10.1016/j.landurbplan.2015.02.021.

Lynch, K. 1960. The image of the environment. *The Image of the City*, 1–13. Cambridge, MA: MIT Press.

Lyon, J., P. Hurley, J. Hall, J. Tsouvalis, D. C. Rose, and R. Little. 2020. Inclusive design of post-Brexit agri-environmental policy: Identifying and engaging the "harder to reach" stakeholders: A quick scoping review. Accessed February 20, 2022. https://doi.org/10.15131/shef.data.12506582.

Marzi, S. 2021. Participatory video from a distance: Co-producing knowledge during the COVID-19 pandemic using smartphones. *Qualitative Research*. https://doi.org/10.1177/14687941211038171.

Møller, M. S., and A. S. Olafsson. 2018. The use of e-tools to engage citizens in urban green infrastructure governance: Where do we stand and where are we going? *Sustainability (Switzerland)* 10 (10). https://doi.org/10.3390/su10103513.

Pallett, H., and J. Chilvers. 2015. Organizations in the making: Learning and intervening at the science-policy interface. *Progress in Human Geography* 39 (2): 146–66. https://doi.org/10.1177/0309132513518831.

Pánek, J. 2016. From mental maps to geoparticipation. *Cartographic Journal* 53 (4): 300–07. https://doi.org/10.1080/00087041.2016.1243862.

Panganiban, G. G. F. 2019. E-governance in agriculture: Digital tools enabling Filipino farmers. *Journal of Asian Public Policy* 12 (1): 51–70.

Pavlovskaya, M. 2009. Non-quantitative GIS. In *Qualitative GIS: A mixed methods approach*, ed. S. Elwood and M. Cope, 13–37. Los Angeles, CA: SAGE.

Pretty, J. N. 1995. Participatory learning for sustainable agriculture. *World Development* 23 (8): 1247–63.

Rawat, P., and J.-E. (Wie) Yusuf. 2019. Participatory mapping, e-participation, and e-governance. In *Leveraging digital innovation for governance, public administration and citizen services*, ed. N. V. Mali, 147–75. IGI Global. https://doi.org/10.4018/978-1-5225-5412-7.ch007.

Reed, M. S. 2008. Stakeholder participation for environmental management: A literature review. *Biological Conservation* 141 (10): 2417–31. https://doi.org/10.1016/j.biocon.2008.07.014.

Reed, M. S., S. Vella, E. Challies, J. de Vente, L. Frewer, D. Hohenwallner-Ries, T. Huber, R. K. Neumann, E. A. Oughton, J. S. del Cino, et al. 2018. A theory of participation: What makes stakeholder and public engagement in environmental

management work? *Restoration Ecology* 26 (1): 7–17. https://doi.org/10.1111/rec
.12541.

Roche, S. 2014. Geographic information science I: Why does a smart city need to
be spatially enabled? *Progress in Human Geography* 38 (5): 703–11. https://doi.org
/10.1177/0309132513517365.

Scottish Government. 2022. Report of the Institutionalising Participatory and
Deliberative Democracy Working Group. Accessed July 27, 2022. https://
www.gov.scot/publications/report-institutionalising-participatory-deliberative
-democracy-working-group/.

Sinclair, A. J., T. J. Peirson-Smith, and M. Boerchers. 2017. Environmental assessments in the Internet age: The role of e-governance and social media in creating
platforms for meaningful participation. *Impact Assessment and Project Appraisal* 35
(2): 148–57.

Smith, K., R. Berry, and L. E. Clarke. 2019. Exploring the potential of Google Earth
as a communication and engagement tool in collaborative natural flood management planning. *Geographical Journal* 186 (2): 1–15. https://doi.org/10.1111
/geoj.12323.

Smith, P. D., and M. H. McDonough. 2001. Beyond public participation: Fairness
in natural resource decision making. *Society and Natural Resources* 14 (3): 239–49.
https://doi.org/10.1080/08941920120140.

Tsamados, A., N. Aggarwal, J. Cowls, J. Morley, H. Roberts, M. Taddeo, and L.
Floridi. 2021. The ethics of algorithms: Key problems and solutions. *Ethics, Governance, and Policies in Artificial Intelligence* 144: 97–123.

Willis, R., A. Yuille, P. Bryant, D. McLaren, and N. Markusson. 2023. Taking deliberative research online: Lessons from four case studies. *Qualitative Research* 23 (4):
921–39. https://doi.org/10.1177/14687941211063483.

Wilson, A., and M. Tewdwr-Jones. 2021. *Digital participatory planning*. New York:
Routledge. https://doi.org/10.4324/9781003190639.

11

Image- and Arts-Based Methods in Natural Resource and Environmental Social Science

Scoping the Domain for Methods That Empower

BRYANNE LAMOUREUX, MELANIE ZURBA, YAN CHEN,
DURDANA ISLAM, AND KATE SHERREN

Image- and arts-based methods are increasingly employed in natural resource and environmental social science research and show great potential to support research processes that facilitate empowerment and equity. This chapter provides a typology of image- and arts-based methods applied in natural resource and environmental social sciences and offers a conceptual model to illustrate how this typology interacts with visual culture. We find that methods where visual data are collectively created with the direct involvement of participants have the greatest potential to produce equity and empowerment outcomes for participants through the research process.

Introduction

Natural resource and environmental social science (NRESS) is practiced by scholars originally trained in a range of disciplines, including sociology, anthropology, and human geography. Like the fields that comprise it, in recent years NRESS has taken a visual turn, looking past text to leverage the

https://doi.org/10.7330/9781646426300.c011

increasing prominence of images and image-making in everyday lives (e.g., Calcagni et al. 2019; Swanson and Ardoin 2021). An example of this is the increasing use of social media images as a source of data for understanding human-environment interactions (Sherren et al. 2017). Images and visual arts (e.g., drawing, painting, photography) present significant research opportunities as well as interpretive challenges. Such work is increasing in amount and diversity in the NRESS literature (e.g., O'Neill and Graham 2016; Muhr 2020; Bentz et al. 2022), in part as an effective means to understand and engage with communities in research (Zurba and Berkes 2014; Rivera Lopez, Wickson, and Hausner 2018). To date, however, such methods have been poorly conceptualized as a domain.

As a subset of such methods, participatory image and arts-based methods can provide new insights about the social aspects of environmental and natural resource challenges, and center and enhance community voices. Such approaches can facilitate informed policymaking, at times by including the policymakers themselves in research and knowledge dissemination processes (e.g., Ranger et al. 2016; Evans-Agnew and Eberhardt 2019). In addition, image and arts-based methods have shown great potential to support research processes that emphasize learning, knowledge co-production, empowerment, and enhancing equity for marginalized groups and/or communities.

For the purposes of this chapter, we define empowerment as a dynamic process that includes thought and action whereby an individual or group can exercise and strengthen their ability to gain control over their life, their community, and their society (Mur 2006). This process of empowerment can lead to more equitable outcomes for individuals and/or groups of people faced with inequities. Equity, which is often used synonymously with fairness and justice, has several dimensions, including the distribution of costs and responsibilities; procedures for decision-making and participation; recognition of distinct histories, values, interests, and knowledge systems; and the influence of context on distribution, procedures, and recognition (Friedman et al. 2018, 3). Research that aims to enhance equity and empower participants should first identify, then aim to reduce (and when possible, eliminate) barriers experienced at both the individual and collective level to provide increased opportunity and capacity for participation in research processes (Morales and Harris 2014; Krupa, Cunfer, and Clark 2019). The process of empowerment provides a pathway by which barriers to equity can be addressed. It is important to note that meaningful participation is needed for empowerment to lead to significant changes in power relations, and that participation itself is an outcome of empowerment (Pettit 2012; Coy et al. 2021).

In this chapter, we seek to answer the following research questions:

1. What image- and arts-based methods are being applied in natural resource and environmental social science research?
2. To what extent do these methods differ in their ability to produce equity and empowerment outcomes?

To establish answers to these questions, we performed a scoping review of the peer reviewed NRESS research literature. We use the results to develop a living typology of the image- and arts-based methods utilized in the field and propose a conceptual model of how they relate to visual culture and its recursiveness. We then review which methods result in empowerment and equity outcomes, and how they relate to our typology.

Methods

We began by searching abstracts from ISSRM conference presentations and papers published in *Society and Natural Resources* (*SNR*) from 2010 to 2020 to identify examples of visual methods utilized in the field. This timeframe was selected in accordance with the purpose of the book to provide a decadal review of the field. This preliminary search allowed us to build an early version of the framework presented in the results section, which assisted in guiding our scoping review. The main scoping review was completed using Arksey and O'Malley's (2005) five-stage framework. This was guided by the two research questions stated in our introduction. The first question guided the scope of the net that was cast while we completed the search, while the second question guided our additional article selection criteria and approach to coding and charting the data.

The databases Agricola, DOAJ, Environment Complete, GreenFILE, JSTOR, ProQuest Central, Scopus, and Web of Science were selected for the scoping review. Search strings consisted of combined keywords related to (i) the field of natural resources; (ii) the relevant themes of equity, empowerment, engagement, and participation; and (iii) visual methods, consisting of both general visual terms (e.g., photo, video, etc.) and specific visual methods identified during the preliminary search (e.g., visual discourse analysis). To address the limited search string space in certain databases, arts-based and image-based terms were rotated through the search string:

["*Visual methods term*"] AND ("natural resource*" OR "environmental resource" OR nature OR environment* OR landscape*) AND ([equit* OR empower* OR diversity] AND [engag* OR participat* OR accessib*])

Articles from these searches were limited to peer-reviewed journal articles and were selected if they addressed NRESS research topics, utilized arts-and/or image-based methods, included attention to equity and engagement issues, and were published between 2010 and 2021. Selected articles also required a sufficiently detailed methods section to clearly understand whether visual data were present in the research process and how they were applied. Articles were not limited to a specific geographic region, however only articles available in English were considered. Articles that could not be accessed through digital downloads were excluded. Since a different chapter in this volume focuses on digital participatory methods (see Hafferty et al. in chapter 10 of this volume), we chose to exclude digital visual methods covered there (e.g., participatory GIS). A total of seventy-two articles were identified and used in our first analysis. We used QSR's NVivo 12 to code information on the types of visual methods applied, the sources of the visual data, and participant interactions during research processes. Visual methods were then organized into categories.

To answer our second research question, we further vetted our sample of seventy-two articles and identified fifty-four articles that explicitly discussed themes of empowerment and equity in relation to the visual methods applied in the research process. We then selected one to two articles per method for a total of seventeen articles to assess evidence of empowerment and equity outcomes in more detail. Articles were selected from each method with the purpose of representing a diversity of geographies, participants, and research topics. The selected articles include research conducted in all continents except Antarctica, and represent participants from various age groups, cultures, and geographies. We then used QSR's NVivo 12 to code for several features including research paradigms (based on Patel [2015]), research design, justifications for the chosen research method(s), and outcomes and limitations related to empowerment and equity.

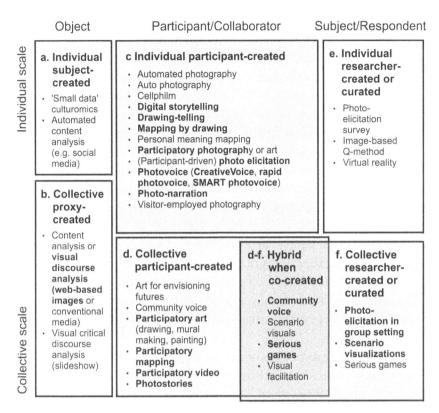

FIGURE 11.1. Typology of visual methods organized based on the role of the target population in the research method (x-axis) and the scale at which data were collected (y-axis). Bolded methods are those represented in the seventeen articles included in our analysis of empowerment and equity outcomes below.

Results

Typology of Visual Methods

We developed a typology of visual methods found in the seventy-two articles in our scoping review (figure 11.1). The x-axis of figure 11.1 is the source of the data relative to the research target population (research objects, participants/collaborators, or subjects/respondents), while the y-axis represents the scale of interest in terms of experiences, preferences, or discourses (individual or collective). The names of methods in the framework are based on those used in the selected articles. These visual methods were often combined with other data-collection methods, mostly to collect qualitative data.

Individual subject-created methods (type a) are those where images are sourced from individual engagement online. Such images and their accompanying captions are important proxies for lifestyles, landscape perceptions, environmental behaviors, and the influence of norms and public discourses. Such methods are increasingly automated using AI but, when manually coded, tend to be sampled and/or filtered "small" rather than Big Data (e.g., Chen et al. 2021). The photo platform Flickr was the most commonly utilized source for social media photos for studying landscape perceptions and human-nature interactions (e.g., Rossi et al. 2020), while Panoramio (photos) and YouTube (video) were also present. The collective proxy-created methods (type b) include a range of explorations of extant images in everyday media such as magazines, advertisements, television/movies, and websites, all of which serve as proxies for a given culture or subculture and its norms. For instance, Bal and Sharik (2019) applied content-analysis to website images to understand demographic participation in professions and activities related to natural resources.

Individual participant-created methods (type c) were the most common in our sample (approximately half of the seventy-two articles) and cover a range of methods. Research of this type is largely phenomenological and asks participants to capture images or other forms of visual data that serve as the basis of interviews or other individual elicitations. Oftentimes, these data are taken a step further and are utilized in a workshop or a community event to work toward a collective vision, plan, and/or action. For example, using drawing-telling, Hensler, Merçon, and Vilsmaier (2021) asked participants to draw their own individual utopias to elicit personal values of nature before bringing everyone together for the creation of a collective vision of a utopia. These were then the basis of the creation of a strategic plan for collective action. In another case, participants were asked to create art based on prompts that were offered by researchers (Zurba and Friesen 2014).

Collective participant-created methods (type d) are collaborative undertakings such as arts-based methods, participatory video, and participatory mapping that often lead to the creation of a collective visual representation (e.g., posters, documentary, community map). With these methods, art or other visuals are used as a boundary object—an object that facilitates communication between different social worlds (Star and Griesemer 1989)—to promote collective and collaborative work that takes place across social divides. For example, Rathwell and Armitage (2016) co-facilitated workshops to help create a collaborative mural with youth, artists, and Inuit Elders with the purpose of bridging knowledge about social-ecological change, planning and future visioning (e.g., Pereira et al. 2019).

Researcher-created or curated methods (type e) utilize visuals that have been created by the researchers for the purpose of stimulating conversations and eliciting feedback. At the individual level, this can involve using photos in an interview to stimulate conversation (photo-elicitation), providing photos for participants to rank, sort, or rate (Q-method), or using virtual reality to convey information and elicit responses from participants, as was done by Fauville et al. (2021) on the topic of ocean acidification. At the collective level (type f), participants interact with these curated visuals in a collaborative space. These visuals can be used to stimulate discussions (photo-elicitation), as well as to convey information to participants, leading to conversation and exploration (scenario visuals, serious games). Photo-elicitation can take place on either level, depending on whether conversations are elicited individually (e.g., via interviews) or collectively (e.g., via group discussion). In one example of the latter, Mikhailovich, Pamphilon, and Chambers (2015) used flashcards with subsistence farmers in Papua New Guinea to elicit storytelling about their experiences in agriculture.

Visual and art-based methods are a complex conceptual space that has not previously been codified. Such methods include primary and secondary datasets, acquired directly or indirectly, actively or passively, synchronously or asynchronously. The people we are interested in understanding through such work may be treated as participants, collaborators, subjects, or respondents or, indeed, their output treated as objects of study. Figure 11.2 presents a conceptual model of the dynamic relationships among the different types of methods (labeled a to f) presented in our typology (figure 11.1), and their links to visual culture. The dotted arrows (a, b) represent the indirect or passive research about populations of interest—individual or organizational—about whom researchers extract data from visual datasets such as social media, conventional media, or institutional websites that capture visuals of desired behaviors. Those individuals or collectives contribute material to visual culture, and are recursively influenced by it, as a by-product of their day-to-day

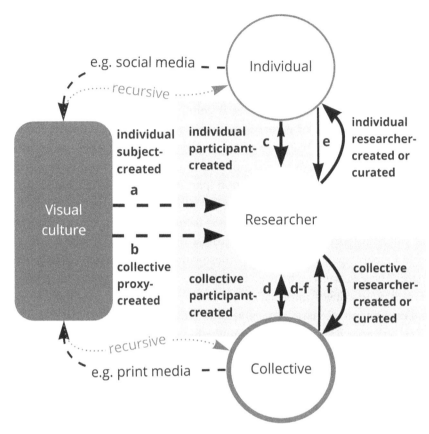

FIGURE 11.2. Conceptual model illustrating the relationships between the typology of visual and arts-based methods, actors, and visual culture.

activities and independent of researcher engagement. The solid arrows represent researcher-driven methods that require direct, active engagement. This includes visualizations requested by the researcher but contributed voluntarily by individuals or groups (c, d), typically synchronously and often in an iterative manner. In others, it is the researcher who creates or curates the visuals (sometimes drawing on visual culture) that are presented to individuals or groups of respondents, whether asynchronously through a survey (e) or more synchronously and collaboratively in a participatory workshop setting (f). Hybrid examples exist where materials are co-created (d-f); indeed, there are many innovative mixes of these archetypes in evidence. Figure 11.2

represents our attempt to visualize visual and arts-based methods in relation to actors and visual culture.

Visual Methods and Implications of Equity and Empowerment

As noted above, fifty-four of the seventy-two articles included content on the role of visual methods in achieving equity and empowerment outcomes. A subset of seventeen articles were selected to represent examples of each of the methods and how they were linked to equity and empowerment outcomes (which are bolded in figure 11.1). Of the seventeen articles, six represented methods in type c, four articles represented methods in type d, two represented methods in type d-f, one in type f, and one in type b. Two additional articles applied methods in both c and d, while one article applied methods in types c and f. No articles from types a and e in our larger sample of articles included discussion of equity and empowerment outcomes. In this section we focus specifically on the subset of seventeen articles.

Most of the studies described in the selected articles were approached from a constructivist research paradigm, though the pragmatist and critical paradigms are also represented. Theoretical perspectives varied, with examples such as ecofeminism and theory of change, and authors utilized a variety of concepts and frameworks from philosophy, geography, gender studies, community development, and Indigenous research. A majority of the selected articles utilized methodologies identified by the authors as participatory, while some also used community-based and/or action research to describe their research approach. Not all articles explicitly stated their research paradigms, theoretical perspectives, and methodologies.

Most commonly, visual methods were utilized to facilitate communication and understanding of complex information among participants, between participants and researchers, and with other stakeholders. They also provided participants an opportunity to share their experiences and express complex issues without the barriers of language and facilitated the creation of collective understandings between participants. Another justification for the use of visual methods was their ability to increase participant engagement in the research process as well as the larger research topic at hand—this was particularly important for youth engagement. A common explanation for choosing specific visual methods was related to cultural context.

Visual methods were commonly utilized to enhance and complement other methods, as they were often accompanied by qualitative data collection methods such as interviews, surveys, participant observations, focus groups, and participant and researcher reflections. Some of these methods directly supported the collection of visual data; for example, a transect walk was done to capture pictures for a photovoice process (Berbés-Blazquez 2012). Visual methods, particularly art-based ones, were often completed with other visual and/or performing arts–based activities (e.g., songwriting in Sonn, Quayle, and Kasat 2015).

Equity and empowerment considerations were also clearly present in the research designs used in these seventeen studies. A focus on building trusting relationships with potential participants before the data collection process began was common. Researchers collaborated with communities, organizations, and participants in designing the research, and cultural and local knowledge were generally considered in the research design. Data collection was often iterative, adaptable, and focused on building skill and knowledge, and data analysis often actively included participants. Building trust and capacity, and considerations of power relations, were present throughout the research processes.

Equity and Empowerment Outcomes

Guided by the definitions of equity and empowerment above, we coded the seventeen articles to identify specific examples of equity and empowerment outcomes experienced by participants as a result of using visual methods in the research process. These outcomes were organized into seven main themes (table 11.1). Since equity and empowerment are intertwined, we do not differentiate between the two in the table but rather give an overview of these outcomes and how they relate to our typology.

These are arguably all desirable outcomes; however, authors also mentioned limitations and challenges related to the use of visual methods to achieve equity and empowerment outcomes. First, equity and empowerment outcomes are generally dependent on participants' engagement in the research process—this means those who are not (or cannot) participate are left out of many of the outcomes in table 11.1. The visual methods themselves do not necessarily remove existing barriers for participating in the

TABLE 11.1. Outcomes of research using visual methods related to equity and empowerment, with links to the typology. The letters in the final column refer to the lettered categories in figure 11.1 and figure 11.2.

Equity and Empowerment Outcomes	Sub-Categories	Description of Outcomes	Link to Typology
Empower participants to engage and actively participate		Participation in the research process, the community at large, and in local government.	c, d, d–f
Empower participants to take action and create change	Tangible change	Creating measurable change (policy changes; decisions made by local organizations)	c, d
	Plan(s) to take action	Strategic planning using participant knowledge and experiences to take (collective) action.	c, d
Facilitate communication and opportunities to be heard	Communicate across boundaries	Communicating across individuals of varying perspectives, across cultures, and to decision-makers.	c, d, f
	Capture diverse interests	Capturing and communicating a variety of interests and perspectives more equitably.	c, d, f, d–f
Shift in power dynamics		Reduction of power imbalances between participant-researcher, participant-stakeholder, and participant-participant.	c, d, f
Empowerment of self		Participants experience a sense of ownership over the research, increased self-confidence, self-reliance, efficacy, agency, and recognized the validity of their own experiences.	c, d
Building capacity	Individual capacity	Participants learn new skills and understand and respond to complex issues.	c, d, f,
	Community capacity	Create understanding at a collective level, an opportunity to build trusting relationships, and a community of practice.	c, d, f, d–f
	Beyond the community	Participants share their learned skills, knowledge, and experiences beyond the community.	c, d
Create a path for increased equity and empowerment		Improves understanding of equity concerns to help plan for increased equity and empowerment.	b

research process. Second, once participants are engaged in the research process, navigating existing power dynamics among participants and between participants and researchers is still a challenge. Third, these methods do not guarantee engagement beyond the research itself, nor can they guarantee that plans to take (collective) action are implemented or that concrete changes (e.g., policy reforms) will occur. Though visual and arts-based methods provide opportunity to advance various equity and empowerment outcomes, they are not immune to existing power relations and barriers in the research context.

Discussion

Image- and Arts-Based Methods in NRESS

Our scoping review demonstrates that a variety of visual methods are being applied in the field of NRESS. The visual methods of photo-elicitation and particularly photovoice were the most common types represented in the articles that met our search criteria. Since these methods have been used for several decades, they have potentially driven the popularity of individual participant-created methods in the field. The well-established method of photovoice is becoming more flexible and being modified to better suit the needs of participants. This is seen in the development and use of rapid photovoice, which addresses financial and time barriers experienced by participants (Mikhailovich, Pamphilon, and Chambers 2015); CreativeVoice, which provides the option for visual expression in art forms beyond photography (Lopez, Wickson, and Hausner 2018), and SMART photovoice, which adds the SMART criteria[1] to the photovoice process (Gervais and Rivard 2013). These modifications were designed to better suit the cultural norms and address barriers present in certain research contexts and have resulted in additional space and opportunities for equity and empowerment outcomes.

More recently, researchers are utilizing a wider variety of visual methods, and new and creative ways to employ art, photos, and other visuals are emerging. Visual research modes can effectively and flexibly bridge cultures, languages, and knowledge systems (Leung 2022; Rathwell and Armitage 2016). As these approaches have increased in number and diversity, the lack

---

1. SMART criteria: "Socio-cultural context informs the procedures; Making participants' priorities the central focus of the consultation question; Analysis process includes women's analysis; Results disseminated by women through participatory exhibition; and Timeframe adapted to participants' schedule drives the logistical process" (Gervais and Rivard 2013, 499).

of a coherent way to categorize them—and a common set of vocabulary for discussing them—has become increasingly problematic.

The typology and conceptualization offered here should help develop the domain by reducing the diffuseness of the literature and facilitating structured literature review and methods instruction. There are important differences depending on both the scale at which visual data are collected and the relationship of participants to the research team. Our framework should also improve the discoverability of specific methods and understanding of the landscape of visual and arts-based methods. Individual methods have characteristics based on the family (i.e., category) to which it belongs, and methodological and design choices have implications for the type of data that will result and outcomes for the participants involved in the research process.

Looking on the horizon, culturomics—the study of human culture through the quantitative analysis of large bodies of digital data (Jarić et al. 2020)—and other uses of social media data will continue to evolve quickly in NRESS research. While some of the methods are passive and thus don't empower *per se*, even these can reveal more diverse perspectives than those represented by people who typically volunteer for research or engagement activities. What is critical is to reflect on who is present and who is absent on the platforms being used and make sure such methods do not replace active engagement but complement it (Sherren et al. 2017). Automated processing approaches such as machine learning present particular concerns in the way that workflows can privilege certain identities over others (Mashhadi et al. 2021).

Equity and Empowerment Outcomes

Our examination of recent publications suggests that certain visual methods more frequently lead to equity and empowerment outcomes than others. Visual methods where participants are directly involved in the creation of the visuals (types c and d) are represented in all equity and empowerment outcomes except one. This indicates an important connection between the inclusion of participants in the creation of visual data and the ability of visual methods to contribute to equity and empowerment. This is similar to Swanson and Ardoin's (2021) findings that visual participatory methods applied in conservation provide an opportunity to build trusting relationships, provide a way to communicate across ways of knowing, lead to the inclusion of a wider diversity of perspectives, and can result in concrete policy change or other actions leading to change.

As noted in table 11.1, all four types of visual methods where data are created or collected at the collective level (types b, d, d-f, and f) can lead to equity and empowerment outcomes. However, papers in our sample that utilize visuals at the individual scale did not report methods where equity and empowerment outcomes were produced unless participants were directly involved in the creation of the visuals (type c), such as in Lopez, Wickson, and Hausner (2018). Though based on a small number of papers, this could indicate that collective-level visuals, even when researcher-created/curated or proxy-created, play a particularly important role in providing opportunities for equity and empowerment outcomes for participants in research processes. As power inequities exist in relation to others in the broader social, governance, economic, and cultural context (Friedman et al. 2018), collective-level interactions facilitated through visuals may provide a way for these power relations to be navigated by supporting and negotiating collective perspectives.

In our sample, only one article from type b (collective proxy–created) included discussion on equity and empowerment outcomes. In this article, website images were analyzed alongside textual data to understand current equity concerns and utilize that information to create a pathway forward to increase equity and empowerment (Lebel et al., 2019). It is the only article included that did not directly involve participants. This example shows that outcomes related to equity and empowerment are still possible when not interacting directly with participants. This is particularly important considering the recent pandemic and ongoing circumstances where face-to-face visual participatory methods are not always possible.

In addition to the selection of specific visual methods, overarching research designs can also affect equity and empowerment outcomes. Participatory action research seeks to transform social inequalities and contribute to a more just and equitable world (Brinton Lykes, and Hershberg 2012), and meaningful participation is needed for empowerment (Pettit 2012; Coy et al. 2021). The fact that many studies in our sample took a participatory approach likely assisted in the creation of equity and empowerment outcomes. Equity and empowerment outcomes are not unique to visual methods; outcomes listed in table 11.1 may also occur through other research methods. Equally important to consider is, as emphasized by Jadallah et al. in chapter 9, participation itself is not enough to address inequities. Nevertheless, similar to Metze (2020), we contend that the visuals themselves encourage individuals to participate, and that the most interactive visual methods (types c and d in particular) offer exciting pathways to enhance equity and empowerment outcomes for participants, particularly when additional contextual dynamics (e.g., power) inform the research design.

Researchers hold a responsibility to shift the power dynamics that have long occurred in research and support research processes that aim for empowerment and enhancing equity for marginalized groups and / or communities. Though equity and empowerment for all participants in a research process cannot be guaranteed, visual methods provide researchers in NRESS with an effective tool to increase these outcomes for participants.

Conclusions, Limitations, and Future Directions

A wide variety of visual and arts-based methods have been deployed in NRESS over the past decade, and this subfield is overdue for categorization. We present a typology, vocabulary, and conceptual model that recognizes distinctions based on the scale of the method (individual or collective), the involvement of target populations in the visuals being used compared to the researcher(s), and the relationship to visual culture. This typology provides some structure but is flexible enough to accommodate new innovations in this growing area.

Our review suggests that not all visual methods lead to equity and empowerment in the same way; methods which directly engage participants in the creation of the visuals result in a wide variety of equity and empowerment outcomes; methods where the research with the visual takes place at the collective scale can also contribute to equity and empowerment outcomes, but to a lesser extent. We conclude that visual methods, particularly those that actively involve participants in the creation of visuals, provide a pathway for producing equity and empowerment outcomes in NRESS research. Visual methods offer an alternative and engaging way of communicating information between participants and researchers, and as a result, provide researchers in the field of NRESS with a wider scope of tools to fulfill their research objectives. When they are combined with appropriate research design and prioritize the voices of participants, visual methods can strengthen empowerment and equity on the ground and provide a pathway for research to lead to meaningful change.

The typology and vocabulary presented here capture and conceptualize the diversity of visual and arts-based methods deployed in NRESS over the past decade, but this will be a "living typology" that will be mutable over time. Additionally, our scoping review captured many types of visual research that have been used in the NRESS literature over the last decade (through the lens of IASNR) but was not designed to provide an exhaustive list. For example, we excluded methods like participatory GIS that could also lead to equity and empowerment outcomes. We also rely on the methodological vocabulary used by article authors to classify visual methods; a closer review of whether the names of these methods are being used consistently would be useful, particularly for methods such as photo-elicitation and photovoice, which can overlap depending on how they are applied. Our search was limited to peer-reviewed articles published over ten years and did not capture non-academic contributions to the field and peer-reviewed sources published outside of this timeline. Expanding the scope of the review could provide additional insights into the typology of visual methods and links of such methods to outcomes of equity and empowerment in NRESS research.

Future research should explore how visual methods interact with other key dimensions of the research design, and how these facilitate or restrict equity and empowerment outcomes, particularly as automated analytical approaches improve for the social sciences. There is also room for additional research on how visuals can be utilized in the dissemination process (e.g., Leung 2022) and how this affects equity and empowerment.

References

Arksey, H., and L. O'Malley. 2005. Scoping studies: Towards a methodological framework.
International Journal of Social Research Methodology 8 (1): 19–32. https://doi-org.ezproxy.library.dal.ca/10.1080/1364557032000119616.
Bal, T. L., and T. L. Sharik. 2019. Image content analysis of US natural resources-related professional society websites with respect to gender and racial/ethnic diversity. *Journal of Forestry* 117 (4): 360–64. doi:10.1093/jofore/fvz023.
Bentz, J., L. do Carmo, N. Schafenacker, J. Schirok, and S. Dal Corso. 2022. Creative, embodied practices, and the potentialities for sustainability transformations.

Sustainability Science 17: 687–99. https://doi-org.ezproxy.library.dal.ca/10.1007/s11625-021-01000-2.

Berbés-Blázquez, M. 2012. A participatory assessment of ecosystem services and human wellbeing in rural Costa Rica using photo-voice. *Environmental Management* 49: 862–75. doi 10.1007/s00267-012-9822-9.

Brinton Lykes, M., and R. M. Hershberg. 2012. Participatory action research and feminisms: Social inequalities and transformative praxis. In *Handbook of feminist research: Theory and praxis*, ed. S. N. Hesse-Bieber, 331–67. Sage. https://dx.doi.org/10.4135/9781483384740.

Calcagni, F., A. T. A. Maia, J. J. T. Connolly, and J. Langemeyer. 2019. Digital co-construction of relational values: Understanding the role of social media for sustainability. *Sustainability Science* 14: 1309–21. https://doi.org/10.1007/s11625-019-00672-1.

Chen, Y., K. Sherren, M. Smit, and K. Young Lee. 2021. Using social media images as data in social science research. *New Media & Society*. https://doi-org.ezproxy.library.dal.ca/10.1177/14614448211038761.

Coy, D., S. Malekpour, A. K. Saeri, and R. Dargaville. 2021. Rethinking community empowerment in the energy transformation: A critical review of the definitions, drivers and outcomes. *Energy Research & Social Science* 72: 1–13. https://doi.org/10.1016/j.erss.2020.101871.

Evans-Agnew, R. A., and C. Eberhardt. 2019. Uniting action research and citizen science: Examining the opportunities for mutual benefit between two movements through a woodsmoke photovoice study. *Action Research* 17 (3): 357–77. https://doi.org/10.1177/1476750318798909.

Fauville, G., A. C. M. Quieroz, L. Hambrick, B. A. Brown, and J. N. Bailenson. 2021. Participatory research on using virtual reality to teach ocean acidification: A study in the marine education community. *Environmental Education Research* 27 (2): 254–78. https://doi.org/10.1080/13504622.2020.1803797.

Friedman, R. S., E. A. Law, N. J. Bennett, C. D. Ives, J. P. R. Thorn, and K. A. Wilson. 2018. How just and just how? A systematic review of social equity in conservation research. *Environmental Research Letters* 13: 053001. https://doi.org/10.1088/1748-9326/aabcde.

Gervais, M., and L. Rivard. 2013. "SMART" photovoice agricultural consultation: Increasing Rwandan women farmers' active participation in development. *Development in Practice* 23 (4): 496–510. https://doi.org/10.1080/09614524.2013.790942.

Hensler, L., J. Merçon, and U. Vilsmaier. 2021. Diverse values and a common utopia: Insights from a participatory art-based plural valuation experience in Xalapa, Mexico. *Ecology and Biodiversity Conservation*: 1–19. https://doi.org/10.1525/cse.2021.1234747.

Jarić, I., U. Roll, R. Arlinghaus, J. Belmaker, Y. Chen, V. China, K. Douda, F. Exxl, S. C. Jähnig, J. M. Jeschkem, et al. 2020. Expanding conservation culturomics and iEcology from terrestrial to aquatic realms. *PLoS Biology* 18 (10): e3000935.

Krupa, M. B., M. M. Cunfer, and S. J. Clark. 2019. Who's winning the public process? How to use public documents to assess the equity, efficiency, and effectiveness of stakeholder engagement. *Society & Natural Resources* 33 (5): 612–33. https://doi.org/10.1080/08941920.2019.1665763.

Lebel, L., P. Lebel, K. Manorom, and Z. Yishu. 2019. Gender in development discourses of civil society organisations and Mekong hydropower dams. *Water Alternatives* 12 (1): 192–220. https://www.water-alternatives.org/index.php/alldoc /articles/vol12/v12issue1/486-a12-1-12/file.

Leung, K. Y. 2022. Reflections on doing cross-cultural research through and with visual methods. In *Co-creativity and engaged scholarship*, ed. A. Franklin, 265–97. Cham, Switzerland: Palgrave-Macmillan. https://doi.org/10.1007/978-3-030 -84248-2_9.

Lopez, F. R., F. Wickson, and V. H. Hausner. 2018. Finding creative voice: Applying arts-based research in the context of biodiversity conservation. *Sustainability* 10: 1778. doi:10.3390/su10061778.

Mashhadi, A., S. G. Winder, E. H. Lia, and S. A. Wood. 2021. No walk in the park: The viability and fairness of social media analysis for parks and recreation policy making. *Proceedings of the International AAAI Conference on Web and Social Media (ICWSM 2021)* 15 (1): 409–20. https://doi.org/10.1609/icwsm.v15i1.18071.

Metze, T. 2020. Visualization in environmental policy and planning: A systematic review and research agenda. *Journal of Environmental Policy & Planning* 22 (5): 745–60. https://doi.org/10.1080/1523908X.2020.1798751.

Mikhailovich, K., B. Pamphilon, and C. Chambers. 2015. Participatory visual research with subsistence farmers in Papua New Guinea. *Development in Practice* 25 (7): 997–1010. https://doi.org/10.1080/09614524.2015.1069260.

Morales, M. C., and L. M. Harris. 2014. Using subjectivity and emotion to reconsider participatory natural resource management. *World Development* 64: 703–12. http://dx.doi.org/10.1016/j.worlddev.2014.06.032.

Muhr, M. M. 2020. Beyond words—the potential of arts-based research on human-nature connectedness. *Ecosystems and People* 16 (1): 249–57. https://doi-org .ezproxy.library.dal.ca/10.1080/26395916.2020.1811379.

Mur, M. H. 2006. Empowerment in terms of theoretical perspectives: Exploring a typology of the process and components across disciplines. *Journal of Community Psychology* 34 (5): 523–40. https://doi.org/10.1002/jcop.20113.

O'Neill, S. J., and S. Graham. 2016. (En)visioning place-based adaptation to sea-level rise. *Geography and Environment* 3 (2): e00028. https://doi.org/10.1002/geo2.v3.2.

Patel, S. 2015, July 15. The research paradigm—methodology, epistemology and ontology–explained in simple language. Accessed December 20, 2021. https:// salmapatel.co.uk/academia/the-research-paradigm-methodology-epistemology -and-ontology-explained-in-simple-language/.

Pereira, L., N. Sitas, F. Ravera, A. Jimemez-Aceituno, and A. Merrie. 2019. Building capacities for transformative change towards sustainability: Imagination in inter-governmental science-policy scenario processes. *Elementa Sciences of the Antropho-cene* 7: 35. https://doi.org/10.1525/elementa.374.

Pettit, J. 2012. *Empowerment and participation: Bridging the gap between understanding and practice.* Sussex, UK: Institute of Development Studies.

Ranger, S., J. O. Kenter, R. Bryce, G. Cumming, T. Dapling, E. Lawes, and P. B. Richardson. 2016. Forming shared values in conservation management: An interpretive-deliberative-democratic approach to including community voices. *Ecosystem Services* 21 (B): 344–57. https://doi.org/10.1016/j.ecoser.2016.09.016.

Rathwell, K. J., and D. Armitage. 2016. Art and artistic processes bridge the knowl-edge systems about social-ecological change: An empirical examination with Inuit artists from Nunavut, Canada. *Ecology and Society* 21 (2): 21. http://dx.doi .org/10.5751/ES-08369-210221.

Rivera Lopez, F., F. Wickson, and V. H. Hausner. 2018. Finding CreativeVoice: Applying arts-based research in the context of biodiversity conservation. *Sustain-ability* 10 (6): 1778. https://doi.org/10.3390/su10061778.

Rossi, S. D., A. Barros, C. Walden-Schreiner, and C. Pickering. 2020. Using social media images to assess ecosystem services in a remote protected area in the Argentinean Andes. *Ambio* 49: 1146–60. https://doi.org/10.1007/s13280-019-01268-w.

Sherren, K., J. R. Parkins, M. Smit, M. Holmlund, and Y. Chen. 2017. Digital archives, big data and image-based culturomics for social impact assessment: Opportunities and challenges. *Environmental Impact Assessment Review* 67: 23–30. https://doi.org/10.1016/j.eiar.2017.08.002.

Sonn, C. C., A. F. Quayle, and P. Kasat. 2015. Picturing the wheatbelt: Exploring and expressing place identity through photography. *American Journal of Community Psychology* 55: 89–101. https://doi.org/10.1007/s10464-014-9686-7.

Star, S. L., and J. R. Griesemer. 1989. Institutional ecology, "translations" and boundary objects: Amateurs and professionals in Berkeley's Museum of Verte-brate Zoology. *Social Studies of Science* 19 (3): 387–420. https://www.jstor.org /stable/285080.

Swanson, S. S., and N. M. Ardoin. 2021. Communities behind the lens: A review and critical analysis of visual participatory methods in biodiversity conservation. *Biological Conservation* 262. https://doi.org/10.1016/j.biocon.2021.109293.

Zurba, M., and F. Berkes. 2014. Caring for country through participatory art: Cre-ating a boundary object for communicating Indigenous knowledge and values. *Local Environment* 19 (8): 821–36. https://doi-org.ezproxy.library.dal.ca/10.1080 /13549839.2013.792051.

Zurba, M., and H. Friesen. 2014. Finding common ground through creativity: Exploring Indigenous, settler and Métis values and connection to the land. *The International Journal of Conflict & Reconciliation* 2 (1): 1–34.

Section Four

Relationships and Place

12

Understanding Environmental Concern, Values, Identity, and Other Drivers of Pro-Environmental Behavior

ROBERT EMMET JONES AND TOBIN N. WALTON

"A good part of the work called 'theorizing' is taken up with the clarification of concepts—and rightly so. It is in this manner of clearly defined concepts that social science is not infrequently defective." Merton (1948) advised us of the importance of learning this lesson a long time ago. This chapter pursues this goal by clarifying, integrating, and organizing the major drivers of pro-environmental behavior.

Introduction

Environmental degradation and public concern for it are certainly not new phenomena (see Glacken, 1967). However, it is clear Catton's (1980) early warning of "ecological overshoot," or the inability of biophysical systems to support the scope and magnitude of human activities, is now a reality as key ecological thresholds are being exceeded at an alarming rate. The rise of this *Anthropocene*, or human-dominated period of earth's history (Lewis and Maslin 2015; see also West et al. in chapter 13 of this volume), now challenges

https://doi.org/10.7330/9781646426300.c012

the way humans are living, how they view nature and themselves, and what they need to do in order to survive and do justice to all of earth's inhabitants (Jones and Wishart 2018). Fueled by unprecedented rates and concentrations of resource extraction, production, consumption, and waste, it has become apparent that human activities are collectively threatening the lives of billons of people and the sustainability of life itself (IPCC 2022). Moreover, these threats are not distributed equally, and instead disproportionately impact the poor and other marginalized communities and groups (Bullard, 2021).

As the nature of environmental problems has evolved, so has public concern for the environment. It has been transformed from a community's unease about the "fouling" of its local environment to global dread over the unravelling of ecological relationships that shape and support social and biophysical systems. Along the way, the "environment" became an "enduring social concern much like health care, education and other basic issues within the United States" (Mitchell 1980, 2). Ultimately, public concern for the environment grew into a strong political movement, major policy directive, and a polarizing issue within the West and within the global community (Dunlap 2002).

Rising public concern for environmental problems ushered in a concerted effort within the social sciences to understand it. Public opinion polls, surveys, and other forms of research on the human dimensions of natural resource management and environmentalism in general, have come to be known by many as either "environmental concern" or "environmental attitudes" studies.[1] Much of this research has tried to identify and understand the way behavior is influenced by values, beliefs, attitudes, norms, and other so-called antecedents, activators, or drivers of pro-environmental behavior (PEB). Generally speaking, PEB includes individual behaviors, sets of actions, and general activities thought to have a positive impact on the health and well-being of social and biophysical systems and environments (cf. Kollmuss and Agyeman 2002).

Researchers have used a variety of constructs, models, and measures in this effort to understand and predict PEB within a variety of settings and contexts. This research has provided many insights into the individual and collective

---

1. Generally speaking, environmental concern (EC) studies and environmental attitude (EA) studies have significant overlap. Both examine public perceptions, behavior, and support for environmental protection. However, EC studies developed more within an environmental social science perspective, while EA studies grew more within a natural resource social science perspective (see Buttel and Field 2004). We use the term *PEB studies* to represent both perspectives.

factors driving PEB, but the diverse ways in which people engage with the environment, and the many divergent ways researchers conceptualize and measure their constructs make it hard to compare studies and establish generalities about them (Van Liere and Dunlap 1980; Heberlein 1981). Dunlap and Jones's (2002) review pointed out these studies seldom built upon each other, and often lacked theoretical grounding. They also made it apparent that this body of research "is complex, continuously evolving and ever expanding, and [this] makes it particularly difficult to map" (Dunlap and Jones 2002, 485).

For example, the accumulation and integration of knowledge about PEB and its drivers has been hindered by the fact that: (1) people and communities engage and express their relationship with the environment in diverse ways, (2) there are numerous constructs used within these studies, (3) they often overlap conceptually and operationally, (4) the names of the constructs are sometimes used interchangeably, and (5) many constructs are used in an ad hoc manner and are not (explicitly) grounded in established social psychological theories (Dunlap and Jones 2002; Castro 2006; McIntyre and Milfont 2016).

Making sense of the richness and variation within this literature could be made easier by clearly defining and distinguishing these constructs, conceptualizing them in a more consistent and coherent manner, and by identifying ways to integrate and organize these constructs so they can be suitably applied across diverse communities, groups, settings, and contexts. We believe these are critical steps to help advance social scientific understanding and theories of PEB. Indeed, as noted in the abstract, Merton (1948) pointed out the importance of following these steps to social scientists a long time ago.

This chapter pursues these goals by first critically reviewing the conceptualizations of the major constructs and models routinely used to predict PEB and then by offering ways to clarify, integrate and organize these constructs within a general exploratory model that should help researchers better understand and predict these behaviors in the future.

Pro-Environmental Behavior and Its Major Drivers

Pro-Environmental Behavior

A wide variety of terms have been used to examine actions, practices, and other human activities thought to be significantly impacting the environment, such as pro-environmental behavior, environmental behavior, environmentally responsible behavior, environmentally friendly behavior, environmentally significant behavior, environmentally sustainable behavior, green behavior, altruistic or prosocial behavior, conservation behavior, and ecological behavior. However, because of its prevalence of use in the literature, we chose the term *pro-environmental behavior* (PEB). These types of activities can be performed by individuals or collectively within households, communities, organizations, governments, and agencies, and within numerous situational, contextual, geographic, and temporal settings. PEBs can be performed in the past or present, or planned for, or undertaken in the future (i.e., intentions). PEB can be based on a single action (known as a single-act behavioral criterion), or multiple acts (known as a multiple-act behavioral criterion; see Fishbein and Ajzen 2010). They can be performed frequently (e.g., purchasing organic foods), less frequently (e.g., setting household thermostats), or once in a while (e.g., installing more energy efficient appliances). Behaviors can be difficult or easy to do, more or less costly to engage in, and have greater or lesser impact on the environment (see Lange and Dewitte 2019).

Behaviors examined in various studies have changed over time as scientific knowledge and public concern for the environment have evolved and new environmental challenges have emerged. The type and magnitude of human activities impacting the health of the planet are also many and the universe of PEBs can be organized by the domain it represents (see Fishbein and Ajzen 2010; Larson et al. 2015; Dunlap and Jones 2002). For example, there are PEBs that promote energy and resource conservation, land stewardship, environmental education, eco-recreation, green consumerism, and those supporting environmental activism, citizenship, and policy (see Stern 2000; Dunlap and Jones 2002; Manfredo and Dayer 2004; Manfredo et al. 2017; Larson et al. 2015). Although there are many ways to organize and define these domains, the simplest way might be to divide them into private and public spheres (Dietz, Stern, and Guagnano1998; Ertz and Sarigöllü 2019). For example, the *private behavioral domain* would cover individual or household practices, activities, and choices (e.g., reducing individual and household energy and resource use, consumption, and waste) that could impact the environment. The *public behavioral domain* would cover actions and activities taken by individuals or collectively in groups, to oppose, support, or change public and/or private organizational policies and management practices that could impact the environment. For example, those supporting or engaging in efforts to clean local water sources, reintroduce native species, divest from fossil fuel industries, or change global environmental policies.

Although other approaches have been used (see Lange and Dewitte 2019), most PEB studies employ mail, online, or in-field surveys of self-reported behaviors that are assumed to improve or benefit some aspect of the environment. Much of this research has tried to identify the internal motivational factors driving individuals to engage in PEB rather than the situational, institutional, structural, technical, and environmental factors external to them that can discourage or encourage their engagement. However, individuals wanting to engage in them often face barriers that lay outside of their volitional control or ability to do so (Kollmus and Ageyman 2002; Dietz, Rosa, and York 2009; Larson et al. 2015; Steg 2016; Nielsen et al. 2021; Sharpe et al. 2022).[2] For example, external conditions may exist which make it harder to perform a given behavior (e.g., not having access to curbside recycling, lack of infrastructure for public transportation), or encourage individuals to engage in PEB (e.g., providing government subsidies for household energy conservation, the availability of local markets for developing green technologies). External conditions can also make it easier or harder to adopt new PEBs (e.g., having access to charging stations for electric vehicles). Consequently, behavior aimed at reducing environmental degradation is driven by a variety of individual (or internal) motivations that are shaped and mediated by sociocultural structures and environmental contexts (or external) that can constrain or encourage PEB (see Steg 2016; Nielsen et al. 2021; Zajchowski, Koenigstorfer and Mostafanezhad 2023). This means that individuals, communities, populations, and groups have differential access to basic democratic practices that may provide them with public information about the environment, opportunities to voice their environmental concerns, and the right to participate in environmental governance and management. In this way, principles of procedural and distributive justice can encourage broader engagement in PEB *and* help address socioecological

---

2. A proxy for estimating the impact of these behavioral barriers are measures associated with the theoretical construct of perceived behavior control found in Ajzen's (1991) theory of planned behavior, later incorporated within Fishbein and Ajzen's (2010) reformulated reasoned action approach. These measures are designed to capture the impact of individual perceptions of these things in impeding or encouraging their behavioral engagement (see figure 12.2).

problems in a more just, equitable, and sustainable manner (see section 1 of this volume.

Future studies need to identify the relative impacts of both external and internal factors on PEB. Researchers also need to make explicit which PEB domain (public, private, or both) is being targeted and the behavior(s) they select to represent it. Researchers (and the public and policymakers) also need to acknowledge the difference between *perceived* environmental impacts of a PEB and its *actual* impacts. For example, perceptions of the socioeco-logical advantages of plastic recycling may not be the actual (immediate and long-term) impacts of engaging in this activity. Therefore, it is important for researchers to identify and target behaviors and collective activities that have *net positive actual impacts* over the short and long term (Dietz, Rosa, and York 2009; Nielsen et al. 2021). Studies investigating energy, carbon emissions, product life cycles, food products, as well as habitat and ecological assessment studies should help researchers identify behaviors having the greatest net-positive impacts, and alert them to the difficulty, demands, costs, and inequities associated with them (see Steg 2016; Nielsen et al. 2021; Rare and California Environmental Associates 2019; Clark et al. 2022).

Drivers of Pro-Environmental Behavior

We define a *driver* of PEB as a hypothesized or theoretical construct thought to represent some aspect of reality that is not directly observable but has been routinely used to identify and understand factors motivating people to engage or not engage in PEB. Next, we critically assess conceptualizations of the major constructs routinely used to predict PEB.

Environmental Concern

Since the earliest studies that examined people's reactions to local air pollution (see Degroot et al. 1966), public concern for the environment, or simply, *environmental concern* (EC), has been conceptualized, defined, and measured in countless ways (see Dunlap and Jones 2002; Schultz et al. 2004; Franzen and Vogl 2013; Cruz and Manata 2020).[3] Researchers have conceptualized EC

---

3. According to Bohr and Dunlap (2018), environmental concern emerged as the most prevalent topic out of twenty-five key topics published in environmental social sciences journals between 1990 and 2014.

as a construct and used it to describe a broad class of research focused on better understanding the drivers of PEB. As a construct, EC has often been defined broadly to "reflect the degree to which people are aware of environmental problems, believe they are serious and need attention, are willing to support efforts to solve them, and actually do things to contribute to their solution" (Routhe, Jones, and Feldman 2005, 878; see also Dunlap and Jones 2002; Steg and de Groot 2012; Tam and Chan 2018). Others have not explicitly defined EC, but operationalized it based on one or more psychological attributes derived from the classical tripartite conceptualization (i.e., affect, cognition and conations) of attitude (e.g., Milfont, Poortinga, and Sibley 2020; see Dunlap and Jones, 2002). In this way, EC has often been used interchangeably with *environmental attitudes* (Cruz and Manata 2020). However, contemporary theory and research have demonstrated the tripartite view of attitude is outdated and instead conceives of attitude more narrowly as one's evaluation (good-bad, desirable-undesirable) of a psychological object (Fishbein and Azjen 2010; Eagly and Chaiken 1993; see the section below).

Dunlap and Jones (2002) proposed EC could be treated as a "multifaceted construct" and conceptually divided it into two major components: *environment* and *concern*. They pointed out that researchers can create indicators drawn from the conceptual "universe of environmental issues" (e.g., water pollution, resource depletion, climate change)—the *environment component*—and from the conceptual universe of expressions of concern (e.g., cognitive, affective, conative, behavioral responses to environmental challenges)—the *concern component*. Both universes are expanding as the scale, magnitude, costs, and forms of environmental impacts change. This means that the way researchers select, combine, and contextualize facets from both universes are innumerable, as are the conceptualizations and measures used to gauge EC.

This wide range of variation, lack of conceptual consistency and theoretical coherence in what researchers claim they are measuring make it difficult to generalize findings on EC, its relation to PEB and to other constructs used to predict it (see Dunlap and Jones 2002; Cruz and Manata 2020). Some of this is because EC has not been easily distinguishable from other established social psychological constructs (e.g., beliefs, attitudes). Given the above review, it appears research on EC suffers from poor construct conceptualizations that can lead to contaminated constructs, ambiguous measures, and other problems impairing our understanding and prediction of PEB (see MacKenzie 2003; Udo-Akang 2012).

The work of Schwartz (Schwartz, Sagiv, and Boehnke 2000; Schwartz 2010) on values may help to narrow the boundaries, meanings and measures associated with the concept of EC (see also Schulz et al. 2004; Steg 2016; Landry et al. 2018). It demonstrates perceived threats to one's values may not only activate personal norms, but also attract attention that can generate worries associated with environmental threats. According to Schwartz, Sagiv, and Boehnke (2000), worries are emotionally charged cognitions (i.e., affects) based on a belief that some domain of life is being threatened or degraded. Theoretically speaking, one could also argue that concern for the environment and worrying about it are conceptually similar and could be related. For example, worries that are more intense and prolonged can become chronic and develop into a major concern that can impact one's well-being and motivate ways to mitigate it.

Indeed, some researchers conceptualize EC only as a person's worry over the consequences of environmental problems or actions (e.g., Schultz et al. 2004). Such a narrow conceptualization could represent an affective and/or emotionally laden reaction (e.g., comfort-discomfort, worry-calm, sadness-joy, concern-unconcern, and other responses associated with fear, anger, pride, and guilt) to perceived socioecological impacts caused by human activities. Future studies operationalizing EC in this manner should employ a variety of these types of *concern* and *care* indicators to determine how they may relate to PEB and its drivers (see Landry et al. 2018; Bissing-Olson, Fielding, and Iyer 2016; Landmann and Rohmann 2020; Bouman et al. 2020).

Environmental Attitudes

Researchers have also conceptualized environmental attitude (EA) in an omnibus and outdated tripartite way. For them, an environmental attitude still represents affective, cognitive, and conative responses people have to an "attitude object" such as water pollution. Indeed, many refer to this research simply as studies of environmental attitudes (see Milfont and Duckitt 2010; McIntyre and Milfont 2016; Domingues and Gonçalves 2020). Other researchers draw on contemporary views of attitude (e.g., Fishbein and Azjen 1975, 2010; Eagly and Chaiken 1993) and narrowly define attitude as one's "disposition or tendency to respond with some degree of favorableness or unfavorableness to a psychological object" (Fishbein and Ajzen 2010, 74). These "objects of evaluation" can be general or specific and include features of the environment (e.g., polluted rivers are bad), environmental policies (decarbonizing the economy is a worthy goal), conservation management practices (e.g., reintroducing elk is foolish), as well as evaluations about specific PEBs (e.g., using organic fertilizers is good). These narrower conceptualizations of environmental attitude would reflect a person's perceived degree of (un)favorableness or (dis)like for each of these environmental objects.

For example, Fishbein and Ajzen's "attitude toward behavior" component within the reasoned action approach (RAA) is designed to gauge a person's overall evaluation of performing a specific behavior (e.g., I like driving less often).[4] In their view, evaluations differ from affect, which has a somatic aspect characterized by some degree of arousal reflected in such things as emotions and moods (2010). While they recognize that the construct of attitude is related to affect, they view them as separate response systems. Given this information, we distinguish EA from EC by the type of response each elicits. The narrower form of EA represents an evaluative response while the narrower conceptualization of EC represents affective-emotional responses to environmental objects. Given this conceptual distinction, we assert the likelihood of performing or not performing a PEB is influenced both by a person's overall evaluation (i.e., EA) of the perceived instrumental and external benefits and costs and by the anticipated internal and experiential feelings or states of arousal (i.e., EC) that may be activated or deactivated by engaging in it. Conceptualizing EC and EA as distinct constructs should increase our ability to generalize the findings across studies and provide a coherent and parsimonious way of employing these constructs to predict PEB.

Environmental Values

Changing people's behavior impacting the environment may not be possible unless their values are reoriented, reprioritized, and ultimately changed.

---

4. The reasoned action approach (RAA) is Fishbein and Ajzen's reformulated version of the theory of reasoned action (TRA) and the theory of planned behavior (TPB). We use the acronym RAA in the rest of this chapter to refer to the general theoretical framework they use to support these models.

Personal values have been defined in many ways but major value theorists such as Rokeach (1968) and Schwartz (2012), define them as fundamental and enduring beliefs about desired goals or end-states of existence (or "terminal values") and modes of conduct for attaining them (or "instrumental values"). In this way, they represent ultimate goals in life worth striving for such as freedom, equality, and unity with nature and the desirable ways for attaining them such as being independent, broadminded, and protecting nature. They operate as general principles that people apply across situations and contexts and help guide the way we view and respond to others and the environment. So, "when we think of values, we think of what is important in life." (Schwartz 2012, 3; Sagiv and Roccas 2021; Sagiv and Schwartz 2022; Steg 2016).

Understanding the roles values play in motivating people to engage or not engage in PEB has been a major focus of research for a long time (Leopold 1949; Dietz, Fitzgerald, and Shwom 2005; Tadaki, Sinner, and Chan 2017). Like other drivers of PEB, the numerous conceptualizations and measures used to examine *environmental values* (see Steg and de Groot 2012) has made it difficult to make sense of them and the "huge array of approaches" used to examine and tap into them (Tadaki, Sinner, and Chan 2017, 6). For example, they have been viewed and measured as a single value (e.g., a dominionistic value), as clusters or classes of values (e.g., self-transcendent values), and as a set of value orientations (e.g., wildlife value orientations). Indeed, Tadaki, Sinner, and Chan (2017, 6) found no broad consensus about "what [environmental] values are, or which approaches to understanding values are useful and legitimate in particular settings."

Making a conceptual distinction between valuation and values-based approaches may be a useful way to organize studies of environmental values (see, Dietz, Fitzgerald, and Shwom 2005; Tadaki, Sinner, and Chan 2017). Environmental valuation studies are usually designed to estimate the worth (or value) of an environmental management program, species, habitat, ecosystem service, or resource. They typically do so by employing willingness-to-pay measures to identify public preferences for potential environmental outcomes, management interventions, or policy goals (see Mitchell and Carson 2013; Loomis 2005). Whereas environmental valuation approaches use economic and ecological concepts and theories to investigate and estimate value, values-based approaches generally draw upon social and psychological concepts and theories to examine how social values are prioritized and shape individual and collective responses to natural resource or environmental challenges.

From a values-based research approach, engaging in PEB is a way to express one's deeply held "environmental values," and performing them can help to validate, prioritize, and routinize them among the general public, other groups, or institutions. A variety of research studies have utilized Schwartz's value dimension of self-transcendence within multivariate models predicting specific PEBs. Transcendence values such as *unity with nature, benevolence, and social justice* seem to direct our attention toward concern for the welfare of other people, nature, and all living things (Steg 2016; Tadaki, Sinner, and Chan 2017). For example, studies employing the value-belief-norm (VBN) model have demonstrated that those who place higher priority on self-transcendence values have stronger altruistic value orientations (i.e., valuing the welfare of others) and biospheric value orientations (i.e., valuing the welfare of the environment) that guide their lives (see Stern et al. 1999; Stern 2000; Dietz, Fitzgerald, and Schwom 2005; Turaga, Howarth, and Borsuk 2010; Lange and Dewitte 2019; Ros and Kaneko 2022).

Values can influence both general and specific forms of PEB (Steg 2016). However, their effectiveness in predicting specific PEBs depends on the presence of situations and contexts that activate them (e.g., threats to one's well-being) and make them more accessible to the person (e.g., by reflecting upon them). Similarly, if a behavior is viewed as an *instantiation of the value* (i.e., it has relevance, symbolic meaning, and can activate emotional arousal), then engaging in it allows a tangible expression of this value and provides the person with an opportunity for fulfilling the goal it represents (see Sagiv and Roccas 2021, for a review of these moderating mechanisms).

Environmental Beliefs

Changing behaviors impacting the environment may not be possible unless humans change their beliefs about the planet, its ecology, human and non-human others, and their place within it. An *environmental belief* (EB) is conceptualized as an individual's presumption that something is true about the qualities, characteristics, or attributes associated with an environmental object (e.g., *the river is polluted*).[5] The widely used new ecological paradigm

---

5. According to Dunlap and Jones (2002, 409), beliefs and knowledge represent different

(NEP) scale represents a set of general environmental beliefs that some people perceive as being true about nature (e.g., nature is balanced, fragile, has limited resources, and humans are destroying it). Researchers also routinely operationalize more specific EBs, which then serve as a causal basis for the formation of attitudes, norms, and other components in their predictive models of PEB.

The NEP scale can help researchers document this type of paradigmatic change in beliefs within society. It is the most widely used measure to gauge public beliefs about environmental problems and numerous studies have helped to establish its validity, reliability, and ability to help predict PEB across multiple societies and cultures (Hawcroft and Milifont 2010; Xiao, Dunlap, and Hong 2019). However, the current NEP scale (Dunlap et al. 2000) and its earlier versions (Dunlap and Van Liere 1978) have been conceptualized in a variety of ways (Hawcroft and Milifont 2010). For example, it has been conceptualized as a paradigm, a worldview, a belief system, a set of primitive beliefs, an attitude, a value, and a value orientation (see Steg and de Groot 2012; Gatersleben, Murtagh, and Abrahamse 2012; Harrison 2019; Cruz and Manata 2020). It has been used as a *measure* of environmental concern (e.g., Unanue et al. 2016), and as a *predictor* of it (e.g., Xiao, Dunlap, and Hong 2019). Moreover, there is "considerable variation" across studies in the number and type of items included from the full fifteen-item NEP scale (Hawcroft and Milifont 2010, 143).

Given the above, the way the NEP has been conceptualized, measured, used, and abused by researchers have been numerous (see Dunlap 2008; Hawcroft and Milifont 2010). Some of this variation is because the NEP was designed as a novel concept (i.e., paradigm) used to describe a domain-specific construct (i.e., ecological paradigm) which had little connection with established theoretical constructs used within any social psychological theory for understanding PEB. However, over time the "amorphous" conceptualization of the "NEP scale" has been clarified by Dunlap and his colleagues to largely represent a general set of *primitive beliefs* about humans and their relationship with the biophysical environment (see Dunlap and Jones 2002,

---

types of cognitions. Cognitive expressions of environmental knowledge potentially have a high empirical probability of being accurate, while cognitive expressions of environmental beliefs potentially have a high intrasubjective expectation of being correct. Although environmental knowledge is important for knowing which actions to take, as a variable it has limited and/or inconsistent effects on PEB (Otto and Pensini 2017).

509; Dunlap 2008). These beliefs are "primitive" in that they are taken-for-granted ways of *seeing* the world more ecologically (e.g., nature is balanced).

NEP was subsequently tailored for children (NEP-C), which, like the NEP, has been translated and widely adopted by researchers in both developed and developing nations. Given the growing evidence of public endorsement of the NEP across many nations and groups, some have deemed it as the "organizing anchor" of an emerging environmental belief system (Xiao, Dunlap, and Hong 2019). Still, there are ongoing questions and concerns about the construct validity, reliability, and generalizability of the NEP and the NEP-C (Rosa, Collado, and Larson 2022; Rosa, Collado, and Profice, 2021). Perhaps a more theoretical challenge is its ability to sufficiently represent this potential environmental belief system. Given that the NEP was designed only to tap into primitive beliefs about human relationship with aspects of biophysical reality, it is unable to tap into primitive beliefs about ourselves and our relationships to others and how they impact the environment and drive PEB. In this manner, the construct of NEP appears to have limited theoretical scope and coverage of this potential environmental belief system as it represents a partial worldview of critical psychological, sociocultural, and ecological relationships that could connect aspects of the self, society, and nature into a broader and more inclusive paradigm. As such, future work will need to reconceptualize and integrate the NEP within a broader, culturally diverse set of socioecological views that represent not just basic beliefs about the biophysical environment but also how others (human and nonhumans) are treated and impacted by socioecological problems. This work could help to identify dimensions of dominant or other worldviews that undervalue and/or exclude basic beliefs that support environmental and social justice, Indigenous and queer ecologies, inclusion and intersectionality, and other realities within our collective socioecological consciousness (see Meija-Duwan and Hoffelmeyer in chapter 1 of this volume and Carter and Roesch-McNally in chapter 2).

Environmental Norms

Changing people's behavior may not be possible unless personal, social, cultural, organizational, and institutional norms are reevaluated and more ecologically informed norms are accepted, strengthened, and widely adopted

(Heberlein 1972, 2012; Dauvergne 2018). Many studies have linked norms to behavior, but unlike EC and the NEP, the concept of norm has long been an established theoretical construct within the social sciences (see Cialdini, Kallgren, and Reno 1991).

Generally speaking, social norms reflect informal internalized and externalized codes or rules of conduct that people widely view as being normal, or commonly approved, and are expected to follow (see Nyborg 2018; Niemiec et al. 2020). They are implicitly or explicitly shared by members of a group or organization who may feel a sense of pride, responsibility, or obligation to support or comply with them (Onwezen, Antonides, and Bartels 2013; Bisson-Olsen et al. 2016). Those who follow norms may experience positive internal reinforcements or rewards (e.g., a sense of pride and belonging) as well as external ones (e.g., greater prestige, status, power, or resources); those who break or violate them may experience negative internal (e.g., a sense of guilt and stigma) and external sanctions (e.g., a loss of prestige, status, power, or resources). In this way, norms help to maintain and promote group cohesion, order, values, and identity, and in doing so secure individual and group benefits and ensure control over resources and others (see Heberlein 2012). Given this, the construct of *environmental norm* (EN) represents what individuals, households, communities, organizations, and so on are expected to do to mitigate the socioecological impact of human activities. On the individual level, there are several different types of norms that are typically examined in these studies; most draw from Fishbein and Ajzen's reasoned action approach (2010), or Schwartz's norm-activation theory (see Niemiec et al. 2020).

According to Ajzen (2012), a perceived norm is the overall perceived social pressure to engage or not engage in a behavior and is determined by two types of normative beliefs: injunctive and descriptive. In relation to the environment, injunctive normative beliefs are a person's perceived expectation that significant or important referents (e.g., family, co-workers, environmental scientists) would approve or disapprove of performing a specific behavior that could impact the environment. Descriptive normative beliefs are a person's perceived expectation that significant and important referents actually perform the specific PEB under question. These types of norms and beliefs are components of Fishbein and Ajzen's reasoned action approach (RAA). It assumes those who feel greater social normative pressure to perform a PEB are more likely to engage in it.

Personal norms (PNs) are another type of norm widely used in these studies. The concept of PN is associated with Schwartz's model of norm activation and research on altruism (Schwartz 1968, 1977; Heberlein 1972, 2012) and later reconceptualizations by Stern and others (see Stern et al. 1999; Turaga, Howarth, and Borsuk 2010) within the value-belief-norm (VBN) model. PNs differ from the norms associated with RAA because they are based on *internalized* personal standards rather than on *externalized* social standards of what others may think is normal conduct (Niemiec et al. 2020). PNs activate and influence behavior when the negative consequences of not acting are known to the person (i.e., awareness of consequences) and the individual attributes personal responsibility (i.e., ascription of responsibility) for acting to address these consequences (Schwartz 1968; Heberlein 1972). Originally, these consequences were restricted to impacts associated with humans (see Heberlein 2012); later, they were extended to include nonhumans and the biophysical environment (Stern, Dietz, and Kalof 1993; Stern and Dietz 1994; see Thøgersen 2006; Abrahamse and Steg 2013; Steg 2016 for reviews).[6] Future work will be needed to try to integrate these different sets of norms into broader and more diverse conceptual frameworks that reflect expected rules of human conduct that can not only impact the environment but also all of its current and future human and nonhuman inhabitants.

Identity, Connectedness, and Place

Changing people's behaviors impacting the environment may not be possible unless people are also willing to change *themselves* and their relationship to nature and others. Viewing ourselves as separate and disconnected from nature has long been identified as a major factor undermining earth's life-support systems (Leopold 1949; Heberlein 1972; Catton 1980; Barragan-Jason et al. 2022). In contrast, people who identify with nature and are more connected to it are more likely to engage in PEB (see Hatty et al. 2020). People are also more vested in environmental issues that implicate the self

---

6. Fishbein and Ajzen (2010) think PNs could be potentially included in the RAA model. They propose that future research should test the utility of using measures of injunctive, descriptive and personal norms to better understand norms and how they influence behavior. Still, they believe PN "is perhaps best viewed as an equivalent to the construct of behavioral intention," which is already included in their model (Fishbein and Ajzen 2010, 284).

(Devine-Wright and Clayton 2010). Over the last decade or so, studies on these and other types of *self-environment* relations have increasingly examined the role people's internalized representations of self (or self-meanings) play in driving PEB.

Researchers from a variety of research traditions have employed a number of theoretical conceptualizations and measures to tap into aspects of self-environment relations (see Hatty et al. 2020). Some of these concepts include *connectedness to nature*, (Mayer and Frantz 2004; Restall and Conrad 2015; Dutcher et al. 2007), *human-nature connectiveness* (Ives et al. 2017), *relatedness with nature* (Nisbett, Zelenski, and Murphy 2009), *inclusion of nature in one's sense of self* (Schultz 2002; Martin and Czellar 2016), *love and care for nature* (Perkins 2010), and *identification* with nature and the environment—or environmental identity (Clayton 2003; Walton and Jones 2018). Not surprisingly, there appears to be significant conceptual, operational, and empirical overlap between these hypothesized constructs (Tam 2013; Brügger, Kaiser, and Roczen 2011; Whitburn, Lankater, and Abrahamse 2020; Barragan-Jason et al. 2022).

Recent theory and research in this area (Walton and Jones 2018; Clayton et al. 2021), however, has pointed out that constructs grounded in theories of identity focus on self-meanings that define one's shared group membership with nature, both directly and indirectly, through the social and ecological relationships that link them together. These self-meanings are related to group membership with nature and particular social groups, the behavioral and role expectations of this membership, and the importance or centrality of one's environmental identity relative to other identities and group affiliations. Although some conceptual diversity exists across these constructs (see Udall et al. 2021), they can be viewed as representing different, but related, forms of environmental identification (EI; see Clayton et al. 2021). For example, an *environmental self-identity* is a behavioral-based form of EI that involves the definition of oneself as belonging to group of people who engage in a particular PEB (e.g., I am a recycler; Nigbur, Lyons and Uzzell 2010). An *environmentalist identity* (e.g., I am an environmental activist) involves self-meanings of identification with political or social groups or movements that advocate on behalf of environmental protection (Dunlap and McCright 2008). Whereas these two forms of EI define the self narrowly in relation to specific behaviors or groups, Clayton's (2003) conceptualization of *environmental identity* (often referred to as EID) and Walton and Jones's (2018) conceptualization of ecological identity (ECO-ID) tap into much more general definitions of the self in relation to broad human and nonhuman groups and biophysical nature. For instance, EID involves seeing oneself as an integrated member of a distinctly nonhuman group, the natural environment, and elements within it (Clayton et al. 2021). ECO-ID is a still broader conceptualization of EI used to describe the extent and ways a person views themselves as being a part of an "integrated *social and biophysical* system" that is "characterized by mutually beneficial processes and nested webs of relationships" (Walton and Jones 2018, 666). In this sense, ECO-ID may represent a wider form of self-identification that integrates aspects of the individual, society, and the environment into a person's overall self-concept.

Constructs grounded in theories of the self-concept and intra / interpersonal relationships with the environment focus more on self-meanings that psychologically *attach* the self—or, more generally, the person—to nature, specific places, or various socioecological settings (see Larson et al. 2018; Eaton et al. 2019; Clayton et al. 2021; Daryanto and Song 2021). Constructs based on personal attachment (or bonding) to some aspect of biophysical reality are grounded on self-meanings and emotions associated with in-nature experiences, and often referred to generically as *connection to nature* (Restall and Conrad 2015; Ives et al. 2017; Hatty et al. 2020; Clayton et al. 2021). Place-related constructs are based on attachment or bonding to specific locations (natural or otherwise) associated with experiences one has within them (Daryanto and Song 2021; see Williams and Miller in chapter 15 of this volume for a more critical view of this idea).

Research associated with connection to nature (CN) taps into the extent a person sees themselves as a part of nature and how this may impact the environment as well as their life. As an umbrella term, CN can be viewed as a domain-specific construct, and similar to EC and EA, conceptualizations of it have often (implicitly or explicitly) been modeled on the traditional tripartite conceptualization of attitude (see Hatty et al. 2020). Indeed, many researchers view CN as a multidimensional construct composed of three components; individual cognitions (e.g., perceptions and knowledge about self-nature relationships), affect (e.g., feelings, emotions, and evaluations related to nature), and behavior (e.g., actions and experiences with/in nature; see Zylstra et al. 2014; Bragg et al. 2013; Whitburn, Linklater, and

Abrahamse 2020; Hatty et al. 2020). This has led to conceptual diversity and inconsistency in the constructs and measures used in these studies. Indeed, a recent meta-analysis of this research identified "several hundred constructs and metrics" used by researchers to examine one or more of these components associated with CN (Barragan-Jason et al. 2022, 3). Most of them overlap conceptually and empirically but nevertheless appear to be tapping into a common psychological phenomenon representing key aspects of self-environment relations (Schultz et al. 2004; Mayer and Franz 2004; Brügger, Kaiser, and Roczen 2011; Tam 2013; Ives et al. 2017; Whitburn, Lanklater, and Abrahamse 2020; Hatty et al. 2020).

Many of these constructs are not based on established psychological constructs associated with PEB (e.g., environmental values, beliefs, attitudes, norms) but have been shown to be moderately correlated to PEB (see Whitburn, Lanklater, and Abrahamse 2020; Hatty et al. 2020; Barragan-Jason et al. 2022). Multidimensional scales of CN that include behavioral measures appear to have stronger links to measures of PEB. Some of this could be attributable to CN studies using one subset of PEBs (e.g., those connected with and/or performed in natural settings) to predict a larger but related set of PEBs (e.g., those connected with the environment and performed at home and other places). Moreover, CN scales that *do not* include a behavioral component have a less overall effect on PEB (Whitburn, Lanklater, and Abrahamse 2020). Indeed, many of the well-known CN-related scales appear to have this type of conceptual overlap and contamination that makes it difficult to determine how CN may be *theoretically* linked to PEB and to its major predictors. Although some rationales have been offered, most have been based on empirical generalizations from correlational studies (see Whitburn, Lanklater, and Abrahamse 2020), and not on an established theory or a model of PEB we were able to identify.

Whereas CN studies tend to focus on the impact of self-in-nature experiences that help people develop bonds with nature, place-based studies focus on the impact of self-in-place experiences within a variety of settings (e.g., natural and outdoor recreational areas, working landscapes, and communities) that help people bond to or attach to them. Unlike CN studies, place-based studies not only examine the physical aspects (e.g., place-based environmental meanings) but the social features (e.g., place-based sociocultural meanings) of these settings (see Williams, Stewart, and Kruger 2013; Brown,

Raymond, and Corcoran 2015). The theoretical framework of sense of place (SOP) has provided a useful lens for identifying factors that can encourage place-based efforts that seek common ground for building local collaborative approaches for governing social and ecological management (see Williams, Stewart, and Kruger 2013; Eaton et al. 2019). Place-based studies regularly employ concepts such as place meaning, place attachment, place identity, place satisfaction, and place dependence in order to understand/ encourage place-based conservation in mostly high amenity and nonurban settings (Williams, Stewart, and Krueger 2013; Mullendore, Ulrich-Schad, and Prokopy 2015; Eaton et al. 2019).

Similar to research on EC and EA, place-based conservation studies have been influenced (either implicitly or explicitly) by the traditional tripartite (and thus broader) conceptualization of attitude. For instance, they are usually anchored to the omnibus and multidimensional construct of SOP, which is designed to cover affective, cognitive, and/or attitudinal relationships between people and places (see Eaton et al. 2019, 828). Others view SOP not as a multidimensional construct but as separate constructs that reflect different, but related, place-based dimensions or components (e.g., place dependence, place identity). So even though there have been concerted efforts to understand how SOP may impact place-based conservation, there appears to be "no singular conceptualization of SOP [that] pervades" this research and no known study that examines all of its components (Eaton et al. 2019, 828). Given this, Eaton et al. (2019, 833) suggest that more theoretical-conceptual work is needed to determine how SOP operates within a more holistic and broader behavioral framework. Williams and Miller (chapter 15, this volume) additionally question the static defaults of such SOP conceptions in a mutable world.

Relatively few studies since Vaske and Kobrin's (2001) groundbreaking study on place attachment in Colorado have examined relationships between place-based constructs and PEB. They demonstrate that place-based constructs are correlated with PEB, especially when the behaviors are directly linked to the place or are viewed as ones that can impact or protect it (Larson et al. 2018; Daryanto and Song 2021). In this manner, place-based conservation practices that individuals or collectives can take to protect or care for the place may be viewed as a subset of PEBs. Future studies need to determine whether or not geographically bound/place-based PEBs and other sets of PEBs—such as household practices—share a common set of drivers (see Larson et al. 2018). There are a variety of rationales offered as to *why* place-based measures of SOP should influence PEB (see Daryanto and Song 2021), but very few studies actually specify *how* they may be causally ordered with established drivers of PEB (Eaton et al. 2019; but see Larson et al. 2018). Finally, based on theory and research (see Fishbein and Ajzen 2010), we would expect that broader or more general measures of SOP are better at predicting an equally broad set of PEBs while place-based values, norms, attitudes, and attachment should be better predictors of PEBs that are aimed at caring or protecting these places.

Models of Pro-Environmental Behavior

Theory and research that combines these and other constructs into models designed to explain and predict PEBs spans nearly four decades. Much of the research has converged around variants of one or two theoretical models (cf. Kaiser 2006). They draw largely from Schwartz's early work on altruistic norms (Schwartz 1968, 1977), his later work on integrated values (Schwartz 2012), and from Fishbein and Ajzen's (2010) and Ajzen and Fishbein's (1975) work using the reasoned action framework.

Schwartzian-VBN Models of PEB

Early PEB studies (e.g., Heberlein 1972; Heberlein and Black 1976; Van Liere and Dunlap 1978) drew upon Schwartz's (1968, 1977), norm-activation model (NAM) of altruism and lent support to the idea that rising public concern about the environment was related to emerging social norms, such as those reflected in Leopold's *Land Ethic* (see Heberlein 2012). NAM stipulates how awareness and perceived seriousness of another person's need for help can trigger the activation of personal norms that spur a moral obligation to take (altruistic) actions to help this person (see Schwartz 1977). As such, its conceptual boundary conditions are limited to understanding interpersonal consequences and actions taken by individuals to help others in moral choice situations. At its core, NAM is grounded in the notion that personal (moral) norms and altruistic behavior will be activated when people "view themselves . . . as the responsible originators of action and are aware that their potential acts may have consequences for the welfare of others" (Schwartz 1968, 233).

Heberlein (1972) extended the boundary conditions of NAM beyond interpersonal behaviors to personal behaviors impacting the environment (e.g., littering, purchasing lead-free gas). His model assumed that personal (*moral*) norms and pro-ecological behavior will be activated when one is aware of some negative consequences to others (i.e., *awareness of consequences*, or *AC*) and ascribes personal responsibility for those consequences (i.e., *ascription of responsibility*, or *AR*) to their own actions (see figure 12.1). In this way, his conceptualization remained faithful to NAM as it asserted that under certain conditions (high AC and high AR) people would engage in PEB for the benefit of *other humans* (see Heberlein 1977, 2012).

Later modifications of NAM would extend the boundaries of the model further to household energy conservation, (Black, Stern, and Elworth 1985), public support for environmental protection (e.g., Stern, Dietz, and Black 1985), environmental activism (Stern et al. 1999), and to benefits to *nonhuman others and nature* (Stern, Dietz, and Kalof 1993; Stern and Dietz 1994). Both earlier and later extensions of NAM remained moral-based motivational approaches used to understand emerging environmental norms, attitudes, and behavior, and public support for environmental protection (see Stern et al. 1999; Turaga, Howarth, and Borsuk 2010). Some analysts thought these moral norms could be linked to deeper changes in the way humans view and value the environment. Consequently, studies included general environmental values and beliefs (e.g., NEP) within more comprehensive models that integrated this earlier work on NAM with Schwartz's later work on social values.

Schwartz's later research emphasizes the psychological content, structure, and relational aspects of social values and value systems. His *theory of integrated value systems* has been tested in many different cultures and groups in over eighty nations and suggests values cluster in a circular fashion comprised of ten broad values organized along two bipolar dimensions (openness to change vs. conservation, self-transcendence vs. self-enhancement). His research demonstrates that these basic values are organized into a coherent and integrated value system "that underlies and can help to explain individual decision-making, attitudes, and behavior" (Schwartz et al. 2012, 664).

Studies have particularly utilized Schwartz's value dimension of self-transcendence within models predicting PEBs. Self-transcendence values, such as *the world of beauty, unity with nature, benevolence, and social justice*, are

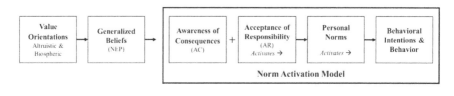

FIGURE 12.1. Value-belief-norm model of environmental behavior. Source: M. Stern's (2018) graphic presentation of the P. Stern (2000) VBN model.

thought to express concern for the welfare of other people, nature, and all living things. These values are opposed to self-enhancement values that are motivated by individual success, power, and control over others. Stern, Dietz, and other colleagues combined aspects of Schwartz's NAM and values theory into an integrative model of environmental concern designed to connect values, beliefs, and norms to specific environmental behaviors and support for the environment (Stern et al. 1995, 1999; Stern, Dietz, and Guagnano 1998). Their VBN model links more distal values and general beliefs to more specific beliefs and norms that are viewed as being more proximate drivers of behavioral intentions and individual actions. Specifically, it assumes that those who place higher priority on self-transcendent values have stronger altruistic and biospheric value orientations that guide their lives and adhere to basic (pro-environmental) beliefs about the world and the environment. These basic and more general beliefs (such as those tapped by the NEP) are posited to then influence specific beliefs about harmful consequences (AC) to someone or something of value associated with a given behavior, policy, or broad practice. If one also ascribes personal responsibility (AR) for relieving this harm to the valued other, a personal norm is activated, and individuals will be more likely to engage in behaviors thought to mitigate the harm (see figure 12.1). This sequence of the direct effects of values on beliefs, and their indirect effects on the activation of norms and behavior has stood up to empirical testing on a wide array of behaviors. But it appears that the VBN model is better at predicting environmental activism and public support for environmental policies than for PEBs performed by individuals in the "private sphere" (see Stern et al. 1999; Stern 2000; Dietz, Fitzgerald, and Schwom 2005; Turaga, Howarth, and Borsuk 2010; Lange and Dewitte 2019).

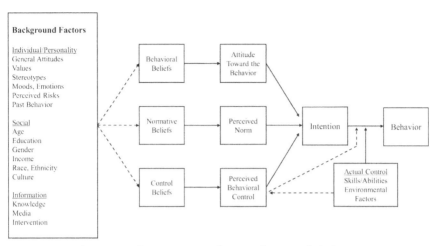

FIGURE 12.2. The reasoned action approach to predict specific behavior. Source: Fishbein and Ajzen (2010).

Fishbein and Ajzen's Reasoned Action Approach

The reasoned action framework (Fishbein and Ajzen 2010, 20–27) is grounded in the notion that one's *intention* to engage in a given behavior is the best predictor of actually doing it. This stands in contrast to a great deal of researchers that tried (quite unsuccessfully), to predict specific behavior with broader *attitudinal-type* measures associated with an object (Sok et al. 2021). Intention is driven by one's *attitude toward the behavior* (AB), *perceived norm* (PCN), and *perceived behavioral control* (PBC), each of which is derived from beliefs and information a person possesses about performing the behavior (see figure 12.2).

AB is defined as one's favorable or unfavorable evaluation of engaging in a targeted behavior. It is determined by *behavioral beliefs* (BB): one's evaluation about a modal set of outcomes (i.e., *outcome evaluations)* they might experience or realize if they perform the behavior and their perceptions that they will or will not occur (e.g., true-false) and the likelihood (e.g., likely-unlikely) of them occurring.

PCN is used to estimate the overall perceived social pressure to engage in a given behavior and it is determined by two types of normative beliefs: injunctive and descriptive. *Injunctive normative beliefs* are a person's perceived expectation that significant or important referents (e.g., family, co-workers, environmental scientists) would *approve or disapprove* of performing a specific behavior.

Descriptive normative beliefs are a person's perceived expectation that significant and important referents are *actually doing* (or not doing) the targeted behavior.

PBC estimates an individual's control over executing the behavior in question. In theory this refers to both *actual control* (ABC) and *perceived control* (PBC) over the behavior, but because of the difficulty of assessing ABC, PBC is typically used as a proxy measure for both while still acknowledging the potential for ABC to moderate behavioral intention (BI) when there is a significant difference between PBC and ABC. PBC contains two components: one is related to a person's perceived *capacity* to execute a given behavior and the other to a person's beliefs about whether they have *autonomy* over whether they can execute the behavior or not.

In addition to these proximal drivers of behavior, Fishbein and Ajzen (2010) argue that a researcher may want to consider more distal background factors as well, especially if researchers believe that the population in question may have different experiences and beliefs due to them or in behavioral domains where they have been found to be important—for example, the impact of environmental values on PEBs. These so-called background factors highlighted in figure 12.2 (e.g., values, identity, culture) include only a short list of an unlimited number of variables that could moderate behavioral, normative, and control beliefs. Those associated with the individual and other types of broad dispositions are thought to have only indirect and limited impact on a specific behavior (see Fishbein and Ajzen 2010, 221–53). Their general framework has been used to successfully explain PEBs in a number of behavioral domains such as traveling and transportation, energy saving, and recycling. A recent meta-analysis of 126 PEB studies determined moral norm, past behavior, and self-identity as the most frequently used in models trying to extend the RAA (see Yuriev et al. 2020).

Each of the frameworks reviewed above have been used effectively to explain specific PEBs. Still, they have very different theoretical lineages and propose different factors influencing PEB. NAM and VBN were developed to explain *normative influences* on behavior resulting from one's beliefs about the consequences of acting or behaving so as to mitigate harm incurred by something of value (e.g., human and nonhuman others). Alternatively, within the RAA, beliefs, attitudes, and norms drive PEB through one's subjective understanding of the cost and benefits *expected to be gained* from engaging in them (Fishbein and Ajzen 2010). Despite this foundational difference in these frameworks, each of them presumes that PEB is driven by both direct (or proximal) influences on PEB, and indirect (or distal) influences on PEB.

There have been recent efforts exploring the way these models may be integrated to better explain PEB (e.g., Han 2015; Gkargkavouzi, Halkos, and Matsiori 2019). Still theory is underdeveloped in this area, and important constructs such as environmental concern and environmental identity have not been considered in these studies. Excluding them in the face of overwhelming impacts of global climatic change is short-sighted. These impacts have become more salient to people and have heightened their concern, worry, anxiety, and fear. Moreover, the socioeconomic and political polarization occurring across the world has often centered on environmental issues. This division is materialized through the adoption of new individual and collective identities that emerge during conflicts over environmental management (Dunlap, McCright, and Yarosh 2016). In this way, environmental concern and environmental identity can powerfully impact not only PEBs but also how people interpret information about environmental issues (Dietz et al. 2018; Clayton, Koehn, and Grover 2013).

Integrating and Organizing the Drivers of PEB into a General Framework

The review above drew upon past PEB research and social science literature to identify ambiguity and inconsistency in the way the major drivers of PEB have been conceptualized in order to understand them in a coherent and consistent manner. Next, we build upon this conceptual foundation to provide a way to integrate and organize these constructs so they can be suitably applied across diverse communities, groups, settings, and contexts. Figure 12.3 illustrates a general exploratory model (GEM) that positions the drivers of both general and specific PEB across four levels. Importantly, whereas past models used to predict PEB (NAM, VBN, RAA) have overwhelmingly focused on explaining specific PEBs, the framework is designed to help explain specific PEBs *and* general engagement in PEB.[7] Thus, both Level 1

---

7. In particular, the framework drew extensively from the following sources: Heberlein and Black (1976); Stern (2000); Dunlap and Jones (2002); Kollmuss and Ageyman (2002); Whittaker, Vaske, and Manfredo (2006); Bamberg and Möser (2007); Heberlein (2012); Steg and de Groot (2012); Schultz and Kaiser (2012); Hines Hungerford and Tomera (1987); Steg (2016); Blankenberg and Alhusen (2019); Lange and DeWitte (2019); Clayton et al. (2021); Yuriev et al. (2020).

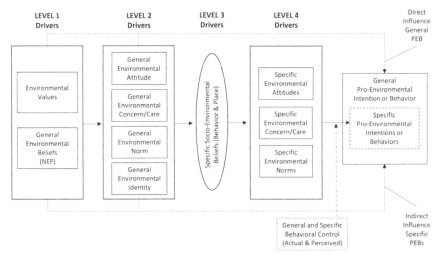

FIGURE 12.3. A general exploratory model (GEM) of pro-environmental behavior and its drivers.

and Level 2 are comprised of constructs that transcend specific situations and behaviors but drive regular engagement in a broad range of activities, situations, and relationships that can impact the individual, others, and/or socioecological systems in general (see Clayton 2003; Walton and Jones 2018; Clayton et al. 2021). Levels 3 and 4 are comprised of constructs that drive performance of specific PEBs.

The full integration of these constructs into the GEM suggests that engagement in both general and specific PEB is driven by valuing and seeing the world more ecologically (NEP). This in turn promotes (1) a deeper identification and connection to nature, environmental landscapes, and others in general; (2) cares and concerns about their well-being; and (3) positive evaluations and normative pressures toward behaviors and lifestyles believed to protect and sustain them.

Level 1 of GEM contains environmental values (EV) and general environmental beliefs (GEB). They are viewed as being the most abstract and general constructs of those included in the GEM. They are presumed to have a direct and strong influence on engagement in broad types of PEB (e.g., taking steps to reduce energy and resource use) and operate indirectly via Level 2, 3, and 4 to influence specific PEBs (e.g., eating less meat). These general values and beliefs are presumed as being the formative influences on the more tangible (but still general) constructs contained on Level 2 (i.e., environmental identity and general environmental attitude, norms, and concern/care). Specifically, through this model we posit that EV and GEB are the foundational drivers of PEB that guide the development of one's environmental identity and their general environmental attitudes, norms, concerns, and cares.

The positioning of EV and GEB within the GEM is supported by research showing them to be causally prior (or distal) to environmental identity and attitude (Walton and Jones 2018; van der Werff and Steg 2016; Gkargkavouzi, Halkos, and Matsiori 2019). This positioning is also theoretically supported because both VBN and RAA identify EV and GEB as distal drivers or background influences to more proximal and specific drivers of PEBs such as attitudes and norms. This illustrates that, although they are "held in the minds of individuals," EV and GEB are deeply embedded in multiple levels of socioeconomic and socioecological contexts and structures that transcend individuals and operate on a much broader level of abstraction (Manfredo et al. 2017, 778). This positioning is also supported by the principle of compatibility.[8] Because of their high level of generality, EV and GEB have stronger theoretical and conceptual correspondence with general multiple-act, rather than specific single-act, behavioral criterion representations of PEB. The general form of PEB represents a broad behavioral domain of PEB such as private sphere behaviors associated with resource conservation (see Fishbein and Ajzen 2010 and Heberlein and Black 1976; Whittaker, Vaske, and Manfredo 2006). Operationalizing PEB in this general way should be useful to researchers and help policy makers identify general patterns or trends across diverse communities, groups, situations, and contexts.

Level 2 of the GEM includes environmental identity (EI) and general environmental concern and care (EC), attitude (EA), and norm (EN). These constructs are viewed as being less abstract than EV and GEB (yet still general) and represent perceptions and responses to *generalized* (and again, transsituational) environmental conditions or threats (e.g., air pollution). They,

---

8. Fishbein and Ajzen's (1974 and 2010), work on the "principle of compatibility" details additional elements of behavioral criteria and predictors that should be aligned (i.e., target, action, context, time). Their work can be generalized to most behaviors, and it has significant empirical support. Full review of this principle is beyond the scope of this chapter, but researchers are strongly encouraged to review it.

too, are seen as directly influencing broad engagement in PEB and operate indirectly via Level 3 and 4 to influence specific PEBs. Specifically, environmental identity, generalized environmental attitudes, norms, and concerns and cares about the environment directly drive this type of broad engagement in PEB. They also contribute to the development of specific socioenvironmental beliefs about behavior and place (i.e., Level 3).

Positioning these constructs on Level 2 of the GEM is supported by research using NAM and VBN models. Through these models we've learned that worries and concerns about environmental problems in general (Level 2) derive from beliefs that some domain of life or value (see Level 1 constructs) is being threatened or degraded from its desired state of existence. (e.g., Schwartz, Sagiv, and Boehnke 2000; Dietz, Fitzgerald, and Schwom 2005; Turaga, Howarth, and Borsuk 2010; Lange and Dewitte 2019; Steg 2016). Past research and theory on individual and collective identities have also shown that identities are supported by positive evaluations (attitude) of the "in-group," and normative pressure to engage in behaviors associated with the group (Ashmore, Deaux, and McLaughlin-Vlope 2004; Schwartz, Luyckx, and Vignoles 2011). Finally, this positioning of Level 2 constructs is also supported by the principle of compatibility because both are conceptualized on the lower (and more general) end of the generality-specificity continuum or hierarchy (see Fishbein and Ajzen 2010; Heberlien and Black 1976; Whittaker, Vaske, and Manfredo 2006).

Level 3 of GEM includes specific socioenvironmental beliefs associated with one's concrete experiences in a particular place and beliefs about performing specific PEB(s). They represent perceptions about the potential impacts or consequences of (not) engaging in, or (not) supporting, a particular activity (e.g., eating beef, voting for a pro-environmental candidate). In this way, specific socioenvironmental beliefs form the basis for the emergence of specific attitudes, norms, concerns, and cares directed at a specific PEB. Numerous studies using NAM, VBN and RAA models use these types of specific beliefs to better understand norms and attitudes and how they influence specific PEB.[9]

---

9. Ideally, these beliefs would be generated by conducting a pilot study similar to the ones recommended by Fishbein and Ajzen (2010). They would ask respondents to list the advantages, disadvantages, risks and benefits, emotions and concerns, and other perceived impacts of performing this behavior to the health and well-being of themselves, others, the environment, and socioecological systems in general. Other beliefs that are

Level 4 of GEM contains specific environmental attitudes, norms, and concerns and cares. These constructs are positioned as the most proximal and direct drivers of specific PEBs. They are directly reflective of specific behavior(s), and they produce an intention or disposition to engage in a specific PEB or sets of specific PEBs. Lastly, in keeping with RAA, one's overall control over engaging in the behavior (perceived and actual behavioral control) given sociocultural structure and context, is modeled as a potential moderating effect between one's intention or disposition to engage in PEBs and actually doing it.[10]

Importantly, the GEM framework can be adaptable to many different forms and types of PEB, and it can be applied when working with diverse communities and groups across different research contexts and objectives. Of particular importance in this regard is for researchers to be cognizant of the degree of familiarity or embeddedness they share with the population of interest. Qualitative research can be vital in helping to ensure that measures of the constructs in the model reflect the particular *socioecological standpoint* (cf. Hartsock 1983; Collins 1986; Smith 1990) through which people and communities engage and express their relationship with the environment and others. It is also important to ensure the conceptualization of the predictors and the behavior criterion are closely matched in their level of specificity or generality. Researchers more interested in predicting engagement in a general PEB behavioral domain will be best served by employing the more general constructs located on Level 1 and 2 but have the option of employing more specific constructs on Level 3 and 4 in their model. Alternatively, researchers more interested in predicting specific PEBs will be best served by employing more specific constructs located on Level 3 and 4 but have the option of employing the more general constructs located on Levels 1

more associated with injunctive and descriptive norms (see above) could be generated asking respondents which specific people, groups, and organizations would encourage or discourage them from engaging in this specific behavior. The most widely mentioned beliefs (or *salient socioenvironmental beliefs*) could then be designed as survey items and used to predict specific norms, attitudes, and concerns after factor analysis and tests of reliability and validity were performed.

10. As noted earlier, the ways in which different elements of sociocultural structural and context impacts engagement in PEB is profound and future researchers are encouraged to apply this framework with measures of it as well in order to get an even broader understanding of PEB and the types of policies, programs, and interventions that can encourage it.

and 2 in their models. In these ways, particular research contexts, objectives, and constraints may not warrant inclusion of some of the constructs in the GEM framework. Future researchers are encouraged to investigate these relationships in more detail to see in what research and situational contexts it is efficacious to model one, two, or all four levels of this framework. In this regard information-theoretic (Burnham and Anderson 1998; Walton and Jones 2018; Riepe et al. 2021) and Bayesian (Gelfand and Dey 1994) methodological approaches may be especially useful in evaluating the efficacy of the model across multiple populations, contexts, and applications.

References

Abrahamse, W., and L. Steg. 2013. Social influence approaches to encourage resource conservation: A meta-analysis. *Global Environmental Change* 23 (6): 1773–85.

Ajzen, I. 1991. The theory of planned behavior. *Organizational Behavior and Human Decision Processes* 50 (2): 179–211.

Ajzen, I. 2012. Martin Fishbein's legacy: The reasoned action approach. *The Annals of the American Academy of Political and Social Science* 640 (1): 11–27.

Ajzen, I., and M. Fishbein. 1975. A Bayesian analysis of attribution processes. *Psychological Bulletin* 82 (2): 261.

Ashmore, R. D., K. Deaux, and T. McLaughlin-Vlope. 2004. An organizing framework for collective identity: Articulation and significance of multidimensionality. *Psychological Bulletin* 130: 80–114. doi:10.1037/0033-2909.130.1.80.

Bamberg, S., and G. Möser. 2007. Twenty years after Hines, Hungerford, and Tomera: A new meta-analysis of psycho-social determinants of pro-environmental behaviour. *Journal of Environmental Psychology* 27 (1): 14–25.

Barragan-Jason, G., C. de Mazancourt, C. Parmesan, M. C. Singer, and M. Loreau. 2022. Human–nature connectedness as a pathway to sustainability: A global meta-analysis. *Conservation Letters* 15 (1): e12852.

Bissing-Olson, M. J., K. S. Fielding, and A. Iyer. 2016. Experiences of pride, not guilt, predict pro-environmental behavior when pro-environmental descriptive norms are more positive. *Journal of Environmental Psychology* 45: 145–53.

Black, J. S., P. C. Stern, and J. T. Elworth. 1985. Personal and contextual influences on household energy adaptations. *Journal of Applied Psychology* 70 (1): 3–21.

Blankenberg, A. K., and H. Alhusen. 2019. On the determinants of pro-environmental behavior: A literature review and guide for the empirical economist. *Center for European, Governance, and Economic Development Research (CEGE) Discussion Papers* (350).

Bohr, J., and R. E. Dunlap. 2018. Key topics in environmental sociology, 1990–2014: Results from a computational text analysis. *Environmental Sociology* 4 (2): 181–95.

Bouman, T., M. Verschoor, C. J. Albers, G. Böhm, S. D. Fisher, W. Poortinga, L. Whitmarsh, and L. Steg. 2020. When worry about climate change leads to climate action: How values, worry and personal responsibility relate to various climate actions. *Global Environmental Change* 62: 102061.

Bragg R., C. Wood, J. Barton, and J. Pretty. 2013. Measuring connection to nature in children: A robust methodology for the RSPB. Accessed February 3, 2014. http://www.rspb.org.uk/Images/methodology-report_tcm9-354606.pdf.

Brown, G., C. M. Raymond, and J. Corcoran. 2015. Mapping and measuring place attachment. *Applied Geography* 57: 42–53.

Brügger, A., F. G. Kaiser, and N. Roczen. 2011. One for all? Connectedness to nature, inclusion of nature, environmental identity, and implicit association with nature. *European Psychologist* 16: 324–33.

Bullard, R. D. 2021. Environmental justice—once a footnote, now a headline. *Harvard Environmental Law Review* 45: 243.

Burnham, K. P., and D. R. Anderson. 1998. *Model selection and multimodel inference: A practical information theoretic approach*. New York: Springer.

Buttel, F. H., and D. R. Field. 2004. Environmental and natural resource sociologies: Understanding and synthesizing fundamental research traditions. In *Society and Natural Resources: A Summary of Knowledge*, ed. M. J. Manfredo, J. J. Vaske, B. L. Bruyere, D. R. Field, and P. J. Brown, 235–47 Jefferson, MO: Modern Litho.

Castro, P. 2006. Applying social psychology to the study of environmental concern and environmental worldviews: Contributions from the social representations approach. *Journal of Community & Applied Social Psychology* 16 (4): 247–66.

Catton, W. R. 1980. *Overshoot: The ecological basis of revolutionary change*. Champaign: University of Illinois Press.

Cialdini, R. B., C. A. Kallgren, and R. R. Reno. 1991. A focus theory of normative conduct: A theoretical refinement and reevaluation of the role of norms in human behavior. *Advances in experimental social psychology* 24: 201–34.

Clark, M., M. Springmann, M. Rayner, P. Scarborough, J. Hill, D. Tilman, and R. A. Harrington. 2022. Estimating the environmental impacts of 57,000 food products. *Proceedings of the National Academy of Sciences* 119 (33): e2120584119.

Clayton, S. D. 2003. Environmental identity: A conceptual and operational definition. In *Identity and the environment: The psychological significance of nature*, ed. S. D. Clayton and S. Opotow, 45–65. Cambridge, MA: MIT Press.

Clayton, S., S. Czellar, S. Nartova-Bochaver, J. C. Skibins, G. Salazar, Y.-C. Tseng, B. Irkhin, and F. S. Monge-Rodriguez. 2021. Cross-cultural validation of a revised environmental identity scale. *Sustainability* 13 (4): 2387.

Clayton, S., A. Koehn, and E. Grover. 2013. Making sense of the senseless: Identity, justice, and the framing of environmental crises. *Social Justice Research* 26 (3): 301–19.

Collins, P. H. 1986. Learning from the outsider within: The sociological significance of Black feminist thought. *Social Problems* 33 (6): 14–32.

Cruz, S. M., and B. Manata. 2020. Measurement of environmental concern: A review and analysis. *Frontiers in Psychology* 11: 363.

Daryanto, A., and Z. Song. 2021. A meta-analysis of the relationship between place attachment and pro-environmental behaviour. *Journal of Business Research* 123: 208–19.

Dauvergne, P. 2018. The power of environmental norms: Marine plastic pollution and the politics of microbeads. *Environmental Politics* 27 (4): 579–97.

Degroot, I., W. Loring, A. Rihm Jr., S. W. Samuels, and W. Winkelstein Jr. 1966. People and air pollution: A study of attitudes in Buffalo, NY. *Journal of the Air Pollution Control Association* 16 (5): 245–47.

Devine-Wright, P., and S. Clayton. 2010. Introduction to the special issue: Place, identity and environmental behavior. *Journal of Environmental Psychology* 30: 267–70. https://doi.org/10.1016/S0272-4944(10)00078-2.

Dietz, T., R. Duan, J. Nalley, and A. Van Witsen. 2018. Social support for water quality: The influence of values and symbolic racism. *Human Ecology Review* 24 (1): 51–70.

Dietz, T., A. Fitzgerald, and R. Shwom. 2005. Environmental values. *Annual Review of Environment and Resources* 30: 335–72.

Dietz, T., E. A. Rosa, and R. York. 2009. Environmentally efficient well-being: Rethinking sustainability as the relationship between human well-being and environmental impacts. *Human Ecology Review* 16 (1): 114–23.

Dietz, T., P. C. Stern, and G. A. Guagnano. 1998. Social structural and social psychological bases of environmental concern. *Environment and Behavior* 30 (4): 450–71.

Domingues, R. B., and G. Gonçalves. 2020. Assessing environmental attitudes in Portugal using a new short version of the Environmental Attitudes Inventory. *Current Psychology* 39 (2): 629–39.

Dunlap, R. E. 2002. An enduring concern. *Public Perspective* 13 (5): 10–14.

Dunlap, R. E. 2008. The new environmental paradigm scale: From marginality to worldwide use. *Journal of Environmental Education* 40 (1): 3–18.

Dunlap, R. E., and R. E. Jones. 2002. Environmental concern: Conceptual and measurement issues. *Handbook of Environmental Sociology* 3 (6): 482–524.

Dunlap, R. E., K. D. Van Liere, A. Mertig, and R. E. Jones. 2000. Measuring endorsement of the new ecological paradigm: A revised NEP scale. *Journal of Social Issues* 56 (3): 425–42.

Dunlap, R. E., and A. M. McCright. 2008. Social movement identity: Validating a measure of identification with the environmental movement. *Social Science Quarterly* 89: 1045–65. https://doi.org/10.1111/j.1540-6237.2008.00573.x.

Dunlap, R. E., A. M. McCright, and J. H. Yarosh. 2016. The political divide on climate change: Partisan polarization widens in the US. *Environment: Science and Policy for Sustainable Development* 58 (5): 4–23.

Dunlap, R. E., and K. D. Van Liere. 1978. The "new environmental paradigm." *The Journal of Environmental Education* 9 (4): 10–19.

Dunlap, R. E., and R. York. 2008. The globalization of environmental concern and the limits of the postmaterialist values explanation: Evidence from four multinational surveys. *The Sociological Quarterly* 49 (3): 529–63.

Dutcher, D., J. Finley, A. Luloff, and J. Johnson. 2007. Connectivity with nature as a measure of environmental values. *Environment and Behavior* 39: 474–93. https://doi.org/10.1177/0013916506298794.

Eagly, A. H., and Chaiken, S. 1993. *The psychology of attitudes.* San Diego, CA: Harcourt Brace Jovanovich.

Eaton, W. M., F. R. Eanes, J. D. Ulrich-Schad, M. Burnham, S. P. Church, J. G. Arbuckle, and J. E. Cross. 2019. Trouble with sense of place in working landscapes. *Society & Natural Resources* 32 (7): 827–40.

Ertz, M., and E. Sarigöllü. 2019. The behavior-attitude relationship and satisfaction in proenvironmental behavior. *Environment and Behavior* 51 (9–10): 1106–32.

Fishbein, M., and I. Ajzen. 1974. Attitudes towards objects as predictors of single and multiple behavioral criteria. *Psychological Review* 81 (1): 59–74.

Fishbein, M., and I. Ajzen. 2010. *Predicting and changing behavior: The reasoned action approach.* New York: Psychology Press.

Franzen, A., and D. Vogl. 2013. Two decades of measuring environmental attitudes: A comparative analysis of 33 countries. *Global Environmental Change* 23 (5): 1001–08.

Gatersleben, B., N. Murtagh, and W. Abrahamse. 2012. Values, identity and proenvironmental behaviour. *Contemporary Social Science: Journal of the Academy of Social Sciences* 9 (4): 374–92. https://doi.org/10.1080/21582041.2012.682086.

Gelfand, A., and D. K. Dey. 1994. Bayesian model choice: Asymptotics and exact calculations. *Journal of the Royal Statistical Society* 56 (3): 501–14.

Gkargkavouzi, A., G. Halkos, and S. Matsiori. 2019. Environmental behavior in a private-sphere context: Integrating theories of planned behavior and value belief norm, self-identity and habit. *Resources, Conservation and Recycling* 148: 145–56.

Glacken, C. J. 1967. *Traces on the Rhodian shore: Nature and culture in Western thought from ancient times to the end of the eighteenth century.* Vol. 170. Berkeley: University of California Press.

Han, H. 2015. Travelers' pro-environmental behavior in a green lodging context: Converging value-belief-norm theory and the theory of planned behavior. *Tourism Management* 47: 164–77.

Harrison, G. M. 2019. Validity evidence against the children's new ecological paradigm scale. *The Journal of Environmental Education* 51 (1): 1–13. https://doi.org/10.1080/00958964.2019.1646202.

Hartsock, N. C. 1983. *Money, sex, and power: Toward a feminist historical materialism.* Boston, MA: Northeastern University Press.

Hatty, M. A., L. D. G. Smith, D. Goodwin, and F. T. Mavondo. 2020. The CN-12: A brief, multidimensional connection with nature instrument. *Frontiers in Psychology* 14: 1566.

Hawcroft, L. J., and T. L. Milfont. 2010. The use (and abuse) of the new environmental paradigm scale over the last 30 years: A meta-analysis. *Journal of Environmental Psychology* 30 (2): 143–58.

Heberlein, T. A. 1972. The land ethic realized: Some social psychological explanations for changing environmental attitudes. *Journal of Social Issues* 28 (4): 79–87.

Heberlein, T. A. 1977. Norm activation and environmental action: A rejoinder to RE Dunlap and KD Van Liere. *Journal of Social Issues* 33 (3): 207–11.

Heberlein, T. A. 1981. Environmental attitudes. *Zeitschrift fur umweltpolitik* 2 (3): 241–70.

Heberlein, T. A. 2012. Navigating environmental attitudes. *Conservation Biology* 26 (4): 583–85.

Heberlein, T. A., and J. S. Black. 1976. Attitudinal specificity and the prediction of behavior in a field setting. *Journal of Personality and Social Psychology* 33 (4): 474–79.

Hines, J. M., H. R. Hungerford, and A. N. Tomera. 1987. Analysis and synthesis of research on responsible environmental behavior: A meta-analysis. *The Journal of Environmental Education* 18 (2): 1–8.

IPCC (Intergovernmental Panel on Climate Change). 2022. Summary for Policymakers. In *Climate change 2022: Impacts, adaptation and vulnerability. Contribution of working group II to the sixth assessment report of the Intergovernmental Panel on Climate Change.* Cambridge, UK: Cambridge University Press. https://doi.org/10.1017/9781009325844.001.

Ives, C. D., M. Giusti, J. Fischer, D. J. Abson, K. Klaniecki, C. Dorninger, J. Laudan, S. Barthel, P. Abernethy, B. Martín-López, et al. 2017. Human–nature connection: A multidisciplinary review. *Current Opinion in Environmental Sustainability* 26: 106–13.

Jones, R. E., and R. Wishart. 2018. Environmental justice. In *Social justice and the sociological imagination: A reader for the twenty-first century,* ed. S. Cable and T. Wall, 122–28, 3rd ed. Dubuque, IA: Kendall Hunt.

Kaiser, F. G. 2006. A moral extension of the theory of planned behavior: Norms and anticipated feelings of regret in conservationism. *Personality and Individual Differences* 41 (1): 71–81.

Kollmuss, A., and J. Agyeman. 2002. Mind the gap: Why do people act environmentally and what are the barriers to pro-environmental behavior? *Environmental Education Research* 8 (3): 239–60.

Landmann, H., and A. Rohmann. 2020. Being moved by protest: Collective efficacy beliefs and injustice appraisals enhance collective action intentions for forest protection via positive and negative emotions. *Journal of Environmental Psychology* 71: 101491.

Landry, N., R. Gifford, T. L. Milfont, A. Weeks, and S. Arnocky. 2018. Learned helplessness moderates the relationship between environmental concern and behavior. *Journal of Environmental Psychology* 55: 18–22.

Lange, F., and S. Dewitte. 2019. Measuring pro-environmental behavior: Review and recommendations. *Journal of Environmental Psychology* 63: 92–100.

Larson, L. R., C. B. Cooper, R. C. Stedman, D. J. Decker, and R. J. Gagnon. 2018. Place-based pathways to proenvironmental behavior: Empirical evidence for a conservation–recreation model. *Society & Natural Resources* 31 (8): 871–91.

Larson, L. R., R. C. Stedman, C. B. Cooper, and D. J. Decker. 2015. Understanding the multi-dimensional structure of pro-environmental behavior. *Journal of Environmental Psychology* 43: 112–24.

Leopold, A. 1949. *A Sand County almanac*. New York: Ballantine.

Lewis, S. L., and M. A. Maslin. 2015. Defining the anthropocene. *Nature* 519 (7542): 171–80.

Loomis, J. B. 2005. Updated outdoor recreation use values on national forests and other public lands. *US Department of Agriculture, Forest Service, Pacific Northwest Research Station* 658.

MacKenzie, S. B. 2003. The dangers of poor construct conceptualization. *Journal of the Academy of Marketing Science* 31 (3): 323–26.

Manfredo, M. J., J. T. Bruskotter, T. L. Teel, D. Fulton, S. H. Schwartz, R. Arlinghaus, and L. Sullivan. 2017. Why social values cannot be changed for the sake of conservation. *Conservation Biology* 31 (4): 772–80.

Manfredo, M. J., and A. A. Dayer. 2004. Concepts for exploring the social aspects of human–wildlife conflict in a global context. *Human Dimensions of Wildlife* 9 (4): 1–20.

Martin, C., and S. Czellar. 2016. The extended inclusion of nature in self scale. *Journal of Environmental Psychology* 47: 181–94.

Mayer, S. F., and C. M. Frantz. 2004. The connectedness to nature scale: A measure of individuals' feeling in community with nature. *Journal of Environmental Psychology* 24: 503–15. https://doi.org/10.1016/j.jenvp.2004.10.001.

McIntyre, A., and T. L. Milfont. 2016. Who cares? Measuring environmental attitudes. In *Research methods for environmental psychology*, ed. R. Gifford, 93–114, 1st ed., Hoboken, NJ: John Wiley & Sons.

Merton, R. K. 1948. The bearing of empirical research upon the development of social theory. *American Sociological Review* 13 (5): 505–15.

Milfont, T. L., and J. Duckitt. 2010. The environmental attitudes inventory: A valid and reliable measure to assess the structure of environmental attitudes. *Journal of Environmental Psychology* 30 (1): 80–94.

Milfont, T. L., W. Poortinga, and C. G. Sibley. 2020. Does having children increase environmental concern? Testing parenthood effects with longitudinal data from the New Zealand Attitudes and Values Study. *Plos One* 15 (3): e0230361.

Mitchell, R. C. 1980. *Public opinion on environmental issues: Results of a national survey.* Washington, D.C.: President's Council on Environmental Quality.

Mitchell, R. C., and R. T. Carson. 2013. *Using surveys to value public goods: The contingent valuation method.* Washington, D.C.: Resources for the Future.

Mullendore, N. D., J. D. Ulrich-Schad, and L. S. Prokopy. 2015. US farmers' sense of place and its relation to conservation behavior. *Landscape and Urban Planning* 140: 67–75.

Nielsen, K. S., V. Cologna, F. Lange, C. Brick, and P. Stern. 2021. The case for impact-focused environmental psychology. *Journal of Environmental Psychology* 74: 101559.

Niemiec, R. M., V. Champine, J. J. Vaske, and A. Mertens. 2020. Does the impact of norms vary by type of norm and type of conservation behavior? A meta-analysis. *Society & Natural Resources* 33 (8): 1024–40.

Nigbur, D., E. Lyons, and D. Uzzell. 2010. Attitudes, norms, identity and environmental behaviour: Using an expanded theory of planned behaviour to predict participation in a kerbside recycling programme. *British Journal of Social Psychology* 49 (2): 259–84.

Nisbett, E. K., J. M. Zelenski, and S. A. Murphy. 2009. The nature relatedness scale: Linking individuals' connection with nature to environmental concern and behavior. *Environment and Behavior* 41: 715–40. https://doi.org/10.1177/00139165 08318748.

Nyborg, K. 2018. Social norms and the environment. *Annual Review of Resource Economics* 10: 405–23.

Onwezen, M. C., G. Antonides, and J. Bartels. 2013. The norm activation model: An exploration of the functions of anticipated pride and guilt in pro-environmental behaviour. *Journal of economic Psychology* 39: 141–53.

Otto, S., and P. Pensini. 2017. Nature-based environmental education of children: Environmental knowledge and connectedness to nature, together, are related to ecological behaviour. *Global Environmental Change* 47: 88–94. https://doi.org/10 .1016/j.gloenvcha.2017.09.009.

Perkins, H. E. 2010. Measuring love and care for nature. *Journal of Environmental Psychology* 30 (4): 455–63.

Rare and California Environmental Associates. 2019. *Changing behaviors to reduce U.S. emissions: Seven pathways to achieve climate impact.* Arlington, VA: Rare.

Restall, B., and E. Conrad. 2015. A literature review of connectedness to nature and its potential for environmental management. *Journal of Environmental Management* 159: 264–78.

Riepe, C., U. Liebe, M. Fujitani, S. Kochalski, Ø. Aas, and R. Arlinghaus. 2021. Values, beliefs, norms, and conservation-oriented behaviors toward native fish biodiversity in rivers: Evidence from four european countries. *Society and Natural Resources* 34: 703–24.

Rokeach, M. 1968. The role of values in public opinion research. *Public Opinion Quarterly* 32 (4): 547–59.

Ros, B., and S. Kaneko. 2022. Is self-transcendence philanthropic? Graded response model approach. *Frontiers in Psychology* 13: 816793.

Rosa, C. D., S. Collado, and L. R. Larson. 2022. The utility and limitations of the new ecological paradigm scale for children. *The Journal of Environmental Education* 53 (2): 87–98.

Rosa, C. D., S. Collado, and C. C. Profice. 2021. Measuring Brazilians' environmental attitudes: A systematic review and empirical analysis of the NEP scale. *Current Psychology* 40 (3): 1298–1309.

Routhe, A. S., R. E. Jones, and D. L. Feldman. 2005. Using theory to understand public support for collective actions that impact the environment: Alleviating water supply problems in a nonarid biome. *Social Science Quarterly* 86 (4): 874–97.

Sagiv, L., and S. Roccas. 2021. How do values affect behavior? Let me count the ways. *Personality and Social Psychology Review* 25 (4): 295–316.

Sagiv, L., and S. H. Schwartz. 2022. Personal values across cultures. *Annual Review of Psychology* 73: 517–46.

Schultz, P. W. 2002. Inclusion with nature: The psychology of human-nature relations. In *Psychology of sustainable development*, ed. P. Schmuck and P. Wesley Schultz, 61–78. New York: Springer. https://doi.org/10.1007/978-1-4615-0995-0_4.

Schultz, P. W., and F. G. Kaiser. 2012. Promoting pro-environmental behavior. In *The Oxford handbook of environmental and conservation psychology*, ed. S. D. Clayton, 556–80. Oxford, UK: Oxford University Press. https://doi.org/10.1093/oxfordhb/9780199733026.013.0029.

Schultz, P. W., C. Shriver, J. J. Tabanico, and A. M. Khazian. 2004. Implicit connections with nature. *Journal of Environmental Psychology* 24 (1): 31–42.

Schwartz, S. H. 1968. Words, deeds and the perception of consequences and responsibility in action situations. *Journal of Personality and Social Psychology* 10 (3): 232–42.

Schwartz, S. H. 1977. Normative influences on altruism. In *Advances in experimental social psychology*, ed, L. Berkowitz, vol. 10, 221–79. Cambridge, MA: Academic Press.

Schwartz, S. H. 2010. Basic values: How they motivate and inhibit prosocial behavior. In *Prosocial motives, emotions, and behavior: The better angels of our nature*, ed. M. Mikulincer and P. R. Shaver, 221–41. Washington, D. C.: American Psychological Association.

Schwartz, S. H., J. Cieciuch, M. Vecchione, E. Davidov, R. Fischer, C. Beierlein, and M. Konty. 2012. Refining the theory of basic individual values. *Journal of Personality and Social Psychology* 103 (4): 663–88.

Schwartz, S. H., L. Sagiv, and K. Boehnke. 2000. Worries and values. *Journal of Personality* 68 (2): 309–46.

Schwartz, S. J., K. Luyckx, and V. L. Vignoles. 2011. *Handbook of identity theory and research*. New York: Springer. https://doi.org/10.1007/978-1-4419-7988-9_1.

Sharpe, E., A. Ruepert, E. van der Werff, and L. Steg. 2022. Corporate environmental responsibility leads to more pro-environmental behavior at work by strengthening intrinsic pro-environmental motivation. *One Earth* 5 (7): 825–35.

Smith, D. E. 1990. *The conceptual practices of power: A feminist sociology of knowledge*. Toronto: University of Toronto Press.

Sok, J., J. R. Borges, P. Schmidt, and I. Ajzen. 2021. Farmer behaviour as reasoned action: A critical review of research with the theory of planned behaviour. *Journal of Agricultural Economics* 72 (2): 388–412.

Steg, L. 2016. Values, norms, and intrinsic motivation to act proenvironmentally. *Annual Review of Environment and Resources* 41 (1): 277–92.

Steg, L., and J. I. M. de Groot. 2012. Environmental values. In *The Oxford handbook of environmental and conservation psychology*, ed. S. Clayton, 81–92. Oxford, UK: Oxford University Press. https://doi.org/10.1093/oxfordhb/9780199733026.013.0005.

Stern, M. J. 2018. *Social science theory for environmental sustainability: A practical guide*. Oxford, UK: Oxford University Press.

Stern, P. 2000. Toward a coherent theory of environmentally significant behavior. *Journal of Social Issues* 56 (3): 407–24.

Stern, P. C., and T. Dietz. 1994. The value basis of environmental concern. *Journal of Social Issues* 50 (3): 65–84.

Stern, P. C., T. Dietz, T. Abel, G. A. Guagnano, and L. Kalof, L. 1999. A value-belief-norm theory of support for social movements: The case of environmentalism. *Human Ecology Review* 6 (2): 81–97.

Stern, P. C., T. Dietz, and J. S. Black. 1985. Support for environmental protection: The role of moral norms. *Population and Environment* 8 (3): 204–22.

Stern, P. C., T. Dietz, and G. A. Guagnano. 1998. A brief inventory of values. *Educational and Psychological Measurement* 58 (6): 984–1001.

Stern, P. C., T. Dietz, and L. Kalof. 1993. Value orientations, gender, and environmental concern. *Environment and Behavior* 25 (5): 322–48.

Stern, P. C., T. Dietz, L. Kalof, and G. A. Guagnano. 1995. Values, beliefs, and proenvironmental action: Attitude formation toward emergent attitude objects. *Journal of Applied Social Psychology* 25: 1611–36. https://doi.org/10.1111/j.1559-1816.1995.tb02636.x.

Tadaki, M., J. Sinner, and K. M. Chan. 2017. Making sense of environmental values: A typology of concepts. *Ecology and Society* 22 (1): 7.

Tam, K. P. 2013. Concepts and measures related to connection to nature: Similarities and differences. *Journal of Environmental Psychology* 34: 64–78.

Tam, K. P., and H. W. Chan. 2018. Generalized trust narrows the gap between environmental concern and pro-environmental behavior: Multilevel evidence. *Global Environmental Change* 48: 182–94.

Thøgersen, J. 2006. Norms for environmentally responsible behaviour: An extended taxonomy. *Journal of Environmental Psychology* 26 (4): 247–61.

Turaga, R. M. R., R. B. Howarth, and M. E. Borsuk. 2010. Pro-environmental behavior: Rational choice meets moral motivation. *Annals of the New York Academy of Sciences* 1185 (1): 211–24.

Udall, A. M., J. I. de Groot, S. B. De Jong, and A. Shankar. 2021. How I see me—A meta-analysis investigating the association between identities and pro-environmental behaviour. *Frontiers in Psychology* 12: 582421.

Udo-Akang, D. 2012. Theoretical constructs, concepts, and applications. *American International Journal of Contemporary Research* 2 (9): 89–97.

Unanue, W., V. L. Vignoles, H. Dittmar, and M. Vansteenkiste. 2016. Life goals predict environmental behavior: Cross-cultural and longitudinal evidence. *Journal of Environmental Psychology* 46: 10–22.

van der Werff, E., and L. Steg. 2016. The psychology of participation and interest in smart energy systems: Comparing the value-belief-norm theory and the value-identity-personal norm model. *Energy Research & Social Science* 22: 107–14.

Van Liere, K. D., and R. E. Dunlap. 1978. Moral norms and environmental behavior: An application of Schwartz's norm-activation model to yard burning. *Journal of Applied Social Psychology* 8 (2): 174–88.

Van Liere, K. D., and R. E. Dunlap. 1980. The social bases of environmental concern: A review of hypotheses, explanations and empirical evidence. *Public Opinion Quarterly* 44 (2): 181–97.

Vaske, J. J., and K. C. Kobrin. 2001. Place attachment and environmentally responsible behavior. *The Journal of Environmental Education* 32 (4): 16–21.

Walton, T. N., and R. E. Jones. 2018. Ecological identity: The development and assessment of a measurement scale. *Environment and Behavior* 50 (6): 657–89.

Whitburn, J., W. Linklater, and W. Abrahamse. 2020. Meta-analysis of human connection to nature and proenvironmental behavior. *Conservation Biology* 34 (1): 180–93.

Whittaker, D., J. J. Vaske, and M. J. Manfredo. 2006. Specificity and the cognitive hierarchy: Value orientations and the acceptability of urban wildlife management actions. *Society and Natural Resources* 19 (6): 515–30.

Williams, D. R., W. P. Stewart, and L. E. Kruger. 2013. The emergence of place-based conservation. In *Place-based conservation: Perspectives from the social sciences*, ed. W. P. Stewart, D. R. Williams, and L. E. Kruger, 1–17. Dordrecht, Netherlands: Springer.

Xiao, C., R. E. Dunlap, and D. Hong. 2019. Ecological worldview as the central component of environmental concern: Clarifying the role of the NEP. *Society & Natural Resources* 32 (1): 53–72.

Yuriev, A., M. Dahmen, P. Paillé, O. Boiral, and L. Guillaumie. 2020. Pro-environmental behaviors through the lens of the theory of planned behavior: A scoping review. *Resources, Conservation and Recycling* 155: 104660.

Zajchowski, C., J. Koenigstorfer, and M. Mostafanezhad. 2023. Human dimensions of air quality: Introduction to the special issue. *Society & Natural Resources.* 36 (9): 1020–27. https://doi.org/10.1080/08941920.2023.2226628.

Zylstra, M. J., A. T. Knight, K. J. Esler, and L. L. Le Grange. 2014. Connectedness as a core conservation concern: An interdisciplinary review of theory and a call for practice. *Springer Science Reviews* 2 (1): 119–43.

13

Theorizing the "Anthropos" in the Anthropocene
Toward Decolonial Practices and Knowledge Co-Production

SIMON WEST, WIEBREN JOHANNES BOONSTRA, AND SASHA QUAHE

Anthropocene debates challenge conventional (Western) approaches to theorizing human-environment relationships. To address these challenges, environmental social scientists need to improve their practices of theorizing. We articulate three principles for better theorizing the "Anthropos" in the Anthropocene: situating theory, practicing theory, and theorizing together.

Introduction

The Anthropocene has become a prominent concept in the environmental social sciences (Hamilton, Bonneuil, and Gemenne 2015), referring to a new geological epoch characterized by the often-destructive effects of human activities in the earth system (Steffen et al. 2004) and acting as a broader sensitizing concept inviting new ways of understanding human-environment relationships (Blumer 1954; Steffen et al. 2011). In its sensitizing role, the Anthropocene partially challenges modernist dualisms of society and nature by marking the geological as inclusive of traditionally social phenomena like

https://doi.org/10.7330/9781646426300.c013

intentionality and meaning, and the social as infused with geo- and biophysical processes (Palsson et al. 2013). Initially developed by geologists and earth
system scientists, the Anthropocene concept has been enthusiastically taken
up in some areas of the environmental social sciences and humanities, where
it has prompted renewed efforts to rethink the traditional categories of agency
(Latour 2014), place (Clark and Szerszynski 2020), and time (Nixon 2011) in
relation to contemporary environmental challenges (Benson and Craig 2014).

Yet the Anthropocene concept, science, and discourse have also been
critiqued for perpetuating modernist knowledge practices that are deeply
implicated in human-environmental destruction. Decolonial, Indigenous,
Black, and feminist scholars, among others, have argued that the universalist
emphasis on a generic "human enterprise" (Steffen, Crutzen, and McNeill
2007, 614) obscures the deeply racialized and gendered dimensions of global
environmental change (Davis and Todd 2017; Whyte 2017; Grusin 2017;
Yusoff 2018). Such perspectives highlight that the Anthropocene has not been
caused by humanity in general but by specific processes of colonialism, capitalism, and industrialization—captured with the compound "modernity/
coloniality" by Mignolo and Walsh (2018, 3)—that have already brought
apocalypse for many Indigenous, Black, and other communities of color
(Ghosh 2016). Consequently, by articulating univocal narratives of human
development and progress, the knowledge practices of planetary science
appear as a continuation of modernity/coloniality (Chakrabarty 2019), even
as, somewhat paradoxically, they become ever more crucial for comprehend-
ing modernity/coloniality's destructive material effects (Belcher and Schmidt
2018). This poses a challenge for environmental social scientists: Is it possible to remain open to the sensitizing nature of the Anthropocene concept,
science, and discourse without inadvertently reproducing the modernist/
colonialist aspects that have characterized them so far? In a now classic paper
of Anthropocene scholarship, Palsson et al. (2013) highlight the need for the
social sciences and humanities to reconceptualize the "Anthropos" in the
Anthropocene in pursuit of thriving futures for all life on earth.

In this chapter, we argue that to address this challenge environmental social
scientists will not just need new theories but will also need to rethink and
reenact their basic practices of theorizing—the ways they observe, reflect,
and make descriptions or explanations about particular phenomena, processes, and events (Swedberg 2014). Many current practices of theorizing

across the social and natural sciences and humanities continue to be implicitly shaped by nature-society dualisms and their corollaries of mind-matter and subject-object; for example, where theorizers are conceived (either positively or negatively) as isolated figures tasked with producing generalizable mental abstractions separate from the "real" or material world (Connolly 2011). At the same time, however, there are efforts to nurture more generative approaches to theorizing. In the social sciences, an emerging literature is drawing on pragmatist philosophy to develop practical suggestions for more creative theorizing (Swedberg 2014). Meanwhile, decolonial approaches aim to "make visible, open up, and advance radically distinct perspectives and positionalities that displace Western rationality as the only framework and possibility of existence, analysis, and thought" (Mignolo and Walsh 2018, 17), and Indigenous scholarship, primarily undertaken in the renewal of Indigenous lands, lives, cultures, and governance systems, is demonstrating the vitality of deeply relational practices of knowing, doing, and theorizing (Betasamosake Simpson 2014). We draw on these diverse literatures to highlight three ways of improving the art and practice of theorizing the Anthropos in the Anthropocene: situating theory, practicing theory, and theorizing together.

Three Ways to Improve the Art and Practice of Theorizing in the Anthropocene

Situating Theory

While Anthropocene science aims to provide a universal, planetary perspective, critics suggest that it more accurately reflects a (natural) scientific understanding of reality originating from knowledge traditions of the Global North (Lövbrand et al. 2015). This reality, or "ontology," reflects what Law (2015) refers to as the "one-world world," where the world is divided into a universal biophysical reality (to which the natural sciences have privileged access) and a pluralistic sociopolitical field of cultural perspectives (the domain of the social sciences). The Northern commitment to a one-world world is closely linked to colonial narratives of modernity and development, which have led to the suppression and eradication of subaltern realities around the world (Escobar 2018). So far, many social science contributions to Anthropocene scholarship, even while ostensibly critical, implicitly reinforce the one-world world. For example, while scholarship as diverse as earth system governance and Marxist environmental history has argued for better recognition of social diversity, it has continued to assume a universal biophysical reality (Galaz 2014; Malm 2016). As de la Cadena and Blaser (2018, 3) note, "It seems almost impossible to imagine a response to the ecological crisis that does not take the world that is responsible for the plausible destruction of the planet as the exclusive starting point in a conversation about the current condition of the planet." One possible alternative response lies in shifting from universal to pluriversal thinking—away from the one-world world and toward "a world where many worlds fit" (Escobar 2020). Emerging at the intersection of decolonial and Indigenous thought, pluriversal scholarship situates the one-world world within the Global North and recognizes the existence of many partially overlapping but distinct realities elsewhere (Blaser 2013; de la Cadena and Blaser 2018). Pluriversal responses to the Anthropocene require environmental social scientists to better situate the ontological distinctions they make in their theories, recognizing that all theories—including those addressing the planetary—are made in the context of particular places, times, and purposes (Hoelle and Kawa 2020).

How might environmental social scientists work to better situate their approaches to theorizing the Anthropocene? A first step might be for theorists to closely reflect on their own assumptions about what exists, how these assumptions relate to their broader social and historical contexts, and the ways in which these assumptions are expressed through their own favored theoretical aims, approaches, and thinkers. Such assumptions are difficult to uncover because they are often implicit and taken for granted. We have found that reflection can be aided through engagement with the history and sociology of science (highlighting the links between theoretical assumptions and the social context of the theorizer) and the emerging ontological turn in social theory (highlighting implicit assumptions about reality, e.g., Blaser 2013). A next step might be for the theorizer to become more familiar with other knowledge systems, including different Northern traditions and, for example, Indigenous, South American, African, or Asian traditions, to get a sense of different possible realities (Escobar 2020). We are not suggesting that Northern theorists necessarily attempt to incorporate such traditions within their own theorizing (there may be good ethical and intellectual reasons not to do so), but rather that they use such familiarity to better understand, locate, and limit what they do in their own work. For example,

Al-Hardan (2018, 545) suggests that decolonial scholarship "holds up a mirror" to social theorists from the Global North. Importantly, situating theory does not require theorists to limit themselves to what Northern scholars often think of as local or place-based theories, but rather requires rethinking conventional associations between the local and the situated, and the planetary and the universal. For example, Clark and Szerszynski (2020) theorize the planetary as plural rather than universal through their dual concepts of "planetary multiplicity" and "earthly multitudes." Indeed, just as planetary science originates from a relatively small network of Northern scientists, so do supposedly local knowledges contain entire cosmologies.

Practicing Theory

Anthropocene science has been critiqued as representative of "disembodied knowledge practices" and "Cartesian habits of mind," where knowledge generation is portrayed as a solely cognitive activity, conducted by scientists at a remove from the real world (Kember 2017, 350). Such assumptions also remain widespread within social theory, with theory often portrayed as an abstract, mental phenomenon that is a necessary precursor to successful practice (Cook and Wagenaar 2012). Decolonial scholars have, however, articulated alternative understandings of theory. Mignolo and Walsh (2018, 7) write, "For us, theory is doing and doing is thinking," before asking, "Are you not doing something when you theorize and analyze concepts? Isn't doing something praxis? And from praxis . . . do we not also construct theory and theorize thought?" These decolonial perspectives resonate in interesting ways with pragmatist approaches to social science theorizing. For Swedberg (2014), theorizing is a practical activity or skill, acquired through embodied processes of learning by doing in the same way as other artful practitioners learn their craft (see, e.g., Mellegård and Boonstra 2020). Sandberg and Tsoukas (2011) suggest that recognizing theory as a practice, and then actively theorizing from the standpoint of practical rationalities, can result in more accurate and useful social theorizing.

How can environmental social scientists let these ideas infuse their own practices? A first step might be for theorists to actively participate in different forms of social action around their topic of interest. Mignolo and Walsh (2018, 18–19) present a picture of the decolonial theorist as engaging in processes of "walking, asking, reflecting, analyzing, theorizing and actioning—in continuous movement, contention, relation, and formation." A next step might be to explicitly nurture the craft of theorizing through practical exercises. Swedberg (2014) encourages researchers to hone their skills through techniques such as inverting their senses of scale and proportion, experimenting with metaphors and analogies, and developing personal sets of heuristics. In the context of Anthropocene scholarship, Clark and Szerszynski (2020, 93–99) suggest that theorists learn from the insights of planetary science as well as from those most directly and experientially attuned to the material forces of the planet, including, for example, weavers, hunter-gatherers, metallurgists, miners, and experimental scientists. Taken together, these ideas suggest a posture for the theorizer that is understood less in terms of distanced theorizing *about* the world, and more in terms of an engaged practitioner thinking creatively *with* and *through* the world of which they are part.

Theorizing Together

Situating and practicing theory challenges the classic Western image of the individual (often male) social theorizer—captured in the image of the "founding fathers" of sociology, Marx, Durkheim, and Weber—and instead situate theorizers within their particular social-ecological context and community. The idea of the individual theorizer is closely linked to linear conceptions of the relationships between science and society, where theorizing is conducted in isolation before the product—in the form of the final theory—is then provided to society. Within such models it is the product rather than the process of theorizing that is considered socially valuable (West, van Kerkhoff, and Wagenaar 2019). The Anthropocene concept has prompted challenges to linear science-society models, with calls for knowledge co-production and transdisciplinary research (Norström et al. 2020). So far, however, knowledge co-production has been oriented to the achievement of instrumental goals, such as the production of management plans and indicators, and there remains a perception that theorizing is something that researchers might do alone before or after the collaborative stage. Indigenous scholars have articulated different understandings of the social role of theorizing. Betasamosake Simpson (2014, 7) writes that in Nishnaabeg thought, "theory isn't just for academics; it's for everyone. . . . [Theory] is generated from the ground up and its power stems from its living resonance within individuals and collectives." Inspired by such approaches, we suggest that extending practices of theorizing to collaborative contexts may be a powerful way of realizing the processual value of theorizing for addressing Anthropocene challenges.

How might environmental social scientists nurture more of a collaborative spirit in their theorizing? As a first step, Swedberg (2014) suggests that theorists should actively seek to work with other disciplines, especially the arts, to develop more imaginative and socially resonant forms of theorizing. Expanding outward from academia, theorists might take inspiration from participatory scenarios and futures thinking, where researchers are thinking together with practitioners, policy-makers, citizens, and communities (Oteros-Rozas et al. 2015). In such work it is vital that researchers become attuned to the power relationships, diverse purposes, and incommensurabilities inherent to situations where those from different knowledges and worlds come together, and that they aim to engage in genuinely good-faith partnerships where differences are respected rather than subsumed under consensual or integrative frameworks (Reed and Abernethy 2018; Turnhout et al. 2021). For example, Verran, Spencer, and Christie (2021) describe a "ground-up" approach to social research in Northern Australia, where Indigenous and non-Indigenous collaborators are working together to generate ontologically unique concepts and categories that can productively advance collective policy and practice challenges, such as water security in remote communities threatened by climate change (Spencer et al. 2019). These ways of doing knowledge co-production without the need for consensus or commensurability—of "doing difference differently" (Verran and Christie 2011)—are, we suggest, more in keeping with complexity-based and pluriversal responses to the Anthropocene.

Conclusion

The Anthropocene concept should prompt environmental social scientists to do things differently in their efforts to grapple with unprecedented global environmental change. Anthropocene debates make clear that academic practices—including practices of theorizing—are never neutral and are shaped by the very changing and power-infused processes researchers seek to understand. Decolonial and Indigenous philosophical praxis, together with old and new perspectives on theorizing in the social sciences, provide sources of inspiration for experimenting with more generative ways of practicing the non-innocent arts of theorizing. *Situating theory* prompts theorizers to begin from pluriversal rather than universal assumptions, recognizing the particularity and partiality of their contributions within a world of many worlds. *Theorizing as practice* encourages theorizers to immerse themselves in the world(s) around them, attending to their craft through continual practices of observing, learning, and doing. And *theorizing together* encourages theorizers to recognize themselves as situated in relational webs and networks, and to explicitly theorize with others in collaborative and co-productive settings. We encourage environmental social scientists to take up the challenges posed by Anthropocene debates to conventional (Western) research practices and to engage in creative theorizing that can begin the task of reconceptualizing the Anthropos in the Anthropocene.

References

Al-Hardan, A. 2018. The sociological canon reconfigured: Empire, colonial critique, and contemporary sociology. *International Sociology Reviews* 33 (5): 545–57.

Belcher, O., and J. J. Schmidt. 2021. Being earthbound: Arendt, process and alienation in the Anthropocene. *Environment and Planning D: Society and Space* 39 (1): 103–20.

Benson, M. H., and R. K. Craig. 2014. The end of sustainability. *Society & Natural Resources* 27 (7): 777–82.

Betasamosake Simpson, L. 2014. Land as pedagogy: Nishnaabeg intelligence and rebellious transformation. *Decolonization: Indigeneity, Education & Society* 3: 1–25.

Blaser, M. 2013. Ontological conflicts and the stories of peoples in spite of Europe: Toward a conversation on political ontology. *Current Anthropology* 54 (5): 547–68.

Blumer, H. 1954. What is wrong with social theory? *American Sociological Review* 19: 3–10.

Chakrabarty, D. 2019. The planet: An emergent humanist category. *Critical Inquiry* 46: 1–31.

Clark, N., and B. Szerszynski. 2020. *Planetary social thought: The Anthropocene challenge to the social sciences.* Cambridge, UK: Wiley.

Connolly, W. E. 2011. *A world of becoming.* Durham, NC: Duke University Press.

Cook, S. D. N., and H. Wagenaar. 2012. Navigating the eternally unfolding present: Toward an epistemology of practice. *The American Review of Public Administration* 42 (1): 3–38.

Davis, H., and Z. Todd. 2017. On the importance of a date, or decolonizing the Anthropocene. *ACME: An International E-Journal for Critical Geographies* 16: 761–80.

de la Cadena, M., and M. Blaser. 2018. *A world of many worlds.* Durham, NC: Duke University Press.

Escobar, A. 2018. *Designs for the pluriverse: Radical interdependence, autonomy, and the making of worlds.* Durham, NC: Duke University Press.

Escobar, A. 2020. *Pluriversal politics: The real and the possible.* Durham, NC: Duke University Press.

Galaz, V. 2014. *Global environmental governance, technology and politics: The Anthropocene gap.* Cheltenham, UK: Edward Elgar.

Ghosh, A. 2016. *The great derangement: Climate change and the unthinkable.* Chicago, IL: Penguin Books.

Grusin, R., ed. 2017. *Anthropocene feminism.* Minneapolis: University of Minnesota Press.

Hamilton, C., C. Bonneuil, and F. Gemenne, eds. 2015. *The Anthropocene and the global environmental crisis: Rethinking modernity in a new epoch.* London: Routledge.

Hoelle, J., and N. C. Kawa. 2020. Placing the *Anthropos* in the Anthropocene. *Annals of the American Association of Geographers* 111 (3): 655–62.

Kember, S. 2017. After the Anthropocene: The photographic for earthly survival? *Digital Creativity* 28: 348–53.

Latour, B., 2014. Agency at the time of the Anthropocene. *New Literary History* 45: 1–18.

Law, J. 2015. What's wrong with a one-world world? *Distinktion: Scandinavian Journal of Social Theory* 16 (1): 126–39.

Lövbrand, E., S. Beck, J. Chilvers, T. Forsyth, J. Hedrén, M. Hulme, R. Lidskog, and E. Vasileiadou. 2015. Who speaks for the future of Earth? How critical social science can extend the conversation on the Anthropocene. *Global Environmental Change* 32: 211–18.

Malm, A. 2016. *Fossil capital: The rise of steam power and the roots of global warming.* Brooklyn, NY: Verso Books.

Mellegård, V., and W. J. Boonstra. 2020. Craftsmanship as a carrier of Indigenous and local ecological knowledge: Photographic insights from Sámi Duodji and archipelago fishing. *Society & Natural Resources* 33 (10): 1252–72.

Mignolo, W. D., and C. E. Walsh. 2018. *On decoloniality: Concepts, analytics, praxis.* Durham, NC: Duke University Press.

Nixon, R. 2011. *Slow violence and the environmentalism of the poor.* Cambridge, MA: Harvard University Press.

Norström, A. V., C. Cvitanovic, M. F. Löf, S. West, C. Wyborn, P. Balvanera, A. T. Bednarek, E. M. Bennett, R. Biggs, A. de Bremond, et al. 2020. Principles for knowledge co-production in sustainability research. *Nature Sustainability* 3: 182–90.

Oteros-Rozas, E., B. Martín-López, T. Daw, E. L. Bohensky, J. Butler, R. Hill, J. Martin-Ortega, A. Quinlan, R. Ravera, I. Ruiz-Mallén, et al. 2015. Participatory scenario planning in place-based social-ecological research: Insights and experiences from 23 case studies. *Ecology and Society* 20 (4): 32.

Palsson, G., B. Szerszynski, S. Sörlin, J. Marks, B. Avril, C. Crumley, H. Hackmann, P. Holm, J. Ingram, A. Kirman, et al. 2013. Reconceptualizing the "Anthropos" in the Anthropocene: Integrating the social sciences and humanities in global environmental change research. *Environmental Science & Policy* 28: 3–13.

Reed, M., and P. Abernethy. 2018. Facilitating co-production of transdisciplinary knowledge for sustainability: Working with Canadian biosphere reserve practitioners. *Society & Natural Resources* 31 (1): 39–56.

Sandberg, J., and H. Tsoukas. 2011. Grasping the logic of practice: Theorizing through practical rationality. *Academy of Management Review* 36: 338–60.

Spencer, M., E. Dányi, and Y. Hayashi. 2019. Asymmetries and climate futures: Working with qaters in an Indigenous Australian aettlement. *Science, Technology & Human Values* 44 (5): 786–813.

Steffen, W., P. J. Crutzen, and J. R. McNeill. 2007. The Anthropocene: Are humans now overwhelming the great forces of nature? *Ambio* 36 (8): 614–21.

Steffen, W., J. Grinevald, P. Crutz, and J. McNeill. 2011. The Anthropocene: Conceptual and historical perspectives. *Philosophical Transactions: Mathematical, Physical and Engineering Sciences* 369: 842–67.

Steffen, W., A. Sanderson, P. D. Tyson, J. Jäger, P. Matson, B. Moore III, F. Oldfield, K. Richardson, J. Schellnhuber, B. Turner II, et al. 2004. *Global change and the Earth system: A planet under pressure*. Berlin, Germany: Springer.

Swedberg, R. 2014. *The art of social theory*. Princeton, NJ: Princeton University Press.

Turnhout, E., T. Metze, C. Wyborn, N. Klenk, and E. Louder. 2020. The politics of co-production: Participation, power, and transformation. *Current Opinion in Environmental Sustainability* 42: 15–21.

Verran, H., and M. Christie. 2011. Doing difference together: Towards a dialogue with aboriginal knowledge authorities through an Australian comparative empirical philosophical inquiry. *Culture and Dialogue* 1 (2): 21–36.

Verran, H., M. Spencer, and M. Christie. 2021. "Ground-up inquiry": Questions and answers about situated research in Northern Australia. Unpublished essay.

West, S., L. van Kerkhoff, and H. Wagenaar. 2019. Beyond "linking knowledge and action": Towards a practice-based approach to transdisciplinary sustainability interventions. *Policy Studies* 40 (5): 534–55.

Whyte, K. 2017. Indigenous climate change studies: Indigenizing futures, decolonizing the Anthropocene. *English Language Notes* 55: 153–62.

Yusoff, K. 2018. *A billion Black Anthropocenes or none*. Minneapolis: University of Minnesota Press.

14

Refocusing Stewardship on Stewards

Place-Based Insights on Diversity, Relationality, and the Politics of Land

JESSICA COCKBURN, NOSISEKO MTATI, AND VANESSA MASTERSON

While the notion of stewardship is seeing a revival in the literature on human-nature relationships, tensions and questions remain about how to put the idea into practice, especially in the Global South. Here we offer insights from place-based empirical cases in South Africa, grappling with questions about how agency, politics, and context influence local stewardship.

Introduction

A golden thread that weaves through the tapestry of stewardship meanings is an aspiration for humans to take responsibility for and care of the social-ecological systems on which we all depend for our well-being (Enqvist et al. 2018; West et al. 2018; Worrell and Appleby 2000). In this chapter, it is the "steward" in stewardship that we are interested in better understanding, supporting, and enabling. We believe that humans have the potential to be positive agents of change for environmental sustainability. We consider this an important counter-narrative to narratives of humans as a destructive force

https://doi.org/10.7330/9781646426300.c014

that are often perpetuated in politically conservative conservation agendas (Robbins 2019). Moreover, we see a need to guard against stewardship becoming focused simply on policies, mechanisms, incentives, and other utilitarian approaches to human-environment relationships, which are coming to the fore (Cockburn et al. 2019a; Tengö et al. 2023); hence our call to refocus stewardship on the needs and perspectives of stewards.

Stewardship has a long history in the literature on society and natural resources. Two central aspects in this history are the contestation around its origins and assumptions (Mathevet, Bousquet, and Raymond 2018; Welchman 2012) and the debate on its multiple interpretations and applications in theory, policy, and practice (Bennett et al. 2018; Enqvist et al. 2018). While these debates are widely discussed in the Global North and from Western scientific and cultural perspectives, there is limited critical engagement with the concept and practice of stewardship from the perspectives of Indigenous peoples, and in postcolonial contexts and the Global South. For example, the notions of stewardship promoted in social-ecological systems literature (Chapin et al. 2009) tend to favour Judaeo-Christian and humanistic interpretations of the idea where individual people are seen as agents of change who can be manipulated to act, as reflected in many national-level policy instruments and western scientific endeavours in post-colonial contexts such as South Africa (Cockburn et al. 2019a) or Australia (Hill et al. 2012).

In this chapter we seek to contribute to a Global South perspective on the stewardship literature, bringing grounded experiences from rural South African landscapes to grapple with the contestations, tensions, and contradictions embedded in stewardship. We extend some of our recent work on these key tensions (Tengö et al. 2023) by grounding our reflections and analysis in three place-based case studies of stewardship initiatives in South Africa, seeking to investigate in a situated manner how agency, politics, and context shape the roles, responsibilities, and actions of local stewards. Each of the three authors have spent years working in, and have in-depth engagement experience with, the context and people in these cases. Our chapter begins with a review of the stewardship literature, then presents three cases through the lens of recent critiques of this literature. We then highlight insights emerging from our efforts to refocus stewardship on stewards, and we conclude with recommendations for future stewardship research, policy, and practice.

Revisiting Stewardship in Social-Ecological Systems

Reviewing the stewardship literature reveals stewardship to be a complex, ever-changing concept with a diversity of meanings in different times and places. While the literature on environmental stewardship has its origins in Western, Judaeo-Christian religious traditions (Berry 2006), the concept has now been widely adopted in a range of different fields, including in environmental sustainability (Enqvist et al. 2018). Previous studies have reviewed the classic Western environmental stewardship literature, exploring a wide range of philosophical interpretations, theories, meanings, policies, and practices (Bennett et al. 2018; Enqvist et al. 2018; Mathevet, Bousquet, and Raymond 2018; Worrell and Appleby 2000).

In this chapter, we focus on stewardship in the context of social-ecological systems and sustainability science, where it is receiving renewed interest and is being refashioned to promote calls for planetary stewardship (Chapin et al. 2009; Folke et al. 2016). Much of this work points to the potential of stewardship as an ideal to enable humanity to engage more responsibly and responsively with ecosystems in the context of rapid global change (Chapin et al. 2009). While we concur with this aspirational vision for more caring and responsible human-nature relationships, these global visions run the risk of abstracting our human relationships with nature (Smith 2019; Tengö et al. 2023) and oversimplifying the relational complexities of stewarding social-ecological systems (West et al. 2018). The origins of stewardship in Western thought traditions means that the notion of stewardship has certain ideological and normative assumptions built into it (Taylor 2017). For example, their reliance on individualistic approaches to stewardship reflects a Judaeo-Christian ethic of individual responsibility (Berry 2006), which is at odds with more collective and relational philosophies typical of many Indigenous societies (Suchet-Pearson et al. 2013; Taylor 2017). The risk of these global discourses is that they universalise and flatten the diversity of contexts, experiences, and realities in different parts of the world, perpetuating over-simplistic and often Eurocentric visions of a shared future for all of humanity (Simangan 2021).

Considering the contestation and tensions inherent in the theory and practice of stewardship, it is important to revisit the concept of stewardship from a critical perspective currently under-represented in the literature, that of Global South and postcolonial contexts. A decolonial lens can assist in revealing troubling assumptions and contradictions in concepts that have wide acceptance in the literature, enabling a more inclusive and plural conversation about their suitability (or unsuitability) in a range of contexts (Amo-Agyemang 2021).[1] A critical, decolonial perspective is particularly pertinent in light of calls for planetary stewardship in response to the challenges of the Anthropocene (Steffen et al. 2011).

In addition, critics of the stewardship concept call for a reframing of the human species as "one of many that make and shape worlds together" (Taylor 2017, 1449). This call is echoed by many perspectives on stewardship from Indigenous groups around the world (Suchet-Pearson et al. 2013; Greeson 2019). While acknowledging the importance of stewardship as a means of expressing and taking responsibility for relations with the natural world (Kahui and Richards 2014), Indigenous systems of knowing and relating to the natural world emphasise a relational ontology in which the role of humans is not to master, manage, and steward but to respond to and live alongside all of nature in ongoing reciprocal relationships (Holmes and Jampijinpa 2013). A relational interpretation of stewardship draws attention to a post-human view that non-humans (plants and animals as well as things and landscapes) in their own right play a role in stewardship (Suchet-Pearson et al. 2013; Gill 2014).

While contextual understandings of the role of individual stewards, and collectives of stewards, is acknowledged and addressed in the literature (Norton 2020; Tengö et al. 2023), there is also substantial work that focuses on philosophical, theoretical, conceptual, normative, and policy matters. The literature appears to lean toward an overemphasis on the latter, running the risk of abstracting and oversimplifying the nuanced human dimensions of stewardship, including aspects related to agency and care, which are so central to understanding and realising the potential of stewardship (Enqvist et al. 2018). In addition, there is often a strong focus on the ecological outcomes of stewardship policies, initiatives, and actions (Barendse et al. 2016), obscuring the motivations, relationships, and lived realities of stewards and the critical role they play in social-ecological sustainability processes (Masterson, Tengö, and Spierenburg 2017).

We therefore build on some of our previous work, where we have suggested a need to refocus stewardship on stewards (Cockburn et al. 2020). This

---

1. While we are inspired by and acknowledge the decolonial scholarship and discourses, we want to be clear that we do not explicitly take a decolonial approach ourselves.

means exploring the agency and context of stewards more carefully. In doing so, it is critical to explore and understand the needs, motivations, interests, and capabilities of stewards (Barendse et al. 2016). This brings us to two important questions about stewardship, around which we focus our analysis of specific cases:

1. What do the realities and voices of local stewards in the rural Global South bring to these renewed debates on stewardship?
2. What might enable or constrain stewards to enact responsibility and care in relation to the social-ecological systems in which they are embedded?

Insights from Place-Based Stewardship in the Global South

Stewardship in South African Landscapes

We now describe three place-based case studies of landscape stewardship from the rural Eastern Cape province in South Africa (figure 14.1; Cockburn et al. 2019b; Masterson, Tengö, and Spierenburg 2017; Mtati 2020). In South Africa, as elsewhere, stewardship includes a range of different interpretations and applications (Barendse et al. 2016). While the term *biodiversity stewardship* has resulted in much stewardship discourse being focused on the outcomes of biodiversity conservation, there are also stewardship initiatives that take a more integrated social-ecological approach to working with local communities, farmers, and resource users toward sustainable resource management in the context of rural development (Cockburn et al. 2020).

Land tenure and reform are deeply emotive, contested, and divisive issues in South Africa (Hall 2009). Discussions about landscape stewardship must confront these complexities (Clements et al. 2021). Centuries of racially based colonial and Apartheid policies have dispossessed the majority of South Africans of land in the name of both agricultural production and biodiversity conservation (Kepe 2009).

In our case studies, land is owned and accessed differentially by actors from different racial,[2] linguistic, and cultural groups, which influences their

---

2. In acknowledgment of the influence of race on relationships to land, we use the race group classifications according to the South African government as relevant in our cases, namely Black (Indigenous people of African descent, in our cases these are mostly people from the amaXhosa ethnic group), White (refers to people of European descent with settler-colonial origins), and Coloured (people of mixed descent). We

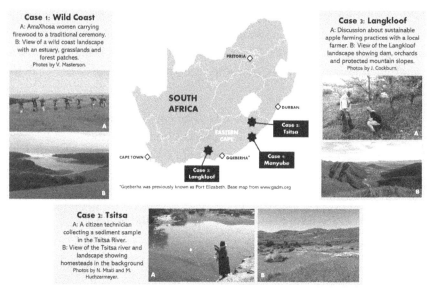

FIGURE 14.1. Map and photographs of the three place-based stewardship case studies in the Eastern Cape province, South Africa.

relationships to land and their role in stewardship. Through colonial and Apartheid land policies, Black South Africans were forcibly allocated land in "homelands" according to ethnic groupings. Despite no longer being a recognised legal jurisdiction or geographic unit, the former homelands have continued to be home almost entirely to Black communities and are plagued by lack of infrastructure, poor service delivery, and governance challenges. Since the end of Apartheid in 1993, communities transitioned away from resource dependence to increasing dependence on state social grants and remittances from migrant workers. While peasant farming is a lifestyle choice for many people, access to land for cropping, grazing, and non-timber forest products can also provide an important safety net or component of livelihoods, especially for the most vulnerable (Shackleton and Luckert 2015). A critical challenge is that traditional leaders govern alongside democratically elected governance institutions and interact with multiple land tenure

recognise that continued use of such categories, which can be argued to be arbitrary and divisive, can be problematic in that they perpetuate race-based discrimination. Nonetheless, since race and land relations are still deeply intertwined and contested, we consider it important to use these labels for the sake of clarity.

and rights systems, within which tenure is insecure for many (Ainslie and Kepe 2016).

Case 1: Manyube[3] Forest and Villages

The Manyube case is based on a study of the diverse senses of place of rural landscapes and how these intersect with a stewardship initiative for community forest conservation. This work was undertaken in the region of the Manubi State Forest in an area known as KwaManyube in the former Transkei homeland. Here conservation and forestry authorities engaged local communities to create a fenced protected area to be stewarded by local (Black) communities through a co-management agreement (figure 14.1). This venture ultimately failed to get communities to agree and the nature reserve was never established. The negotiation process illustrates the importance of engaging with multiple and contested visions of sustainability and relationships with landscape (Masterson, Spierenburg, and Tengö 2019). To convince neighbouring communities to support the forest conservation plan, largely White project proponents emphasised the poverty alleviation aims of the project (e.g., employing game guards and alien invasive clearing teams; potential profit from game breeding and ecotourism), but the questionable economic benefits did not take into account people's attachment to the land under communal tenure. As one community member explained, the forest is stewarded and known through customary ritual practices (such as harvesting particular species) as a cultural symbol of the community's identity, referred to as Xhosa forest:

> That forest is a sacred place to me. There are species that we need for our customary rites and rituals and when addressing the ancestral spirits. [Fencing the forest for a reserve] will affect many people around here because if it's fenced people won't get access to the forest.

Other contestations arose during the process. Conservation authorities and some community members held a strong narrative that the forest and surrounding land was under "threat" from community activities. As one forest ranger described, "What could the [surrounding] community do with the forest? They would only destroy it. The community can't manage this

---

3. Manyube has also been spelt "Manubi."

place on their own. They must go to school and learn more about nature. Otherwise, they can't manage it." These views were driven by pervasive, race-related degradation narratives that "uneducated" communities threaten biodiversity (e.g., through harvesting of rare tree species of important cultural and medicinal value). Other community members (e.g., farmers) opposed the establishment of the fenced reserve, particularly as they did not want to lose their rights to family farm plots, even if they were not currently cultivated. While community members had a reciprocal relationship with the land and intimate knowledge of how their grazing practices affected biodiversity, broader conservation narratives painted small-scale traditional cultivation and grazing practices as degradation and were not considered by the conservation authorities as an option with any ecological value.

Case 2: Tsitsa River Catchment

The Tsitsa case is based on a study of the benefits experienced by community-based river monitors working within the Tsitsa Project, a landscape stewardship and livelihoods initiative (Mtati 2020; figure 14.1). The residents of communal land areas within the Tsitsa landscape (the focus of this study) are characterised by poverty, unemployment, and low levels of education. They rely heavily on government social welfare grants and remittances, and often depend on natural resources to supplement livelihoods through home gardens, cropping, and livestock (Sigwela et al. 2017).

The project supported an environmental monitoring (citizen science) initiative that employed residents from communities living adjacent to the river to collect water samples for studying sediment dynamics and soil erosion in the highly degraded Tsitsa river catchment. These data informed landscape restoration activities implemented by the government. The monitors were called "citizen technicians" and were paid per sample of water collected. This raised an interesting question for project staff: are citizen technicians stewards? The Mtati (2020) study found that citizen technicians experienced numerous benefits from the initiative, including new relationships of trust and reciprocal respect with the Tsitsa Project team and growing confidence in their abilities to contribute to landscape research. In terms of stewardship, some felt a renewed connection to the river, an increased interest in how the landscape works, and a greater appreciation for the role of science in landscape restoration. As one technician reflected, "It made me much more aware of how the river works and all the changes and influence it has got on the banks . . . [the influence of the] big water and dry times. So, it made me much more attentive of my natural environment as such."

The payment received for their work was, however, the primary motivation for their continued involvement, an unsurprising finding considering their socioeconomic context. Most citizen technicians said that they would not continue doing this work if they were not remunerated; that is, they would not voluntarily continue to contribute to stewardship through this monitoring role. While they appreciated that the project team treated them well, the following quote illustrates the power dynamics between the decision-makers (employers) in the project and the technicians: "Bosses should respect their employees. Employers plan and decide the jobs and then find people that have the power to do the job. You may have the plan for the work but if you don't treat people well then you will not have anyone doing the job, yet you cannot do the job alone." While the initiative needed the citizen technicians to do the monitoring, the technicians still saw themselves as subservient to those running the initiative and were not empowered as stewards.

Case 3: Langkloof Region

The Langkloof case is based on a study that investigated collaborative landscape stewardship in the Langkloof region (Cockburn et al. 2019a). The landscape is characterised by high social diversity, inequality, and contestation around the benefits of natural resources.

The history of the Langkloof can be divided into three distinct phases. First, in the pre-colonial era, nomadic San hunter-gatherers and Khoikhoi herders had a localised, transient, and spiritually significant relationship with the landscape and one another. Second, the colonial and then Apartheid eras led to the development of settled agriculture in the form of crop, fruit, and livestock farming, forcing out Indigenous inhabitants. Third, in the democratic era since 1994 there has been increasingly intensive use of natural resources for commercial export fruit farming, including development of large water storage infrastructure (dams) to provide water for the downstream city of Gqeberha (figure 14.1).

Most productive land in the Langkloof is currently owned by White farmers (European settler descendants). Alongside relatively wealthy farmers live dispossessed and marginalised communities of Coloured and Black people, descendants of Indigenous people. Large areas of land are managed as protected areas for biodiversity conservation. While efforts are being made to empower disadvantaged communities to participate in the agricultural economy of the Langkloof and benefit from its natural resources, there are significant barriers to progress, including racial tension between communities and limited agricultural extension support (Hart and Burgess 2006). According to formal land tenure and governance arrangements, commercial farmers and conservation authorities are the actors most directly responsible for stewarding natural resources. Yet, the benefits—which accrue most directly to those with direct access to natural resources—are not being shared equally among all who call the landscape home, raising important questions about social justice and the outcomes of stewardship in contested landscapes.

During interviews, a Coloured Langkloof farmer whose ancestors were forcibly removed from the land by colonial settlers expressed frustration about the persistent unequal sharing of land resources and stewardship responsibilities in the Langkloof. Historical and current political arrangements influence local people's motivation and ability to care for the land. This leads to power imbalances and conflict among land users, decreasing the potential for collaborative stewardship across the landscape. However, this same farmer also expressed a hope for a more collective and respectful approach to working together in the landscape, emphasising the need for a relational understanding of stewarding the land together:

> We must learn to respect each other's culture. You must learn to adapt, to take hands, and go forward together: share and share alike: Ubuntu: It's about living out all our human characteristics to also let others live. All that I can say . . . is that we just grant each other a place in the sun.

Focusing stewardship work on local stewards and their relationships with one another, with the politics of time and place, and with the land and its complex ecosystems is likely to lead to more equitable and sustainable outcomes.

Discussion

These cases present an opportunity to appreciate the realities and voices of local land-based stewards in the rural Global South and to reflect on renewed stewardship debates that ask what might enable or constrain humans to enact responsibility and care in relation to the ecosystems in which they are embedded. All three cases highlight that past and present politics, policies, and land tenure strongly influence who is seen as holding primary responsibility for stewardship and, therefore, for affecting how the costs and benefits of stewarding natural resources are shared. In other words, "stewardship is always entwined with the politics of land" (Gill 2014).

For example, in Manyube, community members all understood who the areas of "abandoned fields" originally belonged to, but those families did not have *de jure* titles to the land, and their claims to access or management authority were not respected by conservation authorities. Similarly, in the Langkloof, natural resources are still owned or controlled by a small elite class, and most people do not have secure access to the basic natural resources needed to gain economic and other benefits from landscapes (Hall 2009). For example, Indigenous people have accessed the mountain slopes for generations to harvest indigenous honeybush tea but are now excluded from this resource due to private land tenure and the establishment of protected areas, preventing them from participating in the use and stewardship of this resource (Polak and Snowball 2017).

The Langkloof and Manyube cases demonstrate that there is a tension between the ideals of stewardship based on ecological actions and outcomes, and principles of social justice, which is intimately connected to access to and capacity to steward land and water resources. Local people's access to resources, capacity to steward them, and a meaningful relationship to their landscape is mediated by conflict and political power, and in the South African context, by race politics. Hence, to address social justice concerns, a social-ecological interpretation of stewardship needs to extend the notion of care not only to ecosystems but also to the diversity of human actors and their relationships (Norton 2020).

The Tsitsa case showed that employing people to participate in environmental monitoring has the potential to re-connect people to the landscape as active participants in stewardship activities. Although this stewardship action is not done on a voluntary basis, it retains the potential to deepen human-nature relationships and care for the landscape, as has been argued in other citizen science studies (Hulbert, Turner, and Scott 2019). On the other hand, despite these potentially positive outcomes, the Tsitsa case also illuminates the possible downfalls of paying people to do stewardship work in the context of a utilitarian relationship characterised by strong power differentials. The initiative is attempting to incentivise local people to become stewards of the land by involving them in paid monitoring work—this is typical of the behaviourist approaches to stewardship which are widespread in western research and policy on stewardship (Chan et al. 2020). As such, it is unlikely to lead to meaningful stewardship since they generally leave local people disempowered and passive. Treating local people merely as "data collectors" or "technicians" (a typical narrative in citizen science initiatives) potentially ignores or undermines their cultural or spiritual relationships to land and water. Taking a relational approach to stewardship would encourage more respectful attention to these relationships; that is, acknowledging that humans and nonhumans co-produce stewardship outcomes and that local people are inextricably constitutive of place (Suchet-Pearson et al. 2013; Gill 2014).

The Manyube case further illustrates that narratives about poverty-reduction and economic incentives can overshadow cultural values of landscapes and nature and that it is important to acknowledge and work with a diversity of stewardship meanings in practice. Community conservation interventions that rely on win-win logic and seek consensus in communities often appeal more to economic aspects of wellbeing and ecological narratives of degradation and may ignore heritage-based stewardship motivations, resulting in failures of conservation interventions. Similarly, in the Langkloof case, inequitable access to land resulted in unequal access to potential stewardship outcomes and raises questions about who is stewarding what and for whose benefit.

There is a tendency in Western-oriented stewardship literature and practice to talk about stewardship as something that everyone agrees on, which ignores the power struggles and issues of agency embedded in complex, heterogenous contexts typical of the Global South and postcolonial contexts (see also Kiaka, Hebinck and Lubilo in chapter 6 of this volume). Moreover, there is a strong assumption, especially in South African conservation and degradation narratives, that poor Black people cannot or do not care about nature (Rosenberg and Le Grange 2020). This shows disregard and disrespect for different cultural perspectives on stewardship meanings, governance, and practices. In the Manyube case, we observed a diversity of habitual cultural rituals and practices such as customary harvesting and cultivation and ways of relating to nature that demonstrate relational values of care toward nature (West et al. 2018) but that were not recognised as stewardship. This illustrates how some stewardship policies can exclude diverse ways of protecting and relating to the environment. More inclusive and context-sensitive policies that meaningfully include local people and are open to alternative framings of stewardship are needed.

We see in both the Tsitsa and Manyube case studies that stewards are often formally labelled as such by government or other organisations but are not in reality able to be active stewards; that is, the idea of stewardship is introduced to communities by outsiders without the capacity or authority to enact stewardship on their own terms. This is not to say the community members were not stewards already (in their own sense of that term) but that their actions were not recognised as stewardship by outsiders who did not take time to understand the context to recognise whether there is any form of stewardship already going on. This highlights a disjunction between different understandings of meaningful stewardship and a privileging of the definitions most prominent in Western scientific and policy discourse (e.g., fencing off biodiversity to protect it from people in Manyube or provision of economic incentives for monitoring the environment in Tsitsa) over Indigenous perspectives and experiences that are more likely based on inextricable spiritual and cultural relations among humans and between humans and more-than-humans. Efforts to validate and support these Indigenous perspectives can deepen and nuance our understanding of a relational approach to stewardship, where reciprocity between more-than-human entities is included, and where landscape is part of identity.

Our cases demonstrate that stewardship is intertwined with the politics of land and is enmeshed within a diversity of place-based meanings, practices, and values held by the different people who inhabit rural landscapes. These empirical insights are consistent with some recent stewardship literature that has focused on the concepts of relationality and reciprocity of stewardship as forms of care (Gill 2014; Norton 2020; West et al. 2018). Our perspectives from the Global South illustrate the importance of relationality to understanding and enabling stewardship at the local level, and the need to critically interrogate questions of politics, inequalities, who is considered a steward, and who sets the agenda for stewardship.

Conclusion

To conclude, we use the *care-knowledge-agency* framework developed by Enqvist et al. (2018) as a lens to consider the implications of our findings. The framework is suitable here as it connects multiple meanings of stewardship and enables a relational understanding of the concept.

Looking at stewardship as *care* raises questions about who is expected to care, who has a meaningful connection to the landscape, and how land tenure, politics, and governance arrangements influence who has access to and responsibility for the natural resources that underpin stewardship actions and care. There is a wide diversity of ways in which people care about the landscape, underpinned by an intricate web of relations among people, and among and between people and their landscapes.

The role of *knowledge* in stewardship processes requires careful consideration, particularly in contexts where there is contestation and a diversity of knowledge forms. Power dynamics among and between forms of knowledge (e.g., knowledge held by conservation officials is often favoured over knowledge held by local people, as seen in Manyube and Tsitsa) can lead to unequal outcomes, or no outcomes at all, for stewardship initiatives.

When considering *agency* and the role and context of local stewards, our cases illustrate that agency is strongly shaped by relationships of power and the politics of land. Diverse connections to land are influenced by cultural practices, migration patterns, governance arrangements, and changing socioeconomic conditions. Land tenure and access to natural resources strongly shape agency for stewardship. The role of traditional knowledge and governance structures needs to be carefully considered, especially where their influence has been eroded by democratization and western conservation narratives. Top-down and bottom-up stewardship policies and processes can often result in local stewards' interests, knowledge, and motivations being sidelined in the interests of broader agendas. These diverse connections to the landscape are also often misunderstood or not valued as stewardship.

Our analysis shows that refocusing stewardship on stewards requires a contextual and relational understanding of the politics of landscapes and an appreciation of the role of diverse forms of knowledge and practice in shaping stewardship. This should be accompanied by critical questioning of who is expected to act as a steward and what can enable or constrain their agency. We have found that stewardship is strongly shaped by how stewards relate to ecosystems and landscapes and simultaneously to other humans through ongoing social, cultural, and political processes. For stewardship to be realised in policy and practice, we call for a better understanding of diversity and relationality while confronting the complexities that emerge from stewardship being deeply intertwined with the politics of land and water.

References

Ainslie, A., and T. Kepe. 2016. Understanding the resurgence of traditional authorities in post-Apartheid South Africa. *Journal of Southern African Studies* 42 (1): 19–33. https://doi.org/10.1080/03057070.2016.1121714.

Amo-Agyemang, C. 2021. Decolonising the discourse on resilience. *International Journal of African Renaissance Studies—Multi-, Inter- and Transdisciplinarity* 16 (1): 4–30. https://doi.org/10.1080/18186874.2021.1962725.

Barendse, J., D. Roux, B. Currie, N. Wilson, and C. Fabricius. 2016. A broader view of stewardship to achieve conservation and sustainability goals in South Africa. *South African Journal of Science* 112 (5/6): 21–35. https://doi.org/10.17159/sajs.2016/20150359.

Bennett, N. J., T. S. Whitty, E. Finkbeiner, J. Pittman, H. Bassett, S. Gelcich, and E. H. Allison. 2018. Environmental stewardship: A conceptual review and analytical framework. *Environmental Management* 61 (4): 597–614. https://doi.org/10.1007/s00267-017-0993-2.

Berry, R. J., ed. 2006. *Environmental stewardship: Critical perspectives, past and present.* London: T&T Clark.

Chan, K. M. A., D. R. Boyd, R. K. Gould, J. Jetzkowitz, J. Liu, B. Muraca, R. Naidoo, P. Olmsted, T. Satterfield, and O. Selomane. 2020. Levers and leverage points for pathways to sustainability. *People and Nature* 2 (3): 693–717.

Chapin, F. S., G. P. Kofinas, C. Folke, S. R. Carpenter, P. Olsson, N. Abel, R. Biggs, R. L. Naylor, E. Pinkerton, D. M. Stafford, et al. 2009. Resilience-based stewardship: Strategies for navigating sustainable pathways in a changing world. In *Principles of ecosystem stewardship: Resilience-based natural resource management in a changing world*, ed. F. S. Chapin, G. P. Kofinas, and C. Folke, 319–37. New Yor: Springer. https://doi.org/10.1007/978-0-387-73033-2_15.

Clements, H. S., A. De Vos, J. C. Bezerra, K. Coetzer, K. Maciejewski, P. J. Mograbi, and C. Shackleton. 2021. The relevance of ecosystem services to land reform policies: Insights from South Africa. *Land Use Policy* 100 (January): 104939. https://doi.org/10.1016/j.landusepol.2020.104939.

Cockburn, J., G. Cundill, S. Shackleton, A. Cele, S. F. Cornelius, V. Koopman, J-P. le Roux, N. McLeod, M. Rouget, S. Schroder, et al. 2020. Relational hubs for collaborative landscape stewardship. *Society & Natural Resources* 33 (5): 681–93. https://doi.org/10.1080/08941920.2019.1658141.

Cockburn, J., G. Cundill, S. Shackleton, and M. Rouget. 2019a. The meaning and practice of stewardship in South Africa. *South African Journal of Science* 115 (5/6): 5339. https://doi.org/10.17159/sajs.2019/5339.

Cockburn, J., G. Cundill, S. Shackleton, M. Rouget, Marijn Zwinkels, S. Cornelius, L. Metcalfe, and D. van den Broeck. 2019b. Collaborative stewardship in multifunctional landscapes: Toward relational, pluralistic approaches. *Ecology and Society* 24 (4): 34. https://doi.org/10.5751/ES-11085-240432.

Enqvist, J. P., S. West, V. A. Masterson, L. J. Haider, U. Svedin, and M. Tengö. 2018. Stewardship as a boundary object for sustainability research: Linking care, knowledge and agency. *Landscape and Urban Planning* 179 (November): 17–37. https://doi.org/10.1016/j.landurbplan.2018.07.005.

Folke, C., R. Biggs, A. V. Norström, B. Reyers, and J. Rockström. 2016. Social-ecological resilience and biosphere-based sustainability science. *Ecology and Society* 21 (3): 41. https://doi.org/10.5751/ES-08748-210341.

Gill, N. 2014. Making country good: Stewardship and environmental change in central Australian pastoral culture. *Transactions of the Institute of British Geographers* 39 (2): 265–77. https://doi.org/10.1111/tran.12025.

Greeson, K. 2019. Pili Oha/Kinship:(Re) imagining perceptions of nature and more-than-human relationality. *Imaginations: Journal of Cross-Cultural Image Studies/Imaginations: Revue d'études Interculturelles de l'image* 10 (1): 353–82.

Hall, R. 2009. *Another countryside? Policy options for land and agrarian reform in South Africa*. Cape Town, South Africa: Institute for Poverty, Land and Agrarian Studies, School of Government, University of the Western Cape.

Hart, T. G. B, and R. P. Burgess. 2006. Across the divide: The impact of farmer-to-farmer linkages in the absence of extension services. *South African Journal of Agricultural Extension* 35 (1): 12–22.

Hill, R., C. Grant, M. George, C. J. Robinson, S. Jackson, and N. Abel. 2012. A typology of Indigenous engagement in Australian environmental management: Implications for knowledge integration and social-ecological system sustainability. *Ecology and Society* 17 (1): 23. https://doi.org/10.5751/ES-04587-170123.

Holmes, M. C. C., and W. Jampijinpa. 2013. Law for country: The structure of Warlpiri ecological knowledge and its application to natural resource management and ecosystem stewardship. *Ecology and Society* 18 (3): 19. https://doi.org/10.5751 /ES-05537-180319.

Hulbert, J. M., S. C. Turner, and S. L. Scott. 2019. Challenges and solutions to establishing and sustaining citizen science projects in South Africa. *South African Journal of Science* 115 (7–8): 15–18. https://doi.org/10.17159/sajs.2019/5844.

Kahui, V., and A. C. Richards. 2014. Lessons from resource management by Indigenous Maori in New Zealand: Governing the ecosystems as a commons. *Ecological Economics* 102: 1–7. https://doi.org/10.1016/j.ecolecon.2014.03.006.

Kepe, T. 2009. Shaped by race: Why "race" still matters in the challenges facing biodiversity conservation in Africa. *Local Environment* 14 (9): 871–78. https://doi .org/10.1080/13549830903164185.

Masterson, V. A., M. Spierenburg, and M. Tengö. 2019. The trade-offs of win–win conservation rhetoric: Exploring place meanings in community conservation on the Wild Coast, South Africa. *Sustainability Science* 14 (3): 639–54. https://doi.org /10.1007/s11625-019-00696-7.

Masterson, V. A., M. Tengö, and M. Spierenburg. 2017. Competing place meanings in complex landscapes: A social–ecological approach to unpacking community conservation outcomes on the Wild Coast, South Africa. *Society & Natural Resources* 30 (12): 1442–57. https://doi.org/10.1080/08941920.2017.1347975.

Mathevet, R., F. Bousquet, and C. M. Raymond. 2018. The concept of stewardship in sustainability science and conservation biology. *Biological Conservation* 217 (January): 363–70. https://doi.org/10.1016/j.biocon.2017.10.015.

Mtati, N. 2020. Towards realising the benefits of citizen participation in environmental monitoring: A case study in an Eastern Cape natural resource management programme. Masters thesis, Rhodes University, Makhanda. http://hdl .handle.net/10962/167562.

Norton, M. 2020. Prawns, justice, and relationships of care in Stilbaai, South Africa. *ICES Journal of Marine Science* 77 (7–8): 2483–90. https://doi.org/10.1093/icesjms /fsaa211.

Polak, J., and J. Snowball. 2017. Towards a framework for assessing the sustainability of local economic development based on natural resources: Honeybush tea in the Eastern Cape province of South Africa. *Local Environment* 22 (3): 335–49. https://doi.org/10.1080/13549839.2016.1196348.

Robbins, P. 2019. *Political Ecology: A Critical Introduction.* 3rd ed. Sussex, UK: John Wiley & Sons.

Rosenberg, E., and L. Le Grange. 2020. Attitudinal difference surveys perpetuate harmful tropes: A comment on Nattrass. *South African Journal of Science* 116 (SPE): 1–7. http://dx.doi.org/10.17159/sajs.2020/8469.

Shackleton, S., and M. Luckert. 2015. Changing livelihoods and landscapes in the rural Eastern Cape, South Africa: Past influences and future trajectories. *Land* 2015 (4): 1060–89. https://doi.org/10.3390/land4041060.

Sigwela, A., M. Elbakidze, M. Powell, and P. Angelstam. 2017. Defining core areas of ecological infrastructure to secure rural livelihoods in South Africa. *Ecosystem Services* 27: 272–80. https://doi.org/10.1016/j.ecoser.2017.07.010.

Simangan, D. 2021. Disrupting the universality of the Anthropocene with perspectives from the Asia Pacific. In *International Relations in the Anthropocene: New Agendas, New Agencies and New Approaches*, ed. D. Chandler, F. Müller, and D. Rothe, 271–90. Cham, Switzerland: Palgrave Macmillan. doi:10.1007/978-3-030-53014-3_15.

Smith, T. S. J. 2019. Ecological ethics of care and the multiple self: Revisiting the roots of environmentalism. In *Sustainability, wellbeing and the posthuman turn*, 63–90. Cham, Switzerland: Palgrave Pivot.

Steffen, W., Å. Persson, L. Deutsch, J. Zalasiewicz, M. Williams, K. Richardson, C. Crumley, P. Crutzen, C. Folke, L. Gordon, et al. 2011. The Anthropocene: From global change to planetary stewardship. *AMBIO* 40 (7): 739–61. https://doi.org/10.1007/s13280-011-0185-x.

Suchet-Pearson, S., S. Wright, K. Lloyd, and L. Burarrwanga. 2013. Caring as country: Towards an ontology of co-becoming in natural resource management. *Asia Pacific Viewpoint* 54 (2): 185–97. https://doi.org/10.1111/apv.12018.

Taylor, A. 2017. Beyond stewardship: Common world pedagogies for the Anthropocene. *Environmental Education Research* 23 (10): 1448–61. https://doi.org/10.1080/13504622.2017.1325452.

Tengö, M., J. P. Enqvist, S. West, U. Svedin, V. A. Masterson, and L. J. Haider. 2023. Stewardship in the Anthropocene: Meanings, tensions, futures. In *Stewardship and the future of the planet*, ed. R. Carnell and C. Mounsey, 234–51. New York: Routledge.

Welchman, J. 2012. A defence of environmental stewardship. *Environmental Values* 21 (3): 297–316. https://doi.org/10.3197/096327112X13400390125975.

West, S., L. J. Haider, V. A. Masterson, J. P. Enqvist, U. Svedin, and M. Tengö. 2018. Stewardship, care and relational values. *Current Opinion in Environmental Sustainability* 35: 30–38. https://doi.org/10.1016/j.cosust.2018.10.008.

Worrell, R., and M. Appleby. 2000. Stewardship of natural resources: Definition, ethical and practical aspects. *Journal of Agricultural and Environmental Ethics* 12 (3): 263–77. https://doi.org/10.1023/A:1009534214698.

15

From Roots to Rhizomes

Place, Transitions, and Translocality in a Less Stationary World

DANIEL R. WILLIAMS AND BRETT ALAN MILLER

In environmental and natural resource social science, place has often been characterized with rootedness and stationarity, which neglects important, dynamic connections between people and place(s). In this chapter, we (1) reexamine certain assumptions in place literature about human-mobility and place-change as necessarily jeopardizing the role of place(s) in our lives and (2) explore how a more relational, pluralistic, and dynamic view of place and place-making can help us navigate accelerating anthropogenic change and uncertainty. We hope that by moving from roots to rhizomes as an organizing metaphor for theorizing people-place relationships, this chapter invites an even more diverse cohort of scholars to examine the critical role of place in social-ecological-technical transitions.

Introduction

What is the future of *place* amid pervasive ecological, economic, social, and technological transitions? We raise this question because place as an object

https://doi.org/10.7330/9781646426300.c015

of study has long been associated with rootedness, stability, and "fixity" (Di Masso et al. 2019). However, as the world we live in becomes ever more mobile and fluid, and ecologically less stationary (Newman et al. 2019), the problems with this rooted concept of place become ever more apparent and demanding of our attention. Understanding place amid rapid changes in human mobility and social-ecological-technical systems (SETS) transitions requires place scholars to reexamine their theoretical understanding of place. To advance that goal, this chapter builds on emerging ideas increasingly being explored by contemporary place scholars (see Manzo et al. 2023). For example, problematizing and pluralizing the concept of place for navigating a wider range of global transitions and disruptions reveal how pluralistic and relational approaches to place have been long neglected (Raymond et al. 2021b).

As a contribution to this volume exploring the state of knowledge on society and natural resources and opening windows to new approaches, we reexamine place scholarship and underlying theoretical and conceptual issues, problematize certain taken-for-granted assumptions about transitioning to a less stationary and less predictable world, and suggest an updated vision of place using the metaphor of a rhizome rather than roots. First, we briefly explain why place scholarship has consistently privileged two problematic notions exacerbated by intensifying transitions: ecological stationarity (Newman et al. 2019) and social sedentarism (Di Masso et al. 2019). Second, we explore the value of a more fluid and relational conception of place to better account for the role of increasing mobilities and SETS transitions in place-making processes. Third, we emphasize how plurality and relationality can highlight the importance of exploring more inclusive and diverse approaches to place-based knowledge in place research. By questioning certain fundamental assumptions about place stationarity and sedentarism, we hope this chapter helps a more diverse cohort of scholars examine the critical role of place to meet the challenges of living in a highly mobile and less stationary world.

We take as our starting point the expanding recognition that, historically, both social and biophysical sciences have been infused with questionable assumptions of stationarity, predictability, knowability, and equilibrium (McKelvey 2021; Williams 2018). For instance, stationarity is often implied in management objectives such as sustained yield forestry or restoring ecosystems to a historical range of variation. By extension, place scholarship historically privileged fixity, stability, and rootedness in a way that normalized social sedentarism—the idea that people are supposed to be securely rooted in a fixed residence, community, and nation (Di Masso et al. 2019; Malkki 1997). Thus, to open new windows of inquiry about the role of place in transitions, we need to critically examine ontological assumptions about the undisturbed earth in homeostatic balance and question the essentialist understanding of people as historically, culturally, and authentically emplaced beings who, in the face of change, are unavoidably at risk of being unmoored, uprooted, or displaced. Moving forward we propose an understanding of place as an uncentered assemblage or constellation of interconnected, networked, fluid, and unfolding relations—nonhierarchical and rhizomatic[1] rather than fixed and rooted—to better account for the role of human mobility and SETS transitions in the constitution and ongoing becoming of place(s).

By giving greater legitimacy to transition, movement, and flow we can reimagine the lived experience of place within more rhizomatic and translocal collections of spaces and experiences. This view offers a more resilient model for building and maintaining ontological security (i.e., expectations about the stability and continuity of one's habits and lifestyle) in the face of uncertainty and change. Not only is a rhizomatic concept of place more useful in a less stationary world but it also helps broaden place scholarship in an epistemologically more inclusive future. We attempt to visualize this difference between a rooted and rhizomatic metaphor of people-relationships by using artificial intelligence image generation, itself a controversial catalyst to uncertain SETS transitions (figure 15.1).

We hope this chapter contributes to place scholarship moving beyond stasis, opening new windows for: (1) engaging with multiple kinds of knowledge and relational ontologies; (2) embracing a broader, more inclusive, democratic, and provisional epistemic orientations; and (3) re-spatializing our lives in ways that are more translocal, inclusive, and resilient.

---

1. The metaphor of the rhizome, drawn from the title of the opening chapter of Deleuze and Guattari's (1987) *A Thousand Plateaus*, has been borrowed widely to contrast substantive ontologies with relational ontologies. It distinguishes "tree-like systems of thinking organized hierarchically with roots, stems and branches" from that of a rhizome "characterized by horizontal lines of movement, networks and connectivity" (Dovey 2020, 24).

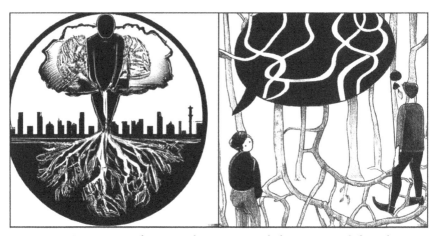

FIGURE 15.1. Two images depicting place as a rooted phenomenon (left) and as a rhizomatic phenomenon (right). The authors generated these images in part with OpenAI's DALL-E 2 artificial intelligence image generation program based on the authors' specific descriptions (OpenAI, 2022). The use of this software is also an exploration of how the authors' description of competing place metaphors would interact with rhizomatic connections by hundreds of millions of images and their associated captions by other people, which is how the DALL-E 2 algorithm works (O'Connor 2022). In the image on the left, a person is shown as rooted and therefore literally place-attached and unable to move. This person is inside a series of "place" containers. These containers represent home, community, country, and the world as a series of nested scales. This version of place is limiting and leaves the rooted person vulnerable. In the image on the right, people are shown moving around a forest of trees. Instead of being rooted to place, the people are mobile and interacting with place. The people are also thinking about what they see (person on the right) and speaking about it (person on the left). These acts of interaction, observation, and social construction are co-creating place as represented by the trees, which are connected underground rhizomatically. The act of co-creation and experience of place is also represented as a rhizome (in the speech/thought bubble). The people are experiencing place and connected to it but not rooted or stationary, and place is connected but not nested.

Place in a Stationary World

Beginning in the second half of the twentieth century, place scholarship emerged as a corrective to overly technocratic approaches that often neglected the authentic character of places and the essential relationships of people to them (Cresswell 2013; Williams 2014). Over time the place literature evolved to address new concerns and new, more diverse perspectives that critiqued the implicit sedentarism and stationarity in place scholarship (Williams and Miller 2021). However, despite challenges to the dominant humanistic paradigm, fixed and rooted notions of place continued to permeate the empirical literature, especially in natural resource sciences and environmental planning (Williams 2014). In this section we briefly outline the early origin of place scholarship and highlight the most problematic consequences for understanding place in transition.

Place Rooted in Sedentarist Metaphysics

A sedentary framing is reflected in the fixed and essentialist notions of place and sense of place advanced by humanistic geographers in the 1970s (Relph 1976; Tuan 1977). Place discourse emerged alongside a hegemonic, sedentarist metaphysics (Malkki 1997) that presumed a normative social order in which people were meant to be geographically and securely rooted beings (Di Masso et al. 2019). Specifically, modernist ideas that minimized the importance of place in geography were challenged by humanistic theories that reasserted the phenomenological importance of place attachment as a rooted, centering, and stabilizing force in people's lives (Cresswell 2013). Accordingly, places were seen as under assault from the uprooting forces of modernity, commodification, and globalization (Norberg-Schulz 1979; Relph 1976) and residential mobility was seen as disrupting the anchoring role of place in people's lives (Brown and Perkins 1992; Fried 1963).

Scholars in natural resource social sciences were attracted to these early conceptions of place for several reasons. One rationale was to overcome an instrumental or commodity bias in characterizing the value of natural resources that left little room for recognizing the emotional and identity bonds people form with specific places (Williams et al. 1992; Williams and Stewart 1998). Another was to highlight the important ways people seek out and create meaning through their transactions with particular places with specific histories (Firey 1945; Williams and Patterson 1996). In addition, some scholars looked at the relationship between community and place to better understand place-dependent values in natural resource politics (Brandenburg and Carroll 1995; Trentelman 2009). These perspectives proved valuable to policy makers as they sought to balance the competing environmental priorities of diverse constituencies (Cheng, Kruger, and Daniels 2003; Yung, Freimund, and Belsky 2003). At the same time, mobility and place transitions threatened the very construction of community, which many scholars conceived of as unavoidably defined by territoriality and locality-relevant or locality-oriented actions (Field and Burch 1988; Luloff et al. 2004).[2]

The Fixed Ecologies of "Authentic" Places

Sedentary thinking about place is also deeply consonant with fixed, stationary notions of ecology, natural processes, and related ontologies that have traditionally divided and reduced the world into various categories of substantive elements (e.g., humans and nature, social and natural, mind and matter, etc.). In the second half of the twentieth century, just as human geographers criticized modernist ideas of place, ecology took on greater social significance as part of a broader environmental movement responding to the environmental consequence of modernity (Walker 2020). This conception of ecology was rooted in the Enlightenment philosophy and transcendentalism (Harvey 1993). Thus, the study of ecology in the United States and Europe emerged from an epistemology that recognized the existence of "nature" and "natural" as real and distinct from humans and human development (Morton 2008).

The close connection between place and ecology was made explicit with the emergence of ecosystem management in the 1990s (Grumbine 1992; Williams and Stewart 1998). Much of ecological thinking as a philosophical discourse about sustainability built on the early notions of fixity and authenticity. Deep ecology and bioregionalism, for example, blended ecological science and environmental ethics to argue for sustaining bioregionally "authentic" ways of acting and dwelling in the world premised on closely linked ecological processes and social practices. The underlying assumption was that greater alignment between social and ecological boundaries promote more sustainable (and therefore more stable) ways of living (Aberley 1999; Thayer 2003).

---

2. The relationship between community and place has prompted considerable debate. In the 1970s researchers began to ask if new technologies allowed people to form and maintain primary ties outside of locality (i.e., place), and promoted a networked conception of community (see Bender 1978; Wellman and Leighton 1979). But it is our estimation that, despite challenges, the link between community and place remains dominant. If community is understood to be place-dependent, then mobility and transition potentially threatened community social order and wellbeing (Wilkinson 1991).

The Challenge of a More Mobile Future (and Past)

As the new century began, a major challenge to sedentaristic metaphysics involved the elevation of mobilities, movement, and flows in constituting modern life that some took to calling the "new-mobilities paradigm" (Sheller and Urry 2006). With circulation and flows of people, goods, and ideas increasingly dominating modern life, identities seemingly no longer required a fixed, authentic essence rooted in a singular home, territory, or nation. Instead, identity formation was seen as an ongoing project of weaving together a coherent but multicentered self-identity narrative (Williams and McIntyre 2001) and raised the possibility of multilayered citizenship (Castles 2002; Lippard 1997). These ideas challenged the way social and environmental transformations often over-simplify place relationships and reaffirm an ethnocentric vision of authentic human habitation that privileges sedentarism and reifies outdated ecological concepts that overestimate the stationarity of past ecological conditions.

The sedentary framing of place often sought to assign people into national, cultural, or other local place-based categories and territorialized their identities (Di Masso et al. 2019). Departures from this presumed norm (e.g., the unhoused, the displaced, refugees, and peripatetic cultures of various sorts) were deemed pathological conditions in need of fixing that justified deliberate, state-imposed processes of sedentarization (Malkki 1997). We believe that this reveals deeply rooted ontological and axiological assumptions about social progress that positions human habitation as developing progressively along a singular path.[3] Based on these assumptions, early attempts to understand the importance of place reified places as static containers of meaning (Cresswell 2013). But this way of thinking about place potentially serves exclusionary and unjust notions about the sanctity and authenticity of certain relationships between specific people and their conceptions of a place, which supports nationalist politics (see Harvey 1993).

With an eye toward the dynamics and asymmetries of power, a relational concept of place emerged in the early 1990s to challenge these notions of place generally associated with humanistic geographers (Harvey 1993;

---

3. According to a simplified, problematic story, people used to be nomadic, then they settled and planted roots (literal agriculture roots as well as cultural and legal ones). This framing marginalizes people displaced by settlement and underestimates the complexity of less sedentary people.

Massey 1993). Writing about the inescapable politics of place, these critical geographers proposed a more open, dynamic, and progressive understanding where places are forged through relational processes constituted from larger networks and flows of people, goods, and ideas of local and global reach that support multiple identities (Massey 1993). Likewise, some natural resource social scientists questioned whether the primacy of a fixed notion of place in constructing community supported unequal power structures and argued instead for a relational understanding of community (Wilkinson 1991). Similarly, sociocultural studies of place emphasized the way landscape features and settings are often symbolically constructed through the meanings ascribed to them by visitors (Williams and McIntyre 2012) and residents (Greider and Garkovich 1994) as well as the intentions of planners, managers, and promotional organizations (Saarinen 1998). Collectively, this place scholarship described how places are subject to complex, contested social processes where various stakeholders struggle to control place meanings, values, and uses (Williams and Patterson 1996; Williams 2014). These emerging relational concepts emphasized the role of discourse and practice in making and remaking places (Di Masso, Dixon, and Durrheim 2014; Pierce, Martin, and Murphy 2011).

As we intend to show in the next section, the relational view of place provides useful leverage for addressing the inexorable complexities and uncertainties inherent to navigating SETS transitions (Williams 2018) and resulting social-ecological precarities (Manzo et al. 2023). Embracing the relational view of place in SETS also provides new opportunities for diversifying the epistemologies of sociospatial scholarship and opens up new ways to re-spatialize our lives that are translocal, multicentric, and resilient.

Place in a Transitioning World

As the western sciences have begun to grapple with the problematic assumptions outlined above, place inquiry has turned increasingly toward more plural and fluid conceptions (Di Masso et al. 2019; Raymond et al. 2021b). In this section we examine the implications of this turn for understanding SETS transitions and how a rhizomatic vision of place can help us understand sustainability in a less stationary world. We do this from three perspectives: ontology (the nature of being or existence), epistemology (what constitutes knowledge), and the everyday lived experience of place, mobility, and transition. An organizing feature across these perspectives is the importance of relationality and a corresponding shift of metaphors from roots to rhizomes.

Ontological Transitions

The shift from place as a fixed entity to a more fluid and dynamic process involves a shift from a substantive ontology and toward a relational ontology. Historically, most of western science has operated from the view that substantive entities (things in the world) are ontologically primary and relations ontologically derivative (Wildman, 2010). In contrast, relational ontologies emphasize how places are in a continuous process of becoming or emergence rather than a collection of fixed (or authentic) meanings. Moreover, this relationality takes on greater ontological significance as the object of inquiry increases in complexity (Polkinghorne 2010). Thus, relational ontologies are particularly useful in thinking about complex, adaptive SETS transitions (Raymond et al. 2021a; Walsh, Böhme, and Wamsler 2021; West et al. 2020). In the field of sustainability science, shifting from substantive to relational concepts can also help transcend longstanding and troublesome binaries such as humans/nature or social/ecological in generating innovative policy approaches to sustainability (West et al. 2020, 306).[4]

One of the main critiques of relational ontologies applied to sustainability science, however, is that they have been hard to put into research practice (Masterson et al. 2017; Raymond et al. 2021a). As a result, some sustainability researchers are increasingly turning to place scholarship for insights on how to apply relational thinking to sustainability (Chapin and Knapp 2015; Masterson et al. 2019; Williams 2018). Likewise, some place scholars have begun to argue that place itself should be understood as a complex adaptive system that engages the sciences of emergence and resilience thinking (Dovey 2020).

In place scholarship, relational thinking has increasingly drawn on Deleuze and Guattari's (1987) assemblage theory and their use of the rhizome metaphor. Specifically, assemblage theory provides a bottom-up framework for

---

4. The emerging interest in relational ontologies within place research and sustainability science shows up in their mutual penchant for adopting assemblage philosophy in the social science.

examining complexity and multiplicities by emphasizing fluidity, exchange-ability, connectivity, and emergence. Assemblage thinking—much like relational thinking and resilience thinking—resists simplification or reduction to a singular definition, theory, or set of propositions, yet it offers powerful advice for addressing complex phenomena in an uneven landscape of power. For example, Greiner, Peth, and Sakdapolrak (2014) applied the relational concept of translocal assemblages to understand the complex relationship between climate change and migration in Africa.

Dovey (2020) recently made the case for place as an assemblage, noting the way assemblage thinking highlights the relational, multi-scalar, and anti-reduction attributes of place as well as the important role of power in place-making processes. First, assemblage thinking adopts what he calls a flat (i.e., non-hierarchical) ontology because it does not recognize a larger transcendent order to which the emergent world can be reduced. At the same time, assemblages are multi-scalar multiplicities, thus a particular place cannot be reduced to the general nor can the local be scaled up to the global. Second, assemblage thinking is radically relational by acknowledging interconnections as preceding the things being connected. Thus, a place is not a thing (nor a collection of things) but the multi-scaled relations of material and flows. The assemblage is not fixed in time or space but is dynamic—trees grow and die, people come and go, buildings are constructed and demolished, meanings are created and lost. Third, assemblage thinking offers an approach to place without the reductionism, essentialism, authenticity, and fixity (i.e., rootedness) of early place theory.

Dovey also notes that assemblage theory allows for empirical examination without reduction to discursive representation, allowing an understanding of the experience of place without the essentialism of phenomenology. Finally, Dovey argues that assemblage thinking understands power as embodied and distributed through material-spatial arrangements rather than as something held by certain agents, which helps reveal why a substantive framing of place necessarily privileges some place-making ideas over others. Since some people in a given place have more privileged access or power over certain place-resources, they have greater power to define these place features, which, in turn, supports their access. Freudenberg (2006) called this a "double diversion" or "disproportionality"—concepts that informed important explorations about place in natural resource social sciences.

Massey (1993) was among the early adopters of assemblage thinking in place research (though she generally used the word *constellation*). She offered a "progressive" view of place that challenged the idea that places have durable, singular identities. Instead, she asserted that places are constituted from a continuously unfolding constellation of local and global processes, flows, and mobilities. Emphasizing the importance of material-spatial relationships, she coined the term *power-geometry* to foreground inequalities that derive from the uneven flow of financial, political, class, and economic power across space. Similarly, Sack's (1997, 1992) relational geographic framework uses the metaphor of *weaving* to describe places as a kind of assemblage of ontological forces and epistemological perspectives. Thus, everyday acts (e.g., consumption) assemble (weave) together forces (e.g., nature, social relations, meaning, and actions) to construct places while simultaneously altering the character of those forces and processes of place-making.

The turn to relationality in human geography is not without criticism, particularly among those deploying non-Western and anti-colonial modes of thought, what is sometimes collectively described as Black, Indigenous, and other people of color (BIPOC) scholarship. Though sympathetic to this relational turn as championed by Massey, Harvey, and other "critical" geographers, Castree (2004) describes how this political and progressive view of relational place-making undermines the rights of some (particularly Indigenous peoples) to assert their own senses of place rather than have them defined for them (see also Barker and Pickerill 2020; Ganapathy 2013; Torgerson 1999). Coulthard (2010) explains how Indigenous senses of place are about more-than-traditional lands having a deep material importance to Indigenous cultures or serving as sites of strong Indigenous attachments. For Coulthard, place is "understood as a field of 'relationships of things to each other' [and] a way of knowing, experiencing, and relating with the world" that often forms the basis of resistance to power relations that too often threaten or obliterate Indigenous senses of place (2010, 79). Although similar to the relational view of place put forth by Massey, Harvey, and others, this understanding "not only anchors many indigenous peoples' critique of colonial relations of force and command, but also [their] visions of what a truly post-colonial relationship of peaceful co-existence might look like" (Coulthard 2010, 80). As place scholars look to improve our understanding of place, taking the time to acknowledge and center these perspectives is important for correcting the problematic assumptions of the past as well as avoiding future ones.

Similarly, Black geographical scholarship has called attention to multiple ways of knowing around relational place-making to underscore the unique experiences of Black peoples in shaping spatial meanings and practices. For example, Allen, Lawhon, and Pierce (2019) argue that Black geographical interest in experience, agency, and non-material spatial practices are very congruent with relational place-making. Accordingly, Black geography "offers an ontological position that maintains the possibilities for multiplicity, considering plural process, and incorporating diverse methodologies and data sources" (2019, 1001). Further, "it enables critiques of the exclusionary constructions of society and place and draws attention to Black articulations of place that seek not only to validate Black experiences but to bring into being these alternative visions" (2019, 1012). Thus, properly articulating place as relational opens up place scholarship to more voices, and thus more critique, which will ultimately improve our understanding of place.

In sum, places are complex adaptive systems, better understood by using relational ontologies instead of substantive ontologies. Thinking of place as constellations or assemblages of relations avoids the binaries of human/ nature and brings to the fore ideas such as emergence, autopoiesis (i.e., self-organization), and the unfolding arrangements of psychological, social, and material actions of many interacting agents capable of learning and adapting. Finally, recognizing relationality in place-making opens up Western scholarship to multiple ways of understanding the ontology of place more widely appreciated in non-Western scholarship and allows for more effective critique.

The Epistemic Transitions: Democratizing Ways of Knowing Place

Taking an ontologically relational approach to place also means extending our epistemological outlook toward more diverse, flexible, or post-normal ways of (co)producing knowledge. Co-producing knowledge about places supports complex adaptive SETS transitions by promoting a more situated conception of knowledge that pays attention to local practice and experience (Bartel 2014; Williams 2018). Interest in ideas such as post-normal science and knowledge co-production are in part the product of a growing epistemic crisis where scholars see more clearly how Western science has been infused with static and ethnocentric assumptions regarding nature, the landscape, and places (Gauchat 2011). The authentic character of places often seems to correspond with the conditions of the past, whether anchored in some pre-Columbian, pre-colonial condition reflecting a "historic range of variability" (McKelvey et al. 2021; Morgan et al. 1994) or favoring the place values of the last generation. For instance, in place literature specifically, scholars have recently begun to document how much place constructs favor a European framing (Lewicka and Dobosh 2021). Likewise, ethnonationalism is reflected in Western anthropology, which, for much of its history, normalized the ideal of sedentary cultures over nomadic ones (Malkki 1997). At the very least it is common for social scientists to assume current conditions or the recent past as the norm against which one might evaluate social change.

In contrast, Raymond et al. (2021b) argued that non-stationary thinking about social-ecological transitions forces scholars to reconsider what they think they know on a fundamental level and reexamine their ways of knowledge-building. They argue that transitioning requires a new epistemic attitude that departs from post-positivist science in three fundamental ways. The first is to replace universalist thinking inherited from the Enlightenment with a pluralistic conception of knowledge better suited to complex systems (Mitchell 2009). The second is to recognize that with pluralism one must also recognize there is no unified "god's eye" position or approach to science that can organize all knowledge. Instead, diverse and generally unreconcilable positionalities or epistemic standpoints exist from which different people observe the world, which can be used to expand our shared understanding (Williams 2013, 2018). The third recognizes that despite our best efforts, deep ontological uncertainties about systems will persist and thus they argue for a more humble, provisional approach to knowledge (Caniglia et al. 2021; Fazey et al. 2020). Embracing a more plural, positional, and provisional approach to knowledge is a key first step toward democratizing the production and acquisition of knowledge on place (Williams 2014).

Rather than continuing to ineffectually resist ecological and social change, a more pluralistic, dynamic, and political view of place and processes of place-making can help foster more productive and inclusive engagement with transitions marked by less stationarity and more ontological uncertainty and anthropogenic system change. Thus, at the heart of reimagining place research to better suit a non-stationary world is the adoption of relational ontologies and pluralistic epistemologies (Williams 2018) that imagine place and place relationships as rhizomatic, changing across time and space based on the experiences and interactions of emplaced, displaced, replaced peoples (Barron, Hartman, and Hagemann 2020).

At this point, we believe it's imperative to openly acknowledge that more relational epistemologies have long existed within different cultures and peoples whose perspectives have not been privileged in academic discourse. For instance, many of the Indigenous peoples displaced by European settlement in North America relied on epistemological frameworks based on a more relational dynamic between the self, others, place, and nature (Kovach 2021) discussed briefly above. But these views did not fit the dominant epistemology of place that favored a substantive framing, which therefore promoted fixed conceptions of a place over others. Place scholars have often noted the irony that in natural resource social sciences, place values rooted in the social construction of early American settlers were privileged as authentic even though these settlers had displaced people with different senses of place (Williams 2002). Thus, recognizing the need for more epistemological diversity in place scholarship serves as the first step toward decolonizing place research.

The emerging recognition of these neglected voices in academia coincides with the increasing recognition in the biophysical sciences of the limitations of Western epistemologies and growing appreciation of insights offered by other ecological epistemologies, such as traditional ecological knowledge (Berkes 1993). Here again, greater inclusion of Indigenous forms of knowledge into biophysical sciences and ecologies may have led to an earlier recognition of the inherently dynamic nature of places outside of socially constructed values (Barker and Pickerill 2020). However, acknowledging our own positionality as non-Indigenousness scholars, trained as we are within the dominant place scholarship, we look to other scholars to offer their conceptions of place and proposals to decolonize place scholarship and natural resource social sciences.

Experiencing Place Transitions: Toward Translocality and Multicentered Identities

Turning from the ontological and epistemic case for relational place-making, we next want to apply relational and rhizomatic thinking to examine how people establish, maintain, and/or restore place-based identities in the face of change. Where the rooted conception of place understood mobility and transition as a threat to ontological security, a rhizomatic conception of place normalizes mobility and transition while revealing the importance of a multiplicity of scales and differences in power. With accelerating system transitions and expanding mobilities, the potential scales at which people belong to or identify with places are similarly expanding (Buckle 2017; Tomaney 2015), increasing the ways people "inhabit the world at a distance" (Sheller and Urry 2006, 115). This expansion has been described in various ways including "translocal" (Ganapathy 2013; Greiner, Peth, and Sakdapolrak 2014) and "multicentered" (Lippard 1997; Williams and Van Patten 2006). While much of the translocality literature emerges at the intersection of post-colonial and migration studies (Hertzog 2021; Verne 2012), globalization and other disruptive forces are driving multicentered inhabitation in various other forms, from tourism and second homes (McIntyre, Williams, and McHugh 2006) to translocal work (Wohlers and Hertel 2017) and electronically mediated (Relph 2021; Taipale 2014), virtual, and imagined experiences of place (Champ, Williams, and Lundy 2013).

Simply put, terms like multicentered and translocality refer to a sense of belonging or identification with more than one location. These terms attempt to capture the interconnectedness and processes that happen between different places and people manifest through a variety of enduring, open, and non-linear processes (Greiner, Peth, and Sakdapolrak 2014). Verne (2012, 15) draws important attention to the complexity of mobility practices, offering a relational view of translocal phenomena in a desire to shift the traditional focus in migration studies from the connected entities to the connections themselves. She further argues for using rhizomatic thinking to better account for this relationality as well as for the complexity, multiplicity, and heterogeneity of translocal connections that are constantly in the making.

Of course, one consequence of transitions and disruptions for many is the detachment of traditional social relations and identities from particular places (e. g., home, community, nation) and a rising ontological insecurity (Devine-Wright et al. 2020; Manzo et al. 2021). Gergen (1991, 215) described this in the context of globalization: "The traditional face-to-face community loses its coherence and its significance in the life of its participants. . . . Their sense of belonging is no longer only, or even primarily rooted in the local soil." The character of how and where people live, work, and play has certainly been disrupted by the "great acceleration" of various human activities (Steffen et al. 2015). By many metrics, people, goods, and ideas are more mobile now than they have ever been (Castles, Haas, and Miller 2014; Di Masso et al. 2019). For some, moving to new pastures is positive (Williams and Van Patton 2006) and mobility a privilege (Wohlers and Hertel 2017). For others, mobility results from a lack of choice to stay in place (Adelman 2008). Increased mobility also means greater economic competition for the same spaces and/or more conflicts over the meaning and use of highly valued places (Manzo 2014; Di Masso et al. 2021). And the impacts of these disruptions are unevenly distributed. For instance, the COVID-19 pandemic has exposed both the precarity and inequality that comes with these disruptions to mobility and access to places (Devine-Wright et al. 2020). Not only do people in positions of privilege have ways to enhance their resilience to spatial change through mobility, that mobility also has consequences for others. In natural resource management, for example, tourism and second homes have been examined as multicentric spatial practices for creating or maintaining place identities in the face of an increasingly fluid and mobilized world (McIntyre, Williams, and McHugh 2006; Williams and Kaltenborn 1999). Accordingly, tourism and the use of recreational spaces more generally are theorized as opportunities to re-spatialize one's ontological security in the face of change and find continuities across a wider range of places, reflecting a more assembled, rhizomatic view of place (Williams and McIntyre 2001).

Various forms of mobility—from tourism, migration, and itinerant work to the environmentally or geopolitically displaced (refugees and unhoused)—are thus a critical nexus around which place meanings are produced, consumed, and contested. They weave together and reassemble various kinds of place meanings and (non-)belongingness (e.g., ancestral, ethno-cultural, refugee, immigrant residential, touristic, and occupational) at different spatial scales. More fluid senses of place are often cultivated through mobility as a way to create greater continuity across various life trajectories such as college, marriage, and retirement (Bailey 2021; Di Masso et al. 2019). Similarly, migration does not necessarily result in the weakening of migrants' bonds with places of origin or destination and, in fact, raises critical questions about the role of strong people-place bonds in navigating the vagaries of living in new places (Greiner, Peth and Sakdapolrak 2014; Hertzog 2021). Hertzog (2021), for example, illustrates how place research has long overlooked the translocal reality of many migrants' lives, particularly in Africa, and shows how transactions and interconnections between places of origin and places of occupation are crucial to shaping identities and senses of belonging.

Reimagining place in a transitioning world also reinforces the post-colonial critique of senses of place literature produced in the Global North (Hertzog 2021; Verne 2012). For instance, uncertainty and change can be an opportunity to disrupt existing (potentially unjust) social orderings as illustrated in how the Maori interpreted an earthquake as disrupting the colonial identity of Christchurch, New Zealand (cited in Manzo et al. 2021; see also Berroeta, de Carvalho, and Castillo-Sepulveda 2021). But it can also create a potential spaciousness to build resilience through cultivation of translocal and multicentered identities, which allow for greater flows of resources and commodities as well as circulations of social remittances of ideas, practices, and identities (Greiner, Peth, and Sakdapolrak 2014; Hertzog 2021). Where a rooted conception of place focused too much on the essential and enduring quality of people-place relations, a rhizomatic view of place offers scholars a flexible vehicle for examining the role of power (or lack thereof) to (re)connect to a multiplicity of places at various spatial and temporal scales.

Certainly, the need for and potential to re-spatialize our lives in response to transitions highlights the ways in which mobility and belonging are often forms of privilege derived from place-based forms of ontological security. Lau, Durrheim, and Young's (2021) study of informal settlements in South Africa serves as a poignant illustration of struggle to "not belong to nonplaces" and reminds us of the way in which sense of place research largely represents the point of view of those who feel attached, safe, and a positive sense of belongingness to home, neighborhood, community, or nation (see Manzo 2014). Structural inequalities and injustices may force some people to move against their will, prevent others from being able to move at will, and empower still others to relocate if they so desire. At the same time, a rhizomatic understanding of people-place relations helps to articulate potential adaptations to these disruptions in which more distributed identities afford individuals more resilient paths for maintaining ontological security within the ongoing making and remaking of places.

Conclusion

Place scholarship is increasingly moving beyond its historical association with essentialism and rootedness. In this chapter we have tried to demonstrate how a more relational, pluralistic, and dynamic view of place and place-making helps to navigate social-ecological-technical transitions marked by non-stationarity, uncertainties, and accelerating anthropogenic change. Also, engaging SETS transitions as a way of understanding place challenges our historically emplaced sense of ontological security, elevates the importance of local and Indigenous knowledges, opens inquiry to more diverse, inclusive (democratic), and provisional epistemologies, and shows us how we might re-spatialize our lives around more resilient, multicentric, rhizomatic networks of places.

Global forces, SETS transitions, and a related epistemic crisis elevate transitional anxieties and unmoor us from our historically situated anchorages of place and identity at many different scales. In fact, these transitional anxieties reveal that our stationarities and fixities were never as solid as we once thought. We can recover or restore some semblance of ontological security by embracing the opportunities of such decentering to reimagine place as more complex and multicentered and offer tools for navigating individual and collective change in a way that is more resilient to uncertainties. Shifting our goal to one of resilience to change through rhizomatic connectivity reveals that what limits human well-being is not change but structural inequalities that limit the ability of individuals to adapt.

Taking a more assembled, rhizomatic view of place allows scholars to understand how place identity can be spatially distributed and therefore how people can adapt to transition. The contemporary age, dominated as it is by deep uncertainties and accelerated transitions, needs to: acknowledge more fluid relations to places by repositioning "place" so that it fits this less certain, less stationary, and more mobile age; build a more pluralistic, dynamic, and political view of place-making; and adopt a more inclusive epistemic attitude that recognizes diverse forms of emplacement, nonplacement, and displacement. Unlike a rooted conception of place that ties people down or roots our inquiry, a more rhizomatic conception of place allows people, society, and academic researchers to seek out and/or maintain ontological security through a multiplicity of connections.

We acknowledge that many of these relational conceptions of place are not so much new as increasingly appreciated in their capacity to conceive a world dominated by transitions, give voice to those marginalized within historical and ethnocentric fixities, forge more inclusive epistemic attitudes, and build more resilient ontological securities. In this endeavor we recognize that in addition to changing technologies, the pursuit of knowledge itself is becoming more plural and therefore more contested and, thus, ideas that were once marginalized are gaining greater recognition. But this transition is also fraught; thus, scholars will need to be intentional to navigate this change. We hope that reimagining place as a rhizomatic rather than rooted phenomenon serves as an invitation to scholars who have previously seen the place literature as too limiting.

Acknowledgments

This chapter was supported in part by the USDA Forest Service Rocky Mountain Research Station. The findings and conclusions are those of the author(s) and should not be construed to represent any official USDA or US government determination or policy. Any use of trade, firm, or product names is for descriptive purposes only and does not imply endorsement by the US government. The authors wish to thank three anonymous reviewers for their insightful comments and suggestions on an earlier draft, which challenged us to be even more explicit in outlining examples of more relational place scholarship by less privileged voices and the exclusion of those voices. We believe this chapter has been significantly improved for these reviews but encourage others to lend and extend their critical perspectives to place scholarship.

We want to thank OpenAI for supporting this chapter by making the use of DALL-E 2 open for research. Although AI assisted, the content of these images is the responsibility of us as authors.

References

Aberley, D. 1999. Interpreting bioregionalism: A story from many voices. In *Bioregionalism*, ed. M. V. McGinnis, 13–42. London: Routledge.

Adelman, H. 2008. *Protracted displacement in Asia: No place to call home*. Aldershot, UK: Ashgate.

Allen, D., M. Lawhon, and J. Pierce. 2019. Placing race: On the resonance of place with black geographies. *Progress in Human Geography* 43: 1001–19.

Bailey, E. 2021. A life course approach to the pluralization of sense of place: Understanding the social acceptance of low-carbon energy developments. In *Changing senses of place: Navigating global challenges*, ed. C. Raymond, L. Manzo, D. R. Williams, A. Di Masso, and T. von Wirth, 156–68. Cambridge, UK: Cambridge University Press.

Barker, A. J., and J. Pickerill. 2020. Doings with the land and sea: Decolonising geographies, indigeneity, and enacting place-agency. *Progress in Human Geography* 44 (4): 640–62.

Barron, E. S., L. Hartman, and F. Hagemann. 2020. From place to emplacement: The scalar politics of sustainability. *Local Environment* 25 (6): 447–62.

Bartel, R. 2014. Vernacular knowledge and environmental law: Case and cure for regulatory failure. *Local Environment* 19: 891–914.

Bender, T. 1978. *Community and social change in America*. New Brunswick, NJ: Rutgers University Press.

Berkes, F. 1993. Traditional ecological knowledge in perspective. In *Traditional ecological knowledge: Concepts and cases*, ed. J. T. Inglis, 1–9. Ottawa: International Program on Traditional Ecological Knowledge.

Berroeta, H., L. P. de Carvalho, and J. Castillo-Sepulveda. 2021. The place-subjectivity continuum after a disaster: Enquiring into the production of sense of place as an assemblage. In *Changing senses of place: Navigating global challenges*, ed. C. Raymond, L. Manzo, D. R. Williams, A. Di Masso, and T. von Wirth, 43–52. Cambridge, UK: Cambridge University Press.

Brandenburg, A. M., and Carroll, M. S. 1995. Your place, or mine: The effect of place creation on environmental values and landscape meanings. *Society and Natural Resources* 8: 381–98.

Brown, B., and D. Perkins. 1992. Disruptions in place attachment. In *Place attachment*, ed. I. Altman and S. M. Low, 279–304. New York: Plenum Press.

Buckle, C. 2017. Residential mobility and moving home. *Geography Compass* 11 (5): e12314.

Caniglia, G., C. Luederitz, T. von Wirth, I. Fazey, B. Martín-López, K. Hondrila, A. König, H. von Wehrden, N. Schäpke, M. Laubichler, et al. 2021. A pluralititc and integrated approach to action-oriented knowledge for stutainaiblity. *Nature Sustainability* 4: 93–100.

Castles, S. 2002. Migration and community formation under conditions of globalization. *International Migration Review* 36: 1143–68.

Castles, S., H. Haas, and M. Miller. 2014. *The age of migration. International population movements in the modern world*. Basingstoke, UK: Palgrave Macmillan.

Castree, N. 2004. Differential geographies: Place, Indigenous rights and "local" resources. *Political Geography* 23: 133–67.

Champ, J. G., D. R. Williams, and C. M. Lundy. 2013. An on-line narrative of Colorado wilderness: Self-in-cybernetic space. *Environmental Communication* 7: 131–45.

Chapin, F. S. III, and C. N. Knapp. 2015. Sense of place: A process for identifying and negotiating poteniallly contested visions of sustainaibltiy. *Environmetnal Science & Policy* 53: 38–46.

Cheng, A. S., Kruger, L. E., and Daniels, S. E. 2003. Place as an integrating concept in natural resource politics: Propostions for a social science reasearch agenda. *Society and Natural Resources* 16 (2): 87–104.

Coulthard, G. 2010. Place against empire: Understanding indigenous anti-colonialism. *Affinities: A Journal of Radical Theory, Culture, and Action* 4 (2): 79–83.

Cresswell, T. 2013. *Geographic thought: A critical introduction.* Chichester, UK: Wiley-Blackwell.

Deleuze, G., and F. Guattari. 1987. *A thousand plateaus: Capitalism and schizophrenia.* Minneapolis: University of Minnesota Press.

Devine-Wright, P., L. Pinto di Cavalho, A. Di Masso, M. Lewicka, L. Manzo, and D. R. Williams. 2020. "Re-placed"—Reconsidering relationships with place and lessons from a pandemic. *Journal of Environmental psychology* 72: 101414.

Di Masso, A., J. Dixon, and K. Durrheim. 2014. Place attachment as discursive practice. In *Place attachment: Advances in theory, methods and applications*, ed. L. Manzo and P. Devine-Wright, 5–86. London: Routledge.

Di Masso, A., V. Jorquera, T. Ropert, and T. Vidal. 2021. Gentrification and the creative destruction of sense of place: A psychosocial exploration of urban transformations in Barcelona. In *Changing senses of place: Navigating global challenges*, ed. C. Raymond, L. Manzo, D. R. Williams, A. Di Masso, and T. von Wirth, 221–33. Cambridge, UK: Cambridge University Press.

Di Masso, A., D. R. Williams, C. M. Raymond, M. Buchecker, B. Degenhardt, P. Devine-Wright, A. Hertzog, M. Lewicka, L. Manzo, A. Shahrad, et al. 2019. Between fixities and flows: Navigating place attachments in an increasingly mobile world. *Journal of Environmental Psychology* 61: 125–33.

Dovey, K. 2020. Place as assemblage. In *The Routledge handbook on place*, ed. T. Edensor, A. Kalandides, and U. Kothari, 21–31. London: Routledge.

Fazey, I., N. Schäpke, G. Caniglia, A. Hodgson, I. Kendrick, C. Lyon, G. Page, J. Patterson, C. Riedy, T. Strasser, et al. 2020. Transforming knowledge systems for life on earth: Visions of future systems and how to get there. *Energy Research and Social Sciences* 70: 101724.

Field, D. R., and W. R. Burch. 1988. *Rural sociology and the environment.* Westport, CT: Greenwood Press.

Firey, W. I. 1945. Sentiment and symbolism as ecological variables. *American Sociological Review* 10: 140–48.

Freudenburg, W. R. 2006. Environmental degradation, disproportionality, and the double diversion: reaching out, reaching ahead, and reaching beyond. *Rural Sociology* 71 (1): 3–32.

Fried, M. 1963. Grieving for a lost home. In *The urban condition*, ed. L. J. Duhl, 151–71. New York: Basic Books.

Ganapathy, S. 2013. Imagining Alaska: Local and translocal engagements with place. *American Anthropologist* 115: 96–111.

Gauchat, G. 2011. The cultural authority of science: Public trust and acceptance of organized science. *Public Understanding of Science* 20: 751–70.

Gergen, K. J. 1991. *The saturated self: Dilemmas of identity in contemporary life*. New York: Basic Books.

Greider, T., and Garkovich, L. 1994. Landscapes: The social construction of nature and the environment. *Rural Sociology* 59 (1): 1–24.

Greiner, C., Peth, S. A., and Sakdapolrak, P. 2014. Decipering migration in the age of climate change: Towards an understanding of translocal relations in social-ecological systems. In *Denaturalizing cliamte change: Migration, mobilities and space*, ed. F. Gesing, A. Meier, S. Klepp, and J. Herbeck, 23–32. Bremen, Germany: University of Bremen.

Grumbine, R. E. 1992. *Ghost Bears: Exploring the biodiversity crisis*. Washington, D.C.: Island Press.

Harvey, D. 1993. From space to place and back again: Reflections on the condition of postmodernity. In *Mapping the futures: Local cultures, global change*, ed. J. Bird, B. Curtis, T. Putnam, G. Robertson, and L. Tickner, 3–29. London: Routledge.

Hertzog, A. 2021. No one is a prophet at home: Mobility and sense of place in West Africa. In *Changing senses of place: Navigating global challenges*, ed. C. Raymond, L. Manzo, D. R. Williams, A. Di Masso, and T. von Wirth, 92–102. Cambridge, UK: Cambridge University Press.

Kovach, M. 2021. *Indigenous methodologies: Characteristics, conversations, and contexts*. Toronto: University of Toronto Press.

Lau, U., K. Durrheim, and L. S. Young. 2021. Place detachment and the psychology of nonbelonging: Lessons from Diepsloot Township. In *Changing senses of place: Navigating global challenges*, ed. C. Raymond, L. Manzo, D. R. Williams, A. Di Masso, and T. von Wirth, 103–15. Cambridge, UK: Cambridge University Press.

Lewicka, M., and O. Dohosh. 2021. Ethnocentric bias in perceptions of place: The role of essentialism and the perceived continuity of places. In *Changing senses of place: Navigating global challenges*, ed. C. Raymond, L. Manzo, D. R. Williams, A. Di Masso, and T. von Wirth, 171–81. Cambridge, UK: Cambridge University Press.

Lippard, L. R. 1997. *The lure of the local: Senses of place in a multicentered society*. New York: New Press.

Luloff, A. E., R. S. Krannich, G. L. Theodori, C. K. Trentelman, and T. Williams. 2004. The use of community in natural resource management. In *Society and natural resources: A summary of knowledge*, ed. M. J. Manfredo, J. J. Vaske, D. R. Field, P. J. Brown, and B. L. Bruyere, 249–59. Jefferson City, MO: Modern Litho.

Malkki, L. 1997. National Geographic: The rooting of peoples and the territorialization of national identity among scholars and refugees. In *Culture, power place: Explorations in critical anthropology*, ed. A. Gupta, and J. Ferguson, 52–74. Durham, NC: Duke University Press.

Manzo, L. 2014. Exploring the shadow side: Place attachment in the context of stigma, displacement and social housing. In *Place attachment: Advances in theory, methods and applications*, ed. L. Manzo and P. Devine-Wright, 178–90. London: Routledge.

Manzo, L. C., D. R. Williams, C. M. Raymond, A. Di Masso, and N. M. Gulsrud. 2023. How a deeper understanding of senses of place can help us navigate place change and uncertainty. *Landscape Journal* 42 (1): 37–52.

Manzo, L., D. R. Williams, C. M. Raymond, A. Di Masso, T. Von Wirth, and P. Devine-Wright. 2021. Navigating the spaciousness of uncertainties posed by global challenges: A senses of place perspective. In *Changing senses of place: Navigating global challenges*, ed. C. Raymond, L. Manzo, D. R. Williams, A. Di Masso, and T. Von Wirth, 331–47. Cambridge, UK: Cambridge University Press.

Massey, D. 1993. Power-geometry and a progressive sense of place. In *Mapping the futures: Local cultures, global change*, ed. J. Bird, B. Curtis, T. Putnam, G. Robertson, and L. Tickner, 59–69. London: Routledge.

Masterson, V. A., J. P. Enqvist, R. C. Stedman, and M. Tengö. 2019. Sense of place in social-ecological systems: From theory to empirics. *Sustainability Science* 14: 555–64.

Masterson, V. A., R. C. Stedman, J. Enqvist, M. Tengö, M. Giusti, D. Wahl, and U. Svedin. 2017. The contribution of sense of place to social-ecological systems research: A review and research agenda. *Ecology and Society* 22 (1).

McIntyre, N., D. R. Williams, and K. E. McHugh, eds. 2006. *Multiple dwelling and tourism: Negotiating place, home and identity*. Wallingford, CT: CABI.

McKelvey, K. S., W. M. Block, T. B. Jain, C. H. Luce, D. S. Page-Dumroese, B. A. Richardson, V. A. Saab, A. W. Schoettle, C. H. Sieg, and D. R. Williams. 2021. Adapting research, management, and governance to confront socioecological uncertainties in novel ecosystems. *Frontiers in Forests and Global Change* 4: 644696.

Mitchell, S. 2009. *Unsimple truths: Science, complexity and policy*. London: University of Chicago Press.

Morgan, P., G. H. Aplet, J. B. Haufler, H. C. Humphries, M. M. Moore, and W. D. Wilson, 1994. Historical range of variability: A useful tool for evaluating ecosystem change. *Journal of Sustainable Forestry* 2: 87–111. https://doi.org/10.1300/J091v02n01_04.

Morton, T. 2008. *Ecology without nature: Rethinking environmental aesthetics*. Cambridge, MA: Harvard University Press.

Newman, E. A., M. C. Kennedy, D. A. Falk, and D. McKenzie. 2019. Scaling and complexity in landscape ecology. *Frontiers in Ecology and Evolution* 13: 293.

Norberg-Schulz, C. 1979. *Genius loci: Towards a phenomenology of architecture.* New York: Rizzoli.

O'Connor, R. 2022, April 19. *How DALL-E 2 actually works.* Accessed June 30, 2023. https://www.assemblyai.com/blog/how-dall-e-2-actually-works/.

Pierce, J., D. G. Martin, and J. T. Murphy. 2011. Relational place-making: The networked politics of place. *Transactions of the Institute of British Geographers* 36: 54–70.

Polkinghorne, J. 2010. The demise of Democritus. In *The trinity and an entangle world: Relationality in physical science and theoology,* ed. J. Polkinghorne, 55–73. Grand Rapids, MI: Wm B. Eerdmans.

Raymond, C. M, R. Kaaronen, M. Giusti, N. Linder, and S. Barthel. 2021a. Engaging with the pragmatics of relational thinking, leverage points and transformations: A reply to West et al. 2020. *Ecosystems and People* 17: 1–5.

Raymond, C., L. C. Manzo, D. R. Williams, A. Di Masso, and T. Wirth. eds. 2021b. *Changing senses of place: Navigating global challenges.* Cambridge, UK: Cambridge University Press.

Relph, T. 1976. *Place and placelessness.* London: Pion Limited.

Relph, T. 2021. Electronically mediated sense of place. In *Changing senses of place: Navigating global challenges,* ed. C. Raymond, L. Manzo, D. R. Williams, A. Di Masso, and T. Von Wirth, 247–58. Cambridge, UK: Cambridge University Press.

Saarinen, J. 1998. The social construction of tourist destinations: The process of transformation of the Saariselkä region in Finnish Lapland. In *Destinations: Cultural landscapes of tourism,* ed. G. Ringer, 154–73. London: Routledge.

Sack, R. D. 1992. *Place, modernity and the consumer's world.* Baltimore, MD: Johns Hopkins University Press.

Sack, R. D. 1997. *Homo geographicus.* Baltimore, MD: Johns Hopkins University Press.

Sheller, M., and Urry, J. 2006. The new mobilities paradigm. *Environment and Planning A* 38: 207–26.

Steffen, W., Broadgate, W., Deutsch, L., Owen, G. and Ludwig, C. 2015. The trajectory of the Anthropocene: The Great Acceleration. *The Anthropocene Review* 2 (1): 81–98. https://doi.org/10.1177/2053019614564785.

Taipale, S. 2014. The dimensions of mobilities: The spatial relationships between corporeal and digital mobilities. *Social Science Research* 43: 157–67.

Thayer, R. L., Jr. 2003. *LifePlace: Bioregional thought and practice.* Berkeley: University of California Press.

Tomaney, J. 2015. Region and place II: Belonging. *Progress in Human Geography* 39: 507–16.

Torgerson, D. 1999. Images of place in green politics: the cultural mirror of Indigenous traditions. In *Living with nature: Environmental politics as cultural discourse,* ed. F. Fischer and A. Hajer, 186–203. Oxford, NY: Oxford University Press.

Trentelman, C. K. 2009. Place attahcment and community attachment: A primer grounded in the lived experience of a community sociologist. *Society & Natural Resources* 22: 191–210.

Tuan, Y. F. 1977. *Space and place: The perspective of experience*. London: University of Minnesota Press.

Verne, J. 2012. *Living translocality: Space, culture and economy in contemporary Swahili trade*. Stuttgart, Germany: Franz Steiner Verlag.

Walker, J. 2020. The age of ecology. In *More heat than life: The tangled roots of ecology, energy, and economics*, 183–92. Singapore: Palgrave Macmillan.

Walsh, Z., J. Böhme, and C. Wamsler. 2021. Towards a relational paradigm in sustainability research, practice, and education. *Ambio* 50: 74–84.

Wellman, B., and B. Leighton. 1979. Networks, neighborhoods, and communities: Approaches to the study of the community question. *Urban Affairs Quarterly* 14 (3): 363–90.

West, S., L. J. Haider, S. Stållhammar, and S. Woroniecki. 2020. A relational turn for sustainaiblity science? Relational thinking, leverage points and transformation. *Ecosystems and People* 16: 304–25.

Wildman, W. J. 2010. An introduction to relational ontology. In *The trinity and an entangle world: Relationality in physical science and theology*, ed. J. Polkinghorne, 55–73. Grand Rapids, MI: Wm B. Eerdmans.

Wilkinson, K. P. 1991. *The community in rural America*. Westport, CT: Greenwood Press.

Williams, D. R. 2002. Leisure identities, globalization, and the politics of place. *Journal of Leisure Research* 34: 351–67.

Williams, D. R. 2013. Science, practice, and place. In *Place-based conservation: Perspectives from the social sciences*, ed. W. P. Stewart, D. R. Williams, and L. E. Kruger, 21–34. Dordrecht, Netherlands: Springer.

Williams, D. R. 2014. Making sense of "place": Reflections on pluralism and positionality in place research. *Landscape and Urban Planning* 131: 74–82.

Williams, D. R. 2018. Spacing conservation practice: Place-making, social learning, and adaptive governance in natural resource management. In *The SAGE handbook of nature*. Vol. 3, ed. T. Marsden, 285–303. London: Sage.

Williams, D. R., and B. P. Kaltenborn. 1999. Leisure places and modernity: The use and meaning of recreational cottages in Norway and the USA. In *Leisure practices and geographic knowledge*, ed. D. Crouch, 214–30. London: Routledge.

Williams, D. R., and N. McIntyre. 2001. Where heart and home reside: Changing constructions of place and identity. In *Trends 2000: Shaping the future*, 392–403. Lansing: Michigan State University.

Williams, D. R., and N. McIntyre. 2012. Place affinities, lifestyle mobilities, and quality-of-life. In *Handbook of tourism and quality-of-life research*, 209–31. Dordrecht, Netherlands: Springer.

Williams, D. R., and B. A. Miller. 2021. Metatheoretical moments in place attachment research: Seeking clarity in diversity. In *Place attachment: Advances in theory, methods and applications*, ed. L. C. Manzo and P. Devine-Wright, 2nd ed., 13–28. New York: Routledge.

Williams, D. R., and M. E. Patterson. 1996. Environmental meaning and ecosystem management: Perspectives from environmental psychology and human geography. *Society and Natural Resources* 9: 507–21.

Williams, D. R., M. E. Patterson, J. W. Roggenbuck, and A. E. Watson. 1992. Beyond the commodity metaphor: Examining emotional and symbolic attachment to place. *Leisure Sciences* 14: 29–46.

Williams, D. R., and S. I. Stewart. 1998. Sense of place: An elusive concept that is finding a home in ecosystem management. *Jounral of Forestry* 96 (5): 18–23.

Williams, D. R., and S. R. Van Patten. 2006. Home and away? Creating identities and sustaining places in a multi-centred world. In *Multiple dwelling and tourism: Negotiating place, home and identity*, ed. N. McIntyre, D. Williams, and K. McHugh, 32–50. Cambridge, MA: CABI Publishing.

Wohlers, C., and G. Hertel. 2017. Choosing where to work at work—towards a theoretical model of benefits and risks of activitybased flexible offices. *Ergonomics* 60 (4): 467–86.

Yung, L., A. Freimund, and J. M. Belsky. 2003. The politics of place: Understanding meaning, common ground and political difference on the Rocky Mountain Front. *Forest Science* 49: 855–66.

CONCLUSION

What Blew in through the Windows?

DOUGLAS JACKSON-SMITH, GLADMAN THONDHLANA,
AND KATE SHERREN

As noted in the introductory essay to this volume, a central goal for this collection was to invite, engage with, and explore emerging and critical perspectives on the legacy of traditional natural resource social science and to outline new research agendas to shape the next generation of work in this space. Our method for inviting contributions aligned with our ethos of providing equity of opportunity and diversity of representation in substance and contributors. We utilized an open invitation approach back in early 2021 to solicit contributions, with some prompts to encourage geographical representation, and encouraged the formation of collaborative author teams that reflected greater diversity in sociodemographics, career stage, and theoretical and methodological perspectives.

We are excited with what blew in through the open windows. Our author list includes larger proportions of authors who are non-white, non-male, from non-US institutions, in early career stages, and from non-academic positions than previous volumes in this series. Notably, we did reasonably well in attracting authors from the Global South—though some are no longer

https://doi.org/10.7330/9781646426300.c016

based there—especially when viewed in relation to the IASNR membership. Equally important, these diverse authors generally adopted critical stances to interrogate some of the core concepts that have long guided scholars affiliated with the IASNR (e.g., stewardship, environmental concern, sense of place, and collaborative resource management), and many are pioneering new methods and theoretical concepts. While generally appreciative of the depth and contributions of classic work on these topics, our contributors highlighted how our traditional approaches frequently reflect worldviews and paradigms shaped by the problems, paradoxes, and puzzles of most interest to the community of the scholars and public land managers who helped found the field of NRSS in the United States.

Emerging Core Ideas

Reading across the final volume, we are struck by the centrality of questions about power that weave throughout most of the chapters. This includes a greater appreciation for the direct and indirect ways that social, cultural, and economic power affect the processes and outcomes associated with traditional natural resource management and policymaking. Chapters also highlight the ways power dynamics have structured and shaped the topical interests and theoretical concepts that have dominated traditional NRSS scholarship in IASNR. Core concepts like place, sustainability, public participation, and management, for instance, frequently privilege the notion of stability, which is a luxury that typically serves the interests of the status quo. The authors in this volume provide examples of how these concepts are power laden, and when executed without a questioning approach can further marginalize those at the margins. These subtle asymmetrical power relations and outcomes are attributed by authors in part to the failure to employ an intersectional approach to understanding the importance of marks of differences (e.g., race, sexuality, and gender) in shaping environmental outcomes. In other words, reductive binary approaches to understanding race, class, sexuality, and gender inevitably result in inequalities and can protect heteronormative narratives. Therefore, a nuanced understanding of intersectionality is needed to address different levels and forms of marginalization within seemingly homogenous identities.

This is similarly manifest in assumptions about who should be involved in natural resource decisions that otherwise tend to focus on populations with relative privilege (landowners, colonial settler populations, government officials and agencies, wealthy and upper-middle-class households, and majority race and ethnic groups), while giving less credence to the needs, perspectives, or legitimacy of Indigenous and/or minoritized racial, ethnic, and gendered populations, and nonhuman actors in complex social-ecological systems. When the role of systemic power is ignored, we also see how many "good" ideas designed explicitly to broaden participation in natural resource management (like CBNRM) are commonly co-opted or corrupted from their original purpose. A key contribution of this book lies in the recognition of marks of differences such as class, gender, and race as more than just demographic categories but as systems of power that can produce different forms of social oppression by privileging some and excluding others. These forms of oppression can manifest even in well-intentioned programs aimed at addressing inequalities and inequitable outcomes.

Most of the future priority research topics and methods outlined by our authors are conscious of these past limitations and call for more transformative or disruptive practices that are likely to challenge conventional assumptions and interests. These include social learning and knowledge co-production, relational approaches that validate Indigenous and non-Western ways of understanding human-nature relationships, building capacity for human dignity, and prioritizing decolonization, antiracism, and antisexist discourse in NRSS work.

Another related observation is that many of the authors are calling for more engagement with diverse communities of interest in conceptualizing, designing, and implementing new research projects in NRSS. We see this as a subtle and important shift away from simple ideas of "public participation" that dominated early scholarship in IASNR (which themselves were developed in response to perceived problems with conventional top-down expert-driven resource management). Best practices for more engaged participatory methods include elevating the legitimacy and authority of non-scientists and experiential ways of knowing.

Missing Pieces

While our volume provides an opportunity for new voices and perspectives to reach a broader mainstream audience in the NRSS community, as co-editors we are aware of important gaps and limitations. Compared to previous decennial volumes, we do not include focused chapters on many of the diverse substantive topic areas that have dominated the *Society and Natural Resources* journal and conference agendas of recent IASNR meetings (e.g., tourism, parks and recreation, wildlife, energy, water, and social-ecological systems). Similarly, while climate change receives attention in many of the chapters, the book does not include a chapter focused squarely on one of the most existential human-nature challenges of our time. The impacts of the global COVID-19 pandemic, growing nationalism and nativist politics, and wars and conflict in Ukraine, Yemen, Ethiopia, and other regions also provide challenges to the inexorable march of globalization that dominated the late twentieth century; it would have been exciting to hear more from scholars exploring how these trends impact human-environment relationships and natural resource management. Other areas that deserve more attention relate to science implementation, particularly integrating diverse ways of knowing, co-development, shared recognition, co-benefits and designing holistic assessments of success.

We also set out with the goal of capturing more of the diverse and growing global NRSS work from non-US or non-European scholars and practitioners. The co-editors did take steps to reach out specifically to colleagues and peers in the Global South but were unable to generate proposals from authors for chapters that could summarize the depth, breadth, and different perspectives reflected in this body of (often non-English language) scholarship. We see global representation as a central challenge and opportunity for the next IASNR decennial volume. This should be bolstered by the recent formation of new regional international "hubs" within the organization that will hopefully catalyze new conversations, knowledge interchange, and creative new directions for the field of NRSS. IASNR's efforts and priorities relating to internationalization, recruitment, and retention provide a good foundation for ensuring sustained growth of a diverse membership. Meaningful efforts are contingent on intentional programs for promoting diversity of membership including providing opportunities for sharing diverse voices, to participate in committees and Council, and to make it easy for minority groups to say yes to invitations to serve in the organization. We hope that academics and professionals reading this volume will find the call for transformative change and action appealing, and work within their organizations to address barriers to entering the field, particularly for marginalized groups and inter-sectional identities. This goes beyond representation but includes efforts to have diverse scholars writing from their own lived experiences. A diverse membership of IASNR will provide a wider pool for potential contributors to future volumes and a more diverse and nuanced set of perspectives when that time comes.

Index

Locators followed by *n* indicate an endnote, by *f* indicate a figure, and followed by *t* indicate a table.

structural change in academia, 77
Structural Transformation of the Public Sphere: An Inquiry into a Category of Bourgeois Society (Habermas), 152
structural view on power, 171, 172
Suchet-Pearson, S., 129
Suškevičs, M., 172–173
sustainability approaches, 126, 136, 297
sustainability plans, government, 78–79
sustainable development, 78
Sustainable Forestry and African American Land Retention Network (SFLR), 53
sustainable grazing, 30–31
Swanson, S. S., 211
Swedberg, R., 265, 266, 267
Szerszynski, S., 265, 266

Tadaki, M., 230
Taking Nature Black Conference, 53
TallBear, K., 21
Tanzania, 108
Taylor, Dr. Dorceta E., 51
Taylor & Francis, 151
teaching experience access to, 78

technocratic approaches, 126
tenure-track faculty positions, 76–77
Thailand, 173
Theoe, D. R., 51
theory: basic practices of, 262–263; decolonial approaches to, 267–268; of integrated value systems, 241; of planned behavior, 225n2, 229n4; practicing, 265–266; of reasoned action, 229n4; role of, 90–91; situating, 263–265; theorizing together, 266–267; trust, 156, 157
Thousand Plateaus, A (Deleuze and Guattari), 291n1
Traditional Authority (TA), 109–110
traditional ecological knowledge, 302. *See also* knowledge
training, academic, 77; push factors, 80
training, for applied careers, 79–80
transcendence values, 231, 241–242. *See also* values
transcendentalism, 294

transitions, experiencing in place, 302–305
transitions, social-ecological-technical systems (SETS), 290, 291, 296–297
translocality, 302–305
trans people, 23
treaty agreements, 47
trophy hunting, 99, 100, 105
trust, 123, 154, 157–158, 159, 190
trust theory, 156, 157
Tsitsa River Catchment case study, 278–279, 281–282, 283
Tsoukas, H., 265
Turner, J. A., 173
typologies: for participation, 181–183; of relationships, 124f, 125, 129, 139–140; of visual methods, 203–207, 203f, 206f, 209t, 213–214

uncertainty, 78, 159
underrepresentation of Asian Americans, 55. *See also* race and racism
UNICEF, 187
Uniform Partition of Heirs Property Act (UPHPA), 53
Union Pacific Railroad, 54
United States Department of Agriculture (USDA), 28, 29
University of Tasmania, 82
UPROSE, 59
US Endowment for Forestry and Communities, 53
utilitarian ethics, 129. *See also* ethics

value-belief-norm (VBN) model, 231, 235, 240–242, 242f, 244, 247, 248
values: in Australian forest management, 135; definitions of, 230; ecological, 278; environmental, 229–231; in human dignity, 73–74n1; in natural resources and recreation, 48–49, 50, 58; place-dependent, 293; in problem framing, 127; in relationship types, 123, 127; representation of, 160; self-transcendence, 241–242; of stakeholders, 159; theory of integrated value systems, 241
van der Ploeg, J. D., 103
Van Paassen, A., 173

Contributors

Evan J. Andrews, Memorial University, Canada

Ian Babelon, Northumbria University, UK

Robert Berry, University of Gloucestershire, UK

Wiebren Johannes Boonstra, Stockholm Resilience Centre / Uppsala University, Sweden

Beth Brockett, Natural England, UK

Jasmine K. Brown, Michigan State University, USA

Angie Carter, Michigan Technological University, USA

Yan Chen, Dalhousie University, Canada

Jessica Cockburn, Rhodes University, South Africa

Michael Dockry, University of Minnesota, USA

Ana Carolina Esteves Dias, University of Waterloo, Canada

Rebecca M. Ford, University of Melbourne, Australia

Madu Galappaththi, University of Waterloo, Canada

Caitlin Hafferty, University of Gloucestershire, UK

Anna Haines, University of Wisconsin–Steven's Point, USA, and chair of the SNRBS editorial board

Paul Hebinck, Wageningen University, the Netherlands / Rhodes University, South Africa (note: posthumous publication)

Sarah Hitchner, University of Georgia, USA

Michaela Hoffelmeyer, Penn State University, now at University of Wisconsin–Madison

James Hoggett, Natural England, UK

Durdana Islam, University of Winnipeg, Canada

Douglas Jackson-Smith, Ohio State University, USA

Christopher Jadallah, University of California, Los Angeles, USA

Robert Emmet Jones, University of Tennessee, USA

Rachel Kelly, University of Tasmania, Australia

E. Carina H. Keskitalo, Umeå University, Sweden

Richard Dimba Kiaka, Jaramogi Oginga Odinga University of Science and Technology / School for Field Studies, Kenya

Christine Knott, San Diego State University, USA

Richard Krannich, Utah State University, USA, and member of the SNR Book Series editorial board

Bryanne Lamoureux, Dalhousie University, Canada

María Andrée López Gómez, Universitat Pompeu Fabra Barcelona, Spain

Rodgers Lubilo, Frankfurt Zoological Society / Zambia Community Resources Board Association and Conservation Coalition Zambia, Zambia

Vanessa Masterson, Stockholm Resilience Centre, Stockholm University, Sweden

Jaye Mejía-Duwan, University of California, Berkeley, USA

Brett Alan Miller, US Forest Service, USA

Maddison Miller, University of Melbourne, Australia

Abraham Miller-Rushing, US National Park Service, Acadia National Park, USA

Nosiseko Mtati, Rhodes University, South Africa

Solange Nadeau, Natural Resources Canada / Canadian Forest Service, Canada

Sarah Naiman, Cornell University, USA

Polly Nguyen, Dalhousie University, Canada

Eliza Oldach, First Light and University of California, Davis, USA

John R. Parkins, University of Alberta, Canada

Courtenay Parlee, Fisheries and Oceans Canada

Archi Rastogi, Green Climate Fund / National University of Singapore, Singapore

Andrea Rawluk, University of Melbourne, Australia

Gabrielle Roesch-McNally, American Farmland Trust, USA

Sasha Quahe, Stockholm Resilience Centre, Stockholm University, Sweden

Prativa Sapkota, University of Melbourne, Australia

John Schelhas, USDA Forest Service, USA

Kate Sherren, Dalhousie University, Canada

William Stewart, University of Illinois Urbana–Champaign, USA, and executive director of IASNR

Gladman Thondhlana, Rhodes University, South Africa

Tobin N. Walton, North Carolina A&T State University, USA

Grace Wang, Western Washington University, USA

Simon West, Stockholm Resilience Centre, Stockholm University, Sweden

Daniel R. Williams, USDA Forest Service, USA

Kathryn J. H. Williams, University of Melbourne, Australia

Melanie Zurba, Dalhousie University, Canada